THE ART OF NATION-BUILDING
Pageantry and Spectacle at Quebec's Tercentenary

In 1908 Canada celebrated its 300th anniversary – the tercentenary of Champlain's founding of Quebec City. In two glorious weeks of parades, ceremonies, balls, and festivities, Canadians commemorated their history in a spectacle that would not be surpassed until the centennial of 1967. The climax of the 1908 celebration was an historical pageant in which 4000 sumptuously costumed citizens re-enacted classic events in Canada's history. Canada's leading painters were also there to capture these memorable scenes for posterity. The past was being celebrated, but with the present and the future in mind.

In *The Art of Nation-Building*, H.V. Nelles uses contemporary literary techniques to convey the scope, colour, and intensity of the tercentenary from various perspectives. Drawing on the intimate diaries and letters of leading social and political figures, he leads us behind the scenes, disclosing the politics of memory, the theatrics of history, and the making of a modern monarchy. Nelles reveals what we actually do when we commemorate, how we use the past, and the multivocal character of mass celebration.

This richly illustrated, thought-provoking interpretation of public celebrations offers a novel perspective on Quebec and on the upcoming celebration of the millennium.

H.V. NELLES teaches history at York University, where he specializes in the study of Canadian political economy and public memory. He has won numerous awards for his scholarship and accolades for his writing.

THE ART OF NATION-BUILDING

Pageantry and Spectacle
at Quebec's Tercentenary

H.V. NELLES

UNIVERSITY OF TORONTO PRESS
Toronto Buffalo London

© University of Toronto Press Incorporated 1999
Toronto Buffalo London
Printed in Canada

Reprinted in paperback 2000

ISBN 0-8020-4271-6 (cloth)
ISBN 0-8020-8431-1 (paper)

Printed on acid-free paper

Canadian Cataloguing in Publication Data

Nelles, H. V. (Henry Vivian), 1942–
  The art of nation-building : pageantry and spectacle at Quebec's
tercentenary

  Includes bibliographical references and index.
  ISBN 0-8020-4271-6 (bound)   ISBN 0-8020-8431-1 (pbk.)

  1. Québec (Quebec) – Centennial celebrations, etc. 2. Québec
(Quebec) – History. 3. Canada – History – 1867–1914. I. Title

FC2946.36.N44 1999   971.4'47103   C98-932763-9
F1054.5.Q3N44 1999

This book has been published with the help of a grant from the Humanities
and Social Sciences Federation of Canada, using funds provided by the
Social Sciences and Humanities Research Council of Canada.

University of Toronto Press acknowledges the financial assistance to its
publishing program of the Canada Council for the Arts and the Ontario
Arts Council.

University of Toronto Press acknowledges the financial support for its
publishing activities of the Government of Canada through the Book
Publishing Industry Development Program (BPIDP).

For Diane

CONTENTS

We have made Italy, now we have to make Italians.

Massimo d'Azeglio

To make a nation there must be a common life, common sentiments, common aims, and common hopes.

Goldwin Smith, *The Bystander*, December 1889

Les fêtes du troisième centenaire de Québec, si grandioses et si populaires, méritaient qu'on en fit le récit fidèle, qu'on en consignât, dans un livre soigneusement préparée.

Le Comité du 'Livre-Souvenir'

I think that we never know the truth by being told it. We have to experience it in some way. That is the abiding grace of history. It is the theatre in which we experience truth. But we have to work at it, because the truth is always clothed in some way by story. History is always parable to the truth.

Greg Dening, *Performances*

THE ART OF NATION-BUILDING

INTRODUCTION: THE MEMORY BOX

Archives of Ontario, 1992

An unexpected burst of colour from a Union Jack and the brilliant scarlet and white uniform of an eighteenth-century British soldier flashed into view as I opened the lid of the dull grey container. When I slid the document out, a matching blue and white clad French soldier, shouldering a flagstaff of golden fleurs-de-lis, faced across the cover page at his British counterpart. Between these two combatants appeared the distinctive image of Samuel de Champlain in cameo. With flowing locks and wispy goatee, the founder of Quebec bore a vague resemblance to a Puritan divine. In the background was an eighteenth-century engraving of Quebec; over the soldiers' heads floated the dates 1608 and 1908. At the bottom of this cover the text proclaimed: 'Souvenir Programme of the National Celebration at Quebec: The Ancient Capital of Canada.'

Turning the page, a striking portrait of the then Prince of Wales, soon to be King George V, fixed me with its gaze. From the head, in dramatic half-shadow, the figure opened out across broad epaulettes and a bemedalled breast, then narrowed progressively through elbows, waist, and braided cuffs to a secondary focus where his hands gently gripped the hilt of a sword.

Several pages of dense type followed this dramatic frontispiece, thick with names of organizers, members of committees, dignitaries, and guests. Turning another page, Frank Lascelles, identified as 'the master of the pageants,' looked melodramatically into the distance above an extensive

Cover of the English-language souvenir program from the tercentenary.

Portrait of His Royal Highness the Prince of Wales in the souvenir program.

plot summary of what seemed to be an elaborate eight-act historical opera. A detailed daily schedule of events stretching over two weeks, a diagram of a grandstand, and information for visitors filled the remaining pages. Neatly tucked into the back cover, a fold-out street map of Quebec City identified the key sites of the 1908 festival. Superimposed over the map of the modern city in pale red and blue ink were thickened parallel lines showing the respective positions of Montcalm's and Wolfe's armies in 1759.

Putting this program aside, I turned back to the other contents of the box: a black-covered scrapbook, some loose pamphlets, more programs and illustrated magazines, a big leather-bound, illustrated history of the festival, and a small, square box, from which protruded the frayed end of a red ribbon. The scrapbook, with its promise of private revelations, begged to be examined first.

The inscription on the inside cover identified the collector of these memories as 'Clare Denison, Heydon Villa, Toronto, Canada.' The daughter of Colonel George T. Denison III and his wife Helen, Clare had travelled to this festival in Quebec City in 1908 with her parents. Turning these stiff pages of yellowed newspaper clippings, neatly organized lithographs, and engraved invitations, one young girl's impression of this event began to emerge.

Clare Denison's memory book begins with Champlain and the founding of Quebec. As a frontispiece to her collection she had selected a heroic print by C.W. Jefferys, titled *The Landing of Champlain, Quebec 1608*. An Indian chief standing on a pine-covered cliff reveals his vast river empire to Champlain and his party. The gold-coated explorer surveys the kingdom, exuding an attitude of satisfaction and possession. An Indian brave, seated in the lower left corner, looks on with apparent misgivings.

'The Pageants' clearly made a profound impression upon the young visitor. Illustrations of this theatrical extravaganza held pride of place in the first section of her scrapbook. She cut out dozens of magazine photographs of elaborately costumed actors; long panoramic postcards of vast scenes with a cast of hundreds had to be pasted in sideways to fit. On these crowded pages dancers at the French court were juxtaposed with Indians on the warpath, ecclesiastical processions, royal retinues, explorers and historic armies.

Then came ships – huge, smoking, battleships bristling with spiky

'The Landing of Champlain, Quebec, 1608,' by C.W. Jefferys. Colour lithograph produced by the Intercolonial Railway as a souvenir of the tercentenary. This is one of Jefferys's earliest historical representations.

masts and powerful guns. At first these images in a young woman's archive were startling. Then, on reflection, they were not so surprising. For although a young girl might not usually be attracted to such things, Clare Denison's father was Canada's foremost military authority, her two step-brothers were soldiers and her uncle was an admiral in the British navy. A report of 'The Torpedo Attack and Naval Fireworks' on Monday 27 July drew four inked exclamation points of excitement. She was quite taken with the ships, and, not surprisingly, with the sailors.

Royalty and the army were inextricably linked in the next section of the scrapbook. The Prince of Wales, in Clare's pictures at least, was usually accompanied by soldiers. The 48th Highlanders of Toronto march past him. Lord Roberts, the renowned British general and former commander-in-chief who won a Victoria Cross during the Indian Mutiny, relieved Kandahar during the Second Afghan War, and commanded British and Imperial troops in South Africa, leads a Roughrider cavalry charge past his reviewing stand. The prince usually appears surrounded by the smart Toronto regiments raised and loudly championed by the Denison family.

Midway through the scrapbook, thematic coherence gives way to a jumble of ships, flags, crowd scenes, portraits, and photographs of dignitaries – with mistakes in the captions corrected in ink. Pages of flaking newspaper clippings describe the major events, trailing long lists of those fortunate enough to be in attendance. The names Lieutenant-Colonel George Denison, Mrs and Miss Denison, where they appear in these accounts, are invariably underlined.

The scrapbook thickens with visiting cards and engraved invitations to dinners, receptions, and balls from Rear Admiral Jellicoe, Vice-Admiral Jauréguiberry, the lieutenant-governor of Quebec, and the governor general of Canada. Precious ephemera – cards, ticket stubs, and passes to the cathedral, the Citadel, and the pageants – fill one page. On the facing page is an item of obvious great importance, an oversize invitation for Mrs and Miss Denison to meet His Royal Highness the Prince of Wales at a ball at Parliament House.

As mementos of visits to luncheons and dances aboard ship and on chaperoned picnics ashore, she collected tallies from sailors' caps embossed in gold with the ships' names: *Russell, Albemarle,* and *Léon Gambetta.* An envelope identified as once containing a set of commemorative postage stamps issued on this occasion now bulges with these cap ribbons. Inside the back cover of the scrapbook is a folded panoramic photograph of eleven enormous battleships anchored in an arc in the river off Quebec City. The sense of power, sweep, and grandeur spilled out beyond the pages of the scrapbook.

There was a great deal more in the document box: pamphlets, brochures, two more official programs, a booklet in French containing the script for the pageants, two special issues of the weekly rotogravure magazines the *Standard* and the *Canadian Pictorial*, and a leather-spined, lavishly illustrated *Commemorative History of the Quebec Tercentenary*. These publications would have to wait while I examined the curious little box which, when I pried it open, contained a red leather case about four inches square and an inch deep. Opening its clasp revealed a large bronze medal resting on wine-coloured velvet with a card: 'Presented by the National Battlefields Commission in Commemoration of the Tercentenary of the Founding of Quebec by Champlain, Quebec, Canada, J. Geo. Garneau, Chairman.'

Lifting the little red ribbon released the hefty medal portraying the raised figure of Champlain, feathered hat doffed in one hand, sword held aloft in the other inverted to resemble a cross rather than a weapon. Champlain is captured in mid-stride in the act of founding a colony, one foot on a ship the other on a rock marked 'Stadacone.' Around the edge runs the inscription: 'IIIᵉ Centenaire de la Fondation de Québec.' On the reverse, two female muses sit under a tree in a garden. The draped figure on the right rests one elbow on the shield of the British royal standard, the figure on the left leans on a box encrusted with fleurs-de-lis. The former gestures upward towards the future, the latter downward towards the past. A ribbon of inscriptions floats through the tree branches overhead: 'Née sous les lis/Dieu aidant l'oeuvre de Champlain/A grandi sous les roses.'[1]

Slipping the medal back into its case, and putting these documents in order again, I reflected on the many layers of memory that had come tumbling out of this box. This was first of all a collection of objects, images, and texts, precious to the memory of a young woman who had witnessed a deeply moving spectacle at which she believed something really important had taken place. With scissors and paste pot, she had neatly sorted her pile of treasured emblems into an ordered sequence in her scrapbook. This act of preservation meant that she wanted the balls,

The two faces of a commemorative medal by Henri Dubois, 'IIIᵉ Centenaire de la Fondation de Québec.' This bronze medal was given to Colonel Denison for his contribution to the tercentenary.

music, vistas, theatrical scenes, shipboard visits, handsome young men in uniform, women in gorgeous gowns, and finally, the prince, to last forever. She clung to these talismanic representations of elegance, grace, glittering society, important personages, and power as if this might be the most important moment of her life. Perhaps it was. She also, I later learned, kept a diary of the event which is not in the collection. Here was evidence of her attempt to make permanent the necessarily evanescent events of a memorable fortnight in Quebec City in July of 1908. It was a futile but very human struggle against forgetting.[2]

Clare Denison's archive testified to much more than a private act of remembrance; it also opened a window upon a great national act of commemoration, in which her father had evidently played an important part. The lavishly illustrated programs, the handsomely published commemorative history, and the medal clearly indicated that this had been much more than a local Quebec City event. The souvenir program said as much, as it proclaimed this tercentenary of Quebec to be a 'National Celebration.' Moreover, the photographs of rich costumes, the cast of thousands, and two packed weeks of orchestrated festivities suggested that no expense had been spared. In the midsummer of 1908 thousands of Canadians had gathered at Quebec for a glorious festival. They encountered each other informally on their holidays but also in scripted roles, in uniforms, costumes, and formal dress. They spoke in symbols; they marched, paraded, and danced. They mingled and displayed themselves in the reflected glory of their next sovereign.

The tercentenary seemed to have been built on the dual propositions that history would make a nation and that history could best be understood in performance. Accordingly, the organizers had gone to considerable lengths to bring history to life by re-enacting great scenes from Canadian history in the specially built Pageant Theatre on the Plains of Abraham. They believed that their past spoke directly to them about their present and pointed firmly towards a collective future.

Ostensibly, it was the past that was being celebrated, but what past? There seemed to be some confusion as to who was being commemorated: was it Champlain, or Montcalm and Wolfe? Was it 1608 or 1759? Or was 1908 itself the object of celebration? Somehow a civic festival had taken on martial and imperial overtones. By a curious logic, the founding of a city in the seventeenth century had become connected in some way to its conquest in the eighteenth century and further linked to a celebration of imperial nationalism in the early twentieth century. Judging from these jumbled images and inscriptions, the festival seemed to be 'about' many things.

This spectacular commemoration in 1908 set me to wondering about the nature of such events. I write this in the Year of Cabot, allegedly the five hundredth anniversary of his landfall in Newfoundland. We commemorate all the time. Scarcely a year goes by without some similar sort of celebration. And even commemorations are commemorated. The centennial in 1967 is now being revisited. What do we do, I asked myself, when we commemorate things?

I could see from these remarkably well-preserved documents and memorabilia that a spectacular celebration of nationhood had taken place during one of the most exuberant moments in Canadian history. This huge gathering at Quebec in the presence of royalty resembled one of those grand festivals during the French Revolution when the nation assembled that it might see itself and its people consecrate a new citizenship. In meeting together they made themselves by remembering together. Commemoration was an act of self-invention.

Clare Denison's treasury of private memory opened a window through time into this wider world of public memory. What she had witnessed was nothing less than an attempt to interpret history before a mass audience in support of a particular vision of what Canada should be and might become. Seen from one angle, the tercentenary was an attempt to shape society around it through spectacle and public performance. The question immediately arose as to whose vision was being projected and the extent to which this effort might have succeeded. However, as I examined the archival detritus of the tercentenary more closely, I could see several different authors at work and many audiences making choices as to what they wanted to see and take away. From this perspective it seemed to me that the primary importance of the event lay not in how it *affected* things, but rather in how it *reflected* the world around it. The tercentenary was politics by other means; it turned social structure into performance art. It did not so much cause other things to happen as demonstrate how many issues, usually studied separately, can come together.

The tercentenary held a distorted glass up to its age. It was not a perfect image of its time. However in this theatre, things I had only grasped in general ways or in abstract terms acquired an immediacy they previously lacked. Here was the naval debate with real ships; here was

French-Canadian nationalism in the round raging *and* laughing; here were princes, prime ministers, politicians, and prelates seen up close in less-guarded moments. All of the great 'isms' of the time (progressivism, liberalism, boosterism, feminism, nationalism in several varieties, imperialism, militarism, historicism, nativism, ultramontanism, racism, modernism, monarchism) came into sharper focus as they struggled through human effort to shape this celebration.

The more I thought about this event the less it appeared to be ephemeral entertainment and the more it seemed a portent. Much of what we as Canadians would become and could not become in the twentieth century was on display in the streets and on the pageant grounds of Quebec in 1908. The then present, strikingly evident in this supposed commemoration of three hundred years of history, disported itself in dissonant, gaudy display. To that extent the celebration foretold much of the future. This was a celebration in a country that would not become a nation state. Here were many different peoples who, unlike their neighbours, would not become one. Here, too, were Canadians preoccupied with domestic arrangements while other principalities and powers aligned themselves for battle. The point is not that politics intruded into the gaiety or interfered with the master plan, but rather that festivals *are* politics. By commemorating we necessarily celebrate ourselves. But more often than not we are plural, and opinion about identity and destiny is divided.

However formal and official things appeared on the surface, I would eventually see that the tercentenary unfolded with divided support, under pro tem agreement, on a negotiated space of repressed differences. Like a stately ritual, national commemoration presented in public view a peculiar kind of politics, with the sharp edges of conflict blunted and differences expressed in polite, coded diminuendo. And somewhat surprisingly, a good deal of middle ground did appear. That too revealed something of the future; a willingness to avoid tough choices and live with contradictions.

But whatever Canadians had done or said to each other during those two weeks in July 1908, and however memorable the occasion might have been, the event itself has nevertheless been forgotten. It occupies scarcely a line in standard histories of the period. Now it hardly seems to have mattered beyond being a 'mere spectacle.' Contrasting the numerous archival collections of ephemera with this silence in the literature, I was struck by this disjuncture between the private clinging to remembrance and the subsequent public forgetting. Why were the Clare Denisons and thousands of others so evidently moved in 1908? If the event had made such an emotional impression, why didn't the mood last? Why was this festival, so important to this generation and evidently designed to be the celebration of the birth and unfolding confidence of a nation, so completely and utterly forgotten? Whatever meaning Clare Denison and thousands like her had found in this linking of their past and present had subsequently been lost.

I soon discovered a surprisingly large number of memory boxes like Clare Denison's in other archives. People as diverse as nuns in Quebec and a socialite in Ottawa kept detailed journals and scrapbook recollections of the tercentenary. One source did fail me: Mackenzie King. Although he took a great interest in the celebration, did some organization on its behalf, and I think I can see him at the festivities in an old photograph, his diary for this period is missing. All sorts of people either went to the tercentenary, or thought it worthy of collecting its memorabilia and keeping it for the rest of their lives. Sometimes these collections were quite extensive; more often the collector clung to only a few fragments, invitations usually, or, for example, the map of the table for the Prince of Wales' dinner aboard the *Minotaur* – fondly kept by the Speaker of the House of Commons.[3]

The tercentenary had been designed to attract thousands of spectators to Quebec. Many more participated vicariously through press reports, as these abundant clippings revealed. Clare Denison's private collection consisted in large part of selections from illustrated magazines, extensive newspaper accounts, programs, and pamphlets. The beautifully designed *Commemorative History*, published by a newspaper as a commercial venture, could not have come into existence without a substantial market of avid readers. Clare, who had been present at most of these events, could read into these static pictures and reams of copy meanings generated by immediate personal contact. Distant readers stood at one remove; for them, the images and text had to explain themselves. The tercentennial event was thus transmuted into words and pictures. Now these public representations were all that remained.

The tercentenary had been a feast for the eye. As such, it was but one of many such presentations that favoured sight over other modes of understanding. History was taught not through books but through re-enactment. Accordingly, the tercentenary of 1908 survived in the archives more as a photographic than as a written record. The Quebec City Archives and the Archives Nationales de Québec both contained large collections of photographs, including splendid portraits by the Livernois studio. At the National Archives in Ottawa I found a half-dozen huge panoramic photographs, the Underwood and Underwood professional photographic collection, snapshots by amateurs, and glorious paintings languishing unseen in the picture collection. The Royal Archives in Windsor Castle contained four magnificently preserved panoramic photographs the Prince of Wales brought home to show his wife, Princess Mary. To my great surprise, the Ursuline Archives in Quebec housed a huge postcard collection, and my own university library at York, as a result of the fortuitous purchase years ago of the Ducharme Collection, had an almost complete set (128 cards) of the Keystone Stereoscopic slide show of the tercentenary. Only the moving picture made of the last scene of the historical pageants, once the property of the National Archives, eluded me, but newsreel footage of some events did turn up. When I eventually assembled all my research materials I found that I had as many photographic images to deal with as letters, memoranda, and other written documents. Much of what I learned about the tercentenary came from the careful examination and manipulation of the many kinds of visual representations of it. Years ago, one of my professors declared that the argument of his book was contained in the adjectives. Here, as the reader will soon discover, a good portion of my argument is borne by the imagery.

In Clare Denison's box of memories time stood still; it was still the summer of 1908. Yet the passage of time between the pasting of these images and stories in her scrapbook in 1908 and my reading of them at the end of the century had changed almost everything. I could not see with her eyes or feel what she felt, of course. But I could see and feel something she could not. What seemed so optimistic, grand, and imperial at the beginning of the century now appeared so fragile, contingent, even innocent at its end.

Four or five generations of change had stripped away the confident certainty exuded by these images. They now seemed more ironic than totemic. Could a modern Prince of Wales pretend to such potency and power? The Empire was gone; war had tarnished all that military hardware; Canada had found its place in the world but it was cramped and less

heroic than expected; Quebec, whose founding was here being celebrated as the birth of Canada, seemed on the brink of leaving. In the
interval, the roles of victors and vanquished have been reversed. The
boldly assertive had, over time, been sapped by doubt. Canada's century,
which had begun with such pomp and circumstance, seemed to be
ending in a whimper.

Beyond that, History itself had been dethroned. In the late twentieth
century the past is now more often a source of shame than pride; it is not
something we seek to relive, but rather to forget as we speed towards an
improved future. How many today would think of appealing to the past
for guidance or inspiration, or think it exciting, romantic, heroic, relevant? One could not help seeing these flaking mementos in the light of
all that had come afterwards. Time had given Clare Denison's collection
other meanings.

Her scrapbook and souvenirs challenged me to write this book in part
because they reminded me of something I had been avoiding. Here I
could see an earlier group of Canadians inside and outside of Quebec
reaching out towards one another, trying within the vocabulary of their
time and in both languages to find some kind of mutual accommodation
but not knowing quite how to go about it. At the turn of the century
historians took Quebec seriously. They may have got it wrong, but they
did not ignore it. And I have to confess that too many historians of my
generation, myself included, have constructed their scholarship in such
a way as to define Quebec out of the picture. How much of Canadian
history spoke only of what is now sadly called the Rest of Canada? In
Quebec, of course, the reverse has been the case for more than a
generation.

Historiographically we have drifted apart; for a long time the historians of our distinct societies have not had much to say to each other. At
the end of the day I did not want to stand accused of this *trahison des clercs*.
There are central questions in our history that must be addressed,
however awkward and uncomfortable the experience might be. And if
critics point out that this is really not Quebec history, but rather a study in
French-English relations, I will not protest too much, except to add that
another people struggles to raise its voice in this history.

This attempt in 1908 to invent and celebrate a new nationality and
thereby, in the imagination at least, establish a new cultural equilibrium
in Edwardian Canada, seemed to be a subject worth exploring, not just

for its own sake, but also for what illumination it might shed on the central unsolved problem of our time. That the tercentenary failed in its larger objectives, while sobering, may offer some lessons. What will our efforts look like reflected in the mirror of history? More darkly, I wonder what the celebration of the quatrocentenary of Canada will be like in 2008 – if there should be one?

I would be reminded of many things and learn much more as I followed these strands of public memory out into other archives and libraries. One of those things I have just admitted to: historians write about the past with the present and future very much in mind. It is no coincidence that I took up this subject during a national crisis, that I found myself in Quebec on the eve of the referendum working in the Bibliothèque Nationale and the Archives of Quebec and wandering across the Plains of Abraham in the first snow flurries of the season. I needed a subject that connected me professionally to something urgent about our present. In these pages, we will find scholars and public figures in another era doing much the same thing.

Somehow the poignancy and immediacy of Clare Denison's memorabilia touched me across the years. These treasured objects piqued my curiosity about the event and the process it represented. This private archive prodded me to think about the ways in which past and present interact in public memory, how history is used in the shaping of nations, and how sometimes history gets in the way of nation-building. Above all, Clare Denison's collection revived in me an enthusiasm for historical narrative. There was a story waiting to be told in this box.

1. A MIDSUMMER NIGHT'S DREAM

Prologue: Quebec City, 12–18 July 1908

Over the weekend, Hurons from nearby Ancien Lorette pitched tepees in the woods at the western edge of the Plains of Abraham. Ojibways from Sault Ste Marie and Iroquois, Mohawks, and Onondagas from reserves on the St Lawrence followed, soon numbering some two hundred men, women, and children.

During the week, another nation also assembled under canvas. Militia regiments and regular soldiers from Halifax to Sarnia, as well as a combined contingent of troops and mounted police from the Northwest, arrived in coordinated waves by steamer and special train. Under the watchful eye of their new Canadian commander, artillery, infantry, cavalry, and engineering units – twelve thousand men in all – filled row upon row of tents covering seven hundred acres at Savard Park and Parc St-Joseph in Lévis.

Unannounced, at seven o'clock on Tuesday evening, a flotilla of British warships steamed into view off the tip of Île d'Orléans. As word spread and onlookers rushed to get a view from the ramparts and terraces, four battleships – the *Albemarle, Russell, Exmouth,* and *Duncan* – and the cruiser *Arrogant* anchored beneath the Citadel under festive arcs of colourful flags and thick plumes of black smoke.

All through the week, horse-drawn carriages and motor cars toiled up the hill from the wharves and railway station, ferrying distinguished guests to their lodgings through streets bedecked with the tricolour of

France, the Union Jack of Great Britain, and festive bunting. The *Empress of Ireland* docked on Thursday evening with a cargo of British aristocrats, notably the Duke of Norfolk, Lord Lovat, Viscount Falmouth, and the popular Field Marshal Earl Roberts, 'Bobs,' and his daughter. Vice-Admiral de Jauréguiberry arrived soon after with the French delegation aboard the jaunty battleship *Léon Gambetta* and took up residence with the lieutenant-governor and Vice-President Fairbanks of the United States at Spencer Wood. Representatives from South Africa, Australia, New Zealand, and Newfoundland, along with the direct descendants of Generals Wolfe, Montcalm, Lévis, Murray, and Carleton joined Canadian dignitaries at the Château Frontenac, headed by Lord Strathcona, Premier James P. Whitney of Ontario, and Edmund Walker, president of the Bank of Commerce. Colonel Denison, his wife Helen, and daughter Clare were already ensconced there in a suite.[1]

The hotels had long since been booked. Visitors filled the guest-houses and spilled into a vast tented city, a temporary summer hotel under canvas. Informal social networks arranged private lodgings. On Friday evening Mrs Crombie arrived from Ottawa, chaperoning four beautiful young women. She dropped two off at the convent where Lady Grey had arranged for them to be guests of the Ursulines, then continued on with her two other high-spirited charges, Lola Powell and Ethel Chadwick, to much more luxurious quarters on the upper floors in the spacious home of William Price on the Grande Allée.[2] Next day, Saturday the 18th, as rain gave way to glorious sunshine, Madame Pasquali, the celebrated contralto from the Metropolian Opera, swept into the gaily decorated town.[3]

A festive stage was set. The cast assembled. Time then for Oberon and Titania to 'awake the pert and nimble spirit of mirth' and for Puck to be about his mischief.

Act One: Competing Homages

The subject of this celebration, Samuel de Champlain, navigator, explorer, colonizer, landed at the site of Quebec City in July 1608 and built a small fortification. After three hundred years, the citizens of Quebec now gathered to honour their founder before the eyes of the world.

The youth of Quebec seized the opportunity to be first to raise their voices in commemoration. After mass on Sunday, 19 July, about five

An honour guard dressed as Montcalm's soldiers lays a wreath at the base of Champlain's statue during the homage of l'Association Catholique de la Jeunesse Canadienne-française.

thousand members of l'Association Catholique de la Jeunesse Canadienne-française assembled. Led by the chief of police on horseback, followed by a contingent of troops of Montcalm's army in historical costume, and a formation of Papal Zouaves, forty-two branches of the organized Catholic youth of Quebec marched up the hill by the Legislative Buildings into the old city to Place d'Armes. There, overlooking the river close to the Château Frontenac, the leaders of the association solemnly laid floral wreaths at the base of the massive rococo monument to Champlain that had been erected in 1897.

The renowned orator Mr Adjutor Rivard opened with a poetic ode invoking Champlain's blessing on his descendants' struggle to build a

French, Catholic nation. Maurice Dupré, president of the association, followed with a eulogy linking Champlain to Bishop Laval, whose bicentennial had been commemorated with a nearby statue only a month earlier. In Champlain's name, Dupré implored the crowd never 'to separate our religious from our national interests because the destruction of the former will entail the ruin of the latter.'

As these red-faced men in tight celluloid collars declaimed mightily in the damp heat, a note of alarm crept into their appeals. Dr Georges Baril, in his evocation of Champlain as a 'worthy founder of our nation,' an 'indomitable soldier of Christ and France,' concluded with a warning. The present generation of youth must take up and complete Champlain's work, he insisted, because Freemasons, appeasers, and enemies were abroad spreading their insidious doctrines, sapping the people's ties to their church. Champlain's valiant spirit must be awakened, he cried, secularism and compromise would 'mean the death of our race, a true national suicide.'

But if this demonstration by l'Association Catholique de la Jeunesse Canadienne-française was part of the official program, where were all the dignitaries? Why were the viewing stands almost empty? Where was the mayor? What official business could possibly demand his attention on such an occasion? Why was there so much indignation in the air?

The ceremony took on the tone of a protest more than a celebration as speaker after speaker hurled his convictions defiantly into the public square. If Québécois were in peril, so too were the French. The youth of Quebec were implored to declare their solidarity with France – not secular France, but the France of the Gospel, the France of St Louis, Joan of Arc, Champlain, Montcalm, and Lévis, the France of Laval, that is, Christian France. It was Canada's duty in the new century, more particularly French Canada's, to save the soul of France. This could be accomplished first by being bold at home. Here in Canada, the crowd was assured, French Canadians must not shrink from asserting themselves. Through their accomplishments in politics and the arts and through their faith, they would eventually earn respect and assume greater control over their own destiny. But to do so they must resist temptation and domination. 'We protest our loyalty to the British Crown,' the last speaker declared, 'but before the interest of the Empire we place the interest of Canada and before all the rest, the love of our Province.'

Amidst much cheering, the singing of 'O Canada,' and 'God Save the

King,' the crowd dispersed, leaving behind its floral tribute to an imagined founding father, puffed with pride at having had the first word in the celebration.[4] Champlain had been honoured, but he had also been symbolically recruited to join an ongoing battle with France, secular liberalism, Anglo-imperialism, and other contemporary enemies of the nation and faith.

Another kind of homage was paid three days later with the triumphal entry into Quebec City of His Royal Highness the Prince of Wales. He too had come to honour Champlain. The crowds turned out in the thousands to pay homage to him. And the messages on this occasion were somewhat different from the Catholic nationalist note struck on opening day.

This time there was ample warning of the ships' arrival. Mobs of citizens and visitors jostled for good viewing positions on the terraces; the cliff face was black with people perched on every ledge. Below, on the King's Wharf, dignitaries in their ceremonial uniforms, gold braid, and cocked hats arrayed themselves in a scene 'of almost medieval splendour': Prime Minister Sir Wilfrid Laurier and his cabinet in their court dress formed up in the centre; to the right, representatives of the provinces along with Robert Borden, leader of the Conservative opposition; to the left, representatives of foreign governments and the navies.

At 2:30 p.m. the cruiser *Minotaur* briskly rounded St Joseph Point, followed by the massive battleship *Indomitable*, from whose topmost mast the royal pennant fluttered. As the ship bearing the prince eased into its mooring and the other vessels already in harbour smartly ran up their colours, a thunderous salute of welcome roared from their guns. Across the water, the playing of 'God Save the King' from the *Léon Gambetta* mingled with the rumble of the great anchor chain of the *Indomitable* and the pealing of church bells from both shores. From the deck of his warship, the Prince of Wales marvelled at the brilliant spectacle – the fleet gleaming on the river, 'the town decorated, & the hills swarming with people in the bright sun.'[5]

As the prince stepped ashore, the band broke into 'God Save the King' and then a visibly excited Sir Wilfrid Laurier waved his plumed hat to encourage three lusty cheers for the prince. Following an inspection of the honour guard, Earl Grey, the governor general, accompanied the prince to a small covered dais at the centre of the welcoming quadrangle of dignitaries, over which towered a gleaming white ceremonial arch from which fluttered the flags of France, Great Britain, and the United States. There a more formal Sir Wilfrid welcomed him in English and

The Prince of Wales upon his arrival at Quebec passes through the ceremonial arch.

French, extolling the heroic deeds of Champlain, the flowering of New France, noting how in the fortunes of war Quebec had passed under British rule, and how fitting it was that the prince could preside over a ceremony by which the Plains of Abraham could be preserved 'as a perpetual memorial, by English and French Canadians, of the great deeds in which both peoples feel an equal pride.'

The prince replied also in English and French, expressing his gratitude for the loyalty of his father's Canadian subjects, his pleasure at the prosperity of the Dominion, and his full endorsement of the memorialization of the hallowed ground of the Plains of Abraham. He recalled from his previous five visits the evidence he had witnessed of the fidelity of the King's French-Canadian subjects. This working together of English and French Canadians, he said, was a source of deep satisfaction to the king and was surely one of the greatest tributes to 'the political genius of England's rule.'

Mercifully, the ceremony under the punishing sun was brief. The speeches over, the Prince of Wales and the governor general climbed into a waiting landau. With Police Chief Emile Trudel and a detachment of Northwest Mounted Police in the van, and the Royal Canadian Dragoons in the rear, the royal procession clattered up the steep streets, narrowed by thousands of cheering spectators in colourful midsummer attire.

As he threaded his way through this throng, the prince was observed to take a particular interest in the palisade at Champlain's reconstructed Habitation and the newly dedicated statue of Bishop Laval. Ethel Chadwick and the irrepressible Lola Powell took in the prince's arrival from their vantage point in one of the dining room windows of the Château Frontenac, sipping champagne sent to them by an anonymous admirer. Ethel later gushed in her diary: 'His Ex saw us as they passed right under our window and bowed & winked, and we all broke out waving our handkerchiefs, cheering wildly our future King.'[6] Looking on from his carriage, the prince noted that the crowds, 'who gave me a most enthusiastic reception,' seemed especially welcoming, 'much more so than when May & I were here 7 years ago,' he happily reported to his father.[7]

The next day the Prince of Wales formally opened the tercentenary in a ceremony of tribute to Champlain at his monument. Simultaneously, on the river below, a reconstruction of Champlain's ship, the *Don-de-Dieu*, accompanied by a flotilla of small craft, sailed gallantly into port, the tiny white-hulled seventeenth-century vessel a diminutive contrast to the grim grey steel of the mightiest battleships of the day. The re-enactment of

Champlain's entry into his city echoed and inverted that of the prince the day before. Native people greeted him aboard his ship and he descended into one of their canoes to be ferried to the King's Wharf. The costumed armies of Montcalm and Wolfe were there to greet Champlain, admirably portrayed by the Honourable Charles Langelier, and escort him to his Habitation.

At the formal dedication ceremony going on in the square above, Mayor Garneau greeted the Prince of Wales on behalf of the city at the feet of Champlain, 'the glorious founder of Canada.' He assured the prince that the patriotism and gratitude of the citizens of Quebec extended both to their beloved France 'to whom they are indebted for their being and their grand traditions,' and to England under whose liberties they have been 'free to expand the full enjoyment of their faith, their language and their institutions.' Concluding with an exclamation of 'God Save the King! God Bless the Prince of Wales,' Mayor Garneau rolled up his address and placed it in a casket of gold which he then presented to the prince as a memento of the tercentenary.

The prince responded in French, eulogizing the immortal explorer, the brilliance of his pen, the beauty of his statue, his high qualities of 'piety and courage, of humanity and strength.' The Dominion, the Mother Country, and the Empire, as well as 'the great nation to whom he owed allegiance,' also joined in the homage. 'Doing honour to the memory of Champlain united in friendship three great, powerful and wealthy nations in a spirit that could only advance the high ideal of universal peace and brotherhood.' Such a celebration, the prince concluded, 'appeals to Canada, to the British Empire, and to the whole civilized world.'

Following a reading by the governor general of many congratulatory telegrams from the four corners of the Empire, the vice-president of the United States conveyed greetings from the neighbours. Canada and the United States he claimed had 'no rivalries except in the ways of peace.' Speaking next as the official representative of France, Admiral Jauréguiberry used the occasion to praise the entente cordiale between the Republic of France and the Government of Great Britain and to emphasize the affectionate esteem of France for Canada. From across the ocean, the citizens of France admired the union 'between two races' as well as the remarkable progress Canadians had achieved, events that necessarily 'increased the glory of their mother country,' he concluded with calculated ambiguity.

Native paddlers in canoes greet Champlain aboard the *Don-de-Dieu*.

To conclude the official ceremony the Honourable Adélard Turgeon, a distinguished orator, spoke for Canada at the special request of the prime minister. In an address whose length tried the patience of most onlookers as much as his rolling rhetorical phrases drew admiration, Turgeon extolled the splendours of the great Dominion, then thanked the Prince of Wales for his presence, the great neighbouring republic for its friendship, the glory of France for benefits of civilization and Christianity, and British liberty which had allowed 'national dualism' to thrive in a bountiful, beautiful landscape.[8]

With that, the prince took to his carriage to move to a new vantage point to observe an elaborate historical procession that had began to file through the square. The two separate ceremonies, one below on the river with Champlain as the centrepiece, and one above on the terrace where the Prince of Wales was the focus of attention, were now joined. At the head of the procession came a contingent of mounted heralds and men of the watch in medieval dress whose appearance as town criers and guides in the streets had elicited much comment. Behind them a cavalcade of Canadian history, beginning with Jacques Cartier and his crew bearing a massive wooden cross, followed by a deputation of native people. Grouped under identifying banners, kings, queens, courtiers, councillors, explorers, soldiers, adventurers, *coureurs de bois*, and habitants wound their way up through the narrow streets, once again packed with onlookers, to the prince's viewing stand by the Château Frontenac.

When Champlain entered the square, he paused briefly to acknowledge his likeness atop the monument with a bow and a flourish of his plumed hat. Champlain, with his wife, partners, and the crew of the *Don-de-Dieu* had other attractions to compete against. For to tumultuous cheers at the climax of the parade, Generals Montcalm and Wolfe rode into view at the head of their respective regiments. The last word of the procession would not be conflict, but rather French-Canadian fidelity to British rule. A small band of French-Canadian militia, commanded by Guy Carleton, who repulsed Montgomery's invasion of Quebec in a December blizzard in 1775, brought up the rear along with three-hundred of de Salaberry's green-clad Voltigeurs, defenders once again of Canada against the Americans at the Battle of Châteauguay in 1812. All told, about four thousand costumed figures filed through Place d'Armes in homage to Champlain. In turn, all of Canadian history and much of that of France passed in review before the heir to the British throne and, thereby, presented itself as prologue to the present.

The François I section of the historical procession approaches Place d'Armes.

Samuel de Champlain, his bride Hélène Boullé, and companions pose during the historical procession.

'I must say the dresses were very good & they were well drilled,' the Prince of Wales wrote to his wife immediately afterwards. He had returned to the Citadel through the cheering crowds 'with the satisfaction of feeling that everything had gone off admirably & that as far as I know everyone was pleased.' He then broke off his narrative in the cool comfort of his fortress to take in the view before him: 'Most lovely sight looking out of my window with ships in the river below & the town on the other side, so quiet and peaceful after the knocking about we have had at sea.'⁹

Meanwhile, in the town all was joyful confusion. With dukes and lords, military officers, politicians in formal attire, soldiers, sailors, and figures in period costumes mingling in the streets with an Edwardian crowd in bright summer clothes, past and present had become inextricably combined, and the precise object of commemoration blurred in an expansive mood of general exaltation.

Act Two: Forest Enchantment

Follow the crowd out through the gates of the old city, along the Grande Allée, up onto the Plains of Abraham, and into the massive grandstand, filled with the sweet fragrance of freshly sawn white pine, to Oberon's enchanted realm where wood nymphs, fairies, and elves dance and the past comes to life in historical pageantry.

The 'stage' in front of the stadium is a wide, flat expanse of lawn sloping down towards the river where, from time to time, the ships of the fleet drift into view. Beyond the river lies the dimpled green landscape of the south shore. For five evenings beginning at 5:00 p.m. – to provide cool, twilit, lengthening shadows in the dramatic gloaming, and more practically to allow actors to assemble after the day's work – the magic of the pageants unfolds. Every day the sky stays blue, the temperatures remain moderate, the sunsets are glorious, and, once, the rain held off until the end of the last scene. It is indeed an enchanted realm.

The audience stills. Attention shifts towards a small group of Indian tepees by the woods to the right. It is the summer of 1534. An Indian chief, Donnacona, emerges from one of the tents. He strides forward, his hand shading his eyes as he peers into the distance. Suddenly he cries out. The villagers rush to his side to catch a glimpse of a strange apparition, three ships sailing up the river. Moments later, French sailors march up the hill singing a jaunty song; the reassuring attitude of these strangers dissolves the natives' fears. Caution quickly gives way to abandon. In

The opening scene of the historical pageant. Donnacona, in the costume of a Plains Indian, sights Cartier's ships.

Nymphs and fairies dance about François I and his queen, who are on horseback under the canopy in the Fontainebleau gardens scene of the first pageant.

delight the natives hurl their bodies into dances of joy, shouting amidst their contortions, 'Agouazi!' welcome. Old and young, warriors and women with babes in arms, crowd up to the newcomers, to feel their clothing and touch their faces.

A humble Jacques Cartier expresses astonishment that the natives take him for a god and prays for forgiveness and strength from his own spiritual master. An old chief, Agouhana, is carried out and begs Cartier to heal him. As Cartier ministers to Agouhana, his crew assemble a large wooden cross bearing the fleur-de-lis escutcheon of the king of France. To the strains of Gounod's 'Road to Calvary,' the cross is slowly raised. In a gesture of understanding, the Indians respectfully place offerings of corn, fruits, and flowers around its base.

Cannons boom from the ships. More sick and ailing are brought out of the village for healing. The crew distribute presents: knives and hatchets to the men, beads, rosaries, combs, and bells to the women; rings and images of the 'Agnus Dei' are flung among the children who scramble for their prizes. Amidst a joyful tumult a young woman is offered to Cartier, then two braves, one of them Donnacona. Cartier, played by the advocate Moise Raymond, strikes a splendid pose with his parting prayer

Panoramic photograph of the scene in which Henri IV commissions Champlain to establish a colony in Canada. Lola Powell and Ethel Chadwick are in the isolated group on the far left just above the inscription.

before the Cross, after which the sailors launch into a spirited chorus of 'À Saint Malo' as they return with their three guests to the ships.

A brilliant fanfare of trumpets marks the beginning of a new scene. The orchestra strikes up a stately processional in the foreground while a scene of unparalleled grandeur begins to unfold in the middle distance. It takes almost ten minutes for the courtiers of François I – nobles, their ladies, officers, equerries, officials, and servants – to wend their way out of the forest, where apparently they have passed an agreeable afternoon. They assemble themselves in glittering array before the grandstand in the imaginary gardens of Fontainebleau in 1536. The king rides up on a horse draped in gold. Fauns and satyrs dance through the gardens. Cartier and Donnacona reappear to be presented to François I. Cartier kneels, Donnacona falls prostrate before the king, then rises to tell a wondrous tale of the new world. Amused and gratified, the king and his court ride off.

In a flurry of activity as stagehands spead a huge pale blue canvas across the grass and erect a backdrop, time moves forward almost sixty years to 1608 and the palace of King Henri IV, the Louvre. The gentlemen and ladies of the court promenade in animated conversation. Their mingling is brought to an abrupt halt by a trumpet fanfare announcing the arrival of the king and queen at the head of a grand procession of

officials, pages, gentlemen, and ladies-in-waiting. Once Henri IV and his queen, Marie de Medici, assume their thrones on a dais to one side surmounted by a royal blue canopy, Sieur de Monts, the king's royal commissioner to New France, presents Champlain to the court. Henri IV grandly commissions Champlain to venture to the new world and found a colony of France.

In celebration, oboes, lutes, and violins sound the first bars of a stately pavane. Thirty or more couples emerge from the assembled courtiers; the dancers file onto the field, wheel, then come together in the centre, the men's swords held aloft flashing in the sunset. The men disengage, form up again with the ladies, then turn once more. The dance concluded, the partners hold their deep curtsies and bows as the king, queen, and court move towards the audience between two columns of halberdiers to a chorus of 'Vivre Henri IV.'

Stately Renaissance music gives way to simple folk tunes as the scenery is swept away and the courtiers disperse on either side of the stadium. Champlain is next seen returning to the colony in 1620 bringing with him his young bride, Hélène Boullé. The entire population of eighty settlers turns out to greet their lieutenant-general and his wife and the natives have prepared a special feast and celebration to mark the occasion. Champlain and his wife take their places; they palaver with the chiefs and smoke the calumet presented to them. Singers and drummers group themselves around the perimeter of a large reed mat and begin their chant. A male dancer takes centre stage, throwing himself into contorted forms, gesticulating with the calumet in his hand. A second warrior strides onto the mat decked out in the accoutrements of war. A mock duel takes place between the two and the warrior of peace, defended solely by the calumet, triumphs in battle over his armed adversary. After the dance Champlain and his wife are led by the settlers and native people to their Habitation.

Rustic sociability gives way to the civilizing power of women and religion in the next pageant scene. The Ursulines, led by Marie de l'Incarnation, and the Jesuits are welcomed to New France by the governor, Sieur de Montmagny, in 1639. The nuns and priests kneel and kiss the soil, then rise and form a procession to a little church to thank God for their safe arrival. En route Madame de la Peltrie kisses Indian children while Marie de l'Incarnation gathers a crowd of settlers' children about her for songs and instruction.

Civilization hangs on the brink in the exciting fourth scene in which the stalwart Dollard des Ormeaux and his colleagues save Ville Marie from destruction in 1660. Dollard and his group ambush a war party of Iroquois on its way to attack the village; the Indians counter-attack and are repulsed. Following a stirring war dance, the Indians overrun the stockade in a massed attack; Dollard and his brave companions perish in the flames. Smoke and sadness fill the air as the Indians form up into a retreating column. As the program notes explain, 'To the beat of drums the train moves off uttering plaintive and mournful sounds and bearing the bodies of the dead in procession, with their scalp trophies elevated on poles.'

A blare of trumpets pierces the gloom. It is 1665 now, and New France has been made a royal colony. Cannons roar their welcome as the new governor, the Marquis de Tracy, leads his regiment, the Carignan-Salières, majestically into the awestruck colony as the orchestra plays Mendelssohn's stirring 'War March of the Priests.' Just as imperiously, Bishop Laval, under a golden canopy surrounded by a splendid retinue, advances to meet the secular power. The marquis kneels, kisses the bishop's ring and the crucifix. Together they make their way towards the cathedral, past twelve vanquished Indian chieftains who lay bows and arrows at their feet to symbolize peaceful submission. Church bells of the city peal out their welcome, and a *Te Deum* is sung. Peace and order have been restored in a joint act of church and state.

Taking possession of le pays d'en haut, the west country, is the subject of the sixth scene of the pageant. A party of voyageurs makes its way

The arrival of the Ursulines in the third historical pageant.

through a progression of friendly Indian tribes to a meeting place near Sault Ste Marie. There the voyageurs barter with the native people for furs, after which Jesuit missionaries bless a cross and pray. The territory is thereby claimed for the king with a prayer 'to thank God on behalf of these rude savages that they are now the subjects of so great and powerful a Monarch.'

It is just before dawn on Monday, 16 October 1690 as the seventh scene begins. Sir William Phips's English fleet of thirty-four vessels is reported to be three leagues from the city. A messenger from Phips interrupts a meeting of the Sovereign Council, imperiously demanding that Quebec surrender immediately. Governor Frontenac jauntily dismisses this arrogant request with his memorable rebuff: 'Je vais répondre à votre mâitre par la bouche de mes canons!' Confounded by such bravery, Phips's squadron retreats in disarray. The colony is once again spared.

In the French-language program, what followed next is described briefly as a 'Grande Parade d'honneur,'[10] but it is more than a mere parade. From opposite sides of the field the two great armies of 1759 appear, the drummers, buglers, and standard-bearers in front. Behind the banners stand row upon row of Montcalm's predominently blue, off-white, and grey-clad ranks. Opposite them in their mitre hats, scarlet coats, and white breeches, Wolfe's regiments form up along with the Fraser Highlanders in full Highland dress. Though the guns of the ships simulate the bombardment of the city, no mock battle between the armies would end the drama. Instead the two generals exchange honours; then together, at the head of a unified army, they march their troops across the field to the strains of 'God Save the King' and, for the first time, 'O Canada' used as a Canadian national anthem. Carleton's Militia and De Salaberry's Voltigeurs join the marching columns. Then all the participants from the previous scenes gather in a glorious finale as children release a flock of white doves of peace.[11]

The crowd in the grandstand is on its feet, applauding, singing, and in many cases crying with joy. They have never seen anything like it before. Outside the stadium, time itself, roles and identities have become merrily jumbled as the audience and actors merge into one excited, chattering body. As the sun sets, the enchanted participants and observers stroll in animated groups across the Plains back towards the now twinkling city. Oberon and Titania can congratulate themselves on a delightful evening of merrymaking.

Artist's impression of the climax of the last scene of the final pageant, the march-past of the two historic armies, their ranks intermingled. In the front rank from left to right: Montcalm, Wolfe, Lévis, and Murray. Note the eleven ships of the fleet in the background firing a salute.

Act Three: Joyful Communion

New smells – leather, horses, gunpowder, and sweat – and new sounds – pipers, bands, brass bands, and fifes and drums – indicated a new order of things on the Plains of Abraham. Early in the morning of Friday, 24 July, the tramp of feet, the clatter of horses, and the rattle of gun-carriages on cobblestones echoed across the city, announcing that twelve thousand militiamen from the three camps had begun to converge on the parade ground. They were joined there by some three thousand sailors from the three-nation fleet. As far as the eye could see, the Plains were covered with a sea of troops and sailors in specially issued white pith helmets to ward off the sun.

Preceded by an escort of dragoons, the Prince of Wales on horseback cantered onto the parade ground. On one side of him rode Earl Grey, the governor general of Canada, and on the other the aged and much beloved 'Bobs,' Earl Roberts. Accompanied by General Otter, the re-cently appointed and first Canadian commanding officer of the Cana-dian militia, the prince trotted slowly along the ranks, past a group of gallant Canadian veterans of various British imperial campaigns. At the end of the royal inspection the prince dismounted at a small pavilion where the governor general was waiting for him. In a brief, simple ceremony the prince handed over to Earl Grey the title deed to the Plains of Abraham along with a cheque for $450,000. This sum, contributed by the citizens of Canada, Great Britain, France, the United States, and the Empire, would preserve forever as a 'shrine of union and peace' these hallowed and historic battlefields where 'two contending races won equal and imperishable glory.' In one elegant sentence, the governor general accepted the prince's present of this 'sacred ground' to mark the three hundredth anniversary of Champlain's founding of Quebec.

The prince took up his position on horseback before a packed grand-stand. Facing him in the place of honour were the Highland regiments; to his right was the naval contingent, and to his left, stretching off towards the jail (whose prisoners had a magnificent view of the pano-rama from their cells), were the massed militia regiments. For the next hour and a half, soldiers, sailors, and militiamen and their bands marched past in review. Earl Roberts brought the cavalcade to a spectacular conclusion as he led an impromptu charge of Royal Canadian Horse Artillery thundering past the reviewing stand.[12] The Plains of Abraham thus became Canada's first historical park through a vast military occupation.

It would be 'sacralized' in a different way on Sunday. Religious beliefs provided a conscious subtext to almost every aspect of the tercentenary. Formal religious ceremonies, however, presented a delicate problem. In Catholic Quebec the Protestant heir to the headship of the Church of England could not take part in a mass. Whatever the prince's own views on the matter, Protestant opinion in Canada would not permit it.[13] Thus without the guest of honour, ten thousand people gathered on Sunday at the pageant grandstand on the Plains to celebrate a magnificent messe solennelle, among them the leading Catholic peer, the Duke of Norfolk, the Marquis de Montcalm, Sir Wilfrid and Lady Laurier, his minister of justice from Quebec, Sir Charles Fitzpatrick, Lomer Gouin, the premier of Quebec, and George Garneau, mayor of Quebec City. Ethel Chadwick, the solitary Catholic in the Ottawa contingent, also attended.[14]

An altar had been built centre stage beneath a crimson and gold canopy; a company of Papal Zouaves was drawn up facing it. Two columns of de Salaberry's Voltigeurs and guards from the Jacques Cartier and Champlain pageants marked the route to the altar. A fanfare of trumpets from the Royal Canadian Artillery Band under the direction of Joseph Vezina stilled the crowd. To the strains of the now familiar 'War March of the Priests,' the ecclesiastical procession paraded majestically up the aisle, led by altar boys in white surplices and red sashes. Then came canons in purple and crimon. Heralds and men-at-arms in gleaming silver breastplates formed an honour guard preceding the archbishop of Quebec, Monseigneur Bégin, in glittering white and gold, followed by his auxiliary archbishop, Paul Roy, and five bishops in scarlet.

It would take the pen of a poet, *Le Soleil* reported, to do justice to the splendour of the religious ceremony. Monseigneur Bégin officiated, assisted by massed choirs. During the service the *Don-de-Dieu* sailed into view on the river. Following the *Te Deum* at the end, the choirs and congregation joined in singing 'God Bless the Prince' – an anthem composed for the occasion – and 'God Save the King.' With a mass of unprecedented glory, the church claimed centre stage in the civic festival and consecrated this sacred ground in its own way.[15]

While this mass was being celebrated on the Plains of Abraham, the Prince of Wales, Lord Roberts, Earl Grey, and others gathered indoors at the English cathedral for a very understated Anglican service. Afterwards

Procession during the messe solennelle.

the prince noted with some weariness: 'On Sunday morning, another very hot day, we went to a Thanksgiving Service in our Cathedral where the Bishop preached, the music & singing quite good & only lasted 1¼ hours but the heat was great.'[16]

The Roman Catholic Church and the crown came to terms informally later, away from public view. Under the pretence of taking a relaxing tour of the countryside, the Prince of Wales spent the better part of Monday as the guest of the apostolic delegate, Monseigneur Sbarretti, and the Quebec bishops at the seminary's country retreat at St Joachim. In the

The royal party returning from the country. The Prince of Wales is closest to the camera in the back of the automobile and is accompanied by the governor general, Earl Grey. Monseigneur O.E. Mathieu, the rector of Laval University, is in the front seat with the driver.

afternoon the Prince of Wales returned by automobile along country roads lined with curious farmers and their families. They gazed in wonder at him. He returned the favour, stopping occasionally for a chat.

Communion and commemoration went together. Joining to worship, eat, sing, dance, march, to be moved to emotional heights, to give and receive honours, the tercentenary of Quebec was an omnigatherum of Canadians. By gathering in fellowship for the common purpose of honouring founders, a people made themselves. The railway companies estimated they carried thirty thousand more passengers to Quebec than usual during the tercentenary. Wealthy tourists arrived in their yachts. All of the hotels were filled, and everyone had guests. Attracted by the rich pluckings, pickpockets and prostitutes mingled with the crowds. Detectives routinely apprehended them and sent them unceremoniously packing.

Spectacle drew people together in common awe of light, art, power, illusion. By day, parades, processions, motorcades of dignitaries, the pageants, fleet movements, and military manoeuvres gathered spectators. By night, the thrill came from being part of a huge crowd jostling in the semi-darkness, surrounded by the tracery of silhouetted buildings, illuminations, powerful searchlights from ships, fireworks, and the sound of music.

Everywhere music could be heard – on the streets, in concert halls, balls, state inners, churches, in open-air concerts, bandshells, and of course at the pageant ground. Joseph Vezina and his music committee staged performances of Felicien David's symphonic ode *Christophe Colomb* for six soloists, a choir of four hundred voices, and full orchestra. Four thousand people attended two performances of this massive oratorio in the Drill Hall. On Saturday evening, Madame Pasquali starred in a gala concert put on by the Symphonic Society featuring the music of Berlioz, Verdi, Weber, Saint-Saens, Massenet, David, and Rossini.

The learned professions dignified the occasion by their deliberations as well. A Congress of French-speaking Physicians gathered for meetings at Laval University. The Royal Society of Canada also assembled especially for the occasion. With the governor general in attendance at the afternoon session, Judge François Langelier, Professor B.P. Mignault of Laval, Professor George Wrong of the University of Toronto, and Mr Adjutor Rivard of la Société de Parler Français were inducted into membership. Two poems of loyalty and optimism for Canada's future were read by the Reverend F.G. Scott. Diplomas were awarded to those who had made special contributions to the organization of the tercentenary, among them Ernest Myrand, author of the script of the pageants, and H.-J.-J.-B. Chouinard, clerk of the city, who had championed the cause of the Champlain tercentenary. And at the evening session the historians focused on Champlain and his legacy.[17]

The tercentenary provided many different degrees of access to membership in the community of celebrants. The majority of those attending the celebrations were merely spectators. But there were also more active forms of participation, those at the highest level being singled out for honours by the crown. Early in the festivities, the prince summoned a select group of men – the governor general, George Garneau, Premiers Whitney and Gouin, General Otter, and a few others to the state ballroom of the Citadel where he presented knighthoods and other honours in the name of the king in a simple ceremony. Colonel Denison modestly declined his honour.[18]

At Quebec, in the presence of their prince, the cream of Canadian society frolicked. The two weeks presented a swirl of balls, formal dinners, garden parties, and receptions at which various elites mingled. Army and navy competed in military games and as hosts. The officers' messes on land and the wardrooms aboard ship competed with one another with dinners, dances, and parties. The mayor hosted a grand dinner at City Hall; the lieutenant-governor replied with a garden party at Spencer Wood. The social highlights of the tercentenary, however, were two glittering state dinners at the Citadel and a magnificent state ball in the Legislative Building.

The first state dinner, given by Earl Grey, was a small, highly select, masculine and mainly military, religious, political affair. The prince reported: '100 in full uniform, no speeches thank God, it lasted over two hours. This was followed by a reception, mostly ladies, all of whom I shook hands with. We all went on the terrace to see the fireworks & the ships illuminated, lovely sight.' The second dinner, held on Saturday evening in honour of the delegations attending from other provinces in Canada and from colonies within the British Empire, was an endurance test of toasts and oratory on the theme of imperial unity. The guest list – all male still – expanded to embrace a broader representation of the Canadian political, financial, university, and judicial elite. Colonel Denison pronounced it 'a great Imperial function.'[19] The prince, after two speeches of his own and a dozen or so by others, rose from the table at midnight confessing to his diary and his wife, 'you can imagine I was pretty tired.'[20]

The men and women were reunited at the state ball given by the Government of Quebec on Friday evening. The Legislative Buildings themselves, outlined in strings of red, white, and blue electric lights, resembled a fabled palace. Dancing to the two orchestras began early, paused for the arrival of the Prince of Wales after the third number, and continued until after midnight. Lola Powell and Ethel Chadwick found the ball too crowded to dance. Ethel retreated to the gallery to 'avoid being squashed to death' and to get a better view of the prince. 'It was really more a reception than a dance,' Ethel sighed upon her return. She preferred lively dancing partners to standing about. 'I couldn't get any supper either, it was too crowded even late when I went down with D'Arcy.'[21] For his part, the prince described it as a 'terrible affair' to his wife: 'the crowd and the heat were both awful & until after supper dancing was quite out of the question. Somebody said that 3000 invitations were sent out, 4000 acceptances received & 5000 people came, judging by the crowded state of the rooms I should think it was true. Anyhow, we didn't stay very long & got home by 12:30.'[22]

The ball was much more exciting seen from the vantage point of sixteen-year-old Clare Denison, who 'came out' at this affair and was presented to the Prince of Wales.[23] By her own account she 'had the time of [her] life.' She renewed acquaintances with all the young officers she had met previously at afternoon dances aboard the *Russell* and the *Albemarle*, especially Sub-Lieutenant Oliphant. She not only filled up her card that night, but also 'had four bids for Monday to the dance on the French Battleship and to see the Regatta on board the *Indomitable, Albemarle* and *Russell.*'

Weary from a week of giving and receiving honours, the Prince of Wales returned to his battleship on the night of 28 July, leaving in the care of the mayor, now Sir George Garneau, a customary purse of $500 for the poor. He would host the last formal dinner of the tercentenary that night under brilliant starlight on the gun deck of the *Exmouth*. Had it not been for the insufferable heat in his cabin, he might have drifted off into a deep and satisfied sleep. The week had passed without incident. Champlain had been well and truly commemorated and the Plains of Abraham consecrated as a historical park.

Epilogue

The fleet slipped away silently in the night. The *Indomitable* bore the prince off at first light. Sailors and soldiers vanished from the streets. Natives and militiamen had quietly decamped. Visitors headed home, among them the squad of Toronto police detectives borrowed by Quebec for the occasion.

The echo of the last pageant slowly died. Costumes of court and country were packed away with wrinkled souvenirs. The grandstand was quickly disassembled to become but a pile of lumber once again. Soon the city resumed its normal workaday aspect in the shimmering August heat. Fading decorations, hanging limp on the lampposts, offered the only clues that magic had been worked here.

The visions inspired by Oberon and Titania had cast their memorable spells; Puck's mischief had threatened but in the end had been confounded. Well might citizens wonder if it had been but a dream, a

momentary heat-inspired delusion of merry disorder, mistaken identity,
and magical righting of the kingdom.

> If we shadows have offended,
> Think but this, and all is mended,
> That you have but slumber'd here,
> While these visions did appear.

And then memory too began to fade.

2. PATRIOTISM

Christmas 1904

Words came easily, even in English. He had, after all been thinking about this for more than two years and words were his stock in trade. Honoré-Julien-Jean-Baptiste Chouinard, a small buffalo of a man, whose squared features were accentuated by a cutaway moustache and florid muttonchop whiskers, sat comfortably at his writing desk situated in the middle of the spacious clerk's office in the new Quebec City Hall. His frosted windows looked out onto the snow-clad square and the shops opposite garlanded for Christmas. Pausing only for ink and inspiration, his hand raced back and forth across the paper. He had a deadline to meet.

Chouinard was writing an article for the special number of the Quebec *Daily Telegraph*. He was writing as a private citizen, as a man of letters and a patriot, not in his official capacity as city clerk. But his object on this day was, it could be said, wholly compatible with his public duty of promoting his beloved city. On Christmas Day 1904, as English-speaking bourgeois families of a Liberal political persuasion scanned the poetry, engravings, short stories, reports from the Holy Land, and seasons greetings from the merchants in the *Daily Telegraph*, they would run across his ambitious proposal. Though 1908 might seem a long way away, he suggested, it was not too soon to start planning.

He had the space, leisure, and learning to work up to his subject. He would begin with a simple analogy, by identifying a person's recollections of childhood in the shaping of identity with the equally important role of public memory of history in the life of a people. Then he would compare the founding myths of other people unfavourably with our own. Other nations might revel in ancient legends and warlike deeds. Canada's birth as a people, by contrast, could be precisely dated in a dignified, evangelical moment whose memory deserved to be written in gold letters in the archives of humanity. With these flourishes he was clearly warming to his task. This people – Canadians – sprang from a missionary impulse: the conversion of the infidel mattered more than the conquest of kingdoms. They owed their beginnings not to a warrior or a tyrant but to a brave mariner and a grand Christian, Samuel de Champlain, imbued with the sublime mission of bringing light to barbarous nations. In the process he acquired a vast kingdom for France and began opening it up to the benefits of Christianity and civilization. That honourable beginning must burn eternally bright in public memory, Chouinard argued, and, on the three hundredth anniversary of the founding of Quebec, it should be suitably commemorated.

Having reached this high ground, Chouinard could now become more expansive and approach his subject from another angle. In the new world, Quebec was uniquely a city of fabled memories: Quebec, the ancient fortress city whose cobblestones had been bathed in the blood of heroes; Quebec, the religious city, peopled with churches and the shades of saints and martyrs; and finally Quebec, the cradle of French civilization in America, temple guardian of a sacred flame, the most French city in the world outside of France.

The city and its French-Canadian citizens had in his rolling prose been elided into one. He must now think of his English readers, for whom he was writing, that 15 per cent of the population who might otherwise think themselves excluded from this story. They had a pride and a history to appeal to as well. For them, Quebec had been the prize in a grand international tournament, fought over by powerful rivals. Now, having been decisively won, Quebec City had become one of the British crown's most precious jewels. Quebec, the trophy of Wolfe, preserved by Murray and Carleton, and held against Britain's enemies by the sons of France, had demonstrated its lasting loyalty to the crown. Quebec had become the Gibraltar of North America, guarding the link between the metropole and the Indies. The English inhabitants who had made Quebec their home had been equally moved by the majesty of the river and the beauty of the countryside such that they too swelled with pride at the sight of the

Union Jack floating over the Citadel, a symbol of domination and power, yes (he must tread carefully here and not forget his other audience), but also respected by everyone as a symbol of liberty and toleration.

The English too could claim Quebec as theirs, and justifiably inherit pride of ownership in its history. French Canadians in turn could claim British liberties, confident in their record of loyalty in time of trial. And so, he scribbled hastily, and somewhat pleased with himself for squaring the circle quite nicely, all Canadians, whatever their origins or ancestry, could welcome the approaching celebration of the third century of the settlement at Quebec. With that he turned with enthusiasm to the details. Now from his pen sprang visions of reconstructed gates, terraces, promenades, vistas, restored fortifications, street improvements, a historical museum, new public buildings, parks, plaques, and magnificent processions.[1]

As he put down his pen and blotted his pages, he was no doubt slightly bemused by the knowledge that to date there were no plans afoot for any kind of celebration on 8 July 1908, and no one but himself seemed much to care. It was enough on this occasion to plant the notion amongst the influential Liberal bourgeoisie of the city in this festive season and give it time to germinate.

Friends

H.-J.-J.-B. Chouinard (he was normally referred to by his initials rather than his given names) had been busy amongst friends and colleagues bruiting the idea about, but in truth, he had not got very far towards realization. Indeed, a full fifteen months would pass before his notion gained any social momentum.

The delay and fitful beginning to the tercentenary celebration could be attributed in part to the somewhat precarious position of its champion in Quebec society and politics. For, despite his public office, Chouinard was neither powerful nor influential and certainly far from being well-off. Rather he, and many others like him, felt themselves to be increasingly marginal figures in the emerging new order of things. But he might be useful, even productive, if he made the most of his opportunities and played his cards right.

Born in Quebec in 1850, Chouinard had been educated at Laval University and trained as a lawyer, but did not enter practice. Instead, he

H.-J.-J.-B. Chouinard, clerk of Quebec City.

immersed himself in politics and history. With a series of speeches before the Institut Canadien on historical subjects (the history of Poland, the founding of Montreal, and the United States' assault on Quebec in 1775, all subsequently published as pamphlets), Chouinard acquired a local reputation as a chronicler, historian, and man of letters.[2] During the 1880s as his ambition shifted with the political winds, he moved away from the radical, anticlerical associations of the Institut towards the more patriotic, conservative, and orthodox Catholic Saint-Jean-Baptiste Society. Under that aegis he published numerous accounts of the celebration of what was coming to be known as La Fête nationale des Canadiens-français, Saint-Jean-Baptiste Day. He also documented the successful movement to erect a statue to Champlain in 1897 and gathered various accounts and documents associated with society activities into a four-volume history of the society from 1881 to 1903.[3]

For more than two decades, then, Chouinard had been at the heart of a patriotic movement dedicated to the celebration on any and all occasions of the survival of a Catholic, French-speaking people in Canada and the preservation of what was rightfully theirs against anglophone incursions. His loyal service to the Saint-Jean-Baptiste Society over the years, his faithful collection and publication of its annals, were rewarded with office. He rose from being a scribe to twice becoming president of the Quebec City branch of the society. In 1904 he was the immediate past president.

The Saint-Jean-Baptiste Society, through its activities on the national day, speeches, pamphlets, demonstrations, and the construction of monuments, represented the aggressive political-cultural side of a nationalist social movement. Under the open patronage of the hierarchy of the church, the society was the intellectual and cultural manifestation of a growing spirit of Catholic nationalism in the province and of course it laboured vigorously to spread the word. Through its activities the society propagated this clerical nationalist ideology throughout the province.[4] In politics, the Castor faction of the Conservative party in the 1880s, and to a lesser extent the 1890s, represented the parliamentary wing of this movement. Bristling with amour propre, Castors in the Quebec legislature and in Parliament at Ottawa fought to defend, preserve, protect, and get-what-was-owing – to the bemusement, befuddlement, and then rage of those who took a different view of their church, history, and country.

After his youthful fling with radicalism, Chouinard gravitated into the orbit of Castor conservatism, his conviction reinforced no doubt in 1884 when he married Louise Duchesnay, daughter of a judge and niece of a bishop. He entered politics first as an alderman in Quebec City from 1880 to 1890. An energetic young man with a facile pen, Chouinard was recruited as a Conservative candidate in the general election of 1882 but was defeated. Later in the decade he was briefly elected to Parliament in a by-election, but he did not contest the general election in 1891. By then a growing family imposed obligations; besides, his social and political activism had finally been rewarded with a secure, honourable, modestly paid but not overly burdensome post as clerk of the Quebec City Council.

From this position in the municipal administration Chouinard had been a worried spectator as the old alliance between the ultramontane Castors and the Conservative party of Macdonald crumbled in the 1890s. He had been a bewildered bystander as the Quebec Conservatives split;

the centrists under the influence of that Judas, Israel Tarte, abandoned ship and by degrees signed on with Laurier's Liberal party.[5] Since Laurier's federal election victory in 1896, thanks in part to the support of former Conservatives in Quebec, the ground had gradually shifted under Chouinard's feet. The power structures to which he owed his position were no longer in place. Laurier's Liberals, an uneasy alliance of former mainstream Conservatives, old Rouges, and an impatient new generation of progressive reformers, were now consolidating their hold over the federal political machinery. Since 1900, Liberals, also controlled the provincial government. A political shift of epic proportions had occurred, reshaping the power structure of Quebec and with it the path to patronage, public appointments, and government favours. By 1904 Chouinard was something of an anomaly, a survivor of the ancien regime in a largely Liberal fiefdom.[6]

Liberal dominance of Quebec looked more secure than it actually was. The Conservative party was still a potent force in Quebec; it continued to receive a respectable 40 per cent of the popular vote in both federal and provincial elections. Secondly, the Liberals were riddled with factions – Rouges, progressives, centrists, and Conservative converts. It was a fractious team that threatened to fly apart with every contentious appointment to be filled or vexing public policy decision to be taken, especially if it involved language, education, or religion.

Finally, the ultramontane nationalist impulse had found a new political outlet. Old Castors turned from the fractured and moribund Conservative party to make new friends and common cause with youthful nationalists in branches of the Saint-Jean-Baptiste Society, and in new organizations such as the Société de Parler Français. These patriotic societies in turn provided the social base for a new political formation. Nationalists, alienated from both the Conservative and Liberal parties, formed the new Ligue Nationaliste Canadienne whose most prominent and enthusiastic supporter was the maverick Liberal MP, Henri Bourassa.

Chouinard maintained contact with this loose coalition of clerical nationalists through his active involvement in the Saint-Jean-Baptiste Society of Quebec, though the new Liberal order required discretion in these matters. He occupied a risky, somewhat vulnerable position in a largely Liberal municipal government. He was in, but not of, the administration. Nevertheless the power structure needed someone to communicate with these nationalist groups and as an elder statesman, literary gentleman, and as a moderate patriot, Chouinard fitted the bill. It was this role as a go-between, negotiator, and conciliator upon which Chouinard's continuing usefulness and therefore continuing employment rested.

Having advertised his plan to the wider public, Chouinard now had to mobilize his friends in these patriotic societies to provide some pressure. That took more work than he expected. He republished his *Daily Telegraph* essay in a French newspaper during the summer of 1905 and he wrote a memorandum expanding upon his newspaper piece in the hope of interesting the municipal administration.[7] No response. It was not until 1 March of 1906 that he managed to catch the attention of his colleagues in the Saint-Jean-Baptiste Society.

And thus with only two years remaining, it was with some sense of urgency that Chouinard presented his commemorative project before the executive committee of the society. This time his associates took up the challenge, and struck a special committee of senior officers of the society which promptly invited him to spell out his proposal in greater detail.

On 6 March 1906 Chouinard once more took up his pen. He sensed the inclination of his audience and pitched his appeal accordingly. The initiative for a festival honouring the three hundredth anniversary of Quebec, he argued, properly belonged to the society which represented the founders of Canadian nationality, the Saint-Jean-Baptiste Society. Their ancestors had come from France and civilized half a continent; it was to their memory that celebration in 1908 should be dedicated. The society had taken the initiative much earlier by erecting the Monument des Braves to honour the French victors in the battle of Ste-Foy; it had led a campaign that had raised the magnificent rococo monument to Champlain in 1898; and currently the society had on its agenda a proposed statue to honour Monseigneur Laval, to be unveiled also in 1908 in conjunction with the two hundred and fiftieth anniversary of the great bishop's death.

It could be left unsaid that, with the Laval celebration in train, the society had its hands full and its resources were already overcommitted. Thus, he reasoned, the burden should be shifted whilst the credit be retained. His strategy was to broaden the scope of the festival and thereby displace responsibility for organizing it. In this instance, the entire population of Canada ought to become involved in commemorating the founding of Quebec, the cradle of the Canadian nation. He recommended therefore that once the society managed to get the Quebec tercentennial festival movement going, it should generously cede leadership to a larger organization capable of making an appeal to a broader constituency in all of Canada.

The report of the special committee, which was discussed at length at a meeting on 13 March, consisted almost entirely of Chouinard's letter. Following the discussion, it was unanimously resolved that a grand celebration ought to mark the three hundredth anniversary of the founding of Quebec, that the Saint-Jean-Baptiste Society, 'which represents the great majority of the citizens of that city' ought to take the initiative in these festivities, and that the resulting celebration should not be of simply a French-Canadian character but rather Canadian in the larger conception of the word. The subcommittee called upon the mayor of Quebec to convene a special meeting of citizens to consider Chouinard's detailed proposal and create a powerful organization to produce a fitting celebration in 1908.[8]

The idea of celebrating the three hundredth anniversary of Champlain's founding of Quebec in 1608 thus originated amongst the members of the Saint-Jean-Baptiste Society of Quebec as another in a series of festivals of national survival and emergence. Bumptious and irrepressible as always, the society threw down the gauntlet to the civic administration and the governments at higher levels to prove themselves to be as worthy and patriotic as it was itself in Champlain's memory. It was a bold gesture, one of many aimed at those in power, by challenging them to earn their office and honour by getting what Quebec properly deserved.

Citizens

Quebec finally had a full-time mayor in 1906, though he was an untried newcomer. Simon-Napoléon Parent had filled the office of mayor for the previous twelve years. During his term he had presided over a number of impressive public works: new parks, paved streets, lighting, bridges, a new library, and a magnificent city hall. But his energies had lately flagged, partly because he occupied two offices. Since 1900 he had also been the premier of Quebec. Five years of this had worn him out, especially the factionalism within the provincial party caused ostensibly

George Garneau, mayor of Quebec City.

by his government's lacklustre efforts to colonize northern Quebec. Both the provincial and municipal administrations were visibly adrift by late 1905. Eventually his enemies within the Liberal party in Quebec deposed him, following which he resigned the mayoralty in a huff. Laurier, ever mindful of past favours, saw to it that he was looked after. In due course he was named president of the National Transcontinental Railway Commission, the proposed publicly owned railway from Quebec City to Winnipeg that would connect with the Grand Trunk in the west.[9] But divisions in Quebec City between the pro- and anti-Parent factions of the Liberal party doggedly persisted.

With Parent out of the way at the provincial level, Lomer Gouin, who was still something of an unknown quantity, emerged to take the leadership of the Liberal party in Quebec and the premiership. As for Quebec City, since 1870 the mayor had been elected indirectly by the city councillors every two years from amongst their number. In February of 1906 the lot fell to the energetic John George Garneau, who had only just himself been elected to council for the first time. The timing of the Saint-Jean-Baptiste Society challenge, therefore, seems to suggest that it was a firecracker hurled into the camp of this younger generation of Liberals as a test of their mettle.

With his high forehead, sweeping lock of curling hair parted to one side, long high-collared neck, Garneau bore a vague resemblance to Sir Wilfrid, who was, in many respects, his political mentor. Pierre Garneau, his father, had been a successful merchant, manufacturer and railway investor. From 1870 to 1874 Pierre had been mayor of Quebec City. He later moved on to provincial politics, where he served as a cabinet minister until 1878 and again in Mercier's government as minister of crown lands and public works until 1891.[10]

John George sprang, therefore, from an impeccable Liberal background, but he himself was a man of the modern world, an engineer-businessman, and not particularly politically inclined. He had graduated in 1884 from the École Polytechnique in Montreal and served his apprenticeship as an engineer on the construction of railways in the Lac St-Jean region. He soon returned to manage the family rubber-manufacturing company in Quebec where he established contacts with the new resource and utilities industries which seemed poised to transform the Quebec economy. For him, the primary role of government was to smooth the way for this job-creating investment. It was therefore a concern for the health of the economy of Quebec, not its soul, that drew him in his forty-sixth year into politics. Fate launched him straight away into the mayor's chair.[11]

The city, it must be admitted, was not in particularly good shape. Its political malaise was perhaps a reflection of its underlying economic decay. For more than a generation, Quebec City had been falling behind as the slow rise of small manufacturing industries failed to compensate fully for the decline of its traditional economic activities – shipping, support of a large military establishment, and squared-timber exports. In the mid-nineteenth century, Quebec City was about three-quarters as big as Montreal; by 1901 it was only a third the size.[12] And its relative decline in the broader Canadian urban system was even more marked. The market for forest products had shifted to the United States, a trade from which Quebec was ill-positioned to benefit. Quebec, if it were to share in the general prosperity of the Dominion, would have to transform itself and to a certain extent turn away from the St Lawrence to do it. The future lay in the new mining, hydro-electric, and pulp and paper industries. To lure investment, the city must make the most of its assets, attract people, open itself for business, connect itself to the rest of Canada – indeed the wider continent – and make its municipal administration a model of efficiency. Old Quebec must, in the view of this new generation of progressive Liberals, re-invent itself, and that, ironically, is where history came in.

Chouinard laid his detailed plan before the Comité du Centenaire which Mayor Garneau organized with commendable speed on 14 May. The enthusiasm of his friends had clearly inflated his ambition. As he now envisioned the festivities, nine committees would be needed to organize events (history, finances, expositions, public works, publicity, transport and lodging, parades and spectacles, games, music, and theatre); three levels of Canadian government would have to coordinate their efforts; France, the United States, and Great Britain would be involved, tourists and travellers from all over the continent would be drawn to the events.

Ironically, commemoration should begin with renovation. For history to be properly appreciated, Chouinard argued, the City of Quebec needed a thoroughgoing makeover. It needed to be made to look both new and old. Much of this transformation had already occurred, but more needed to be done. In Chouinard's report, the occasion of the tercentenary became the reason for pressing these works on to completion with all due haste. So, in addition to processions, historical plaques, and occasions for public speeches, his plan envisioned an expensive program of public works. Citizens would be expected to paint and spruce up their own properties. The city would be called upon to repair its streets, provide sidewalks, and improve public lighting; the province would have to beautify the grounds around the legislature. But that would be only the beginning. It became clear as Chouinard proceeded that the Dominion government would have to bear the greatest responsibility for municipal redecoration.

Through the intercession of Lord Dufferin in the 1870s, the old gates of the city had been preserved (actually widened and relocated to improve traffic flow and rebuilt in a medieval style), and the crumbling ramparts had been reconstructed with finely dressed and neatly pointed stone more suitable for promenades, taking in the sublime views, and romantic, historical reveries.[13] The process of improving upon history and remaking Quebec as a historic city was already well advanced. The terrace which Dufferin had designed in front of the Château Frontenac needed to be completed and extended. Not all of the municipal gates had been built. Rebuilding Quebec to preserve and improve its fortified character, historical associations, and scenic prospects had in the process acquired the patronage of succeedings governors general. The newest arrival, Earl Grey, during his first summer visit in 1905, had expressed great interest in completing what had come to be known as the Quebec City 'embellishments.' One of Garneau's first letters as mayor to Laurier prodded the prime minister, who represented the city in Parliament, to get on with the long-promised Quebec improvements.[14] In Chouinard's hands, the imminent tercentenary of the city now provided new impetus for an emergency program of federal public works.

Work was urgently needed to restore the crumbling Citadel. The adjacent lands on the Plains of Abraham, recently acquired by the Dominion government, needed proper landscaping and a promenade. All these embellishments needed to be pressed to completion, along with the Quebec Bridge carrying the south shore railway across the St Lawrence to the city, so as to be ready for the festivities of tercentenary summer of 1908. The government of the United States had given ample funds to celebrate the birth of the American people at the forthcoming Jamestown festival scheduled for 1907, Chouinard pointedly remarked; surely the government of Canada would wish to put on an equally dignified celebration to mark the third centenary of the birth of the Canadian people.[15]

For Champlain's celebration Chouinard proposed an assembly of warships in the harbour, perhaps a royal visitor, and a reconstruction of Champlain's Habitation guarded by men in period costumes – this last a suggestion from the Quebec Literary and Historical Society. Other historical exhibitions might also be mounted, perhaps under the auspices of this same society. Chouinard also envisioned other reconstructions, and a historical procession of groups in costume representing the first colonists, courreurs de bois, soldiers of the French and English regiments of 1759–60, Canadian militia of 1812, and the sailors of Cartier's and Champlain's vessels (an idea borrowed from the successful depiction of Columbus's crew at Chicago's Columbian World Exposition in 1893). The Champlain celebration, beginning in late June, would last through the entire summer. Though not fully specified in Chouinard's report, the cost of such an ambitious program was understood to run over a million dollars and call for the cooperation of federal, provincial, and municipal governments.[16] It was a breathtaking bill of particulars.

For the new administration at city hall, the tercentenary celebration was an ideal vehicle to lever much-needed civic improvements out of the higher levels of government, continue the revival of the local economy on the basis of the new tourist industry, and incidentally attract the attention of influential Canadians and foreigners to the investment op-portunities of the new Quebec. Shrewdly, Chouinard several times re-ferred to the tourist development potential of his proposed festival. Thus Garneau and his colleagues saw the Saint-Jean-Baptiste proposal not as the mania of a group of troublesome busybodies, but as a business opportunity.

For that reason, the municipal authorities threw their full support behind the idea. The semi-official executive committee that emerged from this public meeting, headed by the mayor, promptly swung into action. The executive committee in turn spawned six subcommittees to refine various aspects of the plan. One of these, a subcommittee of historical experts, known as the Commission d'Histoire et d'Archéologie (Quebec Landmarks Commission), was set the task of advising on what was to be celebrated and how. But before expectations got out of hand it was thought best to check with the prime minister.

Countryman

What, for a politican, was more disconcerting than the warm embrace of friends? By the end of 1906 Sir Wilfrid Laurier had been prime minister for a decade. After three general election victories he was firmly in con-trol of his party and the master of electoral politics. But it had not been easy or without cost, buffeted as he was on one side by anglophone impe-rialists and on the other by anti-imperialist nationalists in Quebec, by those who would restrict French Catholic rights in the broader Domin-ion and those who sought to expand the bi-national, bi-religious compact into the western territories. All the while the economy, though it was boom-ing, needed infrastructure, railways, harbours, post offices, customs houses. Enough could never be done to satisfy everyone, it seemed. Each appointment to public office seemed to breed more enmity than satisfac-

Sir Wilfrid Laurier, with Lady Laurier in the foreground.

tion. Along the way he had parted company with some old friends in both English and French Canada. Beset by his friends and wary of his enemies, Laurier had grown cautious and a little weary in office.[17]

The prime minister had represented Quebec East in the House of Commons since 1877. Not much went on in Quebec without his knowledge; he would have known about this agitation before it came formally to his attention. Of course, as the local member he should expect to be prevailed upon for special projects beneficial to his constituency and he had already been more than generous, he thought. But at the same time he was more than a simple MP; he was also the prime minister with a responsibility to take into account the broader interests of his country and the Liberal party. Of course he had to be sensitive to appearances, particularly regarding any favouritism on his part towards Quebec. Some would say Quebec had already secured more than its share of such patronage over the years. Thus when Sir Wilfrid spied Mayor Garneau and company advancing upon him in the summer of 1906 he sensed not only a raid on the federal treasury, he also smelled trouble.

It was in every respect a proper bicultural, interdenominational Quebec City delegation that waited upon the prime minister in his Ottawa office in June 1906. Besides Mayor Garneau, the party included an abbé from the university, the rector of St Matthew's Anglican Church, a representative of the Literary and Historical Society, and Chouinard as recording secretary. The prime minister seemed in an expansive, welcoming mood. He listened attentively to their florid petition arguing that the history of the city symbolized the 'honour and virility' of all Canadian history and, therefore, that the entire Dominion should take an interest in a celebration of truly national significance.

At the conclusion, the prime minister responded that he would like to know more about what the city planned but he was impressed with what he had heard thus far. They should come back with a more detailed program, some idea of the subsidy that might be required, and a draft of the necessary legislation. It all sounded very encouraging, and the delegates returned to Quebec with the impression that their approach had been favourably received.[18]

Buoyed by Laurier's apparent approval, the subcommittees began to entertain grandiose thoughts over the summer. Besides Chouinard's proposals, all sorts of other ideas were tossed around, from a reunion of all the first families of New France to a world's fair, or perhaps a permanent national exhibition like the CNE in Toronto. The executive committee had to rein in its troops and scale back expectations to the time and resources that might be available.

By November of 1906 the citizens' committee had something like a coherent plan of action with which to return to the prime minister. It was still a fairly extensive proposal comprising a historical procession, plaques for historic buildings and monuments, an exposition of history, archeology, and fine arts, a menu of embellishments demanded of the federal, provincial, and municipal governments, and a deluxe historical publication. The draft legislation, which laid heavy stress upon the national significance of the proposed festival and the need for federal support (not only financially but also for its influence in attracting the possible patronage of the king and the involvement of other governments), set forth the broad outlines of a tripartite national commission appointed by the federal, provincial, and municipal governments to undertake the necessary work.

In this negotiating process Quebec City constructed itself as 'le berceau du Canada.' It busied itself ensuring that its communications imparted 'un cachet national de la Fête,' in this case 'national' referring to Canada as a whole rather than French Canada. The festivities might therefore proceed under the auspices and with the financial support of the entire country. This was absolutely vital because the subcommittee on finance estimated the costs of the festival alone to be something in the order of $500,000.[19]

This time the prime minister seemed more evasive. When Garneau wrote to him in November sending this proposal and the draft legislation, Sir Wilfrid appeared to have had a change of heart. Garneau expressed surprise that the legislation did not meet with Laurier's satisfaction. How should it be changed? The influential committee members who had worked so hard on the proposal, and apparently with the prime minister's support, were feeling very let down.[20]

Eventually Laurier, accompanied by his cabinet colleagues from Quebec, Fisher, Brodeur, and Lemieux, met a small deputation between Christmas and New Year's. When presented with a budget now grown to $630,000, he took exception to the inclusion of $250,000 for the construction of a museum which, in his view, rightly belonged in Ottawa and could not be properly built for less than a million dollars. He thought a park would be a more fitting (and no doubt less expensive) monument.[21]

Somewhat chastened, but nevertheless still filled with hope, Garneau and his colleagues regrouped and made preparations for a mass deputation to Ottawa on 12 February 1907. This time dozens strong, reflecting all of the key constituent groups of the community, they came armed not only with another petition and a day-by-day schedule, but also with the recently published report of the Quebec Landmarks Commission written by Justice François Langelier, E.E. Taché, the provincial deputy minister of lands and forests and a noted architect, and Colonel William Wood, a specialist in the Seven Years' War and former president of the Literary and Historical Society of Quebec. The report focused primarily upon a series of civic improvements that might be carried out to mark the occasion. First and foremost among these was the development on the Plains of Abraham of a park along the lines of Hyde Park, the Bois de Boulogne, Central Park, and the Tiergarten.[22] In justification of state action to preserve historical properties, the commissioners cited American examples such as the creation of Yellowstone Park to protect a natural monument, and Gettysburg Park to commemorate a pivotal battle in the Civil War.

Beyond construction of a historic park at Quebec to mark the tercentenary, the cost of which remained unspecified, Mayor Garneau and his delegation laid out a detailed agenda of public celebrations. His notes for this interview with Laurier show the explicit influence of the contemporaneous Jamestown celebration in the United States which was attracting a good deal of publicity and, he hoped, inciting some envy. Garneau's new and much scaled-down proposal, with sums attached, was as follows:

Historical Procession, sports, games	$40,000
Fireworks, spectacles, music, decorations	$35,000
Receptions, banquets	$28,000
Publicity and security	$15,000
Historical plaques and medals	$12,000
Historical and archeological exhibition	$25,000
Indian encampment	$5,000
Completion of the Dufferin plans	$80,000
Reconstruction of Champlain's Habitation	$10,000
Total	$250,000[23]

Now it was Laurier's turn to feel cornered. The price was closer to being right, but there were some hidden expenses and he would be responsible for that bill as well. The delegation left without a firm commitment but again feeling that the prime minister was nevertheless sympathetic. But by mid-March Garneau still had no definite indication from the prime minister, much to his consternation.[24] Under pressure from the mayor, Laurier craftily replied that he would commit the federal government as soon as the provincial government was also willing to make a generous contribution to the festival. Garneau neatly parried this thrust by obtaining assurances from Lomer Gouin, the premier of Quebec, that the province would generously support the enterprise to ensure the success of such an event of national importance. Laurier wanted to see that in writing.

Returning once again to Ottawa, Garneau came away at last with what he so desperately wanted. Giving in to pressure from all sides, Laurier offered to contribute $300,000 under the control of a federally appointed commission conditional upon the province of Quebec also making a major contribution. Laurier also declared that 'the government of Canada would accept the project of a jubilee on the condition that the festival would represent a truly national character in the broadest sense of the word.'[25] Legislation would have to await his return from Europe, an inconvenience that could not be avoided. The commission could not be appointed and begin its work before the beginning of 1908. That being the case, Sir Wilfrid recommended deferring the festival until 1909 to coincide happily with the expected opening of the Quebec Bridge whose massive diamond-shaped cantilevered sections were rising even now on both sides of the river. Columbus's celebration had, after all, been shifted forward a year from 1892; there was no real need to be literal-minded about dates. The delay, by placing the tercentenary after the anticipated next election, might also defuse potential embarrassment. The mayor and his executive committee gratefully agreed.

Champlain had his uses if his memory could be harnessed to present economic and political purposes. Different interested factions – the Saint-Jean-Baptiste Society, the boosters of the Quebec City Council, the Literary and Historical Society, and eventually the federal government – all had different notions of what those purposes might be. Power to define the event, of course, rested ultimately with those who would foot the bill, but they in turn would have to negotiate for the cooperation of the others. That would involve adding other layers of intent. Fortunately Champlain could be made to have many meanings, almost all of them having to do with the present rather than the past.

By the spring of 1907, therefore, H.-J.-J.-B. Chouinard could take pleasure that his effort had begun to pay off. What his friends in the Saint-Jean-Baptiste Society made of this turn of events can only be imagined. Powerful people with the right connections and access to public funding had taken his project to heart and turned it into a truly national event 'in the broadest sense of the word.' What had begun as an episode in the celebration of local, French-Canadian public memory had evolved opportunistically into a larger celebration of Canadian nationality as sponsorship changed. Something would happen to celebrate the three hundredth anniversary of the founding of Quebec. But it was by no means clear what would be celebrated, or when.

3. A KNIGHT'S QUEST

Wish You Were Here

The prime minister must have smiled as he read a letter in June 1905 from the new governor general in Quebec City. It was the breathless, chirpy prose of a besotted tourist:

> The beauties & Potentialities of Quebec continue to grow upon me & I am becoming tres Quebecois! I am longing to walk along the top of the city walls with you – they can be made easily and at hardly any cost into a Promenade the equal of which cannot be found or produced by any other town I have ever seen & with the exception of Constantinople & Sydney I think I have seen every town which would venture to put itself up in competition against Quebec!

Earl Grey goes on to explain how he has talked to S.-N. Parent, who was the mayor and premier. Together they had walked from the site of the Intendant's Palace in the old city out to Wolfe's Cove talking about their mutual dreams for Quebec. Parent had already accomplished much and Grey expressed admiration for what he had done. Grey in turn had explained his vision for Quebec improvements and Parent had responded enthusiastically. Moreover, following a meeting with the editor and publisher of *Le Soleil*, Grey could report that the press 'has promised to shine on this undertaking.' As Laurier had predicted, Grey had been charmed by Monseigneur Mathieu, rector of Laval University, who, Laurier would be pleased to learn in return, had 'responded with warm sympathy' to the governor general's plans.[1]

But as he read on, Laurier would have grown apprehensive. Fools rush in ...

A Long Row to Hoe

Earl Grey was no fool, but when he wrote the prime minister from Quebec, he had been in the country only a little more than six months. His enthusiasm for all things Canadian, and his overweening desire to be useful, combined to form a potentially dangerous political naiveté. He had much to learn. Gently and deferentially Laurier would teach him. As much as he wanted to learn, and took well to instruction, the governor general nevertheless harboured a steely determination to get his own way on some things. He too had his agenda.

The new governor general had arrived in Canada during the bitterly cold early December of 1904 with a mission to mend the somewhat tattered imperial relationship left by his predecessor, Lord Minto. Controversy over Canada's contribution to the Boer War had provoked a government crisis and left English and French Canada deeply divided. In both camps, Lord Minto had been seen to be a dominant figure, driving government policy, for good in the case of imperialists in English Canada and for ill in the case of nationalist French Canada. Proud and uncompromising, Lord Minto gave the impression to anyone who cared to listen that a weak and vacillating government needed stiffening and direction from him. To the suspiciously inclined, here was evidence of a conspiracy between the Colonial Office and the British army to get Canada more deeply entangled in imperial military affairs to the detriment, according to many French Canadians, of Canada's primary responsibilities at home. To English-Canadian imperial nationalists, such responsibilities provided a golden opportunity for a rising Dominion to assert itself on the international stage and assume a leadership role within the Empire.[2]

Through all this the reputation of the governor general had suffered considerably. Rightly or wrongly – and the burden of the evidence inclined towards the former – he had been seen as a political partisan. The lesson drawn by the Canadian government was that the governor general should be more circumspect or that his role should be more

Earl Grey, governor general of Canada.

narrowly circumscribed. The British government for its part did not think the policy being pursued by Minto wrong, but rather that his execution had been ham-fisted. More tact, subtlety, and gentle persuasion on the part of the governor general might accomplish the goal of closer imperial cooperation on military affairs without putting the relationship at risk. The task of soothing hurt feelings and binding Canada in a functional way into imperial responsibilties, without provoking internal division, fell to Earl Grey.

Outgoing, familiar, and immensely charming, Earl and Lady Grey were a study in contrasts with their predecessors. Earl Grey sought people out for their opinions and listened eagerly to what they had to say. His French was excellent. He had his own views on policy matters, but he kept them scrupulously between himself and the prime minister and he took pains to avoid any public embarrassments. Moreover, the more he knew about Sir Wilfrid the more he admired and respected him and in time the feeling became mutual. Entirely lacking the martinet qualities and self-righteous rectitude of the military-trained Lord Minto, Grey flattered, probed, inquired, adjusted, and moved forward whenever possible with the crab-like manoeuvres of a trained diplomat.[3]

Grey had instructions to do whatever he could to bring Canada more closely into line with British thinking on imperial defence matters, and on naval policy in particular. Typically he approached this issue via a more roundabout route than his predecessor. He chose to address the factors underlying Canadian policy rather than confront the policy itself. As he manoeuvred his way through this delicate minefield, Grey came to believe that concentration upon the emotional and symbolic issues of nation and empire would do more for imperial unity than a dreadnought and, if successful, might in due course produce a dreadnought as well. The problem as he formulated it had two facets: Canada's lack of self-esteem, and French Canada's indifference to the empire ideal. Canada needed some kind of symbolic representation of its nobler self as a nation in order that it might escape the petty internal disputes that made any wider involvement in the world contentious. To do so, Canadians needed to understand their history better. This he saw as a story of two peoples working together and transcending their differences, in order to build a great nation within the world's most powerful empire. There was no necessary obstacle to French-Canadian identification with the British Empire. French Canadians had taken warmly to British political institutions and were great admirers of British liberty. On the matter of the obligations of modern empire, Grey believed, French Canada needed only to be better taught and more warmly appreciated.[4]

In 1905 Grey had been appalled to discover the profound animosities that divided Canadians along linguistic and religious lines. These deep divisions would have to be overcome, he believed, if Canada ever hoped to amount to anything as a nation. At the same time, a united Canada desperately needed some way of feeling more imperial, responding at more of an emotional level to the greater imperial cause than a calculating cost-benefit analysis. If he could help Canadians find that symbol of their common nationality and forge a deeper emotional bond with the Empire, most of the other policy matters would eventually fall into place. That was the legacy he hoped to leave from his tenure in the vice-regal office.

On his first visit to Quebec City in the summer of 1905 Earl Grey began to imagine a way of linking all of Canada more emotionally to the Empire and to do so by striking at the very heart of suspicion. Prompted by the mayor of Quebec on a guided tour of the unfinished 'embellishments,' Grey began to see the opportunity presented by his fully sanctioned, inherited role as non-partisan promoter of the reconstruction of Quebec City. As Parent showed him the new municipal and provincial public buildings begun during his regime, and ever so gently turned to the matter of the unfinished Quebec embellishments, Grey responded with excitement, adding to the list projects of his own. He saw himself inheriting the 'Quebec improvements' mantle of Lord Dufferin. Minto, too, had been alarmed about the shocking state of Quebec's historic sites, particularly the residential and industrial encroachments on the Plains of Abraham. The Quebec politicians were delighted to have a new friend at court in Ottawa. Earl Grey, however, had his own designs for Quebec.

Returning to his summer residence in the Citadel after a brief tour of the Maritimes in August 1905, Earl Grey wrote off to the Dominion archivist, Arthur Doughty, to thank him for sending him historical information on the fortifications of Quebec and, incidentally, to drop a tantalizing hint about his thinking about Quebec. Earl Grey confided that the government of Quebec had adopted his proposal for 'converting the unkempt wilderness on the top of the city walls into a Promenade from Bigot's Palace to the Cove Fields.' But that was only the beginning of his plan: 'I hope that before the end of my term I may be able to obtain the consent of Ministers to the removal of the gaol, the observatory and the factory from the battlefield of Quebec & to the taking of such steps as may be necessary to make Louisbourg the Mecca of the Anglo Saxon race on this side of the Atlantic. But before this consumation is attained there is a long row to hoe & in the hoeing of it I shall require your assistance.'[5]

Grey schemed to improve Quebec, but he planned to add more than masonry and better vistas to Quebec City's charms.[6] He fumed that one of the holiest shrines of British imperialism, a place of unparalleled scenic beauty, the Heights on which Wolfe in an act of immortal heroism had won Canada for the Empire, had been blighted by wanton neglect and desecrated by a factory and a jail. The jail, on the very spot where Wolfe fell, particularly rankled. He would redeem these hallowed grounds and in doing so contribute to what he thought of as a 'fusion of the races.' He would reveal the character of greatness that bound the fates of French and English together in one nation; he would provide this people with an inspiring symbol of their nationality that would help them transcend their differences; and he would draw upon the power and the prestige of the Empire to bring this about. To ensure the Plains of Abraham would remain sacred in perpetuity, the governor general would enlist every man, woman, and schoolchild in the Empire in his crusade. And in doing so he would deepen the emotional ties of Canadians, English and French, to the Empire.

To this end, Grey entered into a delicate conspiracy. First he needed a historian's professional opinion. Who better to turn to than the energetic and ambitious Dominion archivist, a specialist in the history of the Seven Years' War. Arthur Doughty, flattered by the attention, was also all too eager to make the acquaintence of British aristocrats who might smooth the way for his acquisition of precious family historical documents pertaining to Canada. Grey summoned the archivist to Rideau Hall for a talk. An immediate meeting of minds occurred between the amateur and the professional historian, and a mutual conviction developed that the glorious history of Canada deserved to be better and more popularly known.

During one of these conversations between Grey and Doughty, discussion turned to the imminent three hundredth anniversary of Champlain's founding of Quebec in 1608. Would the Dominion archivist be so kind as to suggest the appropriate means of celebrating this momentous event, asked the governor general? Doughty replied with a polished, stentorian memorandum self-consciously written for the ages – three copies are preserved in various collections – in which he delivered his carefully considered judgments. As a document it not so much beseeches as demands quotation. Beginning with a call to all Canadians, whatever their political affiliation, language, or creed, to unite in a dignified national celebration, Doughty describes the glorious train of consequences set in motion by Champlain's founding act:

> Three centuries in the life of a nation is merely a brief pause, but within this magnificent interval how boundless is the vision which arises before one. First there is the picturesque group at the foot of Cape Diamond – the heroic Champlain and his sturdy followers. Before them lies an untamed continent, the domain which France is to conquer for Civilization; beyond them loom majestic mountains silent in primaeval sleep; mysterious forests teeming with savage hordes; mighty rivers rushing onward to unknown

seas, and in a moment, as it were, we behold this vast continent transformed into countless cities, towns and villages peopled by a virile race in
the enjoyment of the highest form of political freedom; leaders in the
world of commerce, unsurpassed in any land in intellectual vigour.

Such a people needed a monument, a place of memory, to commemorate this founding and celebrate its achievement. The tercentenary seemed
the opportune moment, and the Plains of Abraham, more precisely the
site of the jail ('the scene of the last great conflict signifying the passing of
the old regime and the birth of the new'), seemed the obvious place. As
for the form such a monument might take, Doughty was also quite definite. The occasion called for a historical museum of fitting elegance. Support for such a monument ought, he believed, to be readily forthcoming:

> The British Government, the Dominion Parliament, the Provincial
> Goverments, the City of Quebec, the city of Montreal, and the descendants
> of wealthy families connected with the earlier history of this country, would
> cheerfully support such a laudable undertaking, which would emphasize
> our marvellous progress in three hundred years, and the harmonious
> working of a people separated by language and creed, yet unified in their
> efforts to place Canada in the foremost rank of the nations of the world.[7]

As this memorandum corresponded with his own thinking, Grey
promptly forwarded it to the prime minister with his full endorsement.
Any patriotic Canadian on reading Doughty's moving letter would surely
share the belief that something monumental needed to be erected on
the magnificent heights of Quebec to commemorate the founding of
Canada and to symbolize the nobler aspirations of all Canadians. He
personally hoped that the opportunity might be seized to replace the
dreadful jail that disfigured the Plains of Abraham with something more
edifying such as a museum. A magnificent tercentenary celebration,
properly carried off, would have much more than local appeal, and must
have if it were to succeed. Such a celebration could not be conducted in
any 'spirit of provincial exclusiveness,' but rather 'in a manner which will
allow every part of the Dominion, of the British Empire, and of Continental America to actively co-operate.'[8]

To go beyond conception to realization, and in the process move a
curiously reluctant prime minister, Grey had to forge closer links with

groups within Quebec. Somehow he had got wind of the stirrings in Quebec City over the Champlain tercentenary. He may well have heard something of this from Chouinard himself and Parent in the summer of 1905 as he toured Quebec. In any event, Grey kept abreast of events in Quebec through encouraging letters to the new mayor, George Garneau, and discreet inquiries about the cost estimates for further embellishments.[9] He also reminded his correspondents of the very aggressive celebrations being planned at both the national and the local level in the United States. Even St Albans, Vermont, planned to celebrate the three hundredth anniverary of Champlain's arrival! As the Quebec group gathered its resources for a full-scale assault on Laurier in November of 1906, the governor general was kept fully informed by Garneau. His lively interest in the project in turn further raised the hopes of the Quebec delegation.

During the autumn of 1906 Grey made it his business to know what was going on within the Quebec Landmarks Commission, established by the Quebec City municipal authorities. Colonel William Wood had personally conducted the governor general on a tour of the battlefields and would certainly have known Grey's thinking on the matter. It came as no surprise, then, to the governor general (though perhaps it did to some residents of Quebec City), that the core section of the first report of the local commission charged with recommending an appropriate means of celebrating the anniversary of the founding of Quebec in 1608 consisted of a detailed account of the Battle of the Plains of Abraham that occurred 151 years later![10] The principal objective of the Champlain celebration, the commission argued, should be the creation of a national park on this historically significant site. Admirable though this report was in many ways, Grey and his collaborator Doughty were not satisfied. For while the Quebec historians were sound on the matter of the park and the removal of the jail, they said nothing about the equally offensive Ross Rifle factory.[11]

By the fall of 1906, therefore, Grey could congratulate himself that he had managed to bring a fairly powerful set of intellectual and political forces into alignment. The historians were in agreement that a national symbol on the heights of Quebec would be an ideal means of symbolizing Canada's century and that it should be inaugurated in a splendid tercentenary celebration that would surpass that of the Americans had planned for Jamestown. As well, the municipal authorities at Quebec had created

a broadly based movement to organize a festival celebrating the tercentenary with the creation of a historic park and monument. Now it
remained only to bring the government of Canada into line.

At a critical moment near the end of 1906, as Laurier seemed to be
wiggling out of the grasp of the ardent Quebec delegation, Grey inter-
vened directly. Now that the parliamentary session had adjourned, he
hesitated to trespass upon the prime minister's 'leisure,' but he begged
Sir Wilfrid's advice on a proper reply to a letter he had recently received
from the Honourable Thomas Casgrain on the subject of the Champlain
tercentennial. Grey had asked Casgrain about monuments to General
Wolfe, observing in passing that Quebec had fallen short of his expectations in this respect: 'A hero so illustrious in the Annals of Empire, and
associated at all times with the early history of Quebec, is surely deserving
of something better than this insignificant and mutilated memorial,
utterly dwarfed by the huge jail at its site, and not easily found, owing to
the site selected being a side lane.' Casgrain admitted the truth of these
remarks and agreed that something ought to be done to remedy the
situation for the tercentenary.

In his letter to Laurier, Grey enclosed a draft reply to Casgrain. In it he
proposed a national and imperial fund-raising campaign, which he himself volunteered to lead, to create a national historical park on the Plains
of Abraham, to be graced by an appropriate monument. On this latter
point Grey's views had obviously evolved. He appreciated Laurier's reluctance to build a 'national' museum at Quebec City. He therefore proposed
something more grandiose and inspiring: a monumental Statue of Peace
comparable to the Statue of Liberty, to be erected on a commanding position atop Cape Diamond. He begged the prime minister to lead the
campaign. Such a project, he believed, coincided with Laurier's own long-
term goals for Quebec beautification; but, more importantly, the campaign
would also complement Laurier's efforts to unite the two races of Canada.
In his appeal Grey unleashed his considerable powers of persuasion.

> I am aware of the conversations we have had on the subject of Quebec,
> that it is your desire that such steps should be taken as would enable the
> intelligent Tourist to follow the incidents of the past without the assistance
> of a guide, & in a manner which would both feed & stimulate his appetite
> for historical associations & in view of this knowledge it occurred to me that
> it would be much better to assess my unsent letter so that the field should

The Wolfe monument on the Plains of Abraham with the provincial jail in the background.

remain clear to you to suggest as prime minister of Canada, if the idea commends itself to you, a program which would include the points recommended by me to Mr Casgrain. An appeal to the public to commemorate the Champlain Tercentenary in the ways I have suggested as well as in the other ways which may commend themselves to the people of Quebec, would come, if you allow me to say so, with especial grace & appropriateness from yourself – Such an appeal from you would be regarded as another characteristic endeavour on your part to give effect to 'la pensee dominante de votre vie'... harmonising & unifying the two races which together make up the Nation of Canada.

> I have reason to believe that an appeal from you which would touch English as well as French sentiment would be greatly appreciated by the Province of Ontario & be the means of attracting support not only from every part of Canada but from all parts of the U.S. of the U.K. & of Greater Britain outside the Dominion & British Isles.

Grey assured the prime minister that he himself would 'put my back into it' and do his utmost to ensure that the tercentenary transcended a simple celebration of the past to become 'a landmark in the development of that racial fusion on the completeness of which the future greatness of Canada would appear to depend.'[12]

When Laurier returned to Ottawa in a gloomy mood after visiting his dying brother, he dutifully responded to his governor general and his curious obsession. His masterful reply, every bit the equal of Grey's in shrewdness and tact, reminded the governor general that the row to be hoed was much longer than he ever imagined.

Sir Wilfrid had no objection to Grey making the private suggestion of a campaign to build a park and monument on the Plains of Abraham to Casgrain. His government would be entertaining a deputation of citizens of Quebec early in January of 1907 to discuss the form of the celebration, the size of the federal subsidy, and the contributions of the city and provincial governments. And, yes, it was true that he had long hoped 'to mark on the ground the progress & the phases of the two battles of the 13th Sept. 1759 & 26th April 1760 in the manner adopted by the Americans on the battlefield of Gettysburg.' He swiftly added with devastating effect: 'I hardly think however that this idea of mine would fit in the place now in contemplation to commemorate the foundation of Quebec.'

Laurier heartily agreed with Grey about the travesty of the Plains of Abraham. 'It is only too true that the sacred ground around Quebec has been unhallowed in a shocking manner,' Laurier conceded. 'Who would ever have originated the idea of building a common gaol on the Plains of Abraham! Yet, I feel that I cannot too loudly proclaim my indignation since it is my government which is responsible for the Ross Factory.'[13]

Reculer pour Mieux Sauter

The Plains of Abraham had already cost the prime minister more than enough grief and political embarrassment. The Ross Rifle factory, which sullied the supposedly sacred ground, was one of Laurier's major patronage contributions to his home district. The jail, erected in 1867, was entirely a provincial responsibility and it seems unlikely that the new premier would willingly entertain the expense of tearing it down only to rebuild it somewhere else without compensation.

Much earlier in his tenure as prime minister, Laurier had been persuaded by a local committee, led by the members of the Quebec Literary and Historical Society, to lend federal support to a campaign to purchase the battlefield site from private owners who seemed bent upon real estate development. Public meetings had been called, petitions drafted, the rector of the university and members of the Royal Society recruited, and the members of the golf club on the land mollified. The Ursuline Order, who owned the greatest portion of the property, readily agreed to terms, but inevitably other parties held out – an awkward fact that raised the price and entailed much higher transaction fees to the intermediaries. Eventually the site was secured, but recriminations and rumours of scandalous overpayment haunted the prime minister for several years afterward.[14] Having secured the troublesome Plains for posterity, Laurier preferred that they be forgotten. Meanwhile, the land lay dormant.

The Ross Rifle factory was in many respects Laurier's pride and joy. As he pointedly informed Earl Grey, his government had authorized its construction in 1903. But, like a child, it was proving to be awkward as it flourished. He took some satisfaction that this technologically advanced company provided some 10 per cent of the employment of industrial workers in the city. Many of these workers were also his constituents. Moreover, he was under constant pressure from both the company and the local authorities, among them Mayor Garneau, to provide the firm with more land to expand its activities. Even as the governor general appealed for the removal of the factory, nationalist and working-class organizations in Quebec were petitioning their mayor and prime minister to enlarge the factory. Not surprisingly the workers, some of whom lived in the immediate neighbourhood of the plant, felt not only their employment but also their homes were threatened by the governor general's campaign. Leaders of the small Nationaliste political faction took great delight in rising to the defence of the beleaguered workers. For them, expansion of the factory on its present site was a test of government will. This put the prime minister in an extremely awkward position in his own constituency. When Grey learned of this complica-

The Ross Rifle factory on the Plains of Abraham.

tion he professed not to see the problem: 'I quite realize the difficulty attendant upon the grouping of a fairly large class of workmen in a new quarter of the city,' Grey wrote to Garneau, 'but I hope you will, with your characteristic courage, face this difficulty ...' What comfort Laurier and Garneau took from his admonition that they simply gird themselves for this battle is not known.[15]

The jail also served its purposes in that awkward place. Although grim, ugly, and forbidding, it was intended to be. It reminded an entire region of the consequences of crime and the wages of sin. There the condemned criminals of eastern Quebec took their final plunge in the courtyard – as legend had it on the very spot where Wolfe received his fatal wound. The walls of the jail echoed in stone the theme of the fortifications of the city against ancient enemies. The barred windows and the horrid associations of the place spoke of retribution more eloquently than the scriptures. The jail also provided employment, contributed to the local economy, and was conveniently located for visitation. Thus the jail was not without its defenders.

Taken together, these buildings represented fairly formidable impediments to Earl Grey's monumental ambition. But beyond that, Laurier saw dangers the governor general in his misplaced innocence could not have imagined. Grey's friends in Quebec were antediluvian, old school, conservative imperialists, like Casgrain. Laurier had as much reason to be wary of the enthusiasms of an agent of British imperialism as he had of the snares laid by his friends and enemies in Quebec. Nationalism, imperialism, and sectionalism had done enough damage to his party and the national fabric already. Quebec City's grandiose plans, and the governor general's ludic ambition to celebrate the founding of Canada by consecrating the very site of the Conquest raised the further danger of sectional strife. Nor could Laurier be seen to be pandering to Quebec at the expense of the other regions. To these dangers was added the further complication of financing a luxurious entertainment when the Canadian economy was on the brink of a severe recession. Laurier believed Canadians needed fewer lessons about their divisive past and more opportunities to glimpse their glorious future.

At the same time, Laurier could not turn his friends in Quebec down flat; too much had already been invested in the agitation. Garneau had to produce something respectable by way of a celebration. But when it came to the matter of expense, Laurier found himself in the deepest contradiction. Monuments and buildings would cost far more than he could ever hope to produce. On the other hand, the federal government had already gone to the trouble and expense of assembling land for a park. The Plains of Abraham Historic Park, whatever its drawbacks, was in fact the cheapest option. But Laurier would have to align carefully the forces within Quebec and outside, spread the financial burden, and in the process blur the target forming in his critics' sights.

In truth, Laurier and Grey were not as far apart as first it seemed at Christmas, 1906. And in the months that followed, making allowances for the exasperating procrastination of the prime minister, the governor general still harboured hope for his tercentennial project to embellish the Plains of Abraham. He also began to appreciate more fully the treacherous situation into which he had blundered. Grey did learn before he made public mistakes and he came to understand, if he did not always admire, the prime minister's deft handling of the political situation.

For his part, Laurier finally gave agreement in principle to a tercentennial festival. He insisted upon a vehicle, however, to give the federal government full control over the expenditures. By cloaking itself behind a blue-ribbon commission, the government was provided with some security and cover. Laurier also managed the negotiations in such a way that the not entirely cooperative provincial government of Quebec had been manoeuvred into a prior commitment of financial aid. Moreover, he succeeded in his goal of decoupling the celebration from the troublesome historical associations of 1908 to the more upbeat, future-oriented possibilities presented by the opening of the Quebec Bridge in 1909 and, it need not be said, until after the next election – or at least so he thought.

Notwithstanding all these precautions, Laurier maintained a prudent distance from the endeavour. The minister of finance, W.S. Fielding, made the announcement in the House of Commons on 10 April 1907. The prime minister was conspicuously absent on the occasion, and he refused to include a lavish advertisement for the tercentenary in the speech from the throne.[16] Even into the fall he refused to be pinned down on the date for introduction of the necessary legislation or any discussion of its precise terms. Clearly he saw this as a damage control situation in which losses should be minimized and not an opportunity from which credit might be gained.

The governor general drew several lessons from his experience thus far. He had come to understand that he alone could not sacralize the Plains of Abraham without the support of his government. Nor could he unite a nation by loudly commemorating a French defeat. Rather than abandon his plan in the face of opposition, Grey doggedly set about modifying it to obtain the necessary support. He sought to meet the objections of moderate French-Canadian nationalists by embracing one of their fondest beliefs. In Grey's mind, the British victory of 1759 could be paired in commemoration with what one French-Canadian expert on the Seven Years' War called 'the Second Battle of the Plains of Abraham,' the French victory at the Battle of Ste-Foy in the spring of 1760.[17]

Grey had stumbled across one of those rare opportunities for painless magnanimity. He could acknowledge a defeat without surrendering the victory – and purchase some goodwill in the process. There had been a battle at Ste-Foy in April of 1760, a large and bloody one to be sure. More men fell at Ste-Foy than on the Plains of Abraham. And the French army under Lévis emerged victorious; the British under Murray retreated from their mauling to fortress Quebec. Lévis then laid siege to the city; however, the arrival of the British fleet in May negated his efforts and reduced his undoubted military achievements to strategic insignificance. The presence of the British fleet meant that Wolfe's storming of the

Heights in 1759 and the subsequent British capture of Quebec would be decisive.[18] The battle of Ste-Foy had been for naught. However, in 1908 it acquired great political significance. By being raised to the level of symbolic equality with the Battle of the Plains of Abraham, the boil of Conquest could be lanced, the nation united, and the ties of Empire strengthened (or so Grey imagined) without reversing the outcome.

History's message from 1759–60 could be the fusion of two peoples into one in the crucible of war. The Conquest in these symbolic terms could be rendered a draw. Former enemies, worthy adversaries, could emerge from it on terms of harmony. Out of its fearful symmetry flowed the prospects of amity: a French victory answered a British victory; two generals had fallen in battle, one from each side; two lived to fight another day; both armies had distinguished themselves on the field of battle. Both people emerged from war with honour intact. The engagement joined by Wolfe and Montcalm did not therefore end in the superiority of one people over another, but rather in a demonstration on two fields of battle of the equally worthy character of two peoples. On this foundation a great nation might be built. None of this changed history; it only removed its sting.

At first out of necessity and then with enthusiasm, Earl Grey's vision of Wolfe's great empire-building achievement extended to Lévis's redemption of his people. In this way Grey effectively turned a patriotic French-Canadian version of events into a founding myth for a nation composed of two peoples. By acknowledging both of these victories in commemoration, Grey hoped to bring the two peoples together through a reinterpretation of their past. By reclaiming these scenes of glory from public and private misuses Grey also hoped to create a landscape of memory to perpetuate this mutual honour. All of this would take place, however, within the bounded frame of a British Empire which in the eighteenth century had first embraced Canada in conflict. In the twentieth century opportunity abounded for this united people to find a role in that Empire commensurate with their dignity and power.

The Plains of Abraham, Grey readily concluded, were worth another battle, even if it was a British defeat. Inclusion of the Ste-Foy battlefield in the proposed park, not far from the Plains of Abraham and already marked by the Monument des Braves, underscored the claim that the heroic conduct of the armies of both founding peoples was being memorialized and incorporated into a joint vision of Canada.

If the Plains of Abraham were worth a battle, they were also, Earl Grey discovered in 1907, worth a mass. He could not carry his program off without broadening his own base of support in Quebec. He came to realize that his campaign had no hope of popular success without the support of the Catholic Church. He thus began an ardent courtship of the Quebec bishops.[19]

Lastly, Grey realized with alarm that the financial requirements of his program vastly outstripped even the federal government's capacity. The bill for the lands, improvements, and festival soared upward beyond $1.5 million, and that did not include his newly developed enthusiasm for a colossal statue.[20] Ottawa, Quebec, and Quebec City together could not finance the full-scale version of the commemoration. Realization of the greater plan for the Plains of Abraham would require support from all of the provinces, from groups and individuals from all parts of the country, and, for the greatest impact, from throughout the Empire. That would be quite an undertaking even for a governor general of Grey's resourcefulness and energy.

His hopes rose considerably in March of 1907, just as Laurier and the Quebec group were in the throes of their final negotiations, when a long talk in Toronto with premier James Pliny Whitney produced the surprising offer of a possible $100,000 gift from the government of Ontario towards the cost of the celebration. Conversations with Toronto's leading newspaper editors – Willison (*News*), Jaffray (*Globe*), and Wallace (*Mail and Empire*) – proved also to be very encouraging. Both the minister of finance and the minister of agriculture in Laurier's government believed it would be necessary and now perhaps possible to get the other provinces to 'fall in line.'[21] Over the summer on a return visit to England, Grey sounded out all of his friends, who seemed to think an imperial fund-raising campaign a wonderful idea.

By the early autumn of 1907, therefore, the stage seemed to be set. Laurier had committed $300,000, Gouin and Garneau $100,000 each. This should be enough to finance a major tercentennial celebration in 1909 – a year late – at which the historical battlefields park could be suitably inaugurated. The dream of a monumental Angel of Peace and other embellishments would depend upon Earl Grey's national and Empire fund-raising crusade. The province of Ontario's pledge of $100,000 would apply pressure to the other provinces to make proportionate contributions. Grey would use all his connections and guile to prevail upon the other colonies and the elites in Britain. The goal seemed possible.

The Weakest Link

Until, that is, the Quebec Bridge collapsed with a grinding roar and a dreadful loss of life on 29 August 1907.[22] For a time there was nothing but stunned silence. Then the grief, and inevitable finger-pointing, and second-guessing. No one in Quebec could think or talk of anything else. Falling bridges change everything.

Laurier was terribly demoralized by the tragedy. When Garneau pressed him in November of 1907 on the nomination of commissioners for the tercentenary, he stunned the mayor with his sullen response. Since the inauguration of the bridge and the festival were connected, the collapse of the bridge necessitated an indefinite postponement of the Champlain celebration, Laurier wrote. There was no telling when the bridge might be reconstructed. It would be necessary, Laurier concluded dolefully, to wait a while until the situation became clearer.[23]

Garneau felt himself betrayed by the prime minister's sudden change of heart and he poured out his frustrations in an emotional seven-page letter of complaint. How could Laurier forget the impressive display of support from the entire community displayed in the deputation last spring and its stirring memorial? An opportunity for the development of the Canadian spirit would be irretrievably lost. 'Material development alone would not suffice to make a strong nation; it requires also the cult of the ideal, and what a unique occasion presents itself to us in the tercentennial of Champlain's work to unite in harmony the two great races of our country in a spirit of mutual patriotism from which the fruits for the future would be beyond price.' After the cruel shock of the bridge this disappointment would be another large check to Liberal fortunes. At a personal level, Garneau had suffered in silence the constant criticism of portions of even the Liberal press for what he believed to be in the best interests of the city. Now his enemies would become bolder and more unremitting in their attacks.[24]

Laurier upbraided his colleague for the impertinent tone of his letter. No final decision had been taken, he reassured the Quebec mayor, but he thought that Garneau ought to be apprised of the new situation as it presented itself.[25] But it was clear Laurier had developed cold feet and

The wreckage of the collapsed Quebec Bridge in the fall of 1907.

was doing everything possible to back out of what he could only imagine, as the character of the celebration had changed under Lord Grey's urging, to be a source of political embarrassment.

Garneau implored Rodolphe Lemieux, the postmaster general, to intervene with the prime minister. Adélard Turgeon would be sent to Ottawa to plead Quebec City's case, Garneau explained to Lemieux, and it was vital that Laurier hear him out. The choice of a leading figure in the Saint-Jean-Baptiste Society and a member of Gouin's cabinet as spokesperson for Quebec City was cleverly calculated to remind Laurier of the political cost of cancellation, Garneau explained. It was important that Laurier not sacrifice his friends now if he hoped for peace in the future. 'The more he hesitates, the more he gives room to manoeuvre to a certain element who are not disarmed or can never be put out of commission. Yesterday it was the question of the Ross Rifle factory, today it is this tricentennial, tomorrow it will be whatever will provide the greatest opportunity to raise popular passions.'[26] Clearly Garneau felt the hot breath of the Saint-Jean-Baptiste Society. This was a challenge on the eve of several elections, certainly for Garneau as he prepared to present himself in the first popular election for mayor since 1870, but to Laurier as well, who would face the same electors again very soon.

Grey characteristically saw opportunity in the tragedy. He had been pestering the prime minister all fall about the appointment of commissioners and the necessity of a public announcement of the fund-raising campaign. The king had been advised of preparations and sounded out regarding an Empire-wide crusade.[27] He tried to maintain Garneau's spirits by asking him to prepare for what he called 'my big plan.' Grey had a network standing ready to swing into action. 'As soon as you drop the flag,' Grey encouraged his hesitant prime minister, 'I shall start.'

Laurier, who appeared to Grey to be backtracking, objected to a fund-raising campaign in the schools for fear of drawing invidious comparisons between the contributions of French and English children. On this Laurier was fully supported by the bishop of Quebec. The prime minister also fretted about the worsening financial situation that might make it difficult for government to commit such large sums to what might be thought of as a luxury. But Ontario had offered $100,000 of taxpayers' money to be spent in Quebec, Grey shot back. 'Surely to you whose pensée dominante de votre vie it has been to harmonise les deux races, would agree with me that the value to Canada of this Ontario gift was not less than the gift itself.' On the other side, Grey had the support of the Quebec bishops, and he produced copies of letters from Archbishops Bruchési, Mathieu, and Bégin to substantiate this claim.

Far from the collapse of the bridge being a reason for putting off the tercentenary, Grey believed that the festival could now be moved forward to its proper date. Indeed, a festival might help take people's minds off the twisted wreckage. Grey begged the prime minister to reconsider his over-hasty reaction. He was ready to take off his coat and pitch in to raise money governments could not. Could the prime minister willingly turn his back on all of these positive offers of support? 'I have only one desire in the matter & that is to help you & to help Canada ... there are not many ways in which in my official position I can help.'[28]

Laurier wavered. Then late in 1907, after carefully weighing the pros and cons, he and his colleagues decided to go ahead. Yes, if the governor general and the Quebec committee thought it appropriate, the date could be moved forward to the summer of 1908, scarcely six months away. The appointment of commissioners and the introduction of legislation would take some time and require modification of an already crowded parliamentary agenda. If, as Laurier reasoned, English-Canadian imperialists were forcing him to spend hundreds of thousands of dollars in Quebec in the midst of a recession and on the eve of a general election, well, so be it.

4. C'EST TROP JESUITE

Crown Royal

When the king thought of his friend the governor general of Canada, the 4th Earl Grey, he thought of him as Albert and referred to him in that way. Privately Earl Grey knew the king as Bertie, or in wicked moments as Tum-Tum, the randy young buck he had once had to mind touring India, later as the boisterous host of the Marlborough House set, and always as a man whose monstrous appetite for cigars, fast company, and buxom mistresses made for a home life so unlike that of the late dear queen. But Grey would never think of referring to him that way, nor would the king, his friend, countenance it. The king, in this case, was a friend and familiar, but he was also an idea, almost a sacramental conception. For men of Earl Grey's class the fragile web of the civilized society hung on the belief in kings. It was not, therefore, to his friend Bertie that Earl Grey wrote from far-off Canada to enlist his aid, but rather to His Majesty.

In his October 1907 letter to the king, Grey likened the proposal for battlefields preservation at the tercentenary to the much-discussed British-French entente cordiale just concluded which had been attributed in the press (wrongly) to the king's initiative. What the king was doing in Europe between historic enemies, England and France, Earl Grey was echoing in North America. Grey glided easily from this diplomatic high ground to another lofty plane. Kings understood the importance of symbols. Grey thus turned to the theme of the missing monument, or rather the wrong monument:

You can imagine the shock felt by the visitor who approaches Quebec for the first time with emotions similar to those felt by the Mohammedan on his first sight of Mecca, when he looks up to the Plains of Abraham, where the destiny of North America was decided, and the foundations of Your Majesty's Self Governing Dominion across the sea was laid, and sees no inspiring monument like the Statue of Liberty which by the bounty of France has been placed at the entrance to the harbour of New York, but only a great frowning ugly and abominable gaol! and this gaol stands on the very ground over which Wolfe was carried after he had received his third and fatal shot to the spot where he died happy.

There was no more sacred ground than this in all of North America, and now an opportunity presented itself for both English and French to unite to preserve it. Montcalm had scored several victories over the British, might easily have done so again if chance had been on his side, and he too died heroically in the engagement. At Ste-Foy the French had defeated the British in an even bloodier battle than the Plains of Abraham in 1760. Grey claimed that these factors made it possible for the French of Canada to lend their support to the endeavour. 'My proposal,' Grey explained to the king, 'is to throw both battlefields into a National Park, and by so doing to commemorate the two battles in which the two contending races were alternately victorious, and in both of which the vanquished were entitled to as great honour and glory as the victors.' All of this would require money, vast sums of it, perhaps as much as $2 to $2.5 million to clear the site, build a museum for 'the relics of the Old Regime,' and landscape the grounds. He was prepared to lead an Empire crusade which, he hoped, the king would favour with his patronage.

And then he returned to his earlier theme:

I also wish to include in the above scheme the erection of a colossal statue of the Goddess of Peace, standing high against the sky, and offering with outstretched arms a welcome to the incoming immigrant, and as I propose that this statue should stand in a position which will cause it to be the first point of Quebec visible to vessels coming from across the seas, it will offer to the immigrant a welcome more worthy of Canada than that which is now conveyed by the horrible suggestion that Canada's gift to him is his chance of becoming a prisoner in Abraham's bosom![1]

Canadian Club

It could be said that in his enthusiasm to begin fund-raising the governor general sometimes raced ahead of his prime minister's resolve. As the letter to the king indicates, Grey had begun to announce his appeal for funds to save the Quebec battlefields even before the government had settled its mind as to whether a Quebec tercentenary celebration would be held at all. With characteristic impatience, Grey was attempting to force the issue in the late autumn of 1907; and with equally characteristic restraint, Laurier never chided the governor general for his interference or presumption.

Earl Grey wanted the Canadian government to do something; more importantly, he wanted to change the hearts and minds of the people. Grey strove for more than a government grant. The student who admired Mazzini (the romantic who dreamed and fought for a united Italy) and studied at the feet of Cecil Rhodes, Grey knew the importance of capturing the imagination of a people. Somehow every man, woman, and child had to be made to feel connected to the Quebec project. On such efforts mighty works might be then built. In Grey's mind, feeling rather than thinking was the surer route to adhesion to an ideal, in this case a bicultural nation within the British Empire. He would not have been insulted if anyone had dubbed his an act of public theatre. But he was in effect creating a stage upon which an increasingly ceremonial governor general might demonstrate his usefulness.

With instinctive shrewdness Grey opened his Governor General's Appeal before a meeting of the newly organized Women's Canadian Club of Montreal on the night of 12 December 1907. During his many visits to Montreal, where Lord Strathcona had loaned him a spacious house, Grey had made the acquaintence of most of the leading business men of Montreal – and their wives. There he busied himself arranging dinner parties which, to the sometimes strained credulity of his guests, attempted to bring English and French together socially. For the good of the country, he had prevailed upon some of the women to keep up these soirées in his absence.

He took delight in the company of bright, vibrant women. Three women in particular, Elsie Reford, Lady Drummond, and Madame Dandurand, became his protégées. Within the confines of their gender and marriages, their talent sought expression in the public realm. Grey tapped these bottled-up energies, associated as they were with some quite deep pockets. The patriotic men of Canada were then in the process of organizing Canadian Clubs all across the country, men's luncheon clubs at which major issues facing the country might be ventilated. Why should the women of Canada not organize a similar club of their own where they might inform themselves and express their views of public matters? And what more pressing patriotic matter might there be than the redemption of the historic battlefields of Quebec?

Grey honoured the initiative of these Montreal women by inaugurating their new organization with his dramatic appeal. He began by stirring their indignation with his by now familiar obsession with the odious jail. He invited his audience of hostesses to consider the emotions of immigrants being welcomed to their new home in Canada. Steaming past Quebec in a state of high anticipation and hope, passing the most sacred spot of earth on the whole of this continent, all they would see would be a 'black, frowning' building 'associated with all that is darkest in the life of Canada.'

The opportunity now presented itself for the women of Montreal to join forces with the mayor of Quebec City, the premier of Quebec, and the prime minister of Canada to commemorate battles 'in which the contending races were alternately victorious, and in both of which victor and vanquished were entitled to equal honour.' They could help raise the money necessary to remove the gaol, purchase additional land, build a museum, and construct a driveway around the site.

Grey then addressed a plea to the prevailing maternal feminist ideology. Replacing the jail would be a new symbol which would perform the miracle of uniting two people and inspiring immigrants with the Canadian ideal: that symbol would be a woman. The money raised would erect a 'colossal Statue of the Angel of Welcome and Peace, with arms outstretched, offering to clasp to her heart every new arrival from Europe.' On his visit to George Washington's home, Mount Vernon, the previous year he had been impressed by the patriotism of a single woman responsible for its preservation. As a result, thousands of schoolchildren could apprehend their history in a more immediate and telling way than books. Reaching for one of the Canadian 'hot buttons' Grey averred: 'I DO NOT THINK I AM MAKING A MISTAKE IN BELIEVING THE WOMEN OF CANADA HAVE A PATRIOTISM AND COURAGE EQUAL TO THAT OF THE WOMEN OF AMERICA.'

With that he took a paper from his breast pocket with a flourish and read:

THE KING COMMANDS ME TO TELEGRAPH HIS APROVAL OF THE SCHEME
FOR THE CELEBRATION OF THE CHAMPLAIN TERCENTENARY AND TO SAY
THAT HIS MAJESTY WILL GLADLY SUBSCRIBE ONE HUNDRED GUINEAS
TOWARDS THE FUND YOU ARE RAISING FOR THIS GOOD OBJECT.[2]

Bertie had not failed him.

The governor general's speech had a galvanizing effect upon the Montreal women in the audience, who threw themselves into a frenzy of fund-raising. The speech, reprinted verbatim in many newspapers, became something of a sensation. The major metropolitan papers hailed the project. *The Times* and the *Daily Telegraph* reported it prominently in Great Britain. *La Presse* of Montreal offered encouraging support. The name of Wolfe raised no rancour among Quebeckers; Quebec *was* undeniably the site of one of the epic battles in human history, so it was fitting that that ground would now become a hallowed cemetery in which the vicious hatreds that had too long divided English and French might be permanently buried.[3]

Grey followed up this great success with another address to a mass meeting in the Russell Theatre organized by the Canadian Club of Ottawa after the new year. On this occasion he stressed historic battle-fields preservation as a national unifying force. 'It is on the battlefields of Quebec that French and British parentage gave birth to the Canadian nation. To-day the inhabitants of the Dominion are neither English nor French. They stand before the world, not as English or French, but as Canadians.' Stretching history to the point of breaking, Grey claimed that while the Battle of the Plains of Abraham might have determined the fate of North America, the subsequent engagement at Ste-Foy 'won for the French Canadians for all time the absolute right to the sacred enjoyment of their language, their religion and their laws, under conditions such as do not exist in equal degree in any portion of the earth outside the Empire of the British Crown.' Always the subject turned to the supreme benefits of Empire, 'the most potent force for the spread of freedom that the world has ever seen.'

On the rocky crest of this hallowed ground, overlooking the St Lawrence, Grey believed that a properly designed Angel of Peace, not 'banal or vulgar, with flowing windy draperies,' would symbolize this ideal of Canadian nationality within Empire both to the people of Canada and its many hopeful immigrants. To mobilize an audience of bourgeois fathers, Grey unerringly linked his ambition to their two sources of pride – their children and their organizational skills. For such a noble object, he concluded, he hoped 'every boy learns the privilege of contributing' and that the men in his audience would join him in building a national organization to raise funds for the Champlain tercentenary and its project of Quebec Battlefields restoration.[4]

The response was immediate and extremely encouraging. Grey's message was picked up and echoed by the press and also by other prominent individuals. Offers of help and donations poured in from all over Canada and from Britain. The chartered banks cooperated in collecting money. One by one the provincial governments warmed to the project. If only the federal government would cease its agonizing procrastination and put its all-important commission in place. Until then it was a one-man show.

Grey enlisted Lord Strathcona to head a British appeal. Royalty, lords, descendants of Wolfe, and ordinary people would be appealed to for donations. In a wonderful G.A. Henty–inspired dream come true, Grey explained to Strathcona: 'I should like every schoolboy in the Empire to have an opportunity of contributing his shilling in honour of the 300th birthday of Canada and of the ground where the foundations of Greater Britain was laid.' Lord Strathcona cooperated and sent two donations of $1,000 to the cause. Lord Derby, among others, replied directly to Earl Grey asking his name be added to the list. Heartened by this early British response, Grey conspired with the king to wheedle contributions from the numerous colonial governments as well.[5]

The initial Canadian response as a result of the very favourable press coverage of Earl Grey's two speeches also seemed extremely encouraging. Grey led with a $1,000 contribution of his own. The Ontario Historical Society enthusiastically joined the cause. At one end of the country and spectrum of income, the wealthy British Columbian James Dunsmuir sent a donation and ensured the cause received publicity in the local press. From Quebec, Alphonse Desjardins responded. The students of the University of Toronto mounted their own campaign. In Manitoba the minister of education asked that information packages be sent to one thousand rural schools. Provincial governments made promising noises about possible donations. Particularly heartening was the endorsement of the National Trades and Labour Council and the promise to open subscriptions in every local.[6]

In the beginning of 1908, what had seemed highly improbable only a few months before now appeared to be within the realm of the possible. But heroic effort would be required. Grey operated on the assumption that nothing happened without big dreams. In speeches, conversation, and letters to his many correspondents, he began to think out loud about specific details of his project. Designing the Angel of Peace particularly appealed to his romantic sensibility. To a correspondent in England he reported on the favourable response thus far and shared his thoughts on ways to recruit the emotional and financial contribution of all of the schoolchildren of the Empire in his project. Raising an Angel on the Plains seemed most appealing. Inside the statue, he imagined a stairway much like that inside the Statue of Liberty 'which will take visitors up to the head and enable them to look through telescopes from out her eyes over the extensive view; and in the chamber of her bosom there will be kept a register containing the names of all subscribers, alphabetically arranged as to localities – thus every visitor will be able to ascertain how much money has been contributed from the county in England to which he belongs.' (Grey could see the statue in his mind's eye: it would be 'noble, calm, majestic, filled with repose, her arms outstretched forward, with the palm slightly downward as though blessing the incoming ships and the eyes lovingly bent on the people below.') He became so animated about this subject that sculptors began to write seeking the commission.[7]

Grey believed Laurier's stubborn refusal to pass the legislation, appoint the commission, and actually deliver on the federal contribution was frustrating all of his efforts. As long as the federal government held back, so too did other major benefactors. The public campaign was predicated upon governments making major contributions. Government delays gave the appearance of reticence which in turn hindered the public appeal.

To his impatient governor general, Laurier pleaded a full legislative agenda. Then at a key moment Laurier had a falling out with Garneau over the chairmanship of the commission: Laurier wanted to appoint his old friend Parent; Garneau bristled at the implication that nothing could be done in Quebec without the involvement of his superannuated pred-

An artist's impression of the Angel of Peace proposed for the Plains of Abraham, with the two historic armies marching side by side in the foreground and the fleet on the river in the background.

ecessor. Appointment to the commission threatened to reopen old wounds within the Liberal party in Quebec. That fairly settled, Laurier then objected at the last minute to the draft legislation, which seemed to give the authority to contributing governments outside Canada to name members to the commission. All of this had to be delicately sorted out.

To Grey it looked as if Laurier was once again trying to back out, this time using delaying tactics. For his part, Laurier had become alarmed by the imperial tenor surrounding the project, and the vulnerability this created for him amongst the Nationalistes in his own bailiwick. Beyond that, he had serious concerns about implementation. He did not want his government to be isolated; therefore he insisted upon ironclad commitments, especially from Quebec. Gouin did not want to give any hostages to fortune before an election, and so Laurier delayed until premier Gouin put his money on the table.[8] Moreover, Laurier had been burned once with property acquisition scandals on the Plains of Abraham. He did not propose now to put $300,000 in the hands of local people to spend as they saw fit. He knew where that would end. For that reason he insisted upon a national commission of his own appointees who would guard him against any embarrassment arising from overexpenditures or administrative mismanagement. This all took time.

February came and went. In private, the emotional governor general exchanged sharp words with his prime minister.[9] Laurier calmly urged patience. The whole affair took on a melodramatic aspect. Grey could no longer sleep well. After one particularly vexing day he scrambled from his bed at four in the morning and went down to his study to pour out his frustrations and anxieties in a letter to the prime minister. He pleaded with Laurier: 'You will, I know, forgive me if I confess to being a little discouraged by the successive delays that have postponed the taking of the steps necessary to ensure the complete success of the Tercentenary celebrations, which cannot fail to be of the greatest advantage to Canada & the whole Empire if the arrangements are planned & carried into effect with a dignity worthy the occasion.'

Grey reiterated the many steps he had taken himself to get this project off the ground, and the repeated delays of the government in agreeing to participate and then carrying out its undertakings. At his wits' end, Grey scribbled: 'It is now nearly four months since Parliament was opened and we have not even got a commission which is to organize the Tercentenary celebration & in little more than four months the Tercentenary celebra-

Earl Grey at his desk, *c.* 1908.

tions will be upon us! We have been waiting, waiting, waiting & now we are driven to a position in which we shall be obliged to telescope the work of months into days.' Such short notice made it virtually impossible to arrange a royal visit. Responding to the governor general's angst the next morning, Laurier gently chastised him, reminded him of the dangerous political implication of the situation that had to be managed, and promised once again that his commitments would be fulfilled in due time.[10] Grey calmed down.

Then early in March most of the pieces suddenly fell into place. The necessary legislation was introduced in the House of Commons and passed on the 13th after a brief debate. Laurier's appointments to the commission eloquently attest to his need to protect himself politically on all flanks. Mayor Garneau, the champion of the tercentenary, became chairman of the National Battlefields Commission. He was not, as we have seen, Laurier's first choice; but Garneau was the obvious leader of the movement, his party credentials were impeccable, and he could bring local initiatives into line with federal sponsorship. Laurier also named to the commission the recently elected president of the Quebec City Saint-Jean-Baptiste Society, Adélard Turgeon, and George Drummond from the Montreal financial community, to give the organization bottom. From Ontario, to ensure financial probity and perhaps stimulate voluntary contributions, Laurier appointed Edmund Walker, president of the Bank of Commerce, and, somewhat surprisingly, the noted imperialist, soldier, and police magistrate, Colonel George T. Denison. A nationalist, an imperialist, two men of finance of excellent repute, and the mayor of Quebec City: in Laurier's view the commission possessed the necessary balance. Provinces making major contributions could also nominate a board member; both Quebec and Ontario, with their eventual $100,000 contributions, exercised this right.[11]

Grey could barely wait. He called the first meeting of the commission for Government House the same day even before the orders-in-council had been issued. Now at last there was some substance to his campaign. As one of its early acts, the National Battlefields Commission set aside a small amount of money to support the formation of a voluntary fund-raising organization, known as the Quebec Battlefields Association (the plural drawing attention to the two sites of commemoration), which took on the responsibility of breathing life into Grey's private financial appeal. The dual purpose of the commission – to organize a festival and build a historic park – and two organizations – one public, one private, both with similar names – served perhaps to create confusion. But purposes were confused.[12]

The Quebec Battlefields Association Dominion Central Organization swung into action under its paid director, Douglas M. Gibson. It published pamphlets and brochures to explain the goals of battlefields preservation. It issued a blizzard of placards and posters in English and French to advertise the subscription, especially in banks. The association invited members and issued membership cards. It set up subcommittees in major cities and set them gently in competition with one another. It drew upon Grey's existing network of contacts. Mrs Elsie Reford headed the Montreal committee, Mrs Nordheimer its Toronto counterpart. The association supplied question-and-answer materials and draft speeches for meeting organizers. It also welcomed affiliated agencies and recruited existing organizations to the cause.[13]

The Quebec Battlefields Association ended up depending most heavily upon the newly formed Canadian Clubs in various cities. Indeed in many places, Quebec City included, the Quebec Battlefields fund-raising drive was one of the main mobilizing agents to bring Canadian Clubs into existence. Grey, now in harness with the Quebec Battlefields Association and the Canadian Clubs, strove in the spring of 1908 to make reclamation of the Plains of Abraham and the Ste-Foy site *the* defining objective of Canadianism and the measure of Canadian patriotism. The response was encouraging. Distinguished patrons on both sides of politics and from both linguistic communities lent their names in support. Prominent speakers travelling for other purposes offered to speak to Canadian Clubs or other organizations to promote the cause. Mackenzie King, on his way to Asia, made a whistle-stop tour of Canadian Clubs across the west.[14]

By June of 1908, a mere two months before the celebrations were set to take place, something like an organized private fund-raising campaign kicked into gear. Quietly financed by the National Battlefields Commission, the Quebec Battlefields Association and its branches in the main cities employed a network of nationalist businessmen's clubs, the Canadian Clubs, to spread the word, twist arms, and rake in the donations.[15] Schools in many of the provinces took up the cause, as did the Imperial Order Daughters of the Empire. Ministers preached sermons; poetasters filled the newspapers with reams of verse.[16] The association published an expanded version of Grey's thesis in English and French, *The Quebec Battlefields: An Appeal to History* and *Les Champs de Bataille de Québec: La Voix de l'Histoire*, which primed editorial pumps across the country. To calm suspicions in other parts of the country, this pamphlet declared that all of the money collected would be spent on battlefield land acquisition and improvements and flatly promised that not a penny would be spent on the Quebec tercentennial festivities. Sectional jealousies had to be assuaged.

The message certainly penetrated the furthest reaches of the country. The prime minister even received a letter written on birch-bark from a party of foresters in the bush of northern Manitoba. The boys chipped in $10 for what they considered one of the few truly noble Canadian causes, wrote J.R. Dickson, head of a survey party in his forest fastness. He added for effect: 'As I write this the witchery of the Huron's evening carol rolls through the darkening isles of the forest and the mosquitoes – like Night's black agents – to their prey do rouse.'[17]

By this time the political situation in Quebec and Ontario had cleared, both Gouin and Whitney being mightily returned in provincial elections. The announcement of $100,000 gifts from both provinces gave added lift to the campaign. The city councils of Montreal and Toronto chimed in with $10,000 each.[18] At the very last minute, then, the all-important Canadian campaign began to take on life.

Canada Dry

Public appearances to the contrary, fund-raising was going badly every-where. Notwithstanding the heartening financial support and publicity given by some individuals in Great Britain, the British government declined to become involved or make a donation. The British financial community was not more enthusiastic, as the young Winston Churchill learned from Arthur Grenfell, the merchant banker.[19] Governments in other colonies showed a similar financial reticence while lauding the noble goals of the project. In Canada, too, the shower of verbal support for the redemption of the Quebec battlefields did not lead as expected to a flood of donations.

Grey had been duly warned right from the beginning. When he wrote the lieutenant-governor of Ontario in December about the promised $100,000 donation, he was startled by Sir William Clark's brusque indifference. Grey bravely put the best face upon it: 'your letter has been a real cold douche: but it has a wholesome effect upon the system. It gives one a glow and rebraces one up to redoubled effort ... I now realize that a little more education on the subject is required before Mr. Whitney can successfuly approach his Parliament.'[20]

The British ambassador to Washington, Lord Bryce, who had earlier congratulated Grey on his handling of the delicate French-English aspects of this issue, by March had become alarmed at the possibility of a spectacular failure. The president of the Bank of Montreal, Edward Clouston, had recently passed through Washington and had seemed 'depressed' about the tercentenary and the impossibility of carrying it off properly in such a short time. The severe commercial depression into which all of North America had been plunged following the financial panic in New York in October, made it virtually impossible to raise money at this time.[21] Bryce regretted having to pass on bad news, but he thought his colleague deserved to know the mood in Montreal financial circles.

At first Grey thought the problem was a lack of proper organization to solicit donations. The Quebec Battlefields Association answered that concern. The sad truth slowly dawned on him that the well was dry. More troublesome than the financial stringency of the moment in Grey's mind was the fact that the Canadian people didn't seem to care about their history in general and the Quebec battlefields in particular.

Earl Grey made much of the British response and in his private correspondence claimed – no doubt with intended effect – that individuals in England had been more forthcoming than those in Canada. Lord Crewe, the colonial secretary, devoted his Mansion House speech in May to the tercentenary. The printed accounts of that meeting claimed that twenty thousand individuals had contributed, including fifty units of the army. Some two hundred members of the House of Lords subscribed £1,700, the House of Commons £300, the Grand Trunk Railway £1,000, twelve city companies gave £600, the Stock Exchange £520, the *Telegraph*, *Standard*, *Daily Mail*, *Daily Express* had all lent their support, twenty Oxford colleges had donated, as had every boy at Eton, Harrow, and Winchester.[22] Even so, the British response did not measure up to Earl Grey's expectations.

The treasurer of the campaign took a more hard-headed accountant's view of the situation. Promises rained down, but returns came in more slowly. Late in May, J.M. Courtney, the treasurer, reported to the commission that he believed they could only count on $15,000 to date from private sources and that included the king's $3,000 donation. The provinces would pay up after the elections; the public subscription was another matter, he confided to the banker Edmund Walker: 'I am beginning, really, to get frightened at the prospect.' Nor could he imagine any means of extracting any more money from the Canadian people:

> The plain facts are that the inhabitants of the Dominion are not enthusiastic in the matter. Those who for other objects such as the Patriotic Fund and the India Famine Fund could offer hundreds and sometimes thousands are now giving ten and five dollars and many are refusing to subscribe at all. In looking over my lists I have not received a single subscrip-

tion from any member of Parliament and with the exception of Sir George Drummond's subscription of Montreal I do not know of any donation being given by any Senator. This, is of course deplorable, but we may as well once and for all face it.[23]

The commission clamped down tightly on its administration and drew up a budget for a festival which, ruthless economy notwithstanding, would likely consume all of the government grants. The public campaign would have to finance everything else.[24]

The Dominion Central Committee began chiding the chapters in the major cities for lacklustre efforts. The Toronto subscription list, Gibson caustically observed in June, was not as lengthy as might be hoped. Were more pledge forms needed? Toronto must lead or others will not follow. On behalf of the Toronto committee, R. Home Smith offered the excuse that local circumstances combined with a difficult winter hindered their efforts:

> We have been very disappointed in the action of the banks, who at one time seemed to be inclined to contribute handsomely. In some directions the campaign has not been as well managed here as it might have been, but the response has been fairly generous, considering the great number of calls on the City's charity during the past year for the new hospital and especially for the unemployed last Winter. I am also afraid that during the prosperous years a number of our citizens gave sums out of proportion to their means and we have caught the backward swing of the pendulum.[25]

Toronto and Montreal could raise only $30,000 each from private donations.

Characteristically, Earl Grey did not take these facts as given. Rather, he plotted strategies to reverse the flow of events. Attitudes might change with more education. What was needed at this stage of the campaign was a bold gesture, one calculated to turn heads, change minds, redouble effort and release tight purse strings.

To that end, Grey entered into a conspiracy with the wealthy publisher of the Montreal *Star*, Hugh Graham, the stealth and cleverness of which both seemed to enjoy immensely. The publisher of a popular daily revelled in an opportunity to shape public opinion with a dramatic front-page scoop and in the delicious pleasure of sharing the secret with the man who held the keys to higher honours. Graham seems to have dreamed up the idea on an extended visit to New York in May. He sent Grey a draft letter, purportedly from an anonymous American business-man, expressing admiration for the 'pluck and spirit' of Canadians and the positive note being struck by the entente cordiale being shown by the two races in Canada in their joint campaign. 'If the spirit of unity, typified as it will be in the coming celebration at Quebec, is perpetuated, Canadi-ans must become an great and powerful people – a lucky nation.' The author, identified only as 'A Believer in Canada's Destiny,' enclosed a cheque for $10,000.

Such a generous gift from an American would, the conspirators be-lieved, touch the quick of Canadian pride. Everyone had been standing back making excuses. This bolt from the blue should alert Canadians to their responsibilities and have them reaching for their cheque-books too. Delighted by the proposal, Grey redrafted the letter 'to intensify the sting of rebuke which the letter is intended to be to those who are dashing cold water on the scheme.'

The prime minister must have chuckled when the governor general explained the plot to him. Laurier agreed that the public spirit and generosity of the donor deserved wide publicity. But he advised the over-clever governor general against attempting to mislead the Canadian people. Grey reported to Graham that his conversation with Laurier had reinforced some misgivings of his own 'that it would be wrong to convey the impression that an anonymous donor was an American.' The prime minister counselled the conspirators against misrepresentation: 'C'est trop Jesuite,' was Sir Wilfrid's comment on the draft letter Grey reported to Graham.[26] The letter, when it was eventually published, did not say that the donor was American, but by its silences and its New York postmark it opened up that possible reading.

When this magnificent gift was announced and broadcast throughout the Canadian press, the suggestion that the donor was a citizen of the United States had been carefully removed. Grey and Graham counted on innuendo alone to spur national envy. Above all, the two gleeful con-spirators hoped that the size of the donation and the mystery surround-ing the benefactor would cause the sensation needed to turn around the public appeal.

Edmund Walker thought this anonymous gift would energize the campaign as the celebration itself rapidly approached. But he acknowledged the difficulty of raising money. He was even having trouble with his own board at the Bank of Commerce and he hoped that Sir George Drummond would be able to spring large contributions from his colleagues at the Bank of Montreal. But he admitted the reluctance of the Grand Trunk and the Canadian Pacific Railroad, two corporations who stood to benefit handsomely from the festivities, caused others to hesitate.[27]

When the books were finally closed on the public subscription, everyone involved was terribly dispirited. A national organization, patronage from the king, support from the British nobility, public speeches, jesuitical conspiracies, invidious comparisons – every device imaginable had been unleashed to separate Canadians from their money.

A good face could be put on things. The total amount raised reached $766,087.17. However, deducting from that the $300,000 from the federal government and the two $100,000 contributions of Quebec and Ontario, it would appear that the public campaign raised only $266,087.17, including the anonymous $10,000 donation.[28] Included in that sum were smaller contributions from the seven other provinces and the municipal governments of Montreal, Winnipeg, Toronto, and Ottawa. In a sharp financial contraction, with many other worthy causes appealing for funds as well, the governor general's Quebec Battlefields campaign may have captured the public imagination but it certainly failed to command its purse.

Undoubtedly the campaign in Canada and abroad had been a great disappointment to Grey and its supporters. Only New Zealand among other colonial governments made a contribution, of $4,865; the Empire schoolchildren's crusade raised only $3,752. Canadian banks and corporations could only spare $16,396. Individuals in Canada pledged $15,278, in England $5,358. Anonymous donors added $19,735. Special solicitations from among British royalty, nobles, politicians, and colonial financiers raised $34,439. The Quebec Battlefields Association was credited with $84,574. The Quebec City branch netted $6,570, Montreal $42,218, Toronto $25,322, and Ottawa $8,190 – the latter two including their donations from their municipal governments. As the tercentenary approached, Earl Grey must have known that the museum, the driveway, the other embellishments he had proposed, and above all his beloved Angel of Peace, with the inscribed book in her bosom, would most likely have to go.

5. DEBAUCHERY

Seduction

How to woo a French-Canadian bishop? Begin with an appeal to authority, then drift ever so softly to the benefits to the parishioners. With that in mind, Earl Grey drew a long breath and began to dictate:

> His Majesty who takes a deep interest in everything which affects the wellbeing of Quebec will I know be glad to hear that Your Grace agrees with me in thinking that the time has come for a vigorous effort to rescue the battlefields from their present neglected and deplorable conditions, and to put them in shape which will satify the historic sentiment of the stream of visitors who once the plans proposed for the consecration of the battlefields are executed will come in annually increasing numbers to this beautiful city of Quebec which they will rightly regard as the Mecca of North America.

So far, so good. For a second line of attack, consider the view of posterity and authority: 'I should much like to be able to send to the King a letter from Your Grace approving my battlefield proposals, so that it may be preserved among the Royal records as evidence of the support given by the Roman Catholic Archbishop of Quebec to a movement which will be an event of permanent historical interest.' Clever touch, that, an honour with more than a tincture of malice. The bishops must know that their replies will be on the record where it counts. Earl Grey was, to be sure, a consummate courtier. He would learn, however, that if the crown hoped to treat with the mitre, it would have to be seen to kneel.[1]

Wayward Mother

In fact, the bishops had been worrying about the Champlain tercentenary since long before Earl Grey had ever heard of it. Their concern was not born of any fear of imperialist propaganda – that would be in the future – but rather something much more deadly and insidious emanating from inside the family.

It would be impossible to celebrate Champlain's seventeenth-century accomplishments at the beginning of the twentieth century without some formal representation from the former mother country, France. This presented a dilemma to the church in French Canada. The French must be involved, but contemporary France represented all that the French-Canadian church feared most about the course of church-state relations in the modern world.

In the view of the Catholic hierarchy in Quebec, there had been a second French Revolution in the late nineteenth century that confirmed all of the worse possibilities latent in the first. Godless Republican France had stripped the Gallican church of many of its powers and responsibilities, most notably in education. To make proper Frenchmen, Jules Ferry's education reforms in the early 1880s had secularized, radicalized (in the French bourgeois, liberal sense), and nationalized education, pushing church schools to the side. And that was not all. The church had never recovered either its properties or its status following the French Revolution. The state assumed more and more of the social functions the church once performed. Beleaguered, weak, temporizing, the French church found itself in a state of siege within its own country. It looked pathetically outside for help. Or so it seemed from the ultramontane vantage point of Quebec. And Quebec was not alone in this view.

From beyond the mountain the pope and his curia in Rome deplored the situation. Diplomatic notes and papal bulls, however, scarcely deterred the French Republicans bent upon their appointed modernizing tasks. Peasants would be turned into Frenchmen under the aegis of the Third Republic, whose most powerful instruments of change were schools,

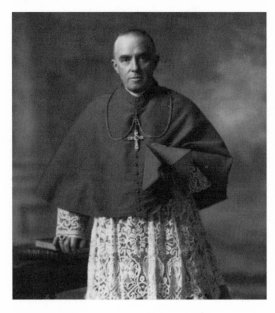

Monseigneur O.E. Mathieu, rector of Laval University.

the army, and roads, whose shock troops were the free-thinking professionally trained school teachers and the gallant engineers of the Ponts et
Chausées.[2]

Here was a tendency that must be fought tooth and nail, according
to the strategists in the Vatican. The tragic fate of the church in France
was scandalous enough, but at all costs this contagion must be kept out of
Canada. For the Mother Church considered Quebec to have struck a finer
balance between church and state, much to the advantage of the former,
of course. Already in Canada there were danger signs that the disease of
secular liberalism might be spreading. During the 1870s and 1880s the
church had gone to extraordinary lengths – some would say extreme – to
stamp out liberal tendencies wherever they might sprout. The bishops and
priests had not hesitated to instruct their parishioners on political as well
as theological dogma. Brave souls – the young Wilfrid Laurier among
them – struggled against received opinion to legitimize a mild form of
classical liberalism. Church authorities and their lay followers developed

openly ultramontane political programs, organized themselves within the Conservative party, and from the pulpit reminded Quebeckers of where their political duty lay: 'le ciel est bleu et l'enfer est rouge.' The battle had been fully joined for more than two decades when in the 1890s liberalism began to show greater strength and boldness within Quebec.[3]

Campaigns for a provincial Department of Education, the first step on the road to state-run schools, had already been mounted by the Liberal vanguard and temporarily checked.[4] Liberalism, which had been successfully driven to the margins of French-Canadian culture in the 1880s, by the 1900s nominally controlled the governments of the province and the country. Nominally, it must be added, because the ideological liberals, who were by no means political radicals on any other scale, had to form coalitions with other forces to obtain power. It was difficult, too, for moderate, outward-looking liberal Catholics who hoped for some kind of acceptable accommodation with Protestant English Canada because their co-religionists and compatriots outside of Quebec *were* under attack. English-Canadian intolerance towards Catholicism and the French language was, if anything, increasing. Even paranoids can have real enemies. And this seems sadly to have been the case in turn-of-the-century Canada.

The apostolic delegate to Canada, Monseigneur Sbarretti, writing from Ottawa, first detected the potential danger of a festival in honour of Champlain soon after the idea was first publicly discussed in 1905. How might France be kept out of this, he asked? He reasoned that the higher the level of the British delegation to such an affair, it would follow that prominent French politicians must necessarily be front and centre too. Sharing a platform with such a delegation would give the appearance of some kind of de facto recognition by the Canadian church to the state of affairs in France, and that would be an abomination. What possibly could be done to prevent this, Sbarretti asked his confidant, Monseigneur Mathieu, rector of Laval University who was closest to the local agitation?[5]

The church authorities maintained a close but unobtrusive watch on the unfolding commemorative campaign, as the numerous documents in the archives of the seminary in Quebec City attest. Of course, as a major force and property owner in the city, the church's views were sought and representatives invited to the organizing meetings. More often than not the church acted through intermediaries, gathering infor-

Louis-Nazaire Bégin, archbishop of Quebec.

mation here, pursuing a strategy by planting something there.[6] It was not the way of the church to press its case in open public meetings. It strove to sway public opinion through private counsel with correct-thinking, right-minded, tractable political leaders who would take up cudgels for the cause in open debate. These politicians in turn were listened to by knowledgeable observers as speaking with the authority of the church. Accordingly, the apostolic delegate, who maintained an unusually close attention to this matter, was reassured by the rector of the university that he would do his utmost to ensure that 'men of sensible ideas' would be placed on the festival committee.[7]

As planning for the tercentenary moved fitfully forward during 1906 and into 1907, the church became more and more exercised about the matter of French representation. Sbarretti and his secretary, Alfred Sinnott, brought intense pressure to bear upon Mathieu to prevent formal invitations being sent to England and France. To Mathieu, the man on the spot, the instructions could not have been clearer. The apostolic delegate hoped and wished, explained his secretary, 'that you *resist all contrary influences* and *absolutely refuse* to *invite* a Government so hostile *so inimical to Religion.*'[8] This was easier said than done. Their first preference was for a celebration that did not require either British or French involvement, but that was clearly not a tenable policy. The church would have to find a second line of defence. When it became clear that some involvement of both Britain and France would be required, the fall-back position was to find some way of having 'Catholic France' represented rather than Republican France. This was an extremely delicate matter, dividing France into the real France to be recognized, and the legitimate government of France that was not to be sent an invitation.

As Lord Grey began to exert his influence, the likelihood of a major British delegation further required a comparable high-level French connection. The more importance Earl Grey poured into this event from a British imperial point of view, the more alarming it seemed to the church hierarchy in Quebec. Mathieu struggled to find some way to avoid the embarrassment.

Louis-Nazaire Bégin, an unreconstructed ultramontane of the old school, had become archbishop of Quebec in 1898. Suspicious, eager to smite liberalism wherever it might sprout, ever alert to threats to the church and the nation – in his mind the two were identical – Bégin usually managed the campaign of eradication against modernism from behind a magisterial cloak of episcopal dignity. By 1908 he had more than ten years of experience on the job. The bishop and the member for Quebec East, Laurier, had been duelling for decades. Bégin had led the fight against the Manitoba Schools compromise in the 1890s; Laurier had outflanked him in Rome. The very presence of an apostolic delegate, whose role was to moderate conflict between church and state, constituted a permanent rebuke to the bishop's authority. Publicly the two maintained appearances, but privately Laurier would have as little to do as possible with the proud and prickly prelate. Bégin considered the apostate prime minister one of the enemy. It is instructive to note that when the time came for the prime minister to make his personal peace with the church in 1899, Archbishop Paul Bruchési of Montreal, a younger man of more flexible mind, served as his interlocutor and confessor. In his discussions with the church in Quebec, Laurier preferred to deal with Bruchési in Montreal, and Monseigneur Mathieu in

Quebec City. Mathieu lacked the weight of an archbishop, but he had influence. In addition to being the most personable member of the hierarchy, Mathieu was the most worldly, most widely read and sophisticated.[9] As befits a university rector, he had a lively, playful mind; he did not fear ideas and relished debate. While he enjoyed considerable latitude on some matters, he too had to answer to authority – his bishop, Bégin, and his superior, the apostolic delegate, Monseigneur Sbarretti.

Thus when Earl Grey came calling on the bishops in 1907, fully briefed by his battle-scarred prime minister, bent upon seeking church endorsement of his grand vision, the bishops had been toiling behind the scenes for more than two years to keep the affair as modest as possible. They were not happy with the turn things had taken, but they could not obviously show their displeasure. The threat of godless Republican France being represented, recognized, and paid homage to in the very bosom of ultramontane Quebec was too much to bear. But no one seemed to be taking the church's concerns very seriously, least of all the governor general. Nevertheless, the bishops were not without resources. When Grey asked for their support of the tercentenary, they had a request to make of him. Would he kindly attend a little celebration they were planning?[10]

Holy Father

At about the same time that the Saint-Jean-Baptiste Society of Quebec inspired planning for the Champlain tercentenary it also launched another patriotic venture, that of erecting a monument to Bishop Laval. The two hundredth anniversary of his death fell in 1908; it was also, coincidentally, the two hundred and fiftieth anniversary of his being named Canada's first bishop.

Since the 1860s the main activity of the society had been to raise consciousness of the survival of French Canada as a people by erecting statues. All over western Europe and North America in the last half of the nineteenth century the statue served as the principal vehicle of public commemoration. In France the phenomenon was sufficiently widespread as to acquire the name 'la statuomanie.' Certainly the last half of the nineteenth century was the golden age of sculptured history, as a glance at any public square reminds us.[11]

Thus when the Saint-Jean-Baptiste Society committed itself to the celebration of French-Canadian survival and national destiny, it thought first of erecting statues. The Monument des Braves to the heroes of the Battle of Ste-Foy in 1860 had been an early project. The Champlain monument in 1898 had been a broader public effort with substantial society support. In the heady ultramontane atmosphere of Quebec, Bishop Laval presented himself as a natural candidate for statuary.

In 1904 a broadly based committee, under the careful guidance of the bishop of Quebec, organized itself to undertake the erection of a suitably heroic image of the first bishop of Canada in an appropriately prominent public place. Municipal authorization was secured, the sculptor Louis-Philippe Hébert was commissioned to build the monument, and a subscription list was opened to receive donations.[12] Through the good offices of the federal and municipal governments, a prominent location was secured not far from the site of the Champlain statue, just down the hill in front of the new post office building on the principal artery connecting upper and lower towns.[13]

Thus from 1905 onward, the Catholic Church and the Saint-Jean-Baptiste Society had as their joint commemorative project the unveiling of the Bishop Laval statue scheduled for 1908. Much hard work needed to be accomplished to bring this ambitious undertaking to a successful conclusion. In these circles the parallel organizing effort for the Champlain tercentenary took a distinct second place.

This became most obvious in the spring of 1907. On behalf of the Champlain committee, Mayor Garneau approached the Laval committee with a request that for maximum effect the unveiling also be delayed until 1909 to coincide with the three hundredth anniversary celebrations. This, he said, was the wish of the citizens of Quebec in general. The refusal of the Laval committee executive to entertain this notion provoked an unusual debate within the committee of the whole on 28 April 1907. Judge Routhier, Monseigneur Têtu, Charles Grenier, and J-C. Magnan defended the executive decision to go ahead: 1908 was the actual anniversary of the bishop's death; invitations had already been issued; the contracts had been let; the subscription promised a 1908 celebration; 1909 would create an anachronism and unnecessary complications; the two celebrations were of quite a different character, celebrated events more than a century apart, and therefore needed to be separated for each to be fully understood; and finally, the committee members happily committed themselves to working also for the success of the much vaster festival being planned for 1909.

The dissidents, led by l'Abbé Roy, Judge François Langelier, and Dr Lessard, responded that the invitations could be easily changed; no one would mind the delay, and the unveiling itself could easily be put off for another year. By coordinating the Laval and Champlain festivals the committee would benefit from the larger publicity effort; public opinion favoured a joint celebration. Finally, including the Laval with the tercentenary would answer those mounting fears that the celebration was becoming 'too English and too Protestant.' The fundamentally French and Catholic festival of the unveiling of the monument to Laval would serve to give the the tercentennial festival the character that Québécois would wish.[14]

When it came to a vote, only four members of the twenty-three-person church-dominated committee favoured cooperation with the Champlain tercentenary. It was perhaps unfortunate but not surprising that the debate pitted men traditionally associated with the liberal, modernizing schools of thought (and the Liberal party), such as Langelier, against an ultramontane hierarchy. The tercentenary was thus doubly damned in the eyes of the conservative faithful: it was a competitor and an imperialist scheme.

When later that year circumstances suddenly conspired to move the Champlain tercentenary back to 1908, a second overture to coordinate the two celebrations, now scheduled to take place a month apart, met the same fate with no debate. Urged on by the governor general, who made a personal visit to Quebec for the purpose, the tercentennial committee formally decided on 13 January 1908, to hold their event at the end of July. Advancing the date called for heroic effort. It also necessarily raised a question about the Laval celebrations. Could they be delayed slightly from June to July to form an integral part of the Champlain celebration? To all of the earlier arguments in favour now was added the unspoken urgency of organizing something respectable, drawing in as many parties as possible.

Monseigneur Mathieu, spokesman for the Laval committee, regretted the date of the monument unveiling could not be changed. Parish priests and members of various patrotic societies had already arranged to meet in Quebec for the Saint-Jean-Baptiste holiday, the highlight of which would be the dedication of the new statue. 'I repeat,' Mathieu added for emphasis, 'we have no ill will'; it was simply impossible to change plans at this late date. To a group proposing to mount a huge festival more or less from scratch in less than six months, this perhaps rang a little hollow. Nonetheless, the press put the best face on the outcome. 'Two Festivals Instead of One,' announced *Le Soleil*'s headline.[15] Quebec would be doubly fêted.

In the most cooperative of spirits and without appearing to have dug in their heels, once again the church and the Laval committee managed to protect the essentially religious and national character of their celebration from contamination by the civic, secular, Canadian, and increasingly imperial tenor of the Champlain festival. By doing so they maintained their distance from the possible embarrassment of having to treat with official representatives of the wretched Third Republic. Two festivals served the purposes of both the church and the patriotic societies better than one omnibus event.

For this reason, the festivities surrounding the unveiling of the Laval monument in June of 1908 can be seen as a counter-cultural event to the Quebec tercentenary a month later. Or at the very least, the Laval celebration serves as an illustration of what the Champlain fête might have been had it remained in Saint-Jean-Baptiste Society hands.

By 9:00 a.m. on Sunday, 22 June, an estimated one hundred thousand people lined the streets and jammed the square in front of the Basilica. At a trumpet's call, a huge procession departed for stately progress through the city. For the first time representatives from all nine parishes in the city took part in this Fête-Dieu, marching beneath banners proclaiming their origins. Among the ranks of the parishioners marched representatives of trade unions, youth groups, temperance societies, charitable and benevolent organizations. Resplendent in their ceremonial uniforms, contingents of Zouaves, Knights of Columbus, the Garde Champlain, Garde Jacques Cartier, and Garde de Salaberry marched smartly through the gaily decorated streets. The cloistered orders were given a special dispensation to march. It was a rare sight; Ursulines, Augustines, and Sisters of the Sacred Heart joined the procession, then promptly repaired to their cloisters. Sir Wilfrid Laurier and two Catholic members of his cabinet, the premier of Quebec and his cabinet, the mayor of the city and the aldermen, followed by the professors of the university in their robes, marched as well. Monseigneur Bégin led twelve Canadian bishops (including the bishop of Toronto but not the bishop of Montreal) on the march. The bishops of Manchester, England, and Orciste in China lent an international flavour to the solemn march. As the procession reached a parish boundary, the bells of that particular church rang out. The procession itself was almost three miles in length and took two hours to pass. At the farthest point on the route from the Basilica, Monseigneur Sbarretti blessed the parade and received the sacraments.[16]

This was a special kind of parade, one in which an institution went out into the streets to connect itself to the resident population. The spectators, the symbols, and the hierarchy and the holy orders left their sacred precincts – the church and cloister. They marched to the people in their neighbourhoods and parishes. The observers did not have to leave their homes to travel to a public space; public things came as close as possible to entering their homes. This procession was thus a powerful reversal of the usual secular parade. It was in a sense an institutional invasion of private space, and, to the extent it was welcomed, it fused the institution and the people in a powerful ceremony.[17]

On Monday the 'apotheosis of Laval' unfolded with great solemnity and ceremony before a huge crowd in Montmorency Park close by the Archbishop's Palace. On this occasion the people had to travel to a public place to view the spectacle. Civil and religious dignitaries, most notably on this day twenty-five bishops, filled two grandstands. In the view of the press, the presence of Earl Grey, on behalf of the Dominion of Canada, and Monseigneur Sbarretti, the delegate of His Holiness the Pope, represented the sympathy felt by both church and state in this glorious event. Papal Zouaves and Gardes took up positions on either side of the veiled monument; a group of Huron Indians situated themselves as the base of the monument. Two regimental colour parties drew up; a troop of riflemen stood at readiness for the salute on a nearby hill. A military band burst into 'God Save the King' followed by Mendelssohn's 'War March of the Priests.' L.-P. Sirois, president of the organizing committee, noted that the presence of the governor general indicated the respect the king voluntarily paid to 'French glories' in Canada, and reminded Earl Grey that Laval, always faithful to his king, had taught French Canadians the virtues of loyalty.

Earl Grey had been made into something of a trophy for the church. He was always prominently on display. Indeed, he would be manoeuvred into unveiling the statue at this national festival to a man who had become almost literally a patron saint of French Canada. Hanging from a golden crown, drapery cloaked the statue. With guns firing in the distance, Earl Grey tugged on ribbons; majestically the veil rose up towards the crown, gradually revealing the statue of Laval, arms outstretched to his flock. From inside the crown a burst of flowers, flags, and firecrackers showered down as a flock of white doves fluttered free.

Earl Grey's speech, delivered in his excellent French and frequently interrupted by applause, opened with the observation that he represented the king, who wished him to pay homage to the everlasting virtues of the French-Canadian people as represented by Bishop Laval. After lauding Laval, Grey seized his moment to preach. It was fitting that the unveiling should coincide with the tercentenary of the city, he observed.

> I rejoice at the thought that the liberality of British institutions has always protected and encouraged the work of Monseigneur Laval. His Holiness ... has reminded you, that thanks to a special protection, your church enjoys perhaps more liberty than it does elsewhere and this special protection has, I am pleased to acknowledge, been rewarded by your unaltered loyalty to the British Crown.

Protestants and Catholics were equals in Canada and he trusted that the education institutions begun by Laval and others would continue to teach 'that great lesson of toleration and peace without which no society can exist.' This, too, would be the message of the coming tercentenary festivities, 'of which this is the happy prelude.' Grey concluded with the hope that the French genius of Champlain and Laval would continue to flourish and expand under the complete liberties of the British crown. The speech was a tour de force of advertisement and a cunning turning of adversity to his advantage.

Grey did not, however, have the last word. Monseigneur Sbarretti countered that through the grace of God, the church in Canada had always triumphed over its enemies, interior and exterior: the Conquest, native paganism, puritan hate, materialism, the loss of respect for authority and the social destruction of alcohol. The Conquest, far from being the tragedy it first seemed, had been God's means of preserving the integrity of French-Canadian society and delivering it from the errors of Gallicanism. Laval, he claimed, was always attached to the Holy See despite opposition from the king of France, an example now followed, he claimed, by all those who had succeeded him as bishops in Quebec. As the representative of His Holiness, Monseigneur Sbarretti prayed that this spirit of Laval, his zeal, courage, and attachment to the Holy See, would remain forever sacred to the church in Canada.[18]

The church had captured the governor general for this 'solemn and grandiose' patriotic celebration. Events of the previous day and the words of the apostolic delegate had imparted the church's ideal of spiritual guidance, social responsibility, and submission to papal authority. Earl Grey, ever the mischief-maker, had played his part but remained his own man. He could not resist using the occasion, he informed the Foreign Office to 'rub it in a little' to the self-centred ecclesiastics who, in all the words they had spilled on this occasion, neglected to mention the advantages they enjoyed under British rule. Still, appearances were enough; he had unveiled Laval. He had allowed himself to be posed within a picture framed by the ultramontane church.

Monseigneur Bégin had every reason to be fulsome in his gratitude to Earl Grey for the honour of his presence at the 'solemnizing of our national feast.' History would record that the memorial to Laval had been unveiled by 'a worthy representative of His Majesty the King.' The bishops thus had Grey in their archive too. His generous eulogy of Laval, the 'appreciation of the good work performed by the church,' and acknowledgment of the many qualities and virtues of the French-Canadian people would certainly 'meet with a grateful acknowledgment in the hearts and minds of my flock.' Monseigneur Bégin concluded his letter of thanks with a florid tribute that demonstrated the church knew how to deal with a governor general too:

> Need I remark that such liberal and generous proceedings are well calculated to strengthen the bonds of loyalty and attachment to the Crown, and that the future will prove, as the past has already done, that our people are not unmindful of the justice dealt unto them, of the regard shown to their

institutions, their language and their laws, and, in this respect likewise, they are faithful to this motto: 'Je me souviens.'[19]

Had the church and the Saint-Jean-Baptiste Society taken responsibility also for the Champlain affair, it is likely that it would have closely resembled the Laval apotheosis. It would have been theatrical, but in a different way – more liturgical and processional. It would have been more religious in leadership and character, more local, verbal, and more narrowly focused on the hero's religious role in the formation of the French-Canadian nation. And certainly it would have had little or no connection with the Plains of Abraham with its recollection of Conquest.

A Grand Duke

When Grey paid an unusual flying visit to Quebec in January 1908, to bring the utmost influence upon the tercentenary committee at a critical juncture, he began to gauge the fears of the church hierarchy, understood the implicit quid pro quo, and sensed a vulnerability which he might shrewdly turn to his advantage. In this struggle he showed himself to be every bit as much the master of ecclesiastical intrigue as the Quebec bishops. While maintaining his full vice-regal dignity he would stoop slightly to conquer by accepting the invitation to the Laval celebration, knowing full well in advance what it entailed. He would ever so gently, and well within the bounds of civility, try to turn the affair to good use. That he did not much enjoy himself was palpable in his official report to the Colonial Office on 'two days of ultramontane debauch.'[20] Nevertheless, he had clenched his teeth and done his duty. Afterwards, Monseigneur Sbarretti and the bishops all came to tea at the Citadel, so beaming and affectionate that Grey 'began to feel positively uncomfortable.'

His presence at the Laval ceremony was part of a tacit agreement between the church and the governor general. His patronage of the church's celebration was the price he would pay for its support of the tercentenary. In truth, the governor general had been greatly disappointed by the bishops' first responses to his October letters. Mathieu said the university was wholeheartedly behind his efforts. The Bishop of Montreal said he was happy to lend his support but wondered where the means would be found for such a grand park and museum on the Plains.

Bishop Bégin of Quebec responded in English, echoing his vision of two peoples destined by providence to live side by side and thanking him for continuing the traditions of his predecessor in promoting Quebec embellishments.[21] The apostolic delegate had also given his quiet endorsement to the event. But there was no life in their responses in Grey's opinion. The bishops were not wholeheartedly with him, he feared, for without their active support the tercentenary was surely doomed as a popular event.

Grey played the game well and was duly rewarded. Belatedly, he explained to the Colonial Office, 'A Papal decree has been obtained from Rome blessing the Tercentenary – but it is all Laval and very little Champlain. There is however a sentence in the decree calling attention to the advantages which The Church enjoys in the Prov of Quebec & attributing them to the influence of the British Crown. This is the sentence wch we must keep to the front.'[22] He would be rewarded right after the Laval unveiling with a pastoral letter from Archbishop Bégin to the clergy providing oblique, conditional, and somewhat backhanded support for the next celebration: 'You desire that the festival might be solemn, popular, enthusiastic, with that religious note which if absent would not dignify either our city or our people, and that being present, faithful to our beloved predecessors, we would take our part in these festivities of the country which would not be complete if the Catholic church were not present.'[23] And on 3 July, the actual date of the tercentenary of Champlain's landing, another mandemant made the church's support of the tercentenary abundantly clear.[24]

The Colonial Office first suggested to Grey that the Duke of Norfolk, the most prominent Catholic layman in Great Britain and said to be a close confidant of the pope, should join the royal party coming to Canada for the tercentenary. The Duke of Norfolk, who had already demonstrated some interest in Canadian church affairs, would be a tremendous coup, he replied to the colonial secretary: 'Norfolk's whisper is, I believe, listened to at the Vatican.'[25] Grey fired off an invitation to the duke, noting that 'It would be a great help personally and politically if you can come [to] Quebec for tercentenary week.'[26] Notwithstanding the fact that the duchess has just given birth to a male heir, the duke, knowing his duty, accepted. 'He can be of real help,' Grey informed the colonial secretary, 'there are unseen currents working against us in the RC Church & it is important they should be stopped.'[27]

Norfolk would be of great use not just by showing that Catholicism could prosper under British imperial blessing, but also by showing up France. Grey relished the embarrassment caused the church by the French situation because Britain would benefit from France's humiliation. As the bishops recoiled from the abomination of French republicanism, they were greeted with open arms by a hearty British duke who, it was rumoured, had the pope's ear. Trump. Grey could not disguise his delight in the irony.

As Grey predicted, the Duke of Norfolk was much lionized by the bishops. With Earl Grey, he enjoyed the vice-regal privilege of visiting the Ursulines and Augustines in their convents. He paid a special visit to the seminary and he dined with the bishops. He was much in evidence at the Basilica and, of course, at the solemn mass at the pageant ground. A photograph of His Grace talking with His Excellency Monseigneur Sbarretti, captioned 'Representatives of Church and State,' figures prominently in the *Commemorative History*.

Grey played the Duke of Norfolk card with great effect. The duke was hard to miss. A full-bearded figure of ample girth and abundant spirit, he made a deep impression on Catholic Quebec. He fully understood the part he was to play and seemed to enjoy it. His presence diminished clerical opposition by emphasizing, in contrast to France, the greater power and liberties enjoyed by the church under British rule. Afterwards Grey was exultant. 'Nobody ever came to Quebec who made himself so generally or so much beloved in so short a time,' he wrote the duke afterwards, adding as a postscript: 'I hope you found the dogs & baby as well as you could desire.' To the colonial secretary, Grey marvelled at the duke's performance: 'Norfolk has been a real brick and has made himself most popular. He has gone to all the balls and been swept out with the Band. He takes back with him the hearts of all Catholics in Quebec.'[28]

Ethel Chadwick, a devout Catholic whose taste in men tended to the slimmer, guardsman type, was initially less impressed. She first laid eyes on the duke from a distance when she attended the open-air mass on Sunday. Though she found the ceremony impressive, and took delight in the sight of Champlain's ship, the *Don-de-Dieu*, passing behind the altar on the river during the celebration, nevertheless, as a confirmed social snob, she could not help but regret performing her devotions amongst 'so few celebrities' – the Protestants being elsewhere. Later in the day she

The Duke of Norfolk with Earl Grey and party being driven through the streets of Quebec at the tercentenary.

The apostolic delegate, Monseigneur Sbarretti, and the Duke of Norfolk photographed in front of the old church at Petit Cap, St-Joachim.

met the duke face to face at a reception and the magic of genuine nobility had its effect upon her judgment: 'he seems very nice, though very ugly, fat & short with a dark beard – but he has a very nice pleasant manner and very unaffected though he is the *first* Duke in England.'[29]

During the Champlain tercentenary the church responded correctly but not necessarily generously. It played the public role expected, but it did not make any extraordinary concessions as it had done during the Laval fête. The church could and did withhold involvement in affairs it considered civic or secular, thereby not leaving the impression among the onlookers of religious subservience to the state. The cloistered orders were not allowed out to see any part of the great spectacle. The Augustines in their garden by the Hôtel-Dieu knew something of the excitement by the sounds spilling over their walls: guns from the ships and the Citadel, the pealing church bells, the distant crump and flash of fireworks, and the cacophony of marching bands criss-crossing the city's narrow streets. Up on Rue Donnacona the bishop did give the Ursulines permission to watch the historical parade through the lace curtains of the upstairs window of their convent. They in turn were overjoyed to observe Montcalm's army through the oriflammes drawn up in front of their convent and salute the mortal remains of their commander interred inside. Both orders received ecclesiastical permission to decorate their façades.[30]

Ecclesiastics who had recently marched miles through the streets of Quebec for Laval downplayed any religious involvement in the historical procession. Thus a historical representation of glorious scenes from Quebec's past fully in harmony with the church's view of history had to make do with only a handful of costumed priests as it paraded through the streets, and they appeared in the retinue of Henri IV, the Protestant convert. The church did, however, participate in the historical pageant. The Ursulines made the costumes for the Marie de l'Incarnation and Madame Peltrie scene. Priests played prominent roles, including of course that of Bishop Laval. Since it was a clerical view of history being declaimed before a huge audience from the Plains of Abraham stage, the church authorities cooperated offering costumed personnel, though only very junior members of the hierarchy. Finally, the church did consent to celebrate a solemn mass. The Plains would be reclaimed and made sacred by state and church, but separately and each in its own way.

Meanwhile the 'sane men' on the organizing committee managed the delicate task set for them by the church of preventing de facto recognition of the government of France. The three metropolitan countries sent asymmetrical delegations, with France being the odd man out. The heir to the throne of Great Britain and a vice-president of the United States did not call forth a comparable high-level French representative. Quebeckers were delighted that the mayors of St Malo and Brouages, the birthplaces of Cartier and Champlain, came, and that the heirs of current heads of the Montcalm and Lévis families accepted invitations to balance the presence of the Wolfes and Murrays. But for reasons of its own, the government of France could not spare a minister; instead it sent a mere conseiller d'état. Known for his anti-clericalism and advanced views on all questions, Louis Herbette thoroughly scandalized all Quebec Catholics by his personal arrogance and indifference to the church. A Protestant as well, Herbette further slighted his hosts by skipping the solemn mass. His appointment even drew a stinging editorial rebuke from the ultra-Protestant Toronto *Telegram,* surely one of the few occasions on which that paper came to the defence of Quebec and the Catholic Church![31] He could, therefore, be readily ignored or dismissed as a typical provocation by the Masonic government of France. While he was present, however, he provided a useful object of jest for the nationalist press.

It fell to the much-maligned arch-imperialist Colonel Denison, whose French was serviceable and manners impeccable, to act as host to the French representative – as seen from Quebec a pariah leading a pariah. The Denisons enjoyed the assignment and savoured the irony of it. Clare Denison later recalled for her children how much time she spent at Quebec with the delightful French delegate.[32] Nevertheless, though not much notice was taken of it at the time, the apostolic delegate refused to take part in any of the civic celebrations at which the French delegate might be present.[33] Monseigneur Sbarretti, however, was quite visible and much photographed in the company of the Duke of Norfolk.

Thus the French delegation was effectively headed by Admiral Jauréguiberry. Seen from the narrow perspective of the church, the symbolism worked well. The admiral was no embarrassment, like Herbette. Rather he was a respectable professional sailor, an honourable representative of the real France. But he was a figure who worked both ways in the iconography. However dignified and courtly his bearing, his unmistakable four-funnelled flagship anchored in the river, the *Léon Gambetta*, advertised by its very name the ignominy of France, named as it was after one of the founders of the Third Republic, a man of the most advanced liberal views, who died appropriately of gunshot wounds.[34]

6. PAPINEAU TROUBLE

The Tutorial

'The position in Quebec province is not satisfactory,' the governor general reported with some urgency to the Colonial Office in May 1908. The prime minister had just warned him that the tercentenary was in trouble. At first Grey was incredulous. All of the major newspapers supported the project. As far as he could tell, only one paper had mounted a persistent opposition, *La Vérité*, an otherwise insignificant weekly which, the Irish Catholic minister of justice from Quebec assured him, 'carried little weight.' At first he thought this was surely another of Laurier's excuses for delay.

Laurier then had to instruct his governor general as to what was really going on in Quebec. It went much deeper than a pesky newspaper. As Grey reported the conversation to London, Laurier told him: 'The priests are stimulating the growth of a Nationaliste sentiment. They are capturing the clever young men in the universities.' According to Grey, the prime minister was visibly saddened by it all. Whereas he had been struggling all his political life to reconcile the two cultures, the church 'had been using its influence in the opposite direction' to keep Quebec isolated from and untouched by progressive forces from outside or from within. This 'retrograde and mischievous movement' Laurier attributed to 'the intrigues of the ambitious Ultramontanes in whose hands the Peasant Pope is a Puppet.'

In Quebec this sentiment was much stronger than it appeared, Laurier claimed, extending far beyond a little newspaper. *La Vérité* was, therefore, not to be taken lightly: 'At present the Priests are heading in a direction which Laurier thinks will eventually lead to another abortive Papineau trouble!' Grey exclaimed with some alarm, then ruefully observed: 'There is nothing the Orangemen of Ontario would prefer better.'[1]

But that was no reason to hold back. Quite the contrary. Having been duly initiated into the intricacies of Quebec politics by his prime minister, Earl Grey now deluded himself that the tercentenary celebration might help liberate Quebec from the iron grip of ultramontane reaction.

Truth

At first glance *La Vérité* didn't seem like the kind of thing to frighten a prime minister. An expensive, flimsy, unattractive four-column weekly whose relentless blocks of type were unrelieved by any concessions to design, its three thousand copies circulated primarily amongst the clergy, religious orders, and devout lay Catholics of the province of Quebec. It looked like a religious tract, and in a certain sense it was.

Founded in 1881 by Jules-Paul Tardivel and largely written by him until his death in 1905, *La Vérité* had by 1908 passed into the control of his son, Paul. The son served up the same weekly diet as the father of sainted memory: the full texts of mandements and circular letters to the clergy, mixed with sensational revelations largely reprinted from other journals, caustic asides on them, letters from subscribers, and biting editorial comment on questions of the day from an embattled ultramontane, nationalist point of view.

The paper accepted no advertising: that would compromise its independence. Nor did it support or accept money from any political party for the same reason. In moments of financial crisis, angels appeared to see it through its difficulties. It remained a one- or two-person operation run out of the Tardivel home on the Ste-Foy Road. A fierce, proud, paranoid, combative us-against-the-world tone permeated its pages. It was filled with diabolical plots, miracles, and frightening outrages.

Opening the pages of *La Vérité*, readers entered a world in which an epic struggle was being waged against evil. The title 'truth' had been chosen to trump the seductive rallying cry of the devil, 'liberty.' When the paper first began, Jules-Paul Tardivel's extreme ultramontanism and aggressive tone embarrassed the archbishop of Quebec. As a layman,

Tardivel could not be disciplined, but his Jesuit mentor and spiritual advisor, Father Joseph Grenier, was banished by Archbishop Taschereau to northern Ontario. Even from that distance he nevertheless continued to guide Tardivel by correspondence. Over time, however, the views of the church and those of *La Vérité* began to come closer together. Though never fully part of the mainstream, Tardivel's tracts and books gradually became suitable material for prizes in schools. Tardivel's sin, or perhaps genius, was his knack of expressing 'in an extreme way what the majority would have put more moderately.' Indeed, on the elder Tardivel's death, the church tried unsuccessfully to purchase the journal from his family, presumably to tone it down.[2]

Jules-Paul Tardivel came to ultramontane, French Catholicism by a curious route. Born in Kentucky to a French father and an English mother, he was sent in his teens to a Quebec seminary. Tardivel was not particularly devout upon his arrival in Quebec in 1868. When he graduated from the seminary of Saint-Hyacinthe, however, he could not abide the anomie of life in the swirling social maelstrom of the United States. He quickly returned to the warm, cloistered, close-knit, organic community of Quebec which he now considered his home. He spent the rest of an active life in journalism fighting to create and protect this nation of his imagination.

Two central beliefs rang repeatedly from the columns of *La Vérité*: that Quebec was essentially a Catholic society and must remain so; and that the French Catholic nation must express itself politically, first as an autonomous province within a decentralized federation, and ultimately as an independent state. It was on this point that Tardivel and his circle broke with more moderate clerical nationalists such as Henri Bourassa and La Ligue Nationaliste Canadienne, who conceived of a more autonomous Quebec within a pan-Canadian nationality. Tardivel imagined that, duly liberated from English-Canadian domination, this church-centred society could expand through colonization into the Laurentian regions, and into adjacent territories in New Brunswick, Ontario, and New England. This was Quebec's mission; to free itself to expand and spread the light of the mother church in the new world. But there were enemies everywhere.

Tardivel's essential Quebec was under attack from many quarters: first and most obviously from the anglicism of the English cultural majority in Canada and North America; secondly from a centralizing federal government whose incursions eroded the capacity of the government of Quebec to protect this distinct society and its institutions. *La Vérité* regularly published lists of barbarous anglicisms that must be stamped out of daily discourse. Brand names and the advertisements in streetcars were a particularly pernicious menace.[3] It warned against the slippery slope of bilingualism. Any proposal for a new pan-Canadian nationality was 'a wicked idea. The French Canadian Race must remain what it is now, with its own language, institutions, traditions, and distinct autonomy.'[4] Tardivel denounced Henri Bourassa for his belief in the possibility of a bicultural, binational Canadian federation.[5]

A constant watch had to be mounted against the centralizing tendencies of the federal government in Ottawa. Only full provincial autonomy in all important matters would allow Quebec to defend its community-building instititutions against the destructive liberalizing and socializing forces abroad in the English-speaking world. In this struggle Laurier and the French-Canadian members of his cabinet were, of course, vendus. Externally the danger lay in the passion of the English majority for imperial adventures which could only end in French-Canadian blood being unwillingly spilled on distant fields, for tawdry territorial trophies or tarnished ideals entirely foreign to French-Canadian sensibilities.

But there were other more insidious demons haunting Quebec. Free Masons and Jews were spreading secular, liberal, and freqently libertine ideologies. *La Vérité* bristled with supposed satanic cults, ritual murders, crack-pot conspiracies, plots, startling revelations of Free Masonry's plans to capture the pope, and supposed Jewish atrocities. Anti-Semitism in its crudest form ran riot in these pages.

However extreme and sometimes intemperate its views, there could be no doubting that *La Vérité* created and reflected deep-seated beliefs. Arthur Silver remarked of Tardivel that 'his underlying notions of religion, society, and the relations of men to each other and to God, were in harmony with those of his province, and indeed, as the international circulation of his writings suggest, with the extreme Catholicism – the militantly defensive Catholicism – of his age.'

The Quebec tercentenary, of course, fitted in perfectly with this notion of an English and imperial plot against Quebec. Right from the beginning, Paul Tardivel and his editor, Omer Héroux (Jules-Paul's son-in-law), led the extreme nationaliste attack against the transformation of the three hundredth anniversary of the birth of French Canada into what they believed it to be, a British Empire festival. During the organizational phase Tardivel and Héroux put aside their fevered campaigns against Jews, Freemasons, Orangistes, Odd Fellows, immigrants, trade unions, anarchists, liberals, and socialists of all stripes to criticize the planning for the anniversary, the imperialist spin being put on the event, and especially the concept of 'race fusion' implicit in the affair.

Paul Tardivel reacted immediately to Earl Grey's speech to the Montreal Women's Canadian Club. Race fusion had only one of two meanings: either it meant the assimilation of one nation by another, or it meant the creation of a new nation out of many nationalities. The latter, Tardivel argued, might once have been possible in the distant past when the integral nationalities of Europe formed themselves. But in the modern era, forging a new nationality out of strong, mature, existing nationalities was an impossibility. One or another nationality must in the end win out. That was the lesson of Canadian history – the assimilation of the minority by the majority; Scots and Irish by the French in Quebec, and francophones by the English in the rest of Canada. Some nationalities could, however, never be absorbed without causing permanent harm. Obviously Earl Grey's real aim was to assimilate French Canada into a larger, imperialist, English majority. However noble or high-sounding his sentiments, race fusion represented a form of race suicide.[6]

As planning for the festival accelerated in January 1908 'Canadien' contributed a full-page 'note mélancolique' on what was happening. Here is that voice in loose paraphrase. In August we will not have a Canadian Catholic fête, nor a celebration of Quebec, but a festival of Canada at large, a festival of Empire. It won't be the founding of Quebec that will be celebrated, but the taking of Quebec by the English. Listen to Grey's discourse at Ottawa. It is not the work of Champlain that is to be celebrated; it is the work of Wolfe. It will not be the three hundredth anniversary of the planting of the cross and the flag of our fathers atop Cap Diamant, it will be the 149th anniversary of the defeat of our heroes by the English troops. We would like to celebrate the beginning of our history; instead we are compelled to celebrate the beginning of British domination in this country.[7]

Each week Canadien, in all probability Tardivel himself, attacked other aspects of the festival. The Plains of Abraham were no proper place for a sacred mass. The battle of Ste-Foy was being slighted. Tricentenaire was another atrocious anglicism; it ought to be rendered in French as 'le troisième centenaire' or 'IIIᵉ Centenaire.' The new park to be created ought to be called by its proper name, not a National Park, but rather a Park of Empire, Colonial Park, or simply the English Park. Canadien deplored the rumour that the farce of the pageants would end with a re-enactment of the battle of the Plains of Abraham, suitable perhaps for American tourists, but an unseemly spectacle of 'poor Canadians aiding in the eradication of their nationhood.' The Quebec Battlefields Associa-tion was nothing but a jingoist organization aimed at brainwashing English-Canadian youth. And inevitably, on 25 April, the troisième centenaire was revealed as a Masonic plot. What else could explain the mysterious forces that propelled the movement forward against the will of the people?[8]

La Vérité from time to time trained its powerful 'jingoscope' upon the effusions of Canadian politicians. The campaign of the Quebec Battle-fields Association provided ample material for analysis by this sensitive instrument. After scrutinizing *The Appeal*, written by Colonel Wood, *La Vérité* concluded: 'It isn't eloquent enough to recruit us to the movement. We will continue to make known the truth about this affair: that is to say to unmask the game of the imperialists. We understand our duty as journalists. We prefer to render service to the country rather than the jingo party.'

The difference between what Quebec really wanted and what it was about to receive thanks to the governor general's energetic meddling presented *La Vérité* with a constant ironic contrast. The old capital, birth-place of French Canada would simply like to gather all of the French-Canadian groups in North America to a solemn and modest celebration. Priests would speak comforting and uplifting words; renowned orators would glorify the name of Champlain; the focus of everything would be on the church and the country. Instead of that, what would French Canada get? One had to admit that the governor general had shown great skill in taking things in hand; he had associated Wolfe with Champlain, 1759 with 1608, and organized a program of military demonstrations and historical masquerades to attract more than one hundred thousand tourists to Quebec. So, instead of an essentially Catholic, French-Canadian fête, com-mercialism had triumphed, and with it imperialism: 'And in case the message escapes us, great efforts are being absorbed by a subscription intended to buy a field by chance neighbouring those where we were eradi-cated. Champlain is evicted: Wolfe dominates.'

The campaign of *La Vérité*, repeated by word of mouth, had a marked effect. In St-Roch, the working-class and commercial district north and east of the old city, a public meeting was held to denounce the celebration. There were even rumblings that George Garneau might be opposed in his nomination for a second term as mayor. The Saint-Jean Baptiste Society, before it would give its endorsement, haughtily demanded to be reassured that 'the 300th anniversary festival will reflect the national character and that their national sensibilities will not be wounded.'[9] *La Vérité* could not suppress its delight at the indifference of the population to the preparations and the general support given to its point of view within the French-Canadian community. It even quoted its proverbial enemy, *La Patrie* of Montreal, to the effect that 'One would prefer to celebrate Champlain otherwise than in the middle of an unwelcome pageant of the conquest of New France.'[10]

Consequences

Popular opposition posed a definite threat to the success of the celebration in the late spring of 1908. *La Vérité*'s campaign had been successful. Yet at this stage there were too many people and a multitude of interests depending upon the success of the tercentenary, the church now included. With the all-too-likely possibility of failure and general embarrassment looming, the church suddenly had to cope with a movement with which it broadly sympathized but which it could not directly control.

As the vultures circled, the tercentenary desperately needed a stout French-Canadian defender. Moreover, the church hierarchy had ever so delicately come to terms with the governor general over the Laval festival. As the success of that event became assured and that of the tercentenary more dubious, it would appear that the church negotiated some sort of truce between the organizers and the nationalists.

Liberal and Conservative newspapers, both English and French, opened their columns for every newsworthy item and gave strong editorial support. The citizens of Quebec would have had no doubts about where their duty lay. Merchants seized on the occasion for special sales, especially the drygoods merchants and department stores. Advertisements for tenders from the National Battlefields Commission dotted the pages.[11] But still the public held back. At length Garneau was forced to call a press conference to beg for public support.[12] A correspondent in *Le Soleil* urged his francophone compatriots to loosen up. If they could not enjoy the opportunity, perhaps they might take advantage of it: 'Let the memory of our past and the gold of the festivals rain without fear on Quebec. The next morning we will wake up still Canadiens.'[13]

Obviously exasperated by Tardivel's crusade in *La Vérité*, and worried by its effectiveness, the respected journalist and historian Thomas Chapais thundered back in the pages of *L'Action Sociale*, a new popular journal funded by the church to spread the orthodox message more widely in the community.[14] It was not so much what Chapais said, but who he was and where he said it, that mattered. A respected, devout, scholar-politician, patron and protector of the Ursuline Convent which backed onto his house, a gentleman Conservative, ardent defender of a Catholic Quebec though not an ultramontane, arguably Quebec's leading historian and chairman of the subcommittee on history and archeology for the festival, Chapais spoke from the pulpit of the church's official newspaper and, presumably, with the church's blessing.

In a moderate, measured tone, he acknowledged the public disquiet and hoped that his essay clarifying the purposes of the event would dissipate the regrettable misconceptions and malicious criticism being spread abroad. Quebec controlled the celebration, he insisted; Champlain had not been lost sight of, and he assured his readers that the festivities would be 'vraiment canadiennes.' It was easier to make criticism than art, he jabbed. And a superb, moving spectacle in which Champlain would be prominently featured was the intended objet d'art. His ship and Habitation would be reconstructed. He would come to life in the procession and pageants. The most eloquent voices in the country, both English and French, would contribute to Champlain's scholarly apotheosis. The voice of authority confidently assured his fellow citizens: 'Champlain, the Founder and the Father of the country will be, and justly so, the central and dominant figure of the tercentenary.'

Turning to the Plains of Abraham, Chapais had nothing but praise for the governor general's laudable campaign. French-Canadian sensibilities need not be wounded by a beautiful park, and certainly the governor general was assuredly a man of generous spirit who did not intend any slight. His gift would be of immeasurable benefit to Quebec, admired by visitors for its incomparable views, its monuments and statues evoking the glory of Quebec's past. It was entirely fitting that a modest celebration take place on the Plains during the tercentenary. What did

Quebeckers have to fear? The Plains would remain the Plains; no one was stealing them, changing their name, stripping them of three centuries of association with French Canada. Nor should French-speaking Quebeckers begrudge their English co-citizens' memories of which they should justly be proud. History did not begin in 1759 nor did it end there.

Chapais asserted that with greater public cooperation and understanding the tercentenary would be an unforgettable popular spectacle of fireworks, religious and musical celebrations, and grand sights that would move the spirit of patriotism in all people. He concluded: 'Those among us who are working silently and incessantly to assure this result are right, and it seems to me their work demands from their fellow citizens a little good will, a little sympathy, and, may I add, a little trust.'[15]

This oration, reprinted widely and commented upon in the Quebec press, seems to have stemmed the tide. The argument, it must be said, was not overpowering. It was the messenger rather than the message that was important. Thomas Chapais was an old Conservative, not a Laurier Liberal. He was not one of the up-and-coming, accommodationist Chamber of Commerce businessmen. After Chapais weighed in, at least there would be some debate on the merits of the celebration.

Probably sensing the seriousness of the situation, the church appears to have gone further. In June, a missive appeared in *La Nouvelle France*, a Catholic journal, with rumoured assurances of ecclesiastical blessing, entitled 'Errors and Prejudices Concerning the Tercentenary of Quebec.' The unknown author (in fact, Raphael Gervais), took an independent tack; he endorsed the festival but not the restoration of the Plains of Abraham battlefield at this time. Nevertheless, he offered a stirring defence of the general intention of using the occasion to bring about greater understanding and mutual respect between the two cultural groups. French Canadians must learn to come to terms with a pluralist milieu while at the same time English Canadians must better understand the history, language, and sensibilities of French Canadians. These lessons could not be learned in culturally separate celebrations, though each community ought to have such events of its own to celebrate. The Laval celebration was an entirely worthy example of this sort of 'within the family' celebration. But French Canadians must also celebrate their wider nationality, Gervais argued, and the tercentenary, which was in danger of failing, was an ideal opportunity: 'It seems to me that a true patriotism, is one that takes into account the general needs of the country, and seeks neither a fusion of the races nor their antagonism, or the preponderance of one race over the other, but rather seeks their mutual accommodation and peaceful cohabitation founded on a perfect understanding and a most sincere respect of their reciprocal qualities.'

The author regretted that parochial resentments of the self-appointed spokesmen of the people had thus far blighted the festival. But that had not, he noted, stopped his English-Canadian counterparts from taking the initiative and showing a true patriotic spirit. They did not seem to be offended by organizing a French and a Catholic event. The Prince of Wales would be neither diminished nor humiliated by the pageant scene in which Frontenac would dismiss the English invaders. Here then was precisely the kind of celebration, in which English Canadians eagerly participated, that French Canadians should join with enthusiasm: 'At the moment, if the programme of the festival remains as it is, and I do not see why it should be modified, the celebration will be well and truly Canadian and at the same time French-Canadian.'[16]

These two essays did not stop the criticism that continued to roll forward under its own momentum. However, a stout defence was important for morale. How otherwise could the organizers rally the mass support required to put on the vast spectacle? As we have seen, Earl Grey's courting of the bishops bought him public support by the church. The Liberal party also mounted a subtle infiltration of nationaliste ranks to turn the tables. During the annual meeting of the Saint-Jean-Baptiste Society, during the Laval demonstrations, Liberal militants managed to elect one of their own, Adélard Turgeon, to the presidency. It was therefore something of an embarrassment to committed nationalists that Turgeon was pushed front and centre by the Laurier forces during the tercentenary as representative of the society.[17] Laurier, it will be recalled, asked that Turgeon speak for him at the Champlain commemoration. The Saint-Jean-Baptiste Society had thus been surreptitiously conscripted for the celebration!

Laughter

The best-known nationalist in Quebec, and Laurier's most tenacious antagonist, Henri Bourassa, said surprisingly little about the tercentenary. While he was considerably more influential than Tardivel and the extremists, and on this matter he shared their views, he did not enter the fray. In the spring of 1908 he was licking his wounds from various run-ins with Laurier's legions and contemplating a turn to provincial politics. He seems to have at first dismissed the tercentenary as a joke, a show that would flare and die leaving little trace. He did not dignify what he considered an empty charade with any comment. But before leaving for France in June he dashed off a few lines to his unlikely correspondent in Toronto, Goldwin Smith, an anti-imperialist of a different stripe and, ironically, a former tutor of the king.

As if he had been privy to Grey's correspondence, Bourassa saw through the governor general's motives but admired his skill at turning a festival of the birth of French Canada into a great memorial to the Conquest. Grey's sole purpose, Bourassa explained, was to impress his friends in London with how 'French-Canadians had grown in the new imperial faith.' His second objective was to change French-Canadian attitudes towards imperialism, and in this, Bourassa acknowledged Grey's shrewdness: 'He has played very adroitly upon what is perhaps the weakest point in our representative men; vanity. He has succeeded in inducing many who will never be imperialists into playing their role in the comedy.'[18]

That weakness became the focus for the barbs of the new popular nationalist daily, *Le Nationaliste*, published in Montreal. At first it followed *La Vérité's* snide, heavy-handed, hard line. Grey's notion of a 'conciliation of the races' was shown to be more a hope than a reality. The name of the National Park was mocked, and ironic bas-reliefs proposed for the base of the Angel of Peace. The term tercentenary was denounced as an anglicism in the bulletin of the Society of French Speakers. At the opening celebration *Le Nationaliste's* headlines proclaimed: 'After many speeches Champlain was completely ignored at the Quebec festival. It was quite simply a vast imperial carnival.' Prominent space was accorded to Edouard Drumont, a French rightist ideologue, who deplored the conduct of the French delegation at Quebec, representing as it did a government of Blocards, Free Masons, and Jews. By a strange inversion he noted that the right of old France now looked to New France for inspiration in its struggle to restore the true France.[19]

Eventually, however, *Le Nationaliste* found its own voice, one more in keeping with the kind of popular paper it hoped to be. It also honed in more accurately on the target identified by Bourassa, the vanity of the Liberal bourgoisie. *Le Nationaliste* had to address the embarrassing fact that large portions of the Liberal and Conservative French-Canadian elite were attracted to the celebration by royalty and by the opportunities for self-promotion it presented. Its pointed barbs, tossed off with a gay spirit, aimed at puncturing pretence.

There is no more savage spirit than laughter. *Le Nationaliste* turned the tercentenary into a source of delicious amusement. Rather than grow indignant or be scandalized, it urged its readers to laugh at the celebration. In March, for example, the paper printed the supposed transcript of the cabinet meeting approving the federal grant to the tercentenary. Laurier opens the meeting by asking his colleagues if the government should take part. Fielding, the minister of finance, supported the tercentenary grant on the condition that the fête be exclusively in English. When Aylesworth, the minister of justice from Ontario, asked what the point of it all was, Fred Borden, the minister of militia, responded the glorification of the Plains of Abraham. Aylesworth came back: 'And you call that a tricentenary?' Fielding interjected: 'You don't know how to count.'

A befuddled Sir Richard Cartwright struggled in his deafness to understand. The minister of railways in all innocence asked his French-Canadian colleagues why they seemed so eager to celebrate their defeat? Sir Wilfrid replied: 'It is necessary to glorify that which one cannot prevent.' Frank Oliver, the minister of the interior from the west, reported that the Doukhobors had promised to send a deputation. Sydney Fisher, the minister of agriculture from the Eastern Townships, snorted that they could not come nude; they would certainly have to put on clothes to walk on Dufferin Terrace. Oliver also wanted to know who was Champlain anyway? The controller of customs replied with a straight face that he was a cadet in Montcalm's regiment.

The proposal to vote $300,000 and control the organization from Ottawa was carried. Sir Wilfrid then enthused:

Laurier: The celebration will be grandiose. It will commence with a
          grand mass.
Cartwright: What? What?
Laurier: There will be a sermon.
Templeman: Hear! Hear!
Laurier: A Grand dinner.
Lemieux: Very fine.

Laurier: Speeches, a splendid ball ...
Fisher: Will the women display plunging necklines?
Pugsley: No, only the men.

Asked if Quebec could hold a half a million visitors, Laurier replied that he didn't know; he hadn't been to Quebec in some time. In any event he thought he might be elsewhere; the west had conquered his affections.[20]

In the middle of the festivities, Le Nationaliste's man-about-town correspondent chanced upon an acquaintance from the race track, Labarrière, consoling himself with beer after beer in a bar on Notre Dame. How come you're not at the fête, our man asked? I've been and returned, Labarrière snarled, and I assure you I'm not very happy. Then out poured a tale of woe as our reporter ministered repeatedly to his friend's abundant thirst.

It seems Labarrière had been poisoned in a restaurant and stung by the watered drinks. He'd taken the lovely Yolande along with him. They were shocked by the prices being asked for rooms and meals. All they had seen were costumed figures rushing about in the streets. The police behaved like Cossacks. The only good thing he'd heard was Mr Turgeon delivering a speech apparently cribbed from Paul Déroulède (a patriotic French, Germanophobe poet whose fanatical anti-Dreyfusard opinions got him exiled for sedition), though he would have preferred to have heard it from the master himself. Apparently Premier Gouin had been admitted by the prince to 'la sirerie,' a turn of events that disappointed orator Turgeon. Labarrière hadn't understood a word of Laurier's welcoming address – it was in English – nevertheless he admired its spirited hand gestures.[21] The prince had responded in French, had he not? Oh yes, someone had convinced him that it was a celebration of Champlain and presented him with a speech in French.

Afterwards, what a noise assaulted the ears from the guns of the fleet. Add to that the punishment to the skin from the black flies. You had to pay for everything; things cost the earth. Nobody seemed to know what was going on.

So you didn't much enjoy the celebrations? our correspondent inquired. 'No, not much,' Laberiere moaned, hoisting another beer, 'but I console myself thinking that things will be much better at the Fourth centennial. Then, if you wish, we will go together.'[22]

Le Nationaliste had another sharp object with which to puncture pretention: the pen of its editorial cartoonist who signed himself 'J. Charlebois.' Before and during the festival weeks Charlebois's spare, deliciously wicked cartoons graced the pages of the paper. Later they were bound and sold as a souvenir of the celebration ('almost a nationalist pamphlet' enthused *Le Nationaliste* in its advertisement).[23] Charlebois aimed his nib not at the prince, who travelled in sublime innocence from one panel to the next, but rather at the bumbling, fawning, locals who swarmed around him, and at Grey.

Charlebois has Laurier and the prince strolling arm-in-arm in evening dress. Laurier remarks: 'Your Highness, Canadians are going to be terribly disappointed; they were expecting to see a Prince in an ermine cape with his crown.' In another drawing, a knot of gentlemen in their Sunday best, gloved, hair slicked, hats in hand, with a perfectly idiotic air about them, arrive at the prince's door expecting to participate in the ceremony of kissing the prince's hand. The valet dismisses them: 'I'm sorry, gentlemen, but you are a little late. His Highness is putting on his pants.' Lord Grey and the prince are enjoying a drink and a cigar together in another cartoon. Suddenly the prince asks: 'What's the real significance of the Tercentenary? I understand absolutely nothing.' The governor general replies with a sardonic smile: 'It's these French Canadians who are celebrating the defeat of their ancestors.'

French Canadian sycophancy and imperialist trickery were the primary objects of Charlebois's barbed jests. His humour did not attack the prince or the monarchy; rather it attempted to puncture the pomposity and cringing ambition of the Liberal French-Canadian elite who had been bamboozled by Anglo-imperialists personified by the governor general. The real spirit of Quebec and the true representatives of its people were not on display for the prince at the tercentenary.

On the day the Prince of Wales arrived, *Le Nationaliste* reverted to a more didactic form in an open letter warning him not to be deceived by appearances. The toadies fawning about him did not really represent the two million people of French Canada. The real French Canada deplored the way in which Grey had inflated a simple family ceremony into an imperial spectacle. 'French speaking Canadians would like to glorify the founder of Quebec. Our Governor prevents us from doing it under the pretext of assisting us with it.' It would be a mistake therefore, to believe on the basis of the demonstrations at the tercentenary that French Canadians had become deeply infected by imperial sentiments. The

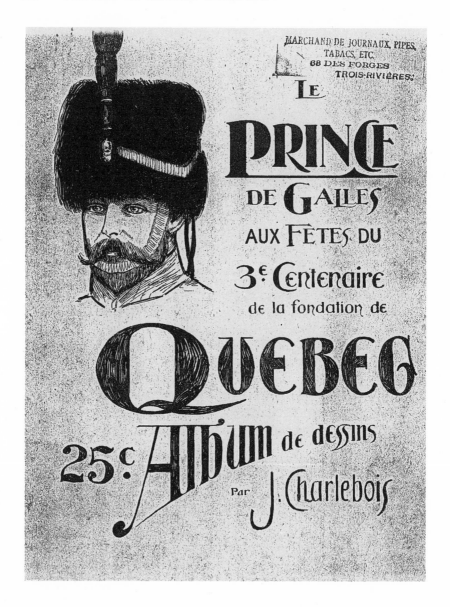

Cover of Charlebois's album of cartoons of the Prince of Wales at the tercentenary.

REMINISCENCES

LE VIEUX CANADIEN.—On l'a ben connu, vot' pére, dans l'temps, en 60, quand il était v'nu pour le pont Victoria.. Est-ce qu'il aime encore les "créatures"?

Le vieux Canadien: 'Your father was well known back in '60 when he came to open the Victoria Bridge. Does he still like the "sweet young things"?'

UN DINER CHEZ M. LE MINISTRE DE LA "MARINE"

LE PRINCE.—Monsieur le ministre, j'aimerais bien goûter un plat du pays, un plat canadien.
M. LE MINISTRE.—Françoise! emporte donc les guertons!

Dinner at the minister of the marine's house.
The Prince: 'Mr Minister, I would very much like to taste a specialty of the country, a Canadian dish.'
The minister: 'Françoise! Bring on the fried pork rind.'

LOYAUX

LE PRINCE.—Hello! hello! Is this you father? Good morning!.....
Si les Canadiens sont loyaux? Je crois bien, écoutez plutôt: Les Canadiens-Anglais sont plus Anglais que le roi, et les Canadiens-Français sont plus Anglais
que les Canadiens-Anglais, ainsi...

The Prince: 'Hello! hello! Is this you father? Good morning! ... Are the Canadians loyal? I'm pretty sure, listen: The English Canadians are more English than
the King, and the French Canadians are more English than the English Canadians, so ...'

French Canadians whom the prince would meet and decorate represented a different generation; they were out of touch with the manners
and sentiments of the people of the province. 'Thank God, we are better
than they. If, in fact, all of the French-Canadians were like them you
would have been right in supposing that we possessed so little dignity as
to be satisfied with Lord Grey's Imperial Masquarade. If we were really
like those people we would indeed be ripe for the grave and this demonstration would be nothing more or less than our funeral.' Be assured, the
letter concluded, that 'The humiliation which has been imposed upon us
by whipping up our national pride, will only serve to hasten the hour of
our awakening. That is the message you should take back to the King.'[24]

When they were a little unbuttoned, Charlebois and *Le Nationaliste*
found their mark and had wonderful fun doing it. This lighter touch
helped negotiate a tricky passage for everyone. Humour decontami-
nated the event and thereby legitimized some form of limited involvement. Grey's game had been unmasked; having been established, one
now participated knowingly, on one's own terms. You could sneer and
stay home if you wished. You could also go out into the crowded streets
and see what was going on with a broad smile. This strategy directed
attention to the folly of the French-Canadian bourgeoisie who had provided Earl Grey with an opening he so cleverly exploited. Laughter
allowed nationalistes to distance themselves from the celebration, to look
down on it with bemused detachment, while at the same time enjoying
the spectacle. Meantime superior spectator-participants could fully sa-
vour the wicked pleasure of watching their political enemies supposedly
make fools of themselves.

In the end, large numbers of French Canadians willingly participated
in the tercentenary. They lined the streets for the processions and parades. They opened their houses to guests; decorated their houses and
shops. Literally thousands of them joined the party, acting in the pageants; thousands more crowded the grandstand. They probably revelled
a little in the presence of royalty, and shuddered at the awesome military
power on display. To all outward appearances the French majority of
Quebec was fully engaged in the work and pleasures of the festival.

Those in the know, of course, were hypersensitive to the reticence
lurking beneath the surface of appearances. Only weeks before the
celebration and after the programs had been printed, the nationalist and
patriotic societies who had turned out in such numbers for the Laval

procession regretted that they could not muster enough strength for the advertised parade at a meeting with the tercentenary organizers. Members of the constituent organizations had been too busy with other aspects of the festival, and had taken too much time off work already, to devote more time to a parade. It was something of a disappointment to the organizers, and diminished the local component of the celebration considerably. Did the nationalists fear being upstaged? Was this a diplomatic regret? Was it an attempt to create a last-minute embarrassment? Was it simply the truth? In any event the tercentenary went ahead without a parade of Zouaves, Catholic Knights, and Saint-Jean-Baptiste Society cadres.

This, it must be said, passed without much notice. It did not, however, go without a reply. The establishment virtually boycotted the Jeunesse Catholique homage to Champlain on the very first day. Mayor Garneau, as we have seen, pleaded other, more pressing commitments. Indeed, after mass at the Basilica he could be seen entering a motor car with the archbishop of Quebec and the rector of the university, for a trip to the church's retreat house at St-Joachim to ensure that all was in readiness for the prince's forthcoming visit.[25] The church, too, needed to distance itself from hot heads and enthusiasts who might, in their ardour, have gone too far.

7. PAGEANTING

The Voice

When Frank Lascelles strode into the Empire Room of the Château Frontenac on 11 April 1908, there could be no doubt that he was a man of the theatre. Abundant, slicked-back hair accentuated the bold facial features of this strikingly handsome, slight, impeccably tailored man. And when he began to speak to this very first meeting of the Canadian Club of Quebec City, his voice carried the message to the farthest corner of the vast room: this man had acted with Irving and studied with Tree.[1]

'It was wonderful to see and hear this distinguished stranger, really "British to the core," pronounce with such a fine accent the French names of our illustrious ancestors,' *Le Soleil* reported in its front-page spread, 'the grand names of Laval, Jacques Cartier, Champlain, Montcalm, Dollard and the Frontenacs, Vaudreuils and Lévis, not to forget "Mary of the Incarnation" and so many others of our glorious people.' With his striking personality and 'with a voice the tones of which fell with melodious cadence upon the ears of his hearers,' he captured the full attention of this audience of business and professional men and stirred their imaginations.[2] He had come to town to put them all on the stage.

Medicine Men

Frank Lascelles had not come to Quebec just to put on a show, but rather to transform society. He was a theatrical medicine man. Theatre, he

Frank Lascelles, master of the pageants at Quebec.

believed, was an elixir for many social ills. In his case the play was not the thing; it was a means to the end.

In theory, a community that put on a pageant necessarily took on a new character in the process. Mass theatre became group therapy: 'History could be made into a dramatic public ritual through which the residents of the town, by acting out a version of their past, could bring about some kind of future social and political transformation.'[3] Frank Lascelles came to town with none of the criminal intent of Professor Hill, the Music Man, or the commercial calculation of Captain Andy with his Showboat, or the gulling lust of Elmer Gantry. He came to heal, to bring people together by having them re-enact glorious episodes from their past on the grandest possible scale. And by re-enacting history, the actors could change the course of history.

Historical pageantry is now a lost art. Echoes of it can be dimly discerned in the peopling of pioneer villages with figures in period costumes, or in the current fad for military re-enactments. Before the First World War historical pageantry enjoyed a considerable vogue, spilling over from England to Quebec and on to New England and the mid-Atlantic states to its American apogee in 1912 at St Louis. The war sapped the social idealism of the movement; later, motion pictures seem to have replaced it as a popular form of entertainment and wonder. The dramatic effect of a historical pageant would not be equalled until the mass rallies of the 1930s or, in a different way, the 'happenings' of the 1960s.

Louis Napoleon Parker, a musician, actor, playwright, and ardent Wagnerian, invented modern English historical pageantry in 1905. Frank Lascelles was a flamboyant follower and sometime rival of the master. Parker inadvertently created the new art form and started a fad when he transformed the anniversary of the founding of Sherborne, where he had once been music master at the school, into an open-air 'folk play' acted out by students, teachers, and townspeople, on the lawns in front of the town's ruined castle. The Sherborne Pageant – the use of the word to cover this new form was also his invention – was an immediate if unlikely success, drawing overflow audiences. For a time Parker built a career as pageant master, as did numerous imitators such as Lascelles, whom he naturally scorned. Although Parker seems to have made up the rules as he went along, with a sense of proprietorial amour propre he later codified his art in twelve imperious commandments. A proper pageant, he pronounced, should be a 'festival of brotherhood' in which social divisions are dissolved in a common effort to re-enact history:

> A Pageant is a Festival of Thanksgiving, in which a great city or little hamlet celebrates its glorious past, its prosperous present, and its hopes and aspirations for the future. It is a Commemoration of Local Worthies. It is also a great Festival of Brotherhood; in which all distinctions of whatever kind are sunk in a common effort. It is, therefore, entirely undenominational and non-political. It calls together all the scattered kindred from all parts of the world. It reminds the old of the history of their home, and shows the young what treasures they are keeping. It is the great incentive to the right kind of patriotism: love of hearth; love of town; love of country; love of England.[4]

In essence, Parker insisted upon the local, democratic and participatory nature of these events. He took great delight in the social mixing and status inversions his folk plays produced onstage. The pageant should be presented not for tourists or for money but to brighten and enoble the lives of the citizens of the community, 'to re-awaken civic pride' and 'increase self respect.' There were to be no sets; the antiquity (preferably ruined) of the community itself was the stage. Self-reliance, local initiative, and learning together were to be put in place of store-bought goods. The pageant was intended to serve as a mass school of arts and crafts: participants had to make their own costumes and properties, research their past, write the script, compose the music, organize the event, and serve as both actors and audience. Here Parker's pageantry joined with the contemporary arts and crafts movement to reawaken pre-industrial skills, revive the 'moral principles associated with the past,' and thereby rekindle a sense of historical organic community.

Above all, a proper historical pageant in Parker's formulation had explicit anti-modern impulses. The aim, apart from community education and entertainment, was to combat the spirit of the age: 'This modernising spirit, which destroys all loveliness and has no loveliness of its own to put in its place, is the negation of poetry, the negation of romance ... This is just precisely the kind of spirit which a properly organized and properly conducted pageant is designed to kill.'[5] Reason and commerce had literally disenchanted society; historical pageantry aimed at nothing less than the re-enchantment of daily life.

In 1906 the London *Times* index contained no references to pageants of any kind. By 1908 it required a full column to itemize articles dealing with a score or more English pageants, including a renowned pageant at Oxford directed by Frank Lascelles, and took more than two columns to index the Quebec tercentenary, including its pageant. Historical pageants had become all the rage. The great actor, Sir Herbert Tree, and his guest, Mark Twain, were so enthralled by Lascelles's Oxford pageant that they lost track of the time. As Tree recalled, 'only by taking a special train back to London, which made me very proud but poorer, was I able to join my own spectacle and serve my own public.' G.K. Chesteron got a little gem of an essay out of the joyful confusions of impersonation he experienced playing Dr Johnson in one of these festivals.[6]

There is no evidence to suggest that in the early planning stages (before January of 1908) the promoters of the Champlain tercentenary knew anything of the development of historical pageantry in England. Influenced by recent American examples and their own experience, they tended, as we have seen, to think of commemoration in terms of formal ceremonies, buildings, reconstructions, and processions. The World's Columbian Exposition at Chicago in 1893 seems to have been the inspiration for some of the early thinking about reconstruction of Champlain's Habitation and his ship, as well as a parade of people dressed up as historical figures.

The idea of putting on a historical pageant as part of the tercentenary celebrations first appeared in the English-language press of Quebec in mid-January of 1908. The Quebec *Chronicle* provided an account of Parker's pageants on 13 January, noting how wonderfully successful they had been: 'They have lowered the distinctions between peers and peasants, between mistresses and servants, between capitalists and workmen. Rich and poor, cultured and uncultured, men and women of low and high estate, have all worked together on a common level for the purpose of picturing before the world some of the great and brilliant deeds in the history of the nation.' The *Chronicle* mused that Canada certainly provided ample material for a pageant, especially the period of the French regime. Moreover, a pageant would be a magnetic attraction for tourists.[7] As this suggestion in the press closely followed a visit of the governor general, brimming with ideas and enthusiasm for a big summer festival, it is likely that he planted this notion.

As various committees worked over the idea, and as the possibilities of federal money provided more scope for the imagination, the notion of 'un grande cortège historique' bringing together in the same procession all of the national societies, allegorical floats, and marching groups recalling 'the most glorious scenes of our history,' evolved towards a theatrical spectacle.[8] By the end of January the subcommittee on history and archeology sketched out not only the elements of a historical procession, but also the scenes for a historical pageant similar to those directed by Frank Lascelles; he was actually named in the report. Speaking for this committee, Thomas Chapais identified the following as suitable subjects for dramatic presentation in the open air: Jacques Cartier at court describing his discovery of Canada; Champlain's return to Quebec in 1633; Dollard at Long Sault; Frontenac dismissing Phips's envoy; Madeleine de Verchères and the Iroquois; and finally Guy Carleton repelling Montgomery's assault in 1775.[9]

As politicians, businessmen, and men of letters had been working themselves towards a more theatrical and spectacular means of representing the past before a mass audience during 1907, those more familiar with the contemporary British cultural milieu had become aware of the current metropolitan fashion – historical pageantry. The good offices of the governor general brought these two currents together at Quebec. Earl Grey undertook to recruit Louis Napoleon Parker himself, who, it turned out, could not come on account of other commitments. However, late in February Frank Lascelles, the famous producer of the Oxford pageant, who had suddenly become available as a result of a cancellation in London, accepted an invitation to direct a pageant at Quebec.[10]

Trouble in River City

When Lascelles arrived in Quebec in March, afer having spent a weekend being briefed by the governor general in Ottawa, he entered a community divided. The Saint-Jean-Baptiste Society had withdrawn to the sidelines, having seen 'its' festival inflated into these gargantuan and in some respects grotesque caricatures. There were ominous rumblings in St-Roch where the nationalists were in full voice. On the other side, the popular press of both parties in English and French urged all citizens to put their differences behind them for once and pull together on behalf of the grand and noble objective.[11] It was certainly a city in need of the elixir of historical pageantry.

Lascelles began an intensive round of discussions with Mayor Garneau, H.-J.-J.-B. Chouinard, and Thomas Chapais and his committee – guardians of a past of which Lascelles knew virtually nothing. In effect the local committee had produced a 'book' from which he could design a pageant. Within days he pronounced himself struck by the dramatic possibilities of Canadian history, the numerous picturesque scenes available for representation, and above all, the Plains of Abraham, an 'incomparable site' for a pageant, he declared: 'It would surpass anything on the continent.'

In a little more than a month some fundamental decisions had been taken. The pageant was sited on the much disputed Plains, close to where Wolfe fell. There were other possibilities, of course, but none so spectacular. Pageantry thus served as another link between Champlain and the Plains. The basic outline of the local historians had been sketched; Lascelles worked closely with them to flesh out the details. But he did make some changes to ensure the maximum dramatic effect. In their deliberations, the local historians had passed over the most obvious scene from Quebec's history, and the one which actually happened on the pageant site: the battle of the Plains of Abraham. The French Canadians on the committee firmly rejected the insulting suggestion that the pageant end in 1759 with a re-enactment of that historic battle. Rather, the more diplomatic episode of French Canadians defending Quebec against the invading Americans in 1775 was deemed a more suitable conclusion. From Lascelles's point of view, theatrical requirements – a stirring climax – supported an 'imperial' ending in 1759. The local committee members could scarcely deny such an important event a place in the pageant; however, they insisted that Carleton's loyal French Canadians of 1775 and de Salaberry's Voltigeurs from 1812 must also take part in the Plains of Abraham scene. To a man of the theatre this seemed a small historical point to concede. The proposal, however anachronistic, lent additional colour to the scene. And so, tagging along in the march-past after Wolfe and Montcalm's armies came deputations from these later conflicts. This did not change the effect upon the casual observer. In Lascelles's reformulation the drama would effectively conclude in 1759–60, but it would not end with a victory and defeat, but rather mutual triumph.

Lascelles met with the newly appointed commissioners for National Battlefields early in April and presented an itemized estimate of $155,850

Frank Lascelles, on the right, gives last-minute directions to Mr C.E. Rouleau, as the Marquis de Tracy.

as the cost of the pageant project. This included the cost of building the grandstand. Initially he hinted that receipts from ticket sales and other revenues might exceed $300,000, which, in no time was reduced downward to a deficit of only $75,000.[12] The commissioners, with a firm budget of a mere $300,000 from the federal government, only promises still from the provinces, and a somewhat lacklustre fund-raising appeal, drew a deep breath and gave Lascelles the go-ahead and a budget of $109,000.

With the full backing of the National Battlefields Commission, the pageants went into production under Lascelles's guiding hand. Ernest Myrand, a member of the Comité d'Histoire et d'Archéologie, a historian and musicologist, set about writing dialogue for each of the scenes and producing appropriate and authentic music. The local artist Charles

Huot was engaged to design the costumes for the historical procession and the pageants. Joseph Vezina and the Symphonic Society were recruited to perform the music. Lascelles went shopping for an exotic list of properties not readily fabricated locally (wigs, hats, muskets, swords, halberds, bows and arrows, cannon, drums, bugles). The commissioners sent out feelers through various networks as to how to recruit native people in suitable quantities. Architects and contractors threw together plans for a temporary stadium for fifteen thousand spectators to be built on the site of the racetrack.

Thus it was as a new celebrity operating a three-ring circus of theatrical activity that Frank Lascelles addressed the Canadian Club, offering a preview of his art. All of this frantic activity quickened interest in what the Englishman was up to. He assured his audience he had not come all this way to put on 'a mere theatrical or spectacular show.' Rather he came to help the city, the country, and the world learn about Quebec's glorious history through a new art form. 'Things seen were mightier than things heard,' he reminded his hearers as he invited them to

> imagine that you dream a dream on a summer's day and see passing before you in quick succession visions of the great heroes who have gone, the peasants, the great founders, the soldiers, the martyrs, and the saints. And you wake up to find that it is really true, there in the flesh and blood before you are their prototypes, living, moving, walking, talking as they used to do and you can hardly believe that you are not dreaming still.

The process of bringing the past to life would, in turn, draw rich and poor into a closer, working relationship, promote mutual understanding, and inspire 'greater sympathy and a greater pride in your common heritage.' The eyes of the world would be on Quebec, Lascelles claimed, perhaps hoping that pride would inspire greater cooperation. Then, after embellishing each scene with melodramatic flourishes, he summoned the city to action with the biblical injunction: 'Let us now praise famous men and the fathers who begat us.'[13]

His speech to the assembled burghers of Quebec was as much a prayer as a promise, for his advance was not uniform along all fronts. At the organization level, things had begun to fall into place in April. Gradually the massive grandstand began to rise from a pile of lumber at the racetrack. Costumes and properties were coming along nicely. Lascelles had everything he needed for the pageant – except his cast of thousands. In his Canadian Club speech Lascelles spoke of the tremendous obstacles he had encountered in his previous engagements from the naysayers, the sceptics, and the timid.[14] Quebec taxed even his abilities. 'I wish I could stir these people up,' Lascelles exclaimed after his address, 'their slowness is heartrending.'[15]

Conscription

Lascelles received a great deal of press attention when he addressed elite men. He shrewdly chose a steering committee of women, however, to organize the pageants. He too wanted to tap into that extraordinary energy associated with middle-class women's emergence into the public sphere. Such women had the necessary time to devote to this ambitious public spectacle, and this was the kind of cultural and social activity which indisputably came within women's supposed domain. They were thrilled by the social opportunities being created as well as the possibility of public show, especially in striking gowns. Women possessed key skills. They could organize, network, design dresses and sew – and there would be a great deal of cutting and sewing to be done. When it came to recruitment, society women in particular could apply pressure to their menfolk to participate. Their stuffier husbands might be understandably reluctant to get dressed up in tights and dance in public.

In this particular case, the women of Quebec were enthusiastic volunteers. Under Mrs L. Williams and Madame Garneau, two committees were set up – costumes and recruitment. Lady Grey herself visited the women in Salle 45, their Parliament Building headquarters ('Le Coin rose') to offer encouragement. The women of Quebec, particularly the anglophone women, pitched in with energy and enthusiasm. Lascelles's secretary, Forbes Dennis, was able to address small groups of women in French. Lascelles spent a great deal of time working with the women and explaining his objectives. He did, however, make one false step; in his estimates he had failed to provide funding for the women to make their dresses – the assumption being, one supposes, women were accustomed to making their own gowns and would therefore donate their own material and labour. The commissioners had to make good this embarrassing oversight.[16]

Using this women's network during March and April, Lascelles was able to block out key elements of the pageants. But there were still too many bystanders, male and female. The middle-class social networks produced the necessary stars and supporting actors, but they could not produce the thousands of extras required for an extravaganza of this sort. As usual, *La Vérité* was fairly close to the mark when it gloated in mid-May that the troisième centenaire was degenerating into a fiasco because 'les incomparables *pageants* de M. Lascelles s'organisent difficilement.'[17]

Things began to change when the two great hierarchies of the city, the one economic and the other ecclesiastical, swung their weight behind the tercentennial effort. On the night of Wednesday, 10 June, William Price, arguably the richest and most powerful businessman in the city, chaired a public meeting at City Hall. The headline the next day in the *Chronicle* said all that need be said: 'Prominent Citizens Delegated to Guide the Destiny of Historical Productions.' At this meeting, with Lascelles present and offering encouragement, responsibility for the casting of each scene was parcelled out amongst individuals and organizations. George Scott and the Quebec Yacht Club took on the nautical Cartier scene (twenty-two performers); J. Burstall assumed responsibility for the mounted scenes in the Henri IV segment and the retail drygoods merchants dealt with those on foot (510 performers). Joseph Savard of the Hunt Club offered to find 464 performers for the François I equestrian scene. The cast for the Champlain pageant would be rounded up by Edouard Laliberté (195 performers). Prominent merchants, brokers, and businessmen had already laid claim to acting as crew on the *Don-de-Dieu* (forty performers). Mr Morency took on the Ursuline episode (218 performers); C.E. Lockwell, representing the Papal Zouaves, promised to find 488 performers for that scene as well. Dollard would be undertaken by Henri Chasse; Mr Couillard volunteered to find 120 actors for the Lusson scene in the pays en haut; George Van Felson and the Knights of Columbus would recruit the 371 performers needed for the Frontenac scene. Finally William Price himself, along with Thomas Vien, Colonel Wood, and M. Blouin took on the onerous task of assembling two armies of 425 performers. A total of 3,150 volunteers would be rounded up by those designated, using whatever means of persuasion that might be at their disposal.[18] Thus the problem of the cast was settled by a theatrical press gang. By the end of June, Lascelles could breathe easier: 'At last we are really moving along.'[19]

Interventions by the economic elite and the bishops had changed the atmosphere dramatically. The nationalistes became comparatively subdued. Amongst the broader population, apathy began to give way to enthusiasm in June. *Le Soleil* reported with some relief: 'It gives us some pleasure to report that for the organization of the historical pageants in particular the apathy manifested earlier especially on the part of French-Canadians has little by little disappeared.'[20] Construction on the stadium and various ceremonial arches proceeded apace. Decorations festooned the streets. The Habitation took shape in Lower Town. In every quarter costumes were being finished; merchants advertised fake fur, jewels, and accessories. Rehearsals for the individual scenes heightened awareness of something coming. When the costumes were distributed, families rushed out to have their pictures taken. By this time people could begin to feel that something truly extraordinary was about to happen.

Having recruited his cast of thousands, Lascelles now had to manage them. Herding these curious, sometimes stubborn, volunteers onto and off the stage at the proper time in another language taxed Lascelles's patience, but gradually things began to take shape out of the shambles. A reporter for the Montreal *Daily Witness* standing at his elbow captured some of the trials and tribulations of a pageant director during the first full-length dress rehearsal. Pacing in his box high above the grandstand, Lascelles held a megaphone in his right hand, while the fingers of his left hand ran nervously through his wavy, light brown hair, grown a full six inches in length since his arrival. He stooped slightly in his blue serge suit, tight trousers cut short in the current English fashion. At 2:30 on the dot he gave the sign to begin, but nothing seemed to go right. During the first scene a white terrier with a blue bow disrupted the native encounter with Cartier. Lascelles barked at his assistant, Forbes Dennis, who in turn shouted orders in French into the telephone. A flirting couple strolling across the ground, oblivious to what was going on around them, ruined the effect of the François I scene. A policeman sent to intercept them threw the audience into fits of giggles. Lascelles, who was by this time literally tearing his hair, smashed down his megaphone in frustration. As pratfall followed travesty, Lascelles lapsed into bitter sarcasm. However, when a brazen cabman, seeing the opportunity of a lifetime, parked his horse and cab right in front of the fifteen thousand spectators, advertising plastered across the buckboards, and sat casually smoking a cigar, taking in the scene like a squire, Lascelles collapsed into helpless accept-

Rehearsal of pageant 1, scene 1, Cartier encounters François I at Fontainebleau. Mr J.E. Boily as the king wore his office attire to the rehearsal.

ance of the absurdity of it all. He laughed until tears streamed down his face. Of course, the colours of the dresses clashed; the bullock refused to cooperate; the speeches droned on too long and had to be cut. Several hundred soldiers from Wolfe's army, growing bored in their isolation, rushed up the cliffs into plain view to observe the excitement of the Dollard des Ormeaux spectacle a century before. His nerves shot, Lascelles nevertheless summoned one last ounce of optimism as he bid farewell to the reporter: 'I hope you won't judge the pageant by this rehearsal. You know what first rehearsals are like, don't you?'[21]

But even in the stress of the dress rehearsals, the evanescent enchantment of historical pageantry began to work its magic, according to the Quebec *Chronicle*:

Emperors and princes, court ladies and lords of high degree, explorers and adventurers, pages, soldiers and Indians, the flower of chivalry and the

pride of court and castle, the heroes of fort and log cabin, and the hardy
campaigners of a bye-gone age, all clad in striking costumes of three
hundred years ago, mingled yesterday with the soberly clad citizens of the
present day, and rode democratically on street cars, or wagons, or walked to
the Plains of Abraham.

On the same day *Le Soleil* commented: 'Full of grace, full of charm, full of
dignity, the public of Quebec City have begun to relive that fascinating
era of three centuries ago, the golden age of chivalry when the finest
flowering of French civilization exerted its greatest influence.'[22]

Modes of Fantasy

The historical pageant presented in July 1908 during the tercentenary of
Quebec was designed to establish and broaden the middle ground of
understanding between English and French Canadians, and to inspire a
new consciousness of shared nationhood. The pageants displayed in the
most powerful dramatic form available a view of Canadian history designed to serve explicit political goals.

The pageants at the Quebec tercentenary fulfilled some of Louis
Napoleon Parker's conditions. They brought back to life a distant, romantic, chivalrous age. They recovered mystical elements – fauns and
satyrs – and thereby brought a natural spirituality to the surface of
bourgeois regimentation. Dance, music, and drama were united. The
costumes were sumptuous, the staging breathtaking. Roles brought forth
new or hitherto disguised talents in doctors, lawyers, wives, and merchants. Past and present mingled in the streets. And the physical setting
was sensational, drawing attention to the dictum that the site itself be
the subject celebrated. A visiting pageant enthusiast, Ellis Oberholzer,
believed the pageant field at Quebec the most beautiful he ever
witnessed.[23]

On the other hand, performance reflects power. On balance, historical pageantry at the tercentenary reflected the balance of power in
Quebec City between the overlapping categories of social class, English
and French, nationaliste and Liberal, church and state, men and women,
historians and dramatists. The tangled origins of the festival, its multiple
purposes, the ability of participants to make a show of their own, and a
culturally divided audience all worked against hegemonic messages from

one side or the other, or subverted them when they occurred. The past as 're-presented' had multiple meanings; even the disagreeable could be confronted if appropriately costumed and choreographed. Some things were more acceptable as theatre than history, and more agreeable as theatre in the form of comedy rather than tragedy.

The pageants were put on by a national commission as a festival of national identity with a view to entertaining and instructing royalty, visiting dignitaries, tourists, and locals. Admission was charged and it was not cheap, leading to some grousing that more performances at lower prices ought to have been arranged to allow orphans and others without means an opportunity to see the spectacle. Lascelles unashamedly aimed for and attained spectacular effects. Props were purchased and the costuming aspect of the affair generated an enormous business amongst the civil and military tailors, seamstresses, milliners, drygoods dealers and merchants of the city. The aim of mixing the classes succeeded in part but was somewhat confounded by recruitment processes that depended upon existing social networks, clubs, organizations, business, or religious associations. Rather than subvert social distinctions, to a certain extent Lascelles's pageant put them on display.

The director did indeed seek out a cast for his script. But by the same token the volunteers made a script for themselves; they determined to a certain extent the balance of representation through the casting. The process of social conscription by which recruiting for this labour-intensive production was carried out to a certain extent worked in opposition to the objective of social mixing. Dramatic necessity *and* social imperatives drove production values.

Statistics offer a dim reflection of the social processes that went into pageant-making at Quebec in 1908. Names are not a reliable indicator of cultural origins, in either direction. And in a bilingual and bicultural setting, characterized by widespread intermarriage between the two dominant groups, cultures change even though names stay the same. That having been said, the classification of the personnel by type of name, gender, and scene does offer some crude insight into the social processes that underlay the pageant.[24] In round numbers, anglophone Quebeckers provided 15 per cent of the starring roles and 33 per cent of the extras; francophones occupied 85 per cent of the principal roles and made up 67 per cent of the extras in the cast of roughly three thousand, almost a mirror reflection of the general population of the city of approximately

85 per cent francophones and 14 per cent anglophones. Although the two cultural groups were mixed in most scenes, some exceptions warrant notice: the principal parts in the Laval and the Ursuline scenes were played exclusively by francophones. Francophones also seemed to make up the ranks of Montcalm's army and anglophones that of Wolfe – though there was more intermixing in the latter. The casting of certain segments provides a better indication of greater anglophone enthusiasm for pageantry. For example, anglophone women, who could afford the expensive costumes more than their francophone counterparts, were comparatively overrepresented in the court scenes.[25]

Several forces seem to have been at work in the selection process: fantasy, identification, inversion, and in all likelihood, coercion. English women in particular satisfied an overwhelming desire to play at being French royalty, princesses, courtiers, and women of quality. Many of them appeared on horseback in the François I and Henri IV scenes. On the other hand, some groups sought to identify themselves with their peers or their organizations in the past. Soldiers from the militia and the garrison made up large parts of the armies; sailors from the Yacht Club manned the *Don-de-Dieu*; businessmen, their wives, families, and children played at being merchants and bourgeois. Priests filled all of the ecclesiastical roles. The same was not, however, the case for nuns. The cloistered orders could not participate. The Ursulines did, however, make the costumes for the scene involving their order, took pains to ensure that the costumes were treated with due respect, and were delighted when young women from good families, graduates of their convent school, were chosen to play the roles of Marie de l'Incarnation and Madame de la Peltrie.[26] There seems to have been some inversion of role too: bourgeoise English women took on the role of French-Canadian peasants. Was it because dressing down might be easier for anglophones, but more problematic for francophones? And there was a good deal of straightforward conscription into the ranks of extras; businessmen used their influence over employees and associates to participate.

The numbers available swelled the ranks of some scenes and left others thinly populated. The court scenes were much larger than might otherwise have been the case on account of the willingness of women to volunteer. Thus women were not invisible in this history, far from it and the court was vastly overblown. This was in part a function of the female power of the organizing committee; it was also a reflection of the organi-

In the foreground the dancers for the pavane rehearse. In the background the actors assemble for the Fontainebleau garden scene. Lascelles directed the rehearsals with a semaphore system suspended on poles at the rear.

zational influence of the female religious orders in the history of New France as seen from a clerical historical perspective.

It is true that the actors were drawn from many ranks of society; however, the pageant made stars mainly out of lawyers, doctors, their wives and daughters, prelates and politicians. Mr Moise Raymond as Cartier received universal praise; the notary Boilly made a striking impression as François I; the avocat Antoine Couillard as Henri IV, and Mme L.A. Carrier as his queen, carried off their roles with panache. Sheriff Charles Langelier as Champlain and Mlle Yvonne de Lery as his young wife formed a heroic couple. L'abbé Vachon recreated the saintly Laval. The reviewer in the *Chronicle* singled out the actor who portrayed Frontenac as one of the most outstanding performances. ('For those who have read with interest the stormy career of haughty Count Frontenac there is a revelation in the acting of M. Dartois that clears away the mists of time.')

For the professional bourgeoisie of the city, acting in the pageants fed their sense of self-importance alongside other powerful social hierar-

Studio portrait of Mr Antoine Couillard as Henri IV and Madame Auguste Carrier as Queen Marie de Medici.

chies and it drew upon their special communications skills. Business people stayed safely in the background. It is impossible to determine the extent to which figures associated with the Saint-Jean-Baptiste Society became involved. Few of the leading participants of the Laval celebration, for example, can be found listed among the participants in the historical pageants. The Laval fête and the tercentenary appear to have involved substantially separate casts. As a working hypothesis, it might be ventured that this was not the full range of Quebec's social structure on display, but rather the Liberal party in costume.

Theatre had a way of spilling out into the streets as intended but not, perhaps, in expected ways. Costumed soldiers from Montcalm's army marched in the nationaliste Catholic Youth parade.[27] At one of the last pageants, the two armies marched out of the stadium to the nearby monument to General Wolfe where they paid their respects. Usually the soldiers from the last scene maintained ranks and marched back through the crowds of the Grand Allée to their dispersal points. On at least one occasion, Montcalm's army marched triumphally through the gaily decorated nationaliste district of St-Roch, prompting requests from anglophone quarters that Wolfe's army do the same thing there. In the streets it was possible to invert meaning. In this sense, the pageants did not end at the Conquest.

As befits the subject, the language of the pageant was entirely French. However logical a decision this might have been, it was nevertheless a bold move in view of the number of anglophone tourists anticipated. The organizers concluded that the inconvenience to unilingual English speakers was vastly outweighed by the offence that might be given if the past were rendered to French-speaking Quebeckers in another language. The English members of the community and the tourists – duly provided with programs and translations of the text if they were interested – made no complaint that was registered. This policy created a few inconveniences for the unilingual Lascelles. His repeated commands in rehearsals to keep off the stage went unheeded. The only exception to the all-French dialogue came in the seventh scene in which Phips's delegate delivers his written ultimatum in English. Frontenac responds: 'Je n'ai jamais été familier avec l'anglais, aussi, M. de Bienville, vous seriez fort aimable de me traduire ce document.' Later in the scene, when the agitated English delegate bursts out in French, Frontenac interjects: 'Monsieur parle le français et bon français, l'aimable surprise! J'en suis ravi. Vous savez encore mieux notre histoire que notre langue. Bravo. Votre geste est charmant.' A serious business, language could also be a laughing matter.[28]

What did the audience make of what it saw? According to *Le Soleil* the crowd watched the simple, opening scene in 'un religieux silence.' Excitement mounted during the frenzy of the Dollard scene (which occupied a disproportionate amount of space in all the newspaper accounts). For Laval, 'les cloches chantent gaiement.' Following Frontenac's boldness, 'Un frisson d'admiration secoue les rangs des milliers de spectateurs.' Then, in a moment of heightened apprehension, the glorious finale unfolded:

> After an interlude of a few minutes the English and French armies arrive marching together and fraternizing in peace. The breeze intertwines the flags of the English and French grenadiers as they march along side by side. The battalions file past, hailed by the cheers of the crowd, and as they leave the ground they leave behind an audience of ten thousand stirring with diverse emotions.

No one present would ever regret being there, *Le Soleil* concluded. The pageants had brought back to life, in full colour and vivid authenticity, three centuries in the life of the Canadian people.[29]

The English press was equally if uncharacteristically rhapsodic. The *Chronicle* considered the climactic last pageant 'the most wonderful, the most magnificent scene ever presented in the history of Quebec.' The Prince of Wales loved the pageants – so he said in a marconigram from the *Indomitable* received at Quebec in which he asked, prompted by Grey, that a moving picture be made of the last scene and shown throughout the Empire. From on board the *Indomitable* he enthused about the pageants in a letter to his wife as well:

> We all went at 5.0 to see the pageant which took place on the Plains of Abraham. We were in a grand box in the middle of the stands. There had been many representations, but this was the State one. I must say Mr. Lascelles who organized & arranged it all, deserves the greatest possible credit, as it was most beautifully done, the dresses excellent & the 4000 people who took part, very well drilled, it was altogether a very fine sight.

Different scenes were enacted beginning with Jacques Cartier & Samuel Champlain 1608 up to Wolfe & Montcalm 1760.[30]

From his point of view the show ended at the Conquest.

From another point on the social compass, Ethel Chadwick expressed her quite different appreciation of the pageant after her first rehearsal: 'It was a lovely sight, all the scenes recalling what had really taken place on that historic ground years ago, it was very French and very Catholic naturally and most impressive in every way. I thoroughly enjoyed it.'[31] Ethel was right: it was Catholic and it was French. Yet the pageant was somehow acceptable to English viewers. That was one of its greatest achievements.

But what of French Canada? What did the more sceptical and sensitive religious and nationaliste critics think? The French-language popular press stressed the dignity and drama of the representation. After its angry denunciations of the imperialist fête, the grudging one-sentence evaluation of the pageants by Tardivel's *La Vérité* speaks volumes: 'Les représentations historiques ont été généralement goûtées.' The weekly Catholic publication, *La Semaine Religieuse de Québec*, went much further: 'We willingly confess to being absolutely incapable of expressing the strong emotions which we experienced during these representations of this incomparable French era of our history.' Seen from this author's perspective, the pageants were particularly important because, as Lascelles had explained, things seen were more powerful than things heard or read:

> We consider the 'pageants' the principal part of the festival because the popular masses, instead of vague notions which they had beforehand, acquired there intuitively a precise knowledge of the most important facts of our history; because our English compatriots from all provinces, and the crowd of visiting tourists above all from the United States, saw with their own eyes the nobility and heroism of the founders of our French-Canadian race. All the English and Americans understood and applauded our French and Catholic glories! Who will say that it was not a great event and that it will not have considerable consequences?[32]

Le Soleil raved about the pageants, in particular the Dollard scene and the grand finale. And in the latter, the ahistorical mingling of several armies was noticed and commented upon:

> The grand parade of honour of Montcalm, Lévis and the regiments of their army and that of Wolfe, Murray and the regiments of their army presented a magnificent spectacle to the huge audience. The scene of De Salaberry and les Voltigeurs de Chateauguay, which best exemplifies the glorious evidence of the fidelity of French-Canadians to the English Crown, is a dignified epilogue to these incomparable historical spectacles.[33]

'Genevra,' the women's columnist for *Le Soleil,* agreed with this assessment. Stretching a point, she also insisted that women had neglected their duties and home, businessmen had neglected their affairs, to bring a distant and noble past to life. English and French had worked together in a theatrical enterprise certain to have lasting effects:

> In each of the exclusively French and Catholic scenes the English were the first to volunteer for roles, leaving to us the most prominent characters, which were ours by right, but which we neglected at first to take. They never laughed in disdain at our religious costumes or the symbols of our culture, they proved that they respected our sincere beliefs. We were able to represent a good part of our daily life ... without sacrifice of our language or faith; without making concessions which would demean our spirit, and to dispel an antagonism as old as the Conquest which now has no more reason to exist.[34]

Perhaps to their surprise, Frank Lascelles did teach the burghers of Quebec how to act. They put on a good show, in their own estimation and also in that of others. The National Battlefields commissioners were similarly thrilled, even though Lascelles went slightly over budget and the ticket receipts did not quite reach his projections. In theatrical terms and as a spectacle, the historical pageant more than met expectations.[35] Earl Grey was tickled pink and commended Lascelles's 'genius for conception' to the king. 'Considering the apathy and indifference which confronted him when he started upon the work of organization, the success which he has achieved is a standing cause of wonder.'[36]

From on board ship when he returned to England, Lascelles, too, expressed his gratitude and satisfaction in all he had been able to accomplish in such a short time: 'The remembrance of the summer spent at Quebec will remain with me all my life, and the days through days of anxiety and toil, will always be a very treasured memory.' The unprecedented celebrations had been, in his mind, 'an unrivalled and brilliant success.' He poured out his thanks to the 'noble spirited patriotism' of the pageant performers and especially the recruiting committees: 'To them we owe everything, for without their ardent & ungrudging support the beautiful scenes of the past history of your city and your country could never have been visualized, and a debt of gratitude, which can never be repaid, will ever be due them from the whole of Canada.'[37]

Sublimated in theatre, history opened up possibilities of multiple interpretations, mutual recognition, acknowledgment of difference, and for some the possibilities of reconciliation and transcendence. Were the French being instructed on becoming Englishmen, or were the English being given a lesson on the essentially French character of Canada? As for empire, Canada, after all, had two imperial heritages. Both were on display, though in different forms. The therapy of theatre, especially in the form of mass participatory re-enactment, taught lessons in different ways, reached new audiences by making them actors, and potentially reshaped public consciousness in such a way that old grievances might be dissolved in a new civic consciousness.

The historical pageant represented a politically correct version of the Canadian past *circa* 1908. From this perspective, pageants taught French Canadians about themselves and delivered a message to English Canada that it would otherwise not wish to hear. At the same time, the historical pageant was a play within a much larger tercentennial pageant in which British imperial social, military and cultural power framed the spectacle, thereby containing its message. In the detumescent glow of the theatrical experience, we can see that the race fusion objectives momentarily succeeded at a sentimental level. A turbulent and violent history could be made to teach tolerance, but what actors and audiences chose to remember is another matter.

8. DRESSING UP

Tehonikonraka

After the pageants on the evening of Wednesday, 29 July, Frank Lascelles gave a dinner party for his leading actors. They in turn honoured him for the opportunities he had given them. The actors were the Indians. They made their English director an Iroquois chief. Both the director and his actors had important things to say to each other; so, they spoke with symbolic actions, dining, and investiture. In that respect this informal ceremony mimicked the whole Quebec tercentenary.

Tables had been set up by the huge black iron cauldrons simmmering over the open fires in the middle of the Indian encampment. In the twilight after the last scene, the Indian cast trooped back with Lascelles to the settlement of brightly coloured tepees in the woods just to the west of the pageant ground. The old men sat down; the young men waited on them. Women and children, also in fringed and beaded buckskin costumes, hung back in circle amongst the tepees. Among them in the shadows lurked one or two eavesdropping newspaper reporters.

Dinner featured the foods of several cultures – soup, meat, pies, ice-cream, fruit, and wine, and at the end tobacco and cigars were passed around. When Lascelles rose to speak in this heady atmosphere, he was at home, an orator among orators, an actor among actors. Together they had realized a noble dream, he began: 'Here on this great river and amid these mighty hills the battleships of three nations had been anchored in peace.' This harmony had been induced by the enchantment of historical pageantry, he claimed, and in particular to the role native people played in it. They had spurred on the hesitant citizens of Quebec with their zeal; nor did they complain or grow cross with one another during the tedium of the rehearsals. From the beginning native people had understood and been faithful to the spirit of pageantry.

Native people had also been magnificent actors. Their singing, dancing, and simulated combat had energized the production and thrilled the crowd. The Prince of Wales himself had 'expressed himself most gratified' with their work as performers. On an occasion when the poetry and romance of the past had been brought to life, the Indians, Lascelles claimed, 'had taken a foremost place, for they had dwelt here amidst these vast forests, primaeval solitudes and mighty lakes long before the white men. When Rome and Greece were young, they were old. All had been thrilled by the part played by the Iroquois in the Pageant.'

The Indians had done much more than demonstrate their prowess as actors; they had, Lascelles believed, made a deep and abiding impression on the consciousness of the white audience. As the reporter's notes recorded, 'he thought there were lessons the white men could learn from the red. The love of country, of hills and forests. The white man was too fond of the town with its hurry and artifice.'

And then, with the pageants drawing to a close and the cast soon to be dispersing, Lascelles became maudlin as he contemplated the honour of becoming an Iroquois chief. He would take back to England with him a native love for the country and its people, now *his* people, the scribbling reporter noted. 'There was a little village in England where he had been born and where his father and mother were laid to rest. When he should be there and see the sun setting far away he would think "beyond that setting sun is Canada, where once the Indians dwelt alone. There live the Iroquois and I am one of them."'

At a signal, the assembly rose from the table and adjourned to the grandstand for another ceremony. At about this time Ethel Chadwick and her friend Lola Powell – looking lovely, a scarlet shawl draped casually over her evening dress – strolled over from the Prices' mansion on the Grand Allée and sat with their host in the nearly empty grandstand to observe the investiture. A fire was set. Chief Scarface started beating his drum. Chief Sazy then looped a string of wampum over Lascelles's neck as a remembrance of this occasion. To the chiefs and warriors he proclaimed that Lascelles had treated the Iroquois well and they in turn wished to treat him honourably. They gave Lascelles a feather. It was explained to him that the English had a flag; this was the native symbol of membership in a community. Lascelles, gripping his feather of belonging, stooped to be crowned with a magnificent head-dress of eagle feathers and to receive the name Tehonikonraka, in English, the Man of Infinite Resources. Five chiefs placed their hands on his shoulders and praised him in song as a worthy warrior. Afterwards all the chiefs performed an initiation dance. Lascelles, visibly moved by the event, shook hands and embraced his new brothers as the songs and dances continued. His assistant, Forbes Dennis, R.J. Blaney, one of the agents who had recruited the native people, and William Price, the Quebec industrialist who had thrown his weight behind the pageants, received similar honours and decorative pins.

Ethel, looking on from the gloomy stadium, saw things in a different light. 'It was a most weird scene,' as she remembered it, 'the Indians lit a fire [and] sat round it; beside them on benches sat the chiefs. The grandstand was all dark except for a few lights about where we and a few other people sat. They sang, danced queer dances, men talked in Indian, and put on queer Indian headdresses, & strings of wampum on the two men who they made chiefs, then they called for Mr. Price to make him one.'

Irony, disgust, and the thrill of the exotic were sentiments more predominant in Ethel's response as she and Lola were invited to join in:

> It was a half funny, half wild sight to see the Iroquois and to think how fierce they used to be sitting calmly among us all. They invited us down to drink milk which I for one only pretended to do, then we all took hands (I was beside an Indian boy and had to take his dirty paw) around the bonfire and sang 'Old Lang Syne' – and 'Good Night Ladies.' Then there were speeches in broken English and at last we came away – we all looked funny in evening dresses among the Indians all dressed up in their native costumes.[1]

If Lascelles's speech indicated a sentimental fusion of native and European sensibilities and stressed the impression native people had made upon the onlookers, Ethel's vague distaste and patronizing language – perhaps more typical of her class than Lascelles's musing – emphasized the distance between the cultures, the 'otherness' of the

Frank Lascelles, centre, at his investiture as an Iroquois chief, Tehonikonraka. Forbes Dennis stands to his left.

natives. As this mixed company circled the fire, hand in hand, hand in 'paw,' singing 'Auld Lang Syne' and 'Good Night Ladies,' many things were true behind the false faces. Native people had declared their presence and insisted that their history and future should also be recognized. Onlookers may have seen something else in their performance, confirmation of deep-rooted racial stereotypes. And it is significant that no French Canadian was honoured.

Cultural Performance

Everyone was an actor at Quebec. The tercentenary was on a very large scale, an example of what anthropologists would call cultural performance. The historical pageant was most obviously a piece of theatre, but so, too, was everything else in the sense that it was an elaborately scripted and staged performance which simultaneously reflected the surrounding culture and tried to influence it. The tercentenary, like other spectacles, could not be ignored; it demanded attention by its scope, grandeur, and awesome powers. Even the unwilling were drawn in one way or another by the crowds, parades, and booming spectacles. It was an entertainment, of course, but it was entertainment with an intent, or rather intentions. Spectators were drawn in at many points of access, becoming in the process participants as well as observers.

Becoming absorbed in a huge mass was itself a novel experience, sometimes inducing a liminal sense of being transported to another realm. People cast off their daily roles, suspended disbelief, entered into an exhilarating collective spirit, adopted new personae, dressed up in unusual clothing, used a formal language, lined up, took their places, played their parts in rituals and dramas. In effect, they told stories about themselves to the members of their group, and to members of other groups. They told stories about the past, intended to impress (teach) the present generation, in the hope of changing the future. Frequently other people are needed to make the story complete, to help a group see themselves more clearly by the contrast. Others often figure in the story as antagonists, friends, or clients. Thus a story about one group often includes a story about another group. As collectivities construct a sense of self and transmit it, they also construct a sense of the other. They in turn might tell their own story back.

Traditionally, historians have tended to overlook events such as the tercentenary as largely ephemeral entertainments or adornments, not in themselves the stuff of history. More recently, scholars have interpreted such events as revealing moments in which societies make profound statements in symbolic language about their deepest beliefs. Anthropologists, who have long studied the meanings of a bewildering variety of these ritualized social dramas, from Balinese cockfights to the modern Olympic Games, have come to believe that cultural performances 'are more than entertainment, more than didactic or persuasive formulations, and more than cathartic indulgences. They are occasions in which as a culture or society we reflect upon and define ourselves, dramatize our collective myths and history, and present ourselves with alternatives, and eventually change in some ways while remaining the same in others.'[2] How much cultural performances shape their societies and how much they merely reflect its contours remains a matter of debate. Nor can intentions be gleaned simply by reading the script; other meanings can be imparted in performance, and by the relative responsiveness or resistance of the audience. Cultural performance can be more or less coherent depending upon the alignment of producers, performers, and consumers.

Quebec combined in one event elements of the four classic kinds of cultural performance; spectacle, festival, rite, and game. Spectacles are things to be seen, vast spectator events intended to awe, masses with symbolic gestures. Actors and audience are usually separate. Apart from a diffuse sense of wonder and awe, spectacles can impart many different moods, from horror to identification to joy. And of course the mood can change during performance.

Festivals, on the other hand, must be light-hearted and joyful to unite audience and actors in joint performance. Festivals are irregular, sometimes calendrical, community events. 'In festival, the roles of actors and spectators are less distinguishable than in spectacle, where the increased emphasis on sight, often at the expense of other modes of participation, seems to increase the threat of oversight.'[3] In the modern world spectacle tends to crowd out festival. Nevertheless, in democratic societies spectacles rely upon festive aspects, such as street demonstrations, concerts, the innate exhibitionism of happy people in groups.

Rites invoke the sacred. Religious services are the most obvious examples of this type of cultural performance, but many public events partake at least to some extent of ritual through the invocation of the gods, or the conscious imitation of or borrowing from religious ceremonies. University convocations, flag ceremonies, oath-takings, services of thanksgiving, or the response to disasters are examples. Public events are frequently structured as ritual and serve as rites of passage for individuals and societies as a whole. Organizations and nations give rise to their own civic religions and rituals.

Games, often also the occasion for spectacle, festival, and ritual, are played by rules which govern play and decide outcomes. Games can be simple or complex, but usually the rewards are intrinsic: winning, participation, performance. Fun and games are often associated; but more often other sensations and emotions are associated with contests. Games are distinguished from life (mere game) as something apart, done in leisure time and as an alternative ethos to the self-interested, anomie of market society. Games also contribute significantly to life in many ways – as a social and physical tonic, as entertainment, as business and politics. Modern societies must have athletic policies at many levels, a politics of games.

While each of these elements can be separately distinguished, often they occur together, combined in the same event. At the tercentenary of Quebec the games aspect was the least emphasized. The crews from the various ships and teams from the regiments did, however, compete in various athletic and military games and boat races. And there was competition on the parade ground and between the ships to look their best. But this was not a prominent aspect of the event. Rather spectacle and festival predominated, and with ritual occasionally added. The fleet, parades, homages, illuminations, decorations, fireworks, displays, native and military encampments, historical pageants, and massing of visitors and residents, and the entry, progress, and retreat of the sovereign-designate constituted the spectacle. Festival can be seen in the balls, street activities, promenades on the terrace, music, celebrations, journeys to and fro. Rituals of different sorts were played out: military rituals of inspection, civic rituals of address and welcome, social rituals of order, conduct, and precedence; sovereign rituals of knighthood, native rituals of investiture, legal rituals of property transfer as occurred between the prince and the governor general on the Plains of Abraham, and of course religious rituals in the churches and in the solemn mass at the grandstand on the pageant ground. As we have seen, the Laval celebration combined these elements (with the exception of games) in a quite different manner.

Historians have been particularly interested in that complex of cultural performances which has played such an important role in creating citizenship, nationalism, and the modern nation. Imagined communities on a massive scale were created and nurtured in the late nineteenth and early twentieth centuries. It has become a commonplace to observe that the traditions that in one sense 'made' modern mass societies had to be invented. From the top down and from the bottom up, national communities were forged in the interactive process of producing and manipulating symbols.

The tercentenary of Quebec in 1908 was a Canadian variant of one of these elaborately staged festivals of national invention that have been the subject of much recent scholarly investigation.[4] Seen from one perspective, the tercentenary was a celebration of an imaginary country, one which the organizers hoped to create. It differed, perhaps, in that a dominant symbol of that new nationality, in this case the Angel of Peace, did not emerge. Several groups of participants and many of the onlookers imagined a different kind of nation. The tercentenary is forgotten precisely because it did not overcome the ongoing social and political divisions within the country, though it seemed to do so at the time. It is interesting not for the single message it presented to the country, but rather because it reflected so well the several Canadas living parallel lives.

Peoples (plural) spoke to each other at Quebec; they did so in costumed formality. There was a script. But the organizers, as we have seen, were not of one mind. They struggled among themselves for control over meaning. Moreover, they did so in an environment of popular indifference or overt hostility; they had to make accommodations of various sorts in the script to attract attention and face down criticism. Actors could in performance give new meanings to the script. In costume one can act out statements that would otherwise go unspoken or if spoken might provoke a hostile response. Nevertheless, there seem to be limits to what anthropologists call reflexivity – the capacity to reflect upon and change behaviour as a result of participation in cultural performances.

Quebec was a great masked ball in which different groups put on costumes to impress one another; they addressed each other in coded language. This is the moment to look more closely at what the actors were doing as they exchanged symbols and to try and parse the meaning of the stories they were telling.

Natives

When organizers began to flesh out the actual program of the tercentenary early in 1907 they hoped to include a settlement of native people as part of the festival.[5] Indians were to live in an encampment with their missionaries throughout the festival, according to one early plan. Indians in costume added colour to otherwise drab, black-coated, celluloid-collared, speech-drowned, formalities. Indians brought joy, innocence, spontaneity, and mystery – the carnivalesque dimensions – to the celebration.

Here the Quebeckers were attempting to recreate the dramatic effect of the 1893 Columbian World's Exposition in which the status hierarchy of the human race was on display in the ethnographic villages on the Midway.[6] The world came to Chicago and people paid admission to see representations of it, including native North Americans in their villages. Visitors could wander about, take camel rides, visit bazaars, temples, and other mysterious places in complete safety, savouring exotic delicacies and forbidden entertainments as they strolled. They could authenticate the sensation for later recollection by having photographs taken surrounded by these anthropological specimens. This sideshow, promoted initially by the Smithsonian Institution, was primarily intended to be of educational value, teaching the hierarchical order of civilization through visual and experiential forms rather than through books. The Columbian Exposition showed, of course, that the exotic proved to have stunning entertainment value as well.

From Chicago onward, two versions of native people competed at public exhibitions: officially sponsored displays of government 'show Indians' in school and employed at useful pursuits on the road to progress; and, more theatrically, commercial displays of a wild people performing feats of derring-do on stage and at ease in native encampments along the entertainment avenues, variously named after different fairs the Midway, the Pan, or the Pike. (The popularity of the term Midway is an enduring legacy of the popularity of the Chicago World's Fair.) The Canadian government discovered and then attempted to discourage the popularity of natives in its late nineteenth-century exhibitions abroad. Unhealthy curiosity about things native obliterated all efforts to impress foreigners with railways, bumper crops, and Canada's empty, beckoning interior.

These conventions of world's fairs and expositions filtered down to state, regional, provincial, and even local fairs. Native people had contributed exhibits and been exhibited in many local fairs. Native people in their own communities in Canada held fairs as well, though they did not overtly put white people on display except as spectators.[7]

Native people had also established a spectacular theatrical presence in the highly popular wild west shows which predated the Chicago World's Fair but gained notoriety because of it. Cowboys lacked drama without Indians. Buffalo Bill Cody's Wild West Show played in Montreal during its second year, 1886. The Notman Studio produced some of the most memorable photographic souvenirs of the tour, featuring Cody and Sitting Bull in numerous heroic poses. In 1897 Buffalo Bill and his troupe of three hundred performers headlined Montreal's celebration of Queen Victoria's Diamond Jubilee. Later in the summer, Buffalo Bill's company paraded through Quebec City leading the excited citizenry to a huge tent illuminated by electric lights set up on the Plains of Abraham.[8] Wild west shows were at the height of their popularity in North America and Europe in the first decades of the century.[9] Having an exhibition, show, or festival and having native people on display just went together. The Miller Brothers's 101 Ranch Real Wild West Show, for example, was the hit of the otherwise lacklustre Jamestown tercentenary in 1907.[10]

The community of French Canada would, as the pageant stressed, forge itself against a native menace. Thus natives had to be present. This sense of an embattled community forming itself in the presence of savage, sudden, blind fury, and cruel, deadly attack, can be grasped visually in the sculpture by Louis-Philippe Hébert, 'Sans Merci,' first shown in 1904, and theatrically in the Dollard des Ormeaux pageant scene. Quebec culture was at this point in what might be called the 'fearsome savage' part of the interpretive cycle. Indians brought to the celebration a sense of contained or implicit danger.[11] Indians were still a frightening people; in school books and stories of saintly martyrdom, Indians continued to represent a more generalized sense of perilous, cultural menace. People from such diverse social and geographical origins as the Duke of Norfolk and Ethel Chadwick were at first frightened when confronted by native people.

Identities in the process of formation were best recognized in the presence of people with visibly different identities. Modern Quebeckers could marvel at how far their civilization had 'progressed' from this more primitive forest existence. In this contrast they could see themselves more clearly as a distinct people. Native people, represented in villages, tents, costumes, and in ritual performances at the tercentenary, would add a progressive symbolism, showing explicitly the measure of civilization's advance. The addition of missionaries framed the scene as a pastorale.

Natives were also objects of temptation, and 'going native' was a forbidden fruit. They represented powerfully repressed sexual anxieties; they were nature amidst the man-made, the mystical outside of the rational. They were, in that sense, beyond history, having been removed from it.[12] Obviously there is also a certain voyeuristic pleasure in the inclusion of this native encampment. There was something vaguely illicit about a gathering of native people. There was a more than slightly shameful aspect to looking at other human beings as objects, which, of course, made the surreptitious visits to the encampment all the more exciting. Of an evening curious city folk strolled out to steal a casual glimpse of what the newspapers referred to as 'Romans of the New World' in their smoky forest encampment – the classical association thereby partially legitimizing the gaze.

The organizers of the tercentenary conceived a functional role for the native people apart from their inherent curiosity appeal. They would participate as welcoming parties for Champlain when he arrived. They would be part of the historical procession. And of course, once the idea of a historical pageant was broached, it became obvious that many native people would be needed as performers.

Of course, native identities too would be largely formulated by the observers.[13] Indians could not simply present themselves as they were or might want to be; they had to look like Indians which, in the popular imagination, meant Plains Indians. The native people from Ancien Lorette in their customary attire of European dress clothes and ragged headgear were not thought to be Indian enough for Quebec tastes. On the other hand, they might have seemed too Indian precisely because they were all too familiar. It had been expected that the Indians would bring their own costumes, that they lived costumed. However, they came as they were. So costumes had to be bought for them, bows, arrows, buckskins, headdresses, just like the costumes of the other players.

Moreover, the Indians were paid actors, the only ones in the pageant. L.O. Armstrong, an official with the CPR, and his assistant, R.J. Blaney,

The native encampment on the Plains of Abraham.

received $5,000 from the National Battlefields Commission to recruit, pay, and transport the native people: Iroquois from Caughnauwaga near Montreal, Ojibway from Sault Ste Marie, and of course other native people from nearby Ancien Lorette. Lascelles incorrectly identified his native guests as Iroquois, but it was perhaps a pardonable mistake, and one which the natives themselves might have accepted. The Iroquois were, in the popular imagination, thought to represent the lordship of the forest, the most athletic, brave, and fearsome of warriors. Probably less than a third of the native people present were in fact Iroquoian.

The presence of the natives energized the rehearsals, especially the Dollard scene. American Horse, a famous veteran of Buffalo Bill's Wild West Shows, directed the native people in theatrical technique. American Horse and his colleagues, decked out by the National Battlefields Commission in gaudy Plains Indian headdresses and leather-fringed clothing, brandishing tomahawks and shouting war whoops, determined to look and act the part expected of them. They would, like good actors, accept the part defined for them by the cultural script, but in their own interests they would make the most of it.[14]

Everyone agreed that the Indians upstaged the other participants. *Le Soleil* in particular went on at great length about the striking impression made by the native people in the drama. This is somewhat surprising since, as originally designed, native people were to be marginal supporting actors. As it turned out, they starred in most of the scenes. The native people had a great deal of artistic leeway; they largely directed their own scenes. And they showed themselves to be extremely pleased with the roles they had been given and could make for themselves.

From another perspective, it is not surprising that the natives made the deepest dramatic impression. They had the most energetic roles and the most exotic costumes. They fulfilled all expectations for nobility as well as savagery. Some of them, after all, were trained actors who knew how to work the crowd. The native people had reason to think well of Lascelles and the pageant. After all, in this Wild West Show they get to win – in the Dollard scene. More to the point, they had key roles in most of the scenes. They did not just greet the European explorers and quietly disappear; they welcomed, guided, resisted, and got to show different aspects of their character. Their cultural differences were displayed on stage to indicate the passage upcountry through different national territories.

Some might think that the 'show Indian' demeaned native people, overshadowing public efforts to educate and train them in modern ways, and that the theatre degraded and sometimes defrauded the individual performers. The National Battlefields commissioners, for example, refused L.O. Armstrong permission to use the grandstand during the tercentenary for 'cultural performances' by native people. Besides a deep aversion to cheap commercialism, the commissioners were also partly reflecting the bureaucratic revulsion against these retrograde performances of native people revelling in their former 'uncivilized' lives, all the more dangerous because they were popular.

Within the conventions of the Wild West Show, Indians made exciting public careers for themselves at a time when other employments seemed dreary and unrewarding; they became 'show Indians' by choice. They created an image of their people as heroic Plains Indians: they assumed the role of skilled horsemen and marksmen, valiant warriors; of a deep, stoic, spiritual, loyal, noble, sagacious, family-oriented people, sensitive to their environment and sceptical of modernity. Reformers and Indian administrators deplored the perpetuation of the wild savage stereotype and the glorification of rebellious violence, preferring to exhibit diligent native schoolchildren, disciplined workers, and prudent farmers at exhibitions as their own 'show Indians.'[15]

It is significant that the ceremony making Lascelles an Iroquois chief took place on the pageant stage. The Indians from several cultural groups manufactured an investiture for the occasion, and the event was as theatrical as everything else about the tercentenary. Even though Lascelles was an actor among other professionals, but he was nevertheless deeply moved by the event. He had his photograph taken in native costume in moody poses in the Indian encampment. In a group photo he clutches a peace pipe and offers a dramatic profile to the camera. He wore his native costume to a formal dinner during the tercentenary.[16] After the festivities he went on a long camping trip into the Laurentian forest. He carried his Indian name, Tehonikonraka, with him as a talisman. His kinship with native people in Canada became part of his legend among his English friends. His art connected diverse cultures and created deep bonds of sympathy between people. The fact that he was an Iroquois chief is indeed mentioned in his obituary thirty years later.[17]

At Quebec, Lascelles found a theatrical device that would serve him well in other commissions. He would go on to produce similar pageants in England, at various World Expositions on behalf of Great Britain, in other divided polities such as South Africa, and at the great Imperial Durbar in India. He would direct another pageant in Calcutta before this same prince, then king, and there too he would divide/unite Hindu and Islam by interspersing between the two a mythological people of warlike and pacific capacities.[18]

The spiritual side of the arts and crafts tradition attracted Lascelles to the natives and created a deep bond of sympathy between the director and these actors at a certain level. Traditionally Lascelles and his colleagues had depended upon fauns, satyrs, nymphs, forest sprites, and other mythical creatures to provide the enchantment of pageantry. Working within the pageant tradition, native people represented the natural, elemental spirits of the land better than fauns. Moreover, they were multi-purpose elements of the drama. They could be used in Christian

A contemplative Frank Lascelles dressed as an honorary chief.

symbolic terms as terrible foes bringing God's retribution. They could bring a genuine tremor of fear to the play. Their wild, flailing dancing counter-balanced the measured civility of the courtly dance. At the same time their presence – singing, dancing, smoking, hunting, guiding – served, like a Greek chorus, as a mordant commentary of the drama being played out. Their encampment was always visible, somewhat incongruously in the photographs, in the woods, stage right.

The continuing presence of native people also effectively mediated and commmented upon the latent conflict between the two dominant cultural groups. Here was a third force struggling to be heard, interspersed between English and French. Within the theatrical conventions, natives were able to present themselves as peoples with a history and a claim to the future also deserving of consideration. It is also clear that 'race fusion' as seen by Laurier and Grey, and 'pan-Canadian nationalism' as seen by the moderate French-Canadian nationalists, much less the separatist vision of the integral nationalistes, did not involve the native people. The pageant, in its own way, said they should be included. It is in that respect that the Indians stole the show. They made it a show about them, and put their collective presence on the cultural agenda.

French Canadians had a story about themselves they wanted to tell, but within their self-construction was an image of native people only insofar as they interacted with French culture. Natives taught the new-comers how to survive, stood in awe of their superior God and culture, became estranged, then became one of the trials to be borne by the small band of faithful in their North American wilderness. The French would survive the onslaught through their faith, God's providence, and supe-rior firepower. Native people, defeated by the gun, would then surrender themselves to tutelage. They became infantalized as wards of Christian charity. The Marie de l'Incarnation scene in which native children repre-sent the future is deeply revealing. At length native people would virtu-ally vanish from the scene, relegated to the shadows as European culture pushed everything to the margins. They would become hangers-on in massed military formations of much more colourful uniforms, leaving a few stoic, silent, knowing, descendants in deep communion with the earth and the seasons, like the native warrior crouching in Benjamin West's famous painting, 'The Death of Wolfe.' It was an effect to be duplicated in tableau vivant at the Laval statue, as we have seen, by having Hurons group themselves at its base during the unveiling.

Almost vanished, docile and loyal: that was the French script, and, perforce, the native people had to play according to it. That, for exam-ple, was the text of the address of the Huron people to the prince of Wales, drafted and presented by their agent, Antoine Bastien.[19] But native people, by their village and their acting, told another story. First they represented themselves as families, in domestic settings. They were a living, reproducing, thriving presence. Photography inadvertently em-phasized this native domesticity as well. The limitations of the camera – slow shutter speeds and slow film – meant that it was extremely difficult to capture native people in action scenes, riding, dancing, charging, or fighting. There are no photographs, for example, of the hugely popular attack on Dollard des Ormeaux's palisade. Instead, the camera's eye came to rest on the more static representations of native life, domestic scenes, sociability, and posed greeting.

A native family preparing dinner in the encampment. Note the grandstand in the background.

Native people also represented themselves as peoples with a rich culture. Rude colonists laid claim to courtly origins, but native people too had ancient airs and dances that were equally admired. They could fight, and win. They lacked science but possessed an elemental wisdom rooted in nature. They may be a people apart, but they had a future if it were not taken from them. Native people expressed awe at Christian symbols, the cross of Cartier and Saint Lusson, and they expected healing powers from the newly arrived European 'Gods.' Europeans also learned from them. They too put their much more animated ceremonials on display.

Organizers scripted a role for native people at the tercentenary. Natives largely played according to the script, living, dressing, and behaving according to dominant cultural perceptions of Indian-ness. But they also seized the opportunity presented by the pageants to make themselves as prominent as possible and present themselves in another though not contradictory way. Their striking presence was universally acknowledged. They forced themselves onto the stage between the two nations and insisted that there be three. They too were a people with a history and a culture. They bore their trials with forbearance and dignity. They had welcomed the newcomers, taught them, shared with them, suffered with them, and when provoked had become worthy adversaries. They too could lay claim to an honourable share of the founding mythology. And they had not vanished; they were still there, in full view, on stage, claiming their share of the present too.

Some observers could see and hear. But performance is ambiguous and can be written off, after all, as only show. And as Ethel's shudder of aversion at a friendly hand reminds us, one could get too close for comfort. What might be accepted as theatre looked altogether different in life when it took the form of a dirty paw.

Newcomers

The French Canadians had stories to tell in cultural performance as well, first to each other as a means of engendering collective solidarity, but also to the visitors from Great Britain, the United States, and other parts of Canada, to impress them with a sense of respect for this identifiable people. French Canadians had more control over their script than native Canadians, but their power in this respect was qualified. Their story had to be played out within the frame imposed by national and imperial constraints on the one hand and in a local climate tinged by nationaliste extremism and the ultramontane church on the other. On the streets, in the presence of the prince, and in the pageants, French Canadians as actors and audience had to negotiate a complex symbolic terrain.

As we have already seen, the goal of historical pageantry was to bring history alive in such a visual and sensory way as to change life. Thus some challenge to audience sensibilities was intended. In a 'Note on the Pageants' printed in the program, Lascelles argued that 'an appreciation of its History and of the deeds of its heroes ranks among the great factors in the development of a nation.' Popular understanding of history therefore should be encouraged and pageantry, in his view, was the most effective means.

Art, to be effective as a civic force, must be allowed certain liberties. Strict adherence to the historical record made for bad theatre. In his prefatory remarks defending his 'art,' Lascelles begged the indulgence of scholars as, from time to time, he exercised some poetic licence:

> In a few places where it has been found necessary to combine in one scene incidents which may have taken place on different occasions, I cannot do better than repeat as an apologia the words used in the prefatory note to the Book of Words of the Oxford Historical Pageant [which he wrote]: 'It is perhaps advisable to point out that a modern Pageant, like an historical play of Shakespeare, is often compelled by reason of space, time, and suitability for representation, to foreshorten history. The critic must not murmur if persons and events are found in a juxtaposition for which there is no absolute warrant in the chronicles, or if fancy sometimes bodes forth possibilities which may never have been realities.'

Pageantry thus conflates, foreshortens, jumbles up, selects the better bits, and sometimes embellishes or invents as it goes about its civic purpose of 'recall in living form.'

What then were the stories French Canadians wanted to tell about themselves through the art of historical pageantry? The main themes could be reduced to the following: that French Canada too had noble origins; that French possession and occupation of New France was just; that civilization had always been a joint responsibility of church and state; that as a people they had survived many trials through faith, strength of character, and boldness; that they had not been conquered; and finally

Actors portraying Henri IV and Champlain flanked by priests.

that their loyalty to Britain had been proven in battle. These were the messages, intended and implicit in the staging.

The royal and noble origins of the colony were greatly embellished in the telling. Or rather, in the telling these aspects of the past stood out on account of the massive cast, spectacular effects of the massed costumes and mounted figures, the elegant dancing. There can be no doubting that Cartier's voyages received royal sponsorship, nor that François took a brief and passing interest in colonizing Canada. However, the representation at Quebec seemed greatly to exaggerate the royal and aristocratic associations of early venturing. The scene between Cartier, Donnacona, and François I falls into the category 'possibilities which may never have been realities.' Donnacona did meet François I; he even gave him a set of moccasins which still survive. But we do not know much more than this. The scene at Fontainebleau then is a complete invention.

While it is true that royal patronage was important to the colony, the reverse was not necessarily true. The colony did not figure much in François's calculations. He was at the time beset by invaders to the south and the north; his crown was at stake on his own territory. Cartier's voyages take up only a page or two of R.J. Knecht's magnificently revised *Renaissance Warrior and Patron: The Reign of Francis I*, and rate only passing mention in the latest biography in French by Jean Jacquart.

It is interesting to note that the producers of the pageant had to rely not only upon their ample imaginations for this scene, but also upon the aspirations of numerous citizens of Quebec. It is said that one hundred and forty men and women appeared on horseback in this scene, veritable knights and ladies. The scene owed its grandeur in large part to the mass participation of Quebeckers in this fantasy of regal pedigree and to a flourishing bicultural Hunt Club, amply supplied with horses and riders. Bourgeois Quebeckers wanted to be courtiers; it flattered them, and expressed their yearnings. Contemporary class striving and cultural pre-tensions fed the process of regal and aristocratic amplification.

That French possession of the new world was just and proper was represented in several ways: through the use of the cross as the symbol of possession; through the response of the native people whose awe and submission was represented as the natural order of things; through the assumption that the French possessed superior powers; and in the self-proclaimed civilizing mission of the Christian French. This can best be illustrated by a reading of the Cartier scene.

Two of Cartier's three voyages are here combined into one. Events that occurred several years apart, on the north shore, Gaspé, in the region of Quebec City and Montreal, are presumed to have occurred in one time and place. This foreshortening of the events of the first two voyages is perhaps pardonable, but staged in this way the elision does tend to stress French power, Christian mission, and native subordination. These are not themes that leap from the pages of the most authoritative source on these encounters, Cartier's *Voyages*, which was well known to the authors of the script.

In many obvious ways the script represented the superiority of Europe-ans. Moreover, it drew upon a deep reservoir of religious iconography to borrow legitimacy and divine sanction for a civilizing mission towards 'lesser' peoples. This effect is most evident in the healing ceremony and the raising of the cross. In both cases the Europeans accept the role scripted for them, in the first instance by the native people, and in the second by their conscience and king. Natives are represented as being in awe of the Europeans though not fearful of them. European power exuded friendship and commanded respect.

We know, of course, and so did the historical advisors, that on many occasions natives contested Cartier's presence. Natives remonstrated against the cross of possession at Gaspé; the one on the north shore was raised in isolation, and that at Stadacona was erected at Easter, following a deadly winter, as an act of thanksgiving for survival. It was an act of desperate men before fleeing homeward.

It is also well known that the Europeans retreated to their pitiful fortification and survived their first winter only with the assistance of the natives. It was the Europeans who became sick and were cured by superior native medicines and powers. Confined to this fort, constantly harassed by natives, the Europeans fled eagerly at the first opportunity.

The French were anything but the superiors in this antagonistic relationship. There is evidence to suggest that European abuse of natives provoked the attacks that pinned them inside their fortifications. The pageant representation omits conflict, which in itself would logically question the premise of natural supremacy. Similarly, references to the obvious weakness of the Europeans, emaciated, trapped inside their crude pallisade, and taunted by native warriors, is also passed over in silence. Lastly, the violence done to the natives by Europeans – in particular the kidnapping of Donnacona and his companions – is transformed into companionate venturing on the part of the native people.

Cartier, it might be noted, takes a more prominent place in a celebration of the founding of Quebec than might be expected. Indeed, in the pageant he shares equal time on the stage with Champlain. His exploits were perhaps better known than those of Champlain as a result of the 1884–5 celebrations of the three hundred and fiftieth anniversary of his voyages and the unveiling of a monument to his memory in Montreal in 1893. He had been recovered from relative obscurity in the 1830s. An image, claiming to be his likeness, was widely circulated. For a time the Saint-Jean-Baptiste Society made something of a cult of Cartier. During the great excitement about Columbus in the 1890s, Cartier served to remind Quebeckers that Canada had been discovered not by an Italian or a Spaniard, but by a Frenchman. He was useful too in scholarly combat with anglophone historians who advanced the prior claims of John Cabot. Cartier was also a more maleable figure than Champlain; less was known about him, but there were no lurking suspicion that he might be a Protestant.[20]

The 1908 pageant representation laid great stress upon Cartier's role

This Livernois portrait of Charles Langelier as Champlain was modelled on a litho.

as an agent of Christianization. This high purpose is not borne out by the testimony, even of Cartier's own *Voyages*. The cross-raisings were quite perfunctory, more civic acts of possession than religious piety. Little or no effort seems to have been spent on Christianizing the Indians on the first two voyages, though on the third, colonizing priests were prominent. Cartier, by his own account, was indifferent to the Christian mission.

The composite cross-raising represented at Quebec, when combined with the healing ceremony, the bread and the wine, makes for a much more sacramental effect than the historical account sanctions. The music accompanying the cross-raising, Gounod's 'Road to Calvary,' underscores the point. Cartier and the French are thus metaphorically likened to Christ on the cross in their devotion to their God and dedication to their calling – in this case bringing the light of civilization to the new world. There is a cost to be exacted, as the crucifixion metaphor implies.

Who is being crucified and for whom is not left in doubt in the representation, nor is the native acceptance of it.

In the pageants, the natives assume a position of natural subordination to the supposedly more powerful Europeans. This is a fairly common theme, one which enters the historical literature as a crude native commodity fetishism. Throughout the pageant the natives stand in awe of the European things and their technology. They marvel at the size of the ships, cloths, guns, embroidery. They willingly present themselves as inferiors. Artistic representations exaggerate the size of the ships, which tower in a golden sheen above the native canoes on the river. Modern observers looking at scale reproductions, the *Don-de-Dieu* in this case and more recently the *Matthew*, marvel at how small these vessels actually were.

By the same token, the native people possess a distinct nobility, grace, poetry, and power of their own. They are not destitute or downtrodden. They are rather lords of their own domain, cognizant of the greater stature of the newcomers. Representation of the St Lawrence native in the more majestic ceremonial costume of Plains Indians further amplified this notion of native potency, thereby further inflating European presumptions of natural supremacy. In this relationship the natives are instinctively friendly; they welcome the newcomers, cooperate with them, and provide useful information. They become, in short, excellent servants.

This collaboration with superior beings is perhaps best represented with reference to the matter of taking native people back to France. Here again, the conflation of the first two voyages muddies the waters somewhat. The native people seem to have been more willing to allow two young men to be taken back to France on the first voyage. There can be no doubt about the second voyage, however. A young girl was offered up as a voluntary migrant, but Cartier and his crew had to deceive and kidnap the others. Donnacona was by no means a willing passenger. Nor did he and the other captives survive the ordeal of removal.

At every stage, the native peoples of the region (with one exception) contested the presumption of possession by the Europeans. At no point were the Europeans regarded with awe; they were often attacked, tricked, and verbally abused. The natives had a premonition of a kidnapping and resisted. When the Europeans deceived the natives into coming on board, then seized them by main force, the native people on shore did everything in their power to redeem the captives.

An artist's rendering of Cartier raising a cross at Quebec.

The one exception to resistance occurred at during Cartier's visit to Hochelaga on what is now the Island of Montreal. There a welcoming and healing ceremony similar to that represented in the pageant did occur. The context is important. Cartier had to break through the Stadacona Indians' resistance to make his way upriver to Montreal; they did not want their power relationship with the Europeans broken. The Hochelagans sought an unmediated relationship with the newcomers and thus were more willing to ingratiate themselves. They seem to have written the script of healing, feasting, and touching. Cartier played his part, quoting from John: 'In the beginning was the Word, and the Word was with God, and the Word was God.' He did not raise a cross on this occasion.[21]

With Champlain and the Ursulines the dual aspects of civilizing the continent begin. The first is colonization; the second is evangelical, teaching the gospel to the native people and claiming the continent for the church. This theme that true community is a joint product of church and state acting in harmony appears several times, most notably in the Ursuline and Laval scenes. When Marie de l'Incarnation and Madame de la Peltrie arrive, gathering native and habitant children around them for instruction, true civilization begins. A scattered band of settlers is drawn together into a nurturing community under the guidance of religion. In this instance the female religious orders are more powerfully featured in this scene of the pageant than the male orders. That changes, however, in scene five when bishop Laval welcomes Governor de Tracy to the colony. When the church represents power, it is male. Here the church meets the state on equal ground, and if anything the church makes the more splendid and imposing impression. Surrounded by priests and altar-boys, under a golden canopy in his gleaming white surplice, Laval receives de Tracy and his noble entourage decked out in their frilled finery. Together they make a solemn procession to a nearby church through a column of natives who symbolically kneel before them and discard their bows and arrows as a gesture of peace. Such is the power of church and state working in harmony. This linkage of church and state appears early, in the use of crosses bearing the escutcheon of fleurs-de-lis to mark initial possession of New France by Cartier. It continues as Saint Lusson uses another cross later on in pageant six to claim possession of the northwest. Peace and order are restored not through the power of the state alone, but by church *and* state. Social redemption is a religious as well as a political accomplishment.

Faith is only one of a series of connected virtues that help the frail plant of New France survive in the hostile wilderness of North America. These ancestors were of resolute good character, the pageants proclaimed in so many different ways. On account of their faith, they could be bold when need be. Faith sometimes demanded the supreme sacrifice. Dollard and his sixteen companions redeemed the entire colony with their heroic resistance. The natives overwhelmed them, but the character of their resistance made a deep impression on the native people. It was not merely a calculation of probable losses alone that made them reconsider an all-out attack on Montreal. Here was a foe to be respected. Thus did heroic deeds speak.

Frontenac, on the other hand, could cavalierly call the bluff of the Bostonnais invader, promising to deliver his answer from the mouth of his cannons. Faith in a divine mission maintained community solidarity in the face of the enemy. A history of fierce fighting in self-defence and a calculation of the costs of brooking that defiance deterred all but the brave or foolhardy. Frontenac gambled that Phips was neither, and won.

Through proud acts of self-defence, the faith and character of the pioneers of New France shone through, a beacon for all succeeding generations. One clear reading of the pageants, especially the final scene, is that in a fundamental sense the spirit of Cartier, Champlain, Marie de l'Incarnation, Dollard, Laval, Saint Lusson, and Frontenac remained undefeated even after 1759. For the battle for New France was marked by parallel victories, the Plains of Abraham in 1759 and Ste-Foy half a year later. The French had not been crushed in the field; they fought on after the siege of Quebec and won a major battle against experienced British troops. The fate of Quebec was not settled on the battlefields of Canada, where brave men and worthy warriors on both sides fought to a draw, but rather on the higher terrain of imperial diplomacy where another kind of calculus prevailed.

The historical pageants did obliquely acknowledge the transference to a new imperial power by turning its consequences into a show of virtue. Citizens of New France were above all faithful to their church and their monarch, English or French. Careful observers of the tumultuous marching in the final scene would notice the presence of costumed French-Canadian militiamen who repelled General Montgomery's invasion in 1775. Marching along with them were De Salaberry's Voltigeurs, the heroes of the battle of Châteauguay in 1813, when once

Frontenac on the right dismisses Phips's envoy. Detail of a panoramic photograph.

again French Canadians rallied to the cause of their new English monarch and drove off the invader. Loyalty had been a distinguishing characteristic of this people, a mark they proudly retained and for which they expected gratitude and respect. The final pageant was not therefore an acknowledgment of defeat but rather a joining of peoples and armies on terms of equality, and solidarity in the face of mutual adversaries. The French press saw this, but not everyone did. Taking in the scene from the sunny grandstand, Ethel Chadwick saw it slightly differently, as she tartly observed in her diary: 'At the end Wolfe and Montcalm's soldiers come onto the Plains together and march and countermarch about but there is no fight – only reconcilement – so as not to annoy the French people.'[22]

The scenes in the historical pageants told these stories about the past of New France in various ways. They sought to move the story of New France out of history onto a timeless didactic plane that drew upon a rich store of shared cultural capital to convey its meaning. The pageants could be read from the outside as a romance, but from inside the community romance became a passion play. That a mass should be said on the same site, using some of the characters and music, drove home the point.

This history of the French-Canadian people presented in the pageants bore more than a faint resemblence to a passion play, an imitation of the life of Christ. French-Canadian society was immaculately conceived; it was not the product of violation or conquest. Quite the contrary, it arose from a natural cession to higher powers. The mission of spreading God's word explained the remarkable geographical scope of the colony at such an early stage. Spreading the faith claimed the interior.

Nevertheless, French Canadians were destined to remain a minority, a small fragmentary people in a huge hostile continental sea. It would not be an easy life, spreading the word. Constant attack was one price of an expansionary missionary role. First native people and then the English beset the community. Although vastly outnumbered, the colony survived its trials. Martyrdom, sacrifice, moral fortitude, and faith allowed the people to survive, even to transcend the ultimate betrayal and abandonment by France. So, too, this people would triumph over the assimilationist torments and temptations of English rule, earning through their solidarity and loyalty the respect of their erstwhile foes for themselves and their religion.

Habitant children from the pageant.

Historians

Lascelles, of course, was a man of the theatre; invention and embellishment came naturally to him. Historians customarily quibble and complain about the distortions and misrepresentation of popular enactments of the past. The past on display in the pageants was, of course, a highly selective, even idiosyncratic representation. The selection of scenes itself emphasized heroism, nobility, grandeur, paternalism, community harmony, Christian sacrifice, mission, loyalty, survival, providential destiny, and transcendence. Royal involvement in the history of New France was greatly exaggerated by the selection and casting. The recently invented Dollard martyrdom was played to the hilt. The romantic aspects of the past were emphasized at the expense of the quotidien. The church appeared not only a central actor, but was also seen through an ultramontane lens. It rivalled the state in both majesty and power. What would the historians make of it?

Thomas Chapais, William Wood, Arthur Doughty, and Ernest Myrand were among the leading historians of their day, a group on the cusp of professionalization. Would they demur? The answer is, surprisingly, not. Men who in their professional lives were particular to the point of pedantry about matters of fact appear to have been quite ready to accept and cooperate in the dissemination of a version of history they knew to be flawed in detail although faithful to the truth in spirit. It is not a question of them not knowing. They were committed to the higher purpose of generating a sense of national history. Doughty, who played a big part in drafting the program and helping with the script, was an unrepentant romantic. He had already written an opera. He and his colleagues in the emerging historical profession were embarked upon a monumental effort not only to give Canadian history a proper documentary base, but also a sweeping, romantic master narrative. Secondly, the historians as a group largely agreed upon the edifying, unifying national purpose of history. Thus what they chose to remember and what they chose to forget is of some interest.

It must be said that the dramatic representation of the past in the pageants was not significantly unfaithful to the spirit of the historiography of the time. Francis Parkman laid out the grand sweep of this view of the past in the previous generation. He had taken a dark view of the attempt by 'feudalism, monarchy and Rome to master a continent,' but he had unquestionably limned with great power and considerable admiration the drama of that heroic but doomed effort. The introduction to his great work, *France and England in North America*, might have served as a preface to the historical pageants:

The French dominion is a memory of the past; and when we evoke its departed shades, they rise upon us from their graves in strange, romantic guise. Again their ghostly camp-fires seem to burn, and the fitful light is cast around on lord and vassal and black-robed priest, mingled with wild forms of savage warriors, knit in close fellowship on the same stern errand. A boundless vision grows upon us; an untamed continent; vast wastes of forest verdure; mountains silent in primeval sleep; river, lake, and glimmering pool; wilderness oceans mingling with the sky. Such was the domain which France conquered for Civilization. Plumed helmets gleamed in the shade of its forests; priestly vestments in its dens and fastnesses of ancient barbarism. Men steeped in antique learning, pale with the close breath of the cloister, here spent the noon and evening of their lives, ruled savage hordes with a mild, parental sway, and stood serene before the direst shapes of death. Men of courtly nurture, heirs to the polish of a far-reaching ancestry, here, with their dauntless hardihood, put to shame the boldest sons of toil.[23]

Writing in French, Thomas Chapais and Benjamin Sulte carried on the heroic tradition of Parkman, by clericalizing it and heightening the notion of the organic unity of the collectivity. They, in effect, turned Parkman on his head for the local audience. New France flourished surrounded by hostile natives and invading English because it was protected by the church and the French state. The fall was not inevitable and certainly not the victory of a superior civilization over an inferior one; the Conquest was reversible. New France passed to the British in the hazards of global warfare and the vague caprice of postwar diplomacy. The Quebec historians retained Parkman's romantic conception of New France but dispensed with his Whig interpretive framework. The pageants represented a version of the history of New France that had been popularized by French-Canadian historians for a generation.[24]

This interpretation resonated in English writing as well. George Wrong published *A Canadian Manor and Its Seigneurs* the year the pageants were produced. Wrong presented the history of New France as a romantic, church-led pastorale. 'From his earliest contacts with Quebec he admired the stability and permanence of its social order and its religious fervour,' writes Carl Berger. 'Church spires dominated his picture of the province, just as they towered over the Laurentian villages.'[25] Wrong believed in the 'perfect equality' between French and English in the House of Commons and the legislature of Quebec – though he did not think this a basis for extending those rights westward. He believed that in time, with greater communications, social interchange, and better understanding, the race question would diminish in importance. To this end, he strove to exorcise extremist views on either side.

Coincidentally an American historian, Frank Tracy, brought out a three-volume history of Canada early in 1908. Hoping to capitalize on this topical event Tracy or his publisher titled it *The Tercentenary History of Canada: From Champlain to Laurier MDCVIII–MCMVII*. The book's emphasis and romantic interpretation also resembled the tercentenary pageants. Frank Tracy admitted to being more emotionally attached to the French than the English period of Canadian history. Indeed, in a letter to George Wrong when his work was in progress, he distanced himself from 'English writers on histories of Canada' who complained that too much space and attention in contemporary historiography was being given to the French period. 'No one who reads Canadian history will deny that the most interesting part of it is the French period,' he insisted, enumerating the bloody wars, the colourful characters, the corruption and boodling, and the splendid documentary evidence. Far too much of the English era of Canadian history had been taken up 'with petty, uninteresting things,' in his view. 'I started out with the idea of spending only about one-third of the time on the French period, but I think before I am through I shall have given the French period at least a half and still leave a great many things unsaid about which there is abundant material and which themselves are very interesting.'[26] As it turned out, the history of New France spilt over from volume one to the mid-point of volume two. If Canadian history was to be made interesting, in the eyes of an American newspaper editor, it must emphasize its Frenchness.

George Wrong's close friend the Dominion archivist, Arthur Doughty, was also hard at work turning the history of New France into the dramatic and stirring origins of a distinctly Canadian nation. Above all, he believed with Wrong that the history of Canada, especially that of New France, must be popularized; once people knew more about their past, their present would flow more smoothly. His *Cradle of New France* was composed in 1907; he actually wrote the preface in Quebec during March of 1908 while he was working on the pageants and battlefields plan.

Most obviously history was altered in its representation at the tercentenary to make it more palatable. As we have seen, there was an ongoing struggle between the local francophone script writers on the one side and Earl Grey's forces, including the English director, on the other, over when the pageants would end. The battle for Quebec in 1759 in the local committee's version melded into other military actions in 1775 and 1812 in which the French Canadians defended the crown. For imperialists such as Earl Grey, history ended and began in 1759; battlefield commemoration was what this was all in aid of. For Lascelles too, for theatrical reasons. Colonel Wood and Doughty in their professional capacities seemed obsessed with the details of the Battle of the Plains of Abraham. But in performance they were less particular and they accepted an ahistorical compromise in part because it corresponded to their own political views. Soldiers might dress up, but they could not fight; they could only express fraternity. The Battle of Ste-Foy was amplified in importance, and made to represent an act of triumphant self-defence in which French Canadians preserved for all time enjoyment of their language, culture, and church. Historians might demur (interestingly, on this occasion they did not), but what actually happened was beside the point. In 1908 both sides won and all the gunpowder, marching, and shouting on the Plains celebrated a century and a half of peaceful cohabitation in mutual respect.

This, of course, was history as someone wanted it to be, not the way it was.

9. ON PARADE

Champs de Mars

What were all of those ships and soldiers doing at Quebec in the summer of 1908 – not to mention the Prince of Wales? There had to be reasons other than Earl Grey's enthusiasms for their presence. Invitations may be sent, but they must also be accepted. The guests had to want to come or thought they should come, for there were many obstacles to be overcome, not all of them physical. It was a long way; it was inconvenient, expensive, difficult to fit into a busy schedule. So it seems that these guests must have wanted to put on a show as well.

Grey's motives were transparent enough. He wanted to make 'a really impressive Imperial splash' to teach Canadians, French Canadians in particular, pride in belonging to the mighty British Empire. For such purposes he thought he needed a clutch of colourful Indian princes and if possible a deputation of Asian or African potentates to show the world scope and exoticism of empire.[1] In his mind he imagined the Quebec tercentenary as a miniature replica of Victoria's jubilee. Ultimately, costumed representatives of the whole Empire would not parade at Quebec. Nevertheless, with the navy in the St Lawrence, the prince in the Citadel, 'Bobs' for the mob, and the Duke of Norfolk for the bishops, Grey had more than enough power and glory for a good show.

At the tercentenary other theatrical performances were being played out besides the historical pageants. Let us call these power plays – dramas about power in which other lessons were being taught, legitimacies claimed, and consequences anticipated. The theatre of power at Quebec in 1908 was every bit as tangled and intriguing as the cultural perform-ances of identity being played out in the streets and on the Plains of Abraham. Empire provided a proscenium arch for the tercentenary. Everything occurred under the cope of British power, in the presence of the prince who became the joint focus of attention, with the fleet visible in the background cruising up and down the river, with military bands and marching columns of soldiers providing order and a colour guard. The tercentenary could be thought of as one big parade.

In this political theatre, Canadians were determined to make a point both about their military competence and their readiness for autono-mous command. The Admiralty wanted to demonstrate its might in convincing, comparative terms to both Canadians and Americans, to hint at looming perils, and literally to attract some Canadian ownership of the British navy.

Attention!

The overwhelming presence of the Canadian militia and representative ships of three navies turned the tercentenary into a continuous military procession. Marching, manoeuvring, competing at games, massing in ranks, soldiers and sailors, with sabres flashing and guns thundering, sought to awe observers, score points, persuade, reassure, and inspire admiration.

Everyone loves a parade. But why? The popularity of a parade stems in part from its compelling representation of an ideal. It is so unlike daily life. A parade presents a structured, ordered world featuring the beauti-ful, fearsome, fraternal, overpowering, totemic, or heroic. Some parades, like those associated with the circus, Christmas, and carnivals, invite spectators to identify by actually joining in or following along in a 'desfile' to some festive place. Most parades pass by, however, thus poten-tially dividing the population into active marchers and passive spectators. In a popular parade the two groups are usually brought together on an emotional plane of admiration. Colour, spectacle, a massing of bodies, ordered formations, and an impelling tempo, by inspiring awe and adulation, dissolve distinctions. Moving together in time to the music transports and unites participants and observers.[2] One way or another, a parade expresses power.

The bands, the uniforms, the huge encampments, the military games turned the tercentenary of Quebec most obviously into a parade of the Canadian militia. The twelve thousand or so troops augmented by the five thousand sailors from the ships gathered on the occasion were both actors and audience to the spectacle. They were there to see and be seen and make a point. Like so many other aspects of the celebration, the participation of the Canadian militia had been the subject of considerable controversy and had to be hastily improvised at the last minute. Without much warning, a local festival turned into a national occasion at which it was imperative that the Canadian militia put on a good show before the prince and the top brass of the British army, not only to impress the people of Quebec but also to lay to rest recent military and political embarrassments.[3]

When the seven thousand or so Canadian volunteers returned from the Boer War with their war stories, both the controversy over the constitutional issue of who determined Canadian policy and what the content of that policy should be had not been buried with the 270 dead. The issues that had divided the country more or less along linguistic lines, and had almost brought down Laurier's government, remained unresolved within Canada and between the governments of Canada and the Great Britain. Differences stemmed from a basic disagreement between Canada and the mother country over the principles of defence policy. British policy, vigorously pressed by governors general and the British-appointed general officers commanding, urged the Canadians to build a proper 'national army' to defend the Dominion against possible attack from the United States and contribute to imperial defence when required. British officers struggled to get Canadians to take their own defence seriously, and reform the patronage-ridden, disorganized militia department.[4] Canadians bristled at interference in domestic affairs. When officers went public to educate public opinion, responsible politicians fumed at insubordination. Benign neglect remained Canadian policy, as the prime minister explained to an astonished incoming major-general: 'You must not take the Militia seriously, for though it is useful for suppressing internal disturbances, it will not be required for the defence of the country as the Monroe doctrine protects us against enemy aggression.'[5]

It is against this background of sharp differences within the country, between the government of Canada and Great Britain, and more precisely between the government and its imperially appointed general officers commanding over defence policy, that the massing of military might at Quebec in 1908 must be seen. After much gnashing of teeth, the Militia Act had been reformed, appropriations slightly increased, and finally, in 1908, a Canadian was given command of the Canadian forces – General William Otter, a veteran of the Battle of Ridgeway during the Fenian troubles in the 1860s, Cut Knife Hill during the Riel Rebellion of 1885, Paardeberg in South Africa in 1900, and many internecine if less lethal bureaucratic quarrels. From a British perspective, the Canadians had a lot to prove; first of all that they could command; secondly that they could summon up the will to fight if need be; and thirdly, that they would commit the resources necessary for a credible defence effort. The Canadians, for their part, wanted to show the world – or at least the British – that what they had done was enough. Thus General Otter's first responsibility, upon taking command of the Canadian forces in March 1908, was to muster as much Canadian military might as possible at Quebec City and put it through its paces before the Prince of Wales, his former commander in South Africa, Field Marshal Lord Roberts, and the top brass of the British army. The purpose of the Quebec tercentenary militia parade was to make Quebec forget the Boer War military controversies by putting a Canadian army (with many French Canadians prominently displayed in it) proudly on display, and to reassure the British that Canada could be relied upon to do what might be necessary for local and imperial defence.

This was the situation that finally evolved; it did not start that way. Indeed, the first step was in the other direction. In the spring of 1908 Otter prudently but ingloriously had to recommend against a massive gathering of Canadian permanent forces and militia at Quebec for what amounted to a local celebration. The Department of Militia could not afford the $937,900 cost of transporting, housing, training, and paying twenty-five thousand men for the two weeks of festivities. Moreover, the railways could not guarantee extra trains to transport such a massive movement of men, equipment, and horses without seriously curtailing other activities at the height of the immigration season. As the government itself seemed to be wavering on its commitment to the festival, the decision of the Militia Council in May, after a month of dithering, to provide for only a local muster of volunteers at Quebec seemed at first reasonable and justifiable.

Then the wind changed. The government finally committed itself through the National Battlefields Commission Bill. With each passing day the size and importance of the British delegation grew and the festivities planned became more spectacular. Then the decision to hold back the militia smacked of bureaucratic cheese-paring.

Early rumours that financial retrenchment within the Department of Militia might lead to a cancellation of the militia muster led to questions in the House. The Quebec papers bristled with outrage. The opposition pounced. Frederick Borden, the minister of militia, scrambled to recover. Otter's old nemesis, the redoutable Colonel Denison, from the lofty height of his appointment to the National Battlefields Commission, loosed a thunderbolt on government indifference to militia affairs.[6] Quebec City and military pressure groups insisted that the Canadian militia be adequately represented at what had now become a national festival. A prince without soldiers and a festival without a military parade were inconceivable. By June, Otter received authorization to muster twelve thousand men at Quebec for the tercentenary. By then he had only a month to do it.[7]

The logistical problems involved in mobilizing and transporting this large body of men across the country, housing, feeding, and providing training for them once there, and then returning them home in orderly fashion, seemed a daunting task. A successful muster of militia on this scale and on such short notice would in itself be an impressive test of the Canadian military mettle.[8] General Otter and his officers set smartly to work once their reservations about spending so much money on a merely ceremonial occasion had been firmly suppressed. Railway and steamship companies coordinated their schedules; camps were erected, equipment prepared, uniforms provided, supplies tendered for and requisitioned, and special white pith helmets secured in great numbers to ward off the summer heat.[9] By the third week in July the various regiments of the small permanent force and the militia began to descend upon Quebec City.

Tramping through the city streets from the railway station and the docks, the troops' gradual assembly contributed greatly to the mounting excitement. Their massive encampments, row upon row of white cone-shaped tents stretching as far as the eye could see, were a thing of wonder. The geography of the three encampments kept the best organized, best drilled, and most prominent English-Canadian regiments to the fore. Quebec's less impressive rural regiments were relegated, along with some maritime detachments, to camps at Lévis across the river.

While officers strolled the promenade in full dress doing their best to maintain the utmost dignity, their more uninhibited troops made a different spectacle of themselves in the streets. So much carefree 'boisterous manhood' seemed to bring the staid city joyfully to life according to one visiting journalist:

> These military fellows are having the time of their lives. They clank their spurs, they cock their hats, they swish the air with swaggers, they ogle the French Canadian girls who cast shy glances at the prettiest uniforms, they blow clouds of blue smoke from cigarettes, they swoop down on every conceivable place where picture postcards are sold, they rush off in mad batches to the post office, they sing songs, they shout, they laugh, they dance – they are mad with the exuberance and they infect others with their madness.[10]

The militia, of course, was intended to be more than decorative. Mass participation in this military tattoo was in and of itself an exercise on rapid mobilization. Once in Quebec the men were expected to be useful as guards and escorts, respectable in their deportment on the city streets, entertaining and inspiring as bandsmen, fearsome in their marching formations massed on the Plains of Abraham, gallant when on horseback – in short, fully worthy of the occasion and the nation. They were there at Quebec to be inspected by the population as well as the top brass.

As was customary, elite corps and their bands welcomed the Prince of Wales in neat formations at the King's Wharf. The prince's first duty was an inspection of his honour guard, the 43rd Duke of Cornwall's Own Rifles from Ottawa. The first Canadian citizens the prince met, therefore, were representatives of its army. The Royal Canadian Dragoons and Royal Northwest Mounted Police provided a mounted escort for his entry into the city. Canadians thus first caught a glimpse of their prince in a parade, bracketed by the forces of order, mounted police, troops, and transported in a bubble of dignitaries. Cavalry trotting fore and aft of the royal cortège added colour, power, and dignity to the spectacle.

It was perhaps regrettable that the Canadian troops lined the route virtually shoulder to shoulder, thereby separating the civilians of Quebec from their prince. Symbolically that was not a popular move, one not likely to enhance public attachment to the militia. Even the correspondent for the militia-mad Toronto *Telegram* observed testily: 'The military and the Church of Rome manage everything in Quebec. Wherever you go looking for a place of vantage you are met by soldiers on guard whose greatest virtue is certainly not their modesty nor their consideration for the rights of civilians.'[11]

Still, this did not quell the popular ardour for further shows of military might in the streets. From the outset, a large-scale military review and military games had been planned for the Plains of Abraham. But seating was limited, expensive, and the best seats were by invitation only. Thus one of the most popular parts of the tercentenary seemed to have been declared off limits to the public. The newspapers began a quiet campaign to rectify this error in judgment. When at the last minute the nationalist patriotic societies of Quebec could not find the organizational zeal to mount a parade of their own within the framework of the tercentenary, a tremendous opportunity for the militia to show off before a popular audience opened up. Here was an occasion for the popular classes to view Canada's militia marching through the streets of Quebec, something the Canadian elite would be able to do later from the comfort of a grandstand on the Plains.[12]

Thus, on the morning of rehearsals for the military review, Otter and his officers arranged to route the departure of the various regiments from the Plains of Abraham through the streets of the city. It was a last-minute, impromptu parade, but no less stirring for that. And the crowds responded warmly to the rousing spectacle of the bands, horses, colourful uniforms, and the precision marching. The procession took more than an hour to pass. First came the Horse Artillery, clattering through the streets hauling their gun carriages; then the mounted divisions of cavalry and hussars, followed by the less decorative but immensely popular rural infantry regiments. The weakest aspect of the militia from a critic's point of view, the rural troops, were thus buried in the middle of the parade, between the permanent force and mounted regiments before, and cadets, troops from the Quebec garrison, city infantry regiments, divisional corps, and Governor General's Foot Guards afterwards. Highland regiments from Toronto and Montreal with their pipe bands were especially applauded. The parade concluded with signals, ambulance corps, the Royal Canadian Regiment, and a striking detachment of Royal Northwest Mounted Police. Stereoscopic photographers found the

Ontario Militia marching in the military parade.

Toronto's 48th Highland Regiment passes in review in front of the official party.
The minister of militia, Frederick Borden, who could not ride a horse, stands to
the left of the Prince of Wales.

military parade particularly suited to their medium; columns of troops filing through crowded streets emphasized the depth of field and thereby enhanced the three-dimensional illusion.[13]

The Quebec *Chronicle* reporter noted solemnly: 'The force of youthful Canada was shown. It inspired respect and perhaps dread – but above all it was imposing.'[14] The popular conservative newspaper *L'Événement*, which had mounted a campaign for a military parade, was naturally overjoyed with the spectacle and the public reaction to it: 'Our troops were applauded by the enormous crowd as they passed and stimulated fierce pride and admiration everywhere they went.'[15] At least in form, this military parade vaguely echoed the procession of the Laval fête. The soldiers marched from their parade ground, past the Basilica, through the main commercial street, then out through the neighbourhoods to dispersal points at the several camps. People did not have to go far to see the spectacle. The militia parade helped bridge some of the popular hostility to the elitism and the imperial aspect of the tercentenary.

A parade impressed by its length and constant variety. A parade passed by; it moved through space. By contrast, the military review on the Plains of Abraham on Friday, 24 June impressed its spectators (as well as its participants) with its sheer massing of humanity in one vast space. It was a static show of force and colour. From the grandstand all fifteen thousand men were in constant view, assembled in their respective groupings across the parade ground. Lord Roberts, one of the guests of honour, knew well the difficulty of carrying off a show of this sort. He had done precisely the same thing himself earlier in his military career in 1887 at the first Indian durbar for the viceroy, Lord Littleton. Quebec posed particular problems quite apart from the distance over which troops had to move to the reviewing ground. The terrain was rough, uneven, and not suitable for precision manoeuvres. And the parade ground was not really large enough for such a vast congregation of humanity. Regiments were constantly getting in each other's way as they marched on and off the central ground. It was also uncommonly hot and dusty.

As the prince mounted his horse at 10:00 a.m. and rode off towards the Plains of Abraham with Earl Grey and General Roberts, he noted with relief that a 'nice little breeze' offered some relief from the blazing sun and that he had been assigned 'a charming quiet horse who didn't mind anything.'[16] On the way he stopped to place a wreath on Wolfe's Monument. He entered the ground, rode down the lines, and then came to the saluting point in front of the stands. A panoramic photographer, perching with his equipment on a telegraph pole high above the parade ground, captured the scene as the prince and his party rode along the length of the massed troops. Following a brief ceremony transferring the title deeds for the Plains of Abraham to the people of Canada, the Prince of Wales rejoined Lord Roberts and General Otter at the saluting point. Then for the next eighty minutes the troops marched past him. First came the French and then the American sailors, followed by a much larger contingent of blue jackets from the British fleet. Delicate diplomacy at the highest levels had been required to obtain the permission for the French and American sailors to be inspected by British officers in an essentially British show. After lengthy consultations, authorization was granted. As a gesture of goodwill, the French were given pride of place, marching first and opening the review, followed by the Americans.[17] These small detatchments were, of course, greatly outnumbered by more than two to one by the British sailors.

In a conscious effort to impress his British visitors, General Otter rearranged the usual presentation of the regiments by seniority so that the review began and ended brilliantly. He ensured that some of the perennially ragged performers were preceded by sharper-looking units, as he had done in the parade the day before. Canadian troops appeared not in hierarchical order, but in an order designed to impress observers with their depth and discipline. Puzzled by the arrangement that had the Royal Canadian Regiment marching last, the Prince of Wales questioned Otter about it. The Canadian general is said to have replied: 'I wanted the tail to be equal to the head.'[18]

Lord Roberts did much to ensure that the review ended in a climax. Though visibly wilting in the heat, the old soldier first rode out to lead General Otter's old regiment, the Queen's Own, past the reviewing stand – he was their honorary colonel-in-chief. With the crowd roaring itself hoarse, the ancient British general brought the military review to a fitting conclusion with a thundering charge of the Royal Canadian Horse Artillery, the billowing dust recalling his youthful heroism in Afghanistan. Unfortunately the old boy overdid things a bit. The heat got to him and he collapsed later in exhaustion.

Everything considered, the Canadian militia put on an impressive show. There were only a few incidents and those that did occur could be quietly dealt with. There were complaints that all the marching disrupted

March-past of the Queen's Own Rifles. This photograph is from Colonel Otter's collection in the National Archives.

This artist's impression improves on the facing photograph by including more participants in the frame, and rearranging geography to eliminate the obtrusive jail and include the fleet. Lord Strathcona is in conversation with Sir Wilfrid Laurier on the extreme left. A figure resembling Zoe, the prime minister's wife, can be seen on the steps of the viewing pavilion, and Frederick Borden's mutton-chops are visible beyond the hindquarters of General Otter's steed. This illustration of the Queen's Own Rifles passing in review captures both the individuals of the official party and the sense of massed humanity missing from more tightly focused photographs.

the schedule of the street railway. Private Stevenson from the 90th Regiment drowned while swimming in the St Charles River; Private Roberts of the Governor General's Foot Guards took ill and died in hospital of some intestinal disorder – beginning a rumour that bad water had killed an unspecified number of visitors. The 3rd Cavalry Regiment apparently caused havoc one evening in a brothel on Ste-Cecile Street and the district was henceforth declared off limits. Some boisterous troopers from the 3rd Cavalry, careening drunkenly in the street, smashed a few windows and frightened the shopkeepers.[19] This was more or less to be expected.

Quebeckers took some satisfaction from the fact that thousands of rabid Orangemen from Ontario had been in their midst for several weeks with nary a provocative incident on either side. For their part, the soldiers returned from the heart of French Canada to their towns and cities with stories of the warmth of their reception. Grey hoped and prayed that this mass migration to Quebec, most of it by militiamen, would dispel irrational prejudices and bigotry in other parts of the country and calm anxieties in Quebec.

Grey, not surprisingly, was exultant in his report to the Colonial Office. Everything had gone off without a hitch:

The proceedings concluded with a march past when the smartness, smoothness and precision of the movements of the Canadian militia and the excellence of their horses were a source of great satisfaction to His Royal Highness, a surprise to Lord Roberts, and a revelation to all. Hundreds of militia had left their farms in order to march past the Heir to the Throne at a time when the hay crop required their labour. The greatest enthusiasm prevailed.

The huge field of troops greatly impressed the Prince of Wales. The march-past, he noted in his diary, 'considering they were Militia with very little training was most creditable, the horses excellent.' For publication, at least the British visitors were more enthusiastically impressed. Grey triumphantly telegraphed Lord Roberts's opinion of the review to the king along with the old soldier's concluding judgment: 'Canada appears to me to be dealing adequately with the problems affecting her militia and with care and improved organization to be building up a very useful force.'[20]

Present Arms!

There was, however, another perspective on military matters and another military agenda. Seen from the point of view of a modern military strategist, all of this marching on the Plains of Abraham amounted to little more than fighting the last war. The future lay elsewhere, or so it was thought. In this instance it was to be found in the St Lawrence River, in the form of the great looming menace of the dreadnought, the newest of which, the *Indomitable*, was kept plainly in view. The British Admiralty sought to impress the colonials with the might and majesty of the navy by putting a parade of the latest military hardware on water. It hoped that by doing so it might kindle a greater sense of local ownership in the imperial navy and a shared vision of the urgency of maintaining the strategic two-to-one ratio of naval superiority over any potential enemy.

At that very moment an aggressive German naval construction program was creating a political and financial crisis in Great Britain. Technological change had suddenly rendered obsolete most of Britain's huge fleet, and political ambition turned that into a new arms race. Advances in metallurgy, ballistics, power and propulsion systems had created a new weapon, the battleship or dreadnought, essentially a vast floating gun platform. Now the issue was not the size of the fleet, but rather its composition. Whoever had the most battleships held the keys to Europe. For maximum effect, a fleet had to be concentrated in home waters rather than scattered across the globe. The Admiralty calculated that to maintain strategic supremacy Britain would have to build at least eight dreadnoughts a year. The formidable cost of such a program had already rocked Campbell-Bannerman's Liberal government and was in the process of tearing apart that of his successor, Herbert Asquith. As the British agonized over the precise number of capital ships that must be built, it became clear that the cost of any policy would be staggering.[21]

In some circles it was thought that the Empire might be brought to bear to redress the growing strategic imbalance in Europe by making direct financial contributions to the imperial navy. The matter had come up at the 1902 Imperial Conference. Grey had been sent out to Canada in 1904 with instructions to keep naval policy issues to the fore. As he explained to the new colonial secretary in 1906, Grey set about to 'water a plant of promising but tender growth,' by encouraging whenever possible 'the self-respecting desire to contribute to the fleet, which exists

I am glad to believe in many quarters.'[22] The tumultuous events that wracked political life at home since his appointment served only to re-emphasize the importance of educating Canadians to their naval responsibilities.

But in life nothing is simple. Rapidly changing technology, in this case the torpedo, also validated smaller, speedier vessels and by implication local navies. Seen in this light, colonies might be able to add to the strategic balance with such ships, weapons, trained sailors, and local docking facilities. This was the position of the First Sea Lord Sir John Fisher's principal opponent, Lord Charles William Beresford. In this case, Canadians should be chivvied along towards building a modern navy of their own. British policy had not yet settled on this issue. One way or the other, either by the Australian model of a mobile local navy readily integrated into imperial command in time of war, or the New Zealand model of direct contributions to British home defence, the colonies would henceforth be expected to play a much greater role. It was, nevertheless, a sideshow. Fisher concentrated mainly upon the daunting task, which seemed to produce more enemies than friends, of scrapping as many obsolete vessels as quickly as possible, rapidly restructuring command, improving gunnery training, and rebuilding the British navy around battleships – the key to which was finding political support to sustain a mind-boggling program of constructing eight dreadnought-class ships a year.

The Canadian government had yet to settle its mind on naval policy, in part because the issue had not yet been forced upon it. The looming naval crisis had been discussed at the 1902 and 1907 Imperial Conferences.[23] Contributions to the navy had been asked for; Laurier politely refused and there the matter rested. Canada preferred not to hear about potentially divisive and expensive defence-related problems. Canadian policy on naval matters, to the extent that it had one, leaned towards self-defence at the minimum possible cost. Laurier seriously suggested that Canada contributed to imperial naval defence by building the Canadian Pacific Railway which created closer contact with the Pacific. Recently Canada had inherited Britain's old naval establishments at Halifax and Esquimault, but had done nothing with them. The Department of Marine and Fisheries operated a number of icebreakers to assist shipping and several light armoured vessels for fisheries patrol duties. A larger vessel, HMS *Canada*, had recently been delivered. While some colonial governments seemed receptive to the idea of direct contributions to the imperial navy, Canada conspicuously was not among them. But on the other hand, Canada did not seem much interested in building a navy of its own.[24]

A hostile critic could be forgiven for believing Canada wanted a free ride, in the form of protection from the British navy for which it was not prepared to pay. Seen from the Canadian government's perspective, either the United States remained an ally of Great Britain and therefore a friend and protector of Canada under the Monroe Doctrine – in which case Canada lived in a fireproof house – or in the event of Britain and the United States becoming enemies, the situation was hopeless and the fire insurance of an expensive navy would be useless. Under the circumstances, in naval as well as army matters, doing the bare minimum had much merit: maintenance of armed forces on a modest scale kept Canada out of imperial entanglements and kept defence costs down so that money might be spent on other priorities.

Though the ships of the Atlantic Fleet from time to time made stops at Quebec – always a popular spectacle – the appearance of eight huge ships, including the navy's newest and fastest vessel, did not happen by chance. The British government and the Admiralty had their own reasons for wanting to put on a good show at Canada's tercentennial celebration. Seen from the hawkish big-ship admirals' point of view, a colonial self-defence naval force would add nothing to the strategic balance. Britain needed capital ships in home waters. For naval policy, 1908 was a crucial moment. The British government and the Admiralty anticipated having to approach the colonial governments for direct contributions to the imperial navy in either ships and money or an aggressive local naval defence program. The question was about to be put; positions had not yet been taken. This, then, was the optimum moment for influence. A visit by the fleet was a tangible way of inspiring greater Canadian awareness of the naval problem. On the river, therefore, the British were doing their utmost to impress the Canadians.[25]

In March of 1908 the Admiralty ordered a squadron of the Atlantic Fleet to make preparations to sail to Quebec for the July festivities. A second contingent, detached from the Channel Fleet and bearing the Prince of Wales from England, would rendevous with these ships at Quebec. Initially the prince was to be conveyed to Canada aboard the cruiser *Duke of Edinburgh*. However, when the *Indomitable*, one of the first

Panoramic photograph of the fleet assembled at the Quebec tercentenary diminishes the size of the ships.

ships to be completed under Admiral Fisher's accelerated construction program, became available for sea trials later that spring, the Admiralty seized the opportunity to show off its newest dreadnought to the colonial audience.[26]

Impressing folk came at a price. Ships alone would not do. The Treasury had to approve funds for 'suitable entertainments.' The Admiralty barge had to be readied and shipped over for the dignified ferrying of the Prince of Wales and the admirals to and from shore. Fireworks had to be bought specially for the occasion, and ceremonial rockets requisitioned from naval stores; the latter alone cost £6,000. Carpets for staterooms, awnings for the decks, tables, chairs, linen, crystal, and china for formal dinners had to be found. Live cattle were hoisted aboard to be slaughtered to supply fresh meat to the prince and his guests. The possibility of an international regatta required the services of fast cutters and gigs. Massive quantities of coal had to be ordered to be ready to hand at Quebec to replenish the fleet.[27] It added up.

The British navy could best be seen by comparison with other navies. Thus the Admiralty's desire to show off fitted neatly into Grey's determination to make the tercentenary an international event. France had been invited out of necessity, the United States out of neighbourliness. In addition to deputations of politicians, both then should be invited to

send a naval contingent as well. Inevitably the ships would not be as large, modern, or as numerous as their British counterparts. The Foreign Office issued the formal invitations; the Admiralty handled the delicate business of protocol and coordinating the movement of ships from three navies in narrow waters. (Would a French admiral accept orders from a British vice-admiral? Who would take precedence on formal occasions?) The French navy offered to send two cruisers; the request to the Americans was for 'a warship,' which was readily accepted.[28] Thus, the naval representation at Quebec (eight British warships, two French, and one American) more or less reproduced in actuality the ideal of British policy of a two-to-one superiority over its potential rivals.

The *Indomitable* steamed serenely into position below the Citadel at 2:30 p.m., right on time, on 22 July. It had been a rough crossing; she had been badly knocked about in a North Atlantic gale. The discomfort visited upon most of the passengers and crew by the pitching and pounding were compounded by further misfortune: the *Indomitable* leaked. When the bow plunged into massive waves and seas raged over the decks, water flooded into the gangways. Everyone got drenched *in* their cabins. A wobbly, nauseous British deputation disembarked at Quebec. Being a sailor by profession, the prince claimed that he did not get seasick. It nevertheless took several days for even the prince's appetite to recover. Notwithstanding the miserable passage and the soaking, the prince nevertheless loved the new ship and he took a great interest in its operation.[29]

The ships created a sensation as they assembled in the harbour. When they were all present they stretched for several miles in their anchorages in midstream. The 'foreign vessels,' the *Léon Gambetta, Admiral Aude,* and the USS *New Hampshire,* were grouped directly opposite Lévis and the commercial districts of Quebec, but well away from the docks so as not to interfere with regular shipping. The British warships formed up in pairs upstream: the *Arrogant* and *Venus,* the *Duncan* and *Russell,* and the *Exmouth* and *Albermarle.* The mighty *Indomitable,* flanked by the *Minotaur,* had pride of place opposite the Citadel. This remarkable assembly drew vast crowds. The thunder of the guns as the ships saluted arrivals and departures startled residents and provided a constant reminder of the presence of the navy, even to those far from the scene. The press and casual visitors were not welcome aboard. But otherwise, everything possible was done to make the visit of the British fleet friendly, not threatening, and to use the spectacle to educate the uninitiated Canadian population in naval affairs. Officers were under orders to provide any Canadian authorities who might be interested with instruction on naval matters. To encourage hospitality, the officers were relieved by the Treasury of the obligation to finance shipboard entertainments themselves.

However, the untrained eye could not easily grasp the message of British naval mastery. The French cleverly despatched a vessel of unusual design, with two funnels forward and two aft. The USS *New Hampshire,* gleaming in white in the shimmering midsummer heat, looked extremely handsome. But the general effect was overpowering. As the ships assembled in port onlookers gasped at the might on display. The press groped for metaphors: 'monarchs of the ocean,' 'powers of the deep,' 'death-dealing, damnable machines.' The limitations of photography as a medium scarcely conveyed the overpowering impact of the flotilla on spectators. Panoramic photographs spread the ships out in a long, thin line, only those directly in front of the camera showed their massive bulk to good effect. And, by chance, the focus fell on the French warship. Photographs of individual ships, however striking and awe-inspiring they might be, failed to convey a sense of the mass of warships assembled. Artists filled the gap with sketches of the impossible scenario of all twelve ships steaming abreast in the narrow channel past the Citadel, an event, which had it occurred, would have resulted in a spectacular shipwreck!

A drawing by William Whittington captures the massed power of the fleet.

Even though the Prince of Wales took up residence at the Citadel, much of his entertaining took place aboard ship. An ardent proponent of a big navy himself, the prince kept the focus on the fleet. On Saturday, 25 July, under brilliant sunny skies, a grand naval review took place on the St Lawrence, the seafaring equivalent of the military review on the Plains of Abraham the day before. It opened with an ear-shattering explosion of gunnery that sent every dog in the city scurrying for cover. The prince greatly enjoyed the 'fine sight' of the fleet in perfect weather. 'At 10:30 I embarked with [the] Governor General & party from here at King's Wharf, (in frock coat and epaulettes),' the prince noted in his diary, 'and went on bd Arrogant, Capt. Huddleston, all ships saluting as the standard was broken. We got under weigh & steamed twice down the lines of fleet, each ship cheering as we passed, beautiful sight.'[30] As the *Arrogant* sailed past each gallantly decorated warship, bands playing the national anthem, and the sailors lining the rail gave him a lusty cheer. He returned their salute with a jaunty wave of his plumed admiral's cocked hat. Present, but not much noticed in this formidable company, was Canada's navy, almost all of it: the icebreaker *Frontenac* (ferrying the press) and the tiny unarmed fisheries protection vessel, HMS *Canada*. Another point deftly made.

Ethel Chadwick and Lola Powell were also there bobbing along in the prince's wake, guests aboard the yacht of a rich American visitor. When the prince came into view, the Americans played 'God Save the King' across the waters on their portable gramophone. Ethel allowed as how the occasion had been 'very inspiring,' but on the whole she was more taken with the fine spread of turkey, ham and salad decorated with Union Jacks they munched as afterwards they sailed on up the St Lawrence. The prince was deeply moved and immediately signalled his satisfaction to Vice-Admiral Curzon-Howe, the officer commanding: 'I desire to express my entire satisfaction with the appearance and discipline of the Atlantic Fleet and I am much pleased to hear from you that the conduct of the men has always been a credit to the splendid service to which I am proud to belong.'[31]

Once the ships arrived, the French-language press, *L'Événement* and *Le Soleil*, tended to ignore them, although events aboard the *Léon Gambetta* were fully reported. Having the French ships present also served the useful purpose of giving French Canada a non-British angle on a navy. The ships usefully drew attention to the recent Anglo-French entente, as did the convivial mingling of French and British sailors in the streets. The English-language papers, *The Chronicle* and the *Telegraph*, were on the whole more attentive to the military aspects of the tercentennial. Surprisingly, the metropolitan newspapers, especially the Montreal *Gazette* and the Toronto *Telegram*, appeared fascinated by the warships. Readers in those distant places received much more information and more vivid writing about the fleet than did residents of Quebec who could see the spectacle with their own eyes.[32]

Gazing at the ships in harbour as they manoeuvred, took on coal, and exchanged signal traffic became a popular pastime. But the fleet actively commanded attention and contributed to the festive atmosphere as well. Ships' guns punctuated public events. They performed the distant audio-effect of bombardment in 1759 for the last scene of the pageants. Music from the bands drifted across the water. Small craft scurried about giving visitors closer looks at the monstrous vessels. Sailing and rowing competitions between the crews attracted throngs of spectators. And the simulated torpedo-boat attack caused a sensation. Not only did it draw four exclamation points in Clare Denison's diary, but the prince himself called it 'magnificent.'

The fleet could be seen to even greater effect at night. In the darkness each ship was outlined in electric lights. The *Indomitable* pleased the crowd with a giant illuminated replica of three plumes from the Prince of Wales's heraldic device suspended in its rigging that bore more than a passing resemblance to a fleur-de-lis. The *Minotaur* countered with the outline of a bull. In the darkness, signal lamps winked messages. Powerful searchlights pierced the sky and cast a ghostly light over the city. Fireworks from the shore were answered by the ships. The sweet smell of coal smoke and gunpowder scented the evening air. The rockets' red glare silhouetted the superstructures in a scarlet flashes; bombs burst in golden showers. Together these missiles seemed to simulate a fierce overhead battle until, after a climax of exploding colour, darkness swallowed up the ships once more, leaving only the delicate tracery of lights.

The fleet was one great free entertainment for the whole population. And there was more to do than simply look at it; it was an interactive amusement. On the streets, the high spirited sailors of all three nations did the things that sailors always do. Providentially, they could upon occasion be seen visibly playing out the intent of the entente cordiale by fraternizing with each other.

The naval fireworks display.

The attraction of the fleet also crossed gender lines. After the naval officers finished paying courtesy visits to each other, they turned to entertaining local dignitaries and being entertained on shore by the locals. The ships were vast floating ballrooms. Dances on the deck in the afternoon, then in the evening under the stars. Teas in the afternoon, coveted invitations to manly dinners in the officers' wardrooms. Both Lola Powell and Ethel Chadwick were much in demand at these occasions. Following an afternoon dance aboard the American flagship, Ethel made a hasty note in her diary about 'James, a Virginian, who says he saw me in the pageant,' and observed 'all the important Canadians were aboard.' A few days later Ethel toured the *Indomitable*. She was in truth more impressed by the dance aboard the *Minotaur* later in the day. She first danced with an American flag lieutenant on the deck in her yellow silk dress – an exception to her general view that the American sailors were detestable – and then became quite smitten by Mr Money, a lieutenant aboard the *Minotaur*, who took her to his cabin to show her 'some photos & silhouette portraits he had made.' Dallying too long, Ethel noticed 'a stillness seemed to fall over the ship & I rushed up to find our party all going.'

Ethel's pageant duties kept her away from the dance aboard the *Léon Gambetta*, but Clare Denison was there, chaperoned by her mother. The Denisons, who were unusually well connected with the British navy – Colonel Denison's brother John being a now-retired rear admiral – were frequent guests on the ships. They dined with Sir John Jellicoe on the *Albermarle* on 17 July. Clare considered Jellicoe's flag lieutenant, Buxton, 'remarkably handsome.' On the 20th the Denisons took tea on the *Russell*, where Sub-Lieutenant Oliphant gave Clare a cap tally from his ship. On the 24th she danced with Oliphant aboard the *New Hampshire*. After the naval regatta on the 27th she once again danced the afternoon away with Oliphant aboard the *Léon Gambetta*. On the 21st the lieutenant-governor of Quebec answered with a ball for the fleet at which Clare had her dance card completely filled up. Ethel and Lola, needless to say, enjoyed themselves, surrounded by three navies, but things were slow starting: 'At first it did not look as if we were going to have a good time, there were heaps of sailors but no one to introduce them, but in the end it was lovely.' Lola took things in hand. Before long Ethel, too, had a long list of dancing partners. Social activities, in particular dancing, focused attention on the navy. The prince gave his farewell dinner and his last night at Quebec al fresco under the guns on the quarterdeck of the *Exmouth*. As a parting gesture and to ensure that the navy not be forgotten in the winding down of the festivities, he sent marconigrams of thanks to his hosts.[33]

And when the fleet weighed anchor silently in the dead of night, it left a void. Ethel awoke at 3:00 a.m. thinking she heard noise from the river although a reporter present wrote that 'not a sound heralded the movements of the British fleet.' 'Glory Is Departed,' ran the headline in the Montreal *Gazette*. Quebeckers were startled to look out on the river in the morning to see only the two French ships.

From his cabin in the mid-Atlantic, Vice-Admiral Curzon-Howe could take some satisfaction in a job well done. The fleet had put on a good show. The men had, on the whole, behaved well on shore leave. There had been only one minor collision between the vessels and the fleet put to sea with only thirty-nine desertions. While British superiority in all things had been demonstrated – including the racing competitions –

Curzon-Howe could not suppress a complaint that the French seemed to have better underwater sounding equipment for running in fog. So, for that matter did the Cunard liners. Such instruments would have come in handy as he fought his way through thick smoke from forest fires and fog at the mouth of the St Lawrence.[34]

On the gentle cruise down the St Lawrence ('perfectly heavenly day, not a breath of wind, dead calm, nice tempr about 68° very pleasant change from the heat of yesterday') the prince brought his diary up to date, wrote a long letter to his princess, napped, walked about the deck, and had long talks with his advisors about the effect of the tercentenary. Once through the Straits of Belle Isle, as the *Indomitable* gingerly picked its way through a field of monstrous icebergs gleaming white, green and blue in the sun, the prince took great interest in the preparations for the ship's high speed trials. Curiosity took him deep into the ship: 'I went down to the engine room & into the stokeholds,' he reported – an excursion he found 'dirty & disagreeable' – but circumstances would soon bring him back.[35]

Let us leave him there, sweating and shielding his eyes in the hot belly of his beast, for a brief reflection on these respective military performances. People *were* impressed by the parades, that is clear. But was anybody fooled? Did the 'performance' of the military, the Canadian militia, and the British navy, change anyone's mind about imperial defence? That is a more difficult question, but the answer must surely be no, or at least very little. Pith helmets and artful staging made the Canadian militia look good and the British went away duly impressed by the quality of their drill – at least so they said. But a rip-roaring show on a Friday afternoon did nothing to alter the broader strategic situation. Despite it all, Canada remained defenceless. The march through the streets, by popular demand, probably did much to assuage tender feelings in French Quebec on militia concerns, but it seems unlikely a parade would influence public opinion on participation in British colonial wars.

Earl Grey characteristically followed up the visit of the fleet with a concerted campaign of charm and suasion directed towards L.P. Brodeur, the minister of marine and fisheries. He hoped to convert the occasion to some form of action by the Canadian government, one way or the other. Even the German naval scare in 1909 only produced a rather tepid bipartisan resolution from the House of Commons on 9 March that recognized 'the duty of Canada, as the country increased in numbers and wealth, to assume in a larger measure the responsibilities of national defence ... in co-operation with and close relation to the Imperial Navy.'[36] As events were subsequently to reveal, nothing had shaken conviction in French Canada that a naval build-up led inevitably to subservient service in Britain's imperial wars.

In both instances there were strict limits to the power of public relations. Spit and polish went only so far. The fleet could be a popular attraction, even carry away broken hearts, without converting minds.

10. OF CABBAGES AND KINGS

Reflections

After a quick visit to the hairdresser on the morning of Monday, 27 July, Ethel Chadwick went down to the wharf to be taken out for a tour of the *Indomitable*. She couldn't stay for tea because, as she explained, she had to hurry back and dress for the pageant. Nevertheless, she wanted to take up the invitation of one of the officers she had met to see the mighty ship – and, being Ethel, the officer. The venerable author of popular Quebec stories, Sir James Le Moine, escorted her. As they stood waiting on the pier, a passing group of French sailors gallantly ferried them out to the British ship.

Once aboard, charming sailors competed to escort her. In the company of a certain Mr Warre, Ethel clambered all over the ship and even peaked into the Prince of Wales's quarters! As she tiptoed about these private rooms, Ethel did a surprising thing. She went straight to his mirror and stared into it. She squirmed with delight as she told her diary before bed: 'we were able to look into the mirror *George* [her emphasis] looks in to tinten his *beautiful* face.'

A more apt metaphor for the perfect melding of identities between the crown and its people would be difficult to find. She called the prince by his first name. She thought him gorgeous. She wanted to dissolve her self in his image through the looking-glass. This kind of adulation did not just happen; it was consciously cultivated and then constantly fed. It did not come naturally for members of the royal family

Ethel Chadwick, *c.* 1908.

Ethel Chadwick's best friend, Lola Powell, vamping in the photographer Topley's studio as Elinor Glyn's woman on a tiger skin sometime shortly after 1908.

to expose themselves in public and have their private rooms pried into. Apart from the danger – and there was some – one had to get used to being a spectacle. That had to be taught and willingly learned. During this period, the modern British monarchy turned deference into affection and popular indifference to intense mass loyalty. A people came to see themselves in their king. Carefully staged events like the tercentenary contributed greatly to the transformation of the monarchy into an object of popular mass idolotry.

But there was another aspect of the symbolism of that trip to the *Indomitable* that deserves attention. An English Canadian in the company of a French Canadian (albeit the most English of them) visits a British warship. Here was Earl Grey's fantasy of race fusion within the Empire being realized. Canadians were learning to love their future monarch; they were also, perhaps for the first time, getting to know each other across vast distances. Not all Canadians, of course. But the ties between members of what might be called a national class of political, literary, business, social, and professional Canadians were being gently stretched across geographical, linguistic, and religious chasms. A king was being made; so, too, it was hoped by some and feared by others, was a people.

A Social Body

In the fall of 1907 Earl Grey went to Toronto to present an honour to a member of the Ontario cabinet, Colonel J.S. Hendrie. He returned to Ottawa somewhat shaken by the experience, as he later reported to the prime minister. Grey had naturally turned conversation towards plans for the upcoming Quebec tercentenary. He asked Hendrie if Premier Whitney's earlier promise of $100,000 still stood, fully expecting an enthusiastic answer in the affirmative. To the governor general's surprise and disappointment, Hendrie expressed grave doubts. A grant of that size for Quebec would not be very popular with the taxpayers of Ontario or the Conservative members of the Assembly, Hendrie replied: 'Remember, not 15 or perhaps 10% of our members have ever been to Quebec! & are very Orange. Before such a proposal can be made,' he added, 'a good deal of education will be required.' Hendrie was not alone. The lieutenant-governor poured cold water on the scheme a few weeks later for essentially the same reasons. Grey also discovered to his horror that certain narrow-minded capitalists of Montreal and Ontario begrudged every cent that left Montreal and Ontario 'to feed the parochial necessities of Quebec.'[1]

Grey was astounded not only by the bigotry of these Ontario public men, but also by their openly confessed ignorance of Quebec. Canadians, he was discovering, had very little direct personal experience with other parts of their country beyond their own regional bailiwicks. They did not travel much; they had never met many people from outside their region. Their knowledge of other parts of the country came mainly from the newspapers, political parties, and religious bodies – agencies renowned more for fanning flames of intolerance and emphasizing differences than promoting harmony and understanding.

As the tercentenary approached, editorials, speeches, and sermons in support began to appear, especially in English. Grey sent an otherwise exemplary sermon by a Presbyterian minister from Montreal to Sir Arthur Bigge, the prince's private secretary, first to show the beneficial effects the tercentenary seemed to be engendering, and secondly the ease with which good intentions could turn suddenly sour in this poisonous atmosphere. He urged Bigge to read the sermon, a glowing tribute to the achievements of the French pioneers in Canada, to appreciate how careful the prince would have to be to avoid inadvertently insulting someone. According to Grey, 'the Archbishop of Montreal told me that all the good done by Dr. Barclay's most appreciative reference to the achievements of the RC Church had been undone by a single unnecessary sentence in which he said something about regarding the doctrine believed in by the RC Church as erroneous!' Canadians, it seemed, could not resist an opportunity to score points. They could not accept compliments without careful scrutiny. They could never forget past wrongs.

Thus when Grey wrote to the Prince of Wales explaining the purposes of the tercentenary, so that these might be incorporated into the prince's own public statements, he laid the primary emphasis upon what in our time would be called the national unity objectives. His first goal was 'to fuse the two races of the Dominion'; his second was 'to weld more closely the 9 provinces to the Dominion.' After that came strengthening ties to Britain and uniting the various parts of the Empire.[2] More pointedly, he explained to the Prince of Wales's speech writer: 'One of the chief advantages resulting from the Quebec tercentenary movement will be the quietus it will help to give to that miserable, narrow, selfish spirit of greedy unimaginative provincialism, which is the curse of the Empire in every portion of it, not excluding England.'

As Grey daily discovered the depths of religious intolerance and regional resentment that divided Canadians, he came to appreciate even more Sir Wilfrid Laurier's nation-making passion as well as his unerring tact in negotiating these dangerous counter-currents. Laurier's evasiveness frustrated him; the prime minister had grown tired and overcautious in office, and his administration seemed in the eyes of the country to be growing lazy. This the governor general readily conceded. Nonetheless, Grey recognized in Laurier a noble ideal he also burned to promote. Born French, Laurier had been educated in English and was perfectly at home in both cultures. He struggled against intolerance and suspicion at home in Quebec as well as in the other provinces. And Laurier, as a Canadian, had a profound respect for British political traditions and, so Grey believed, the moral purpose of the British Empire. In his own mind Grey imagined that his initiatives at Quebec might in the longer run serve to further the prime minister's own program of national unification and in so doing strengthen the connection of a united Canada to the Empire.

If there were obstacles to national unity in Ontario and English Montreal, there were also troublesome tendencies in Quebec. The Duke of Norfolk, because he was a Roman Catholic, would have an important influence on the religious side of things in Quebec. But as Grey thought about the question further, he began to understand why Laurier was more interested in getting the great South African leader, General Louis Botha, to come out for the celebration. Botha represented in some respects the Canadian ideal; a Boer leader who had come to honourable terms with the British Empire; a member of a linguistic minority who had achieved a leadership role in imperial affairs; and at home a man who had worked to diminish the postwar animosities that divided the white settlers in South Africa. Laurier knew him personally and had come to like him at various Imperial Conferences.[3] Such a man would, in the prime minister's eyes, be very useful in Quebec, a province, which if anything, identified more closely with the Boers than with the British. 'Laurier is most anxious to get Botha out here for the tercentenary,' Grey reported to the colonial secretary early in June 1908:

He thinks his presence here would help him towards the attainment of that

Race Fusion which has been the dream of his life. At the present moment there is an unfortunate little Nationaliste agitation for keeping Quebec an isolated unit in a backwater of its own outside the main currents of National Life – This mischievous agitation is being improperly encouraged by the cures who are tres ultramontanes. As the RC Church has nothing to gain but everything to lose in the Province of Quebec the attitude of the Nationaliste Ultramontane Cures is inconceivably silly. The Protestants of Canada led by the Orangemen of Ontario will not be slow to accept anything which may be interpreted as a challenge. The presence of Norfolk will be useful qua Church as is Botha, if he can be persuaded to come, qua the people.[4]

To the great regret of both Laurier and Grey, Botha could not come to Quebec on such short notice.

But how then do you go about making a people? In recent years historians from diverse ideological backgrounds have begun to explore the 'social construction' of nations.[5] Hegemony cannot be asserted; it must be negotiated between citizens and elites through the creation and manipulation of symbols. The instruments of nation-making are most notably flags, anthems, idols, monuments, and civic architecture. But these pieces of cloth, music, and stone must be given emotional life by shared perceptions of their meaning. The collective past, enshrined in histories, re-enacted in commemorations, memorials, and national days, gives meaning to the present and points towards a future. Loyalty to this broader community cuts across many other conflicting local identities. Though the predominant carriers and propagators of nationalism come from the burgeoning commercial and professional middle class, the identity of 'le peuple' transcends class. Citizenship involves a development of a sense of self in society, and of society in relation to the nation.

Identities are often best formed in opposition to other identities, and are frequently therefore forged in battle, or the sentimental equivalent of war, sports. In the British case, the French performed this adversarial role: Britishness and Frenchness were both defined in mutual antagonism. Under Disraeli's diversionary instigation, the supremacy over a vast globe-girdling empire became an integral element of national identity and pride.[6] 'Britishness' became bound up not only with the domestic social characteristics of a people in their homeland, but also with their historic mission to repel oppression from their shores and expect submission from others. This conception of the character of the nation extended from the concert hall to the music hall. Indeed, it was in the Edwardian music hall these beliefs were most warmly nurtured.[7]

Britain, it might be said, had been 'made' by the turn of the century, though of course the process was ongoing and allowances had to be made for Ireland. Canada had not yet been 'made,' as many domestic and foreign observers had sensed. In Canada, Grey perhaps unconsciously followed a program that would have been familiar to him from home. He, like Disraeli, was a romantic, a man of passions and grand gestures, who believed symbols and bold strokes made nations. A nation needed occasions in which people were drawn out of their narrow social circles, brought together to mingle, to discover other parts of the country first hand, and to break down those largely imaginary barriers that divided them.

He had already initiated a dialogue of sorts between the English and French elites in Montreal soon after his arrival.[8] A small step, to be sure, but one that had not yet been taken, in his view. The tercentenary was to be one of his Montreal style parties, but on a much grander, national scale. The meetings of learned and professional societies, formal and informal dinners, teas, garden parties, participation and observation, the honours, balls, and access to the royal personage were carefully designed to bridge the solitudes, mix the two cultural groups, and thereby help to create what might be called a national class.

Grey believed that the best way to distinguish this national class was with royal honours, peerages, knighthoods, and decorations. But nothing vexed Laurier more. 'Sir Wilfrid does not like the subject of honours,' Grey informed the colonial secretary. 'His recommendations are so frequently ignored & his amour propre wounded.' However, Grey placed the utmost importance on such symbolic matters. The three-cornered correspondence between the governor general and the prime minister on the one side, and the governor general and British officials in the Colonial Office and the Palace on the other, reveals the several different ways of thinking about the making of an honours list. Grey wanted the tercentenary to be the occasion for a dramatic bestowal of knighthoods and other honours on notable Canadians with a view to emphasizing the bi-national character of the country, and thereby linking both peoples more firmly to the crown and empire.[9] Laurier took a more narrowly functionalist approach. If honours must be given – and he could not prevent it – then they should be given to people like Edward Clouston, the president of the Bank of Montreal, who in his view had almost single-handedly saved the credit of the Dominion during the recent monetary crisis. Grey sought to make a nation with honours; Laurier wanted to repay debts.

The Palace would not give Grey the number of honours or the ranks he desired. Australia, he groused, managed to get many more decorations for less cause. Secondly, Laurier protested that his proposed list of honourees was biased too much towards French Canadians for his comfort. The lieutenant-governor of Quebec was thus stricken from the list.[10] The Palace refused honours for Clouston because it insisted the honours be given for notable contributions to the Champlain tercentenary itself.[11] It frustrated Grey that Laurier himself refused further royal distinction: 'Unlike a Frenchman he has a soul above Ribbons,' Grey confided to the colonial secretary, 'but I think as the Premier of Canada he must consent – there is no other way in which the Sovereign can honour Canada except by a peerage Laurier will not accept.'[12]

In the end, then, the list of honours settled upon was a compromise of sorts in which the faint echo of nation-making is somewhat diminished by the blare of other trumpets. The list represented only a portion of what Grey sought; the prime minister exercised veto power and did so to create a perception of balance. The recipients had to accept the honours proffered – it will be remembered that Colonel Denison declined his. The king insisted upon giving the highest honour to Grey himself for his energetic promotion of the celebration and imperial integration, and to Grey's aide-de-camp, John Hanbury-Williams. Grey received the Grand Cross of the Victorian Order and became a Privy Councillor; Hanbury-Williams a Knight Companion of the Victorian Order. Canadians, therefore received lesser ranks, hardly the message the governor general wished to convey. Grey's vanity here worked somewhat against his other purposes.

Grey's nation-making goals could be seen more clearly in the second rank of honours. Lomer Gouin and James P. Whitney, premiers respectively of Quebec and Ontario, were each made Knight Bachelor. French and English speakers, Catholic and Protestant, provincial politicians whose governments had contributed mightily to a national celebration – these in Grey's view were model members of the national class. Included in their number as a Knight Bachelor was George Garneau, the bilingual

businessman, engineer, mayor of Quebec, and champion of the tercentenary – another model of the new citizen. Further down the ranks, but
similarly balanced as to region, language, and occupation were to be
found a general, a Montreal industrialist, a Toronto banker, a Quebec
patriotic orator, and a federal public servant.[13] From such stuff a social
body might be fashioned for the political skeleton of the country.

On the whole, the British placed more stock in honours and titles than
did Canadians. Laurier's ambivalence and Denison's refusal reflect a
profound sense of unease about distinctions of 'quality' in a democratic,
North American culture. The French-language and English-language
newspapers reflected some pride and satisfaction in these honours – they
were front page news in both[14] – but the nationalist press made jokes
about the local nobs being inducted into 'the sirerie.' This system of
national honours had its limitations as a binding force. Purged of these
associations in later years, would such a system be any more powerful?

The attempt to develop a new sense of Canadian citizenship extended
beyond the somewhat flawed instrument of conferring titles. The joining
and making of the national class was attempted most obviously by invitations to the tercentenary's receptions, dinners, and dances. In these
meetings and social gatherings, the new national class of people from the
military, professional, learned, business, and political world would get to
know one another better. This class, valuing the things they had in
common as much as the particularism that set them apart, would transcend regional antagonisms born of prejudice and thereby lead in the
creation of an imagined community. A political creation, the country,
might thereby creep towards social cohesion, or simply a nation.

When Grey thought about practical models of this new citizenry, he
thought naturally of people like himself and the prime minister. Worldly,
cultured men, more or less at ease in two cultures – though Grey betrayed deep-rooted beliefs in the moral and political if not cultural
superiority of one over the other. But there were others. Doughty would
have come to mind: assiduous to a fault, and a multi-talented man of
letters. Of English background, he had functioned in both languages as a
public servant in Quebec before being appointed Dominion archivist.
The list would go on; old Thomas Chapais, of course, in Quebec City, and
the newly knighted Garneau. Edmund Walker seemed a fellow spirit, as
did George Wrong the historian in Toronto. Colonel Denison was both
well-read and well-connected, wasted of course in his police magistracy,

but an excellent companion, a man of many parts, and a resolute champion of the Empire. What these men had in common was a breadth of view, some learning, a sense of Canada's place in the wider world, and familiarity with Quebec.

It could be said that the Royal Society represented something approximating the ideal of a national class. In the mind of its fellows the society consisted of distinguished men of letters, above the current political fray, concerned with higher things, dedicated to the advancement of science, knowledge, culture, and civilization. Drawn from across the country, from the churches, professions, universities, and the arts, they might be men of mixed social origins but they shared values and achievements. Above all, it was a confraternity of merit yearning to exert its intellectual influence in a wider public sphere. This society, after all, had championed the cause of historic battlefields preservation.[15] From the nation-making perspective, it was exemplary too in its recognition of English and French cultural achievements; the two cultures were indeed institutionalized in two academies. The Royal Society agreed to hold a special meeting of its fellowship on the occasion of the tercentenary. This brought the sanction of the Canadian scientific and literary community to the commemoration of Champlain and dedication of the battlefields. In return, the tercentenary directed attention towards the Royal Society as a model national body. The society played its part by inducting an equal number of French-speaking and English-speaking fellows at its convocation, and honouring Champlain in learned papers in both languages.[16]

If the working class made itself on the shop floors, on strike, in struggles with bosses, on baseball diamonds, in chapels and taverns, this new masculine national class was consolidated in the ritual of formal dinners. Here uniforms, clothing, manners, appropriate speech, acknowledgment of hierarchy, and access to the guest of honour served to bond the celebrants together. Amidst a torment of knives, forks, and etiquette, and under a deluge of verbose toasts, men bonded into distinct societies. Over menus of a dizzying number of courses but some care with regard to temperance, they discoursed on important questions of the day with what they considered commendable good judgment. They congratulated each other on their sound views. They looked out from their smoky bastions with a mighty sense of public purpose and they grumbled confidentially at the seditious and backward forces that beset them, with wary glances and due regard to the company present.

The desire to make a mutually respectful national community at the Quebec tercentenary was not fully reflected in the make-up of the guest lists to the numerous formal dinners. Certainly efforts were made to balance the English and French representation. But other guests had also to be entertained, such as the prince, and the representatives of France and the United States, the mayors of Brouages and St Malo, the descendants of Wolfe, Murray, Montcalm, and Lévis, and the extensive British and foreign military contingent. Because the tercentenary attracted a large sample of lieutenant-governors, judges, premiers, prominent federal and provincial politicians, mayors of the major cities, high-ranking officers in the militia, and leading Canadian bankers, industrialists, railway managers, and businessmen, French-Canadian guests were always greatly outnumbered by the English-Canadian, imperial, and foreign deputations.

Taking five dinners for which the guest lists were printed as a sample, it is possible to calculate rough percentages of the three groups of invitees – those from abroad, English Canadians, and French Canadians[17]:

Event	Date	Abroad (%)	Eng Can (%)	Fr Can (%)
Lord Roberts's dinner	July 20	8	75	17
Grey's dinner for the prince	July 23	35	50	15
Mayor's luncheon	July 24	45	40	15
British Empire dinner	July 25	20	62	18
Earl Grey's dinner	July 27	35	45	20

The French-Canadian contingent never exceeded 20 per cent of the guests invited from all other groups combined. The overall effect, then, could only have been to overwhelm the local French-speaking community. British and imperial representatives, princes, aristocrats, knights, admirals, and generals were not only more numerous, they were clearly seen to be 'more important.' At no point did French-speaking guests exceed 30 per cent of the Canadian invitees, their proportion in the country at large. Thus, however gratified some of the French Canadians would have felt at being included in this illustrious company, they would most certainly have come away with the sense of having been at a largely English-speaking, imperial affair. They were a minority even at home. Native people, so prominent in the pageants, processions, and in their Plains of Abraham encampments, were not invited at all. Citizenship did not extend to them. The intentions of creating a pan-Canadian social body, then, were not necessarily realized in the performance. Or rather, the social bias of that citizenship was reflected in the inclusions and exclusions.

The state dinners, however, suffered from another major deficiency: they represented only half of the nation. No women were present, just as they were then absent from the body politic. Nevertheless, even in the bifurcated world of separate spheres, there remained one domain in which society made and reproduced itself and over which women ruled – the ballroom.

Dance and drill have much in common, as W.H. McNeil, the great historian of western civilization, has so elegantly pointed out.[18] Coordinated mass movement to a beat or rhythm creates in both situations a powerful sense of collective cohesion. The analogy holds best, of course, for the formal stately dances with set steps of an earlier era. The self gets absorbed in the camaraderie of the movement in unison of the platoon. In dance there are several levels of surrender: first to the rhythm; then to the choreography of the group, and finally to a swirling partner. Participants float over space in or on each others' arms, moving together in time. If drill made armies, dancing made society, and together they made nations.

Dance and drill share much more than this psychological state of suspended individualism and collective emotional bonding. They share as well an obvious hierarchy, command structure, uniforms, and in many instances the same musicians. Two military bands provided the music, for example, at the tercentenary ball. Formal dance is not unlike a march, although there are important differences. In the case of the tercentenary, save for one significant exception, women ruled the ballroom. They organized it beforehand; on the evening they were the stars. They ruled not by fiat or command, but by their beauty. Men were important accessories; it was important that they look smart in their formal attire or dress uniforms. But it was the occasion at which each woman strove to be her most beautiful, to be remarked upon, to have her dance card filled – to be the belle of the ball. That is why Charlebois's cartoon of the ball was so wicked; it struck at anxieties and vulnerable vanities. Compare his satire with the *Commemorative History*'s décolleté beauties. The Canadian women imagined themselves to be fashionable and beautiful. In Charlebois's vignette the ball is peopled by fat or hatchet-faced women and stolid, plain men in dinner jackets. The prince,

An artist's rendering of the state ball in the legislature.

LE GRAND BAL

LE PRINCE.—Vous avez du bien beau monde à Québec... en vérité.

Charlebois's jaundiced view of the beauty on display at the state ball.

absorbed in conversation with a truly handsome woman, ignores the multitude. He can be overheard observing to the singular beauty something patently not the case: 'Oh my, you are all very fashionable here in Quebec.'

In some strait-laced Canadian circles, dance was directly associated with reproduction and was thus frowned upon if not banned. Other less literal-minded Canadians eagerly took the risks of moving together in time. At the upper reaches of the social structure dance did, however, play an integral functional role. Young women came out at formal dances. Girls became women and passed from the arms of their fathers into the embrace of suitable suitors in a rhythmic, choreographed, dance.

From the very small sample of Ethel Chadwick and Clare Denison, however, the dancing served not to introduce them to French-Canadian men, but rather English naval officers such as Sub-Lieutenant Oliphant and Mr Warre. It seems quite likely that the powerful military and imperial presence undermined the agenda of social integration across national lines and generations. It is more likely that the French and the English guests kept their own company, the young people included, or that the young women were distracted by the British, French, and American officers.

The balls, garden parties, teas, and soirées at the Quebec tercentenary were intended to forge more lasting ties than the homo-sociability of the state dinner, the smoking room, and the officers' mess. Here young men and women might establish unions that would give birth to a new generation. Children of the next national class might thereby be imagined if not conceived. At dances another generation formed up, in couples, squares, and circles, held together by melody and steps. In the gaiety, property and status were affirmed and, if possible, enhanced. For Clare Denison, the tercentenary, in particular coming out into society before the Prince of Wales, surrounded by handsome sailors and the haute monde of Canada, was without question one of the most exciting moments of her life.

At these balls the unbalanced social account set by the male dinners was, to a certain degree, rectified. In these affairs, with their huge guest lists, local society predominated, and as a result the French-Canadian presence could be more strongly felt. The oversubscription of the state ball at the legislature, an affair fully under local control, perhaps indicates compensation for exclusion from other events.

A national spirit must be expressed in music. The tercentenary also presented Canada with a putative national anthem. For, as the two historic armies marched back and forth across the Plains of Abraham before the crowded grandstand, the orchestra played 'God Save the King,' and then 'O Canada.' The melody was familiar, of course in French Canada, having been composed for a competition to create a patriotic song for the Saint-Jean-Baptiste Society by Calixa Lavallée in 1880. It had subsequently been frequently sung, with various words in French, at national fêtes in Quebec. It was much less familiar, though not unknown, in English Canada. The song was first performed outside of Quebec at Belleville, and then at the 1901 review of the troops on the Garrison Common at Toronto, with the Prince of Wales present on that occasion.

At Quebec in 1908, however, the song passed from being a patriotic hymn of French-Canadian nationalism, into being a proto-national anthem for all of Canada. Calixa Lavallée's stirring melody certainly fit the bill. There were, however, problems with the words, especially for a Protestant population. For example, a literal translation of 'Car ton bras sait porter l'épée, Il sait porter la croix!,' 'Amour sacrée du thrône et de l'autel,' and 'Et répétons comme nos pères, le cris vainquer: "Pour le Christ et le Roi!"' presented obvious difficulties. Judge Routhier, author of the French words, tried with 'O Canada! Our Father's Land of Old,' in 1906. T.B. Richardson revised his text for publication soon afterwards, and it was this version that was printed in the official program of the tercentenary. Another judge, Robert Stanley Weir, produced what became the standard and copyrighted version, significantly also in 1908. The later tangled history of Canada's national anthem need not concern us here. What is important is that 'O Canada' emerged as a musical symbol of Canadian nationhood at the Quebec tercentenary of 1908.[19] As the throng in the grandstand raised their discordant voices together in English and French to sing these two anthems, 'O Canada' and 'God Save the King,' the songs reminded them that if they could not fully agree on the nature of the former, perhaps they might jointly but separately share an allegiance to the latter, the monarchy.

Modern Monarchy

Freud's biographer, Ernest Jones, searching for an example of the irrational power of the monarchy over the masses even in a modern democratic society, recalled an incident from his early clinical training in Canada. An angry woman demanded to know by what right her husband had been confined to a lunatic asylum. A doctor, who knew the circumstances of the case intimately, answered not by giving her a rational explanation, as Jones remembered, but rather 'he made a histrionic gesture and declaimed "I do so in the name of the King."'[20] She apparently calmed down and resigned herself to her husband's involuntary committal. She did not take it as evidence of tyranny, as might have been the case in an earlier era, nor did she consider the response irrelevant, as might be the case now. She accepted the fact that the agents of the crown, acting at the behest of a benevolent father, were doing what he deemed best for the family.

The point here is that the king was known to have authority, and that his authority was unquestioningly accepted by someone in the far-off colonies who knew the king only by reputation. That reputation had to be established. The king too had to be made. It so happened that the king in question, George V, had figured as the centrepiece of the 1908 tercentenary as Prince of Wales.

The monarchy was not particularly popular in the nineteenth century. The young Victoria only barely snatched the institution from the jaws of terminal disgrace early in the century. Then her extended mourning following the death of Prince Albert did much to destroy the relationship that had gradually developed between the queen and her people. The stern old woman in the Palace, and the scandalous Prince of Wales galloping through the bedrooms and gaming salons of the aristocracy, served for a time to revive a nascent republican movement. In the memorable phrase of Philip Ziegler, 'Absentee Queen and libertine heir provided the matter for innumerable denuciations.' Only when she was persuaded to come out of seclusion – which she did only with the greatest misgivings – and present herself to her people at the end of the century, did the people warm to the monarchy and vice versa. At her Diamond Jubilee celebration in 1897 this 'dumpy figure in mourning black' received a tumultuous welcome as her carriage passed through the streets of London. 'No one ever, I believe, has met with such an ovation as was given to me,' she recorded afterwards in her diary, 'the crowds were quite indescribable, and their enthusiasm truly marvellous and deeply touching. The cheering was quite deafening, and every face seemed to be filled with real joy.' That last point is worth underscoring. Her people had come to love her, and seeing her brought profound pleasure to masses of them.

Her son, Prince Edward, recognized the importance of spectacle as an instrument for forging a stronger bond between the monarch and the people. His triumphant return to England with his Danish bride, Princess Alexandra, in 1863 had given him an early sensation of the potentialities of what Ernest Jones much later called 'this mystical identification of king and people.' He had tried unsuccessfully for many years to persuade his mother to take a carriage ride about London during her visits. Her people, he promised, 'would be overjoyed – beyond measure.' His concern ran deeper than just the popularity of the queen; her seclusion threatened the social order: 'We live in radical times and the more *the People see the Sovereign,* the better it is for the *People* and the *Country.*'[21]

Edward VII was by nature theatrical. Popular monarchy required style; not for him his mother's dark weeds. A proper king set the stylistic tone for his era through his choice of clothing, hair styles, manners, sports, entertainments, and enthusiasms. He believed that the monarch should not merely appear, his appearance had to be properly stage-managed. When he frequently ventured out into public, the hierarchical relationship between the crown and his people had to be fully reflected in the staging of the event. The monarch must be cast above but not beyond it all. Obviously, the king must be the focus; everything should lead up to and away from his presence. During the late Victorian and Edwardian era the British monarchy acquired some brilliant producers and directors, one of whom was the Duke of Norfolk, the Earl Marshall of England, who had staged Edward's coronation and later George's. A previously private and often bungled occasion, the coronation became the occasion of something akin to a national sacrament as the mystical bond between crown and people was renewed amidst great pomp and circumstance. Costumes, music, setting, supporting casts were all brought together in one blazing climax of popular adulation. Royal marriages and funerals were constructed with the same intent.[22]

This Prince of Wales – after 1910, George V – learned from his father, an excellent teacher. He would travel extensively. This would be his sixth visit to Canada, something he repeatedly reminded his audiences at Quebec. In 1905 he had toured India as his father had before. His biographer notes that it was during this triumphal tour of India that

George, too, came to believe 'that there existed some almost mystical association between the Sovereign and the common people.'[23] George V would take public appearance one step further than his father. With his popularity more or less secure, he could venture forth in less formal settings, and in particular, into working-class districts and workplace settings. Though not immune to glorious spectacle, he also sought out frequent, smaller opportunities to cultivate the link between the working class and the monarchy. Later, in wartime he sought out the company of the troops and of the veterans. He was determined to bring the monarchy closer to the people, and it was in that connection that he would much later use the new medium of the radio to talk directly to the people on his Christmas Day broadcasts. In time it was said that George V became a 'father' to his people. His own unblemished home life gave him the added dimension of moral authority. His death was an occasion for genuine grief.[24]

The Prince of Wales worked hard during his apprenticeship to learn and extend the principles of the modern monarchy. He did not always like what he had to do, and sometimes he balked. But he believed that by presenting himself at suitable public occasions, where he might see and be seen by masses, served both the people and the country. Thus when the governor general of Canada asked if the king and queen might be persuaded to come out to Canada to crown the tercentenary festivities, the Palace took the opportunity as an occasion for the further grooming of the future king. The prince did not particularly want to go; he preferred the company of his wife and family. But he did go when duty called. And for a time he confessed to being quite miserable and lonely. 'I miss you here,' he wrote to his wife from the Citadel, 'everything reminds me of you, & I really feel quite lost without you at the various functions & have nobody to walk with or stand beside now & I own I feel very homesick & wish you were here terribly.'[25]

Of course, the Prince of Wales had to do more than simply be present; he had to present himself in public. His family, the court officials, and the colonial secretary were concerned primarily with his safety in such circumstances. This was an era of assassinations. Britain too suffered its troubles, and royalty, as supreme symbols of the state, were obvious targets. Quebec, situated in the vicinity of large, expatriate Irish nationalist communities in Boston and New York, presented a clear security issue. Then there was the much less threatening issue of dissident French-

Canadian nationalists. And what of lurking anarchists, with no cause at all but disorder? As the colonial secretary handled the details of the royal visit, he stressed in his correspondence with Earl Grey the importance of vigilance. In a secret despatch, Lord Crewe warned Grey that British intelligence sources had information that the Clan-na-Gael faction posed a 'possible danger' to the prince. Grey assured Crewe with a Privy Council minute giving instructions to the head of the Dominion police, 'to use all diligence to avert any possible danger.' Beyond the troops on hand, extra police were brought in from Toronto to keep track of known troublemakers. Nothing could be done to prevent a mad suicide bomber, the governor general admitted, but he attempted to reassure the nervous British officials that 'every room at the Château Frontenac from which a rifle could be pointed at the Champlain platform will be in occupation of friends & under strictest surveillance in addition. In the Citadel he is as safe as on his battleship.'[26]

Presenting oneself in public in the colonies, especially such a fractious place as Canada, imposed considerable demands upon the prince. Grey, having persuaded the Palace to send out the popular heir to the throne, immediately set about tutoring him through the prince's private secretary on what to do to avoid missteps and to attract maximum favourable public attention. Canada was a minefield, as Edward VII well knew from his riotous 1860 tour during which his sympathetic response to the Catholic hierarchy in Quebec aroused the ire of the ever-vigilant Orangemen in Ontario. But beyond avoiding error, Grey demanded certain things of the prince – as he had of his father on the trip to India – to kindle affection in French-Canadian hearts. At several points the prince expressed reluctance, and had to be cajoled. Grey persisted. He was determined to stage-manage the royal tour to create a much more direct emotional bond between the French-Canadian people and the monarchy whether the prince liked it or not.

As a first step, the prince would have to speak French. Of course, the British upper classes all spoke French; it was not only the language of an aristocratic education, it remained the language of diplomacy. The new foreign secretary, Sir Edward Grey, was the first politician to occupy that post who could not speak French fluently.[27] When the prince was informed he would have to give public speeches in French at Quebec he demurred. Through his office he protested that 'he cannot do so well in French after 25 years of disuse.'[28] Grey nevertheless insisted and sought the support of Lord Elgin, a confidant of the prince, in his struggle: 'My Prime Minister attaches great importance to the use of French as well as English on the first day. I am aware of the objections to this course but it is customary in the king's speech at the opening of Parliament when the Governor General reads his speech in both languages. I hope His Royal Highness may agree to the arrangement.'[29] Local custom and the needs of state overrode the prince's private wishes. He was, as the colonial secretary confessed, 'not easy on such matters.' It took some work, but Sir Francis Hopwood, an intimate of the prince's circle who knew how to handle him, conspired to convince the reluctant prince that 'speaking in French is an agreeable pastime.' The prince would speak French.

What he said in either language had to be carefully vetted as well. After four years of sometimes painful experience, Grey instructed the prince's speech-writer on words and phrases to avoid in public. Do not under any circumstances use the word 'colonial,' he advised Arthur Bigge. Similarly, steer clear of 'French Canadian' which Grey believed caused offence: 'We do not talk of an Englishman with Norman blood as French Englishmen – neither should we talk of a French Canadian.' Grey recommended the phrase 'Canadians of French and British descent.' The governor general amused himself at the double standard; Canadians might use these phrases, but an Englishman could not: 'It took me 3 years to discover that I ought not to employ the term French Canadian, which is in general use.' It might be better, Grey concluded, simply to refer to French-speaking Canadians as *Canadians.*

When Grey received the first draft of the prince's address, he immediately spotted another gaffe, the treacherous word 'loyalty.' The word appeared three times in the address, Grey pointed out. Canadians were particularly sensitive on this point. As he recommended padding the speech with a few more references to the Battle of Ste-Foy, Grey pointed out that loyalty to Great Britain was natural, expected, and not to be commented upon as if it were surprising. French Canadians bristled at the imputation of possible disloyalty; English Canadians expected their loyalty to be taken for granted.

Through this process of transatlantic tutoring, the prince's speeches were drafted and redrafted with a view to creating the maximum positive effect and avoiding the many pitfalls lying in wait, perhaps unseen by the distant British authorities. Similarly, the king's written communications on the occasion of the tercentenary passed by Grey's careful eye before being finally approved for delivery.[30] The prince actually expressed some surprise at the words being put in his mouth and those to be spoken to him. Laurier and his cabinet apparently took his views into consideration but in the end did not revise the address of welcome significantly. Again Grey strongly counselled the prince to accept it 'without amendment.'[31]

Then there was the awkward matter of Champlain. The prince, who wished to keep his public engagements to a minimum, at first balked at the elaborate ceremonies planned for the foot of Champlain's statue. If he must go, he insisted upon a brief appearance. And he most certainly objected to the number of people who would be speaking after him. If the crown was to be the focus, surely all of the others would detract from that purpose. Grey remained adamant that the prince attend and that the others speak with him present. The prince's wishes ran counter to everything Grey hoped to achieve, as he explained to the colonial secretary:

> I am most anxious as you know to meet every wish of HRH in the fullest possible way, but, as my cable will have explained, the difficulties are considerable. To persuade the Canadians of French descent to agree to, nay more, to propose the celebration of the Champlain tercentenary by the consecration of the Plains of Abraham, was no ordinary achievement, and you can easily understand that we are continually up against a little sore racial feeling on this subject and ever on our guard against its assertion.

The celebration before the statue of Champlain would, from a Quebec point of view, be the most important and impressive incident of the week. The prince would simply have to be there; to do otherwise would represent an unpardonable slight. For the same reason, it was important that the representative of the United States, Vice-President Fairbanks, and also that of France, be able to pay the respects of their countries to the hero of French Canada and by extension French Canadians themselves. Grey bombarded British officials with ammunition to use in their campaign. He was as persuasive with the crown as he was with bishops. As we have seen, the prince not only attended the celebration, and tolerated the endless speeches from other delegations, he stayed on in his carriage at the feet of the great explorer, as the historical procession passed in review.[32] The private desires of the prince came second to what was deemed to be his public responsibility for cultivating a greater taste for monarchy amongst the French-speaking population of Quebec.

Following up a suggestion from Sir Wilfrid Laurier to further enhance the prince's standing amongst 'Canadians of French descent,' Grey urged the Palace to appoint a French Canadian as the prince's aide-de-camp during his stay at the Citadel. 'The duties would be nominal but it would be a compliment to French Canadians.' The Colonial Office agreed with this public relations gesture. Lieutenant-Colonel Roy was proposed and accepted by the prince. This compliment and the formal honour Roy received from the prince was duly noted in the French press.[33]

There remained, finally, the touchy matter of the prince's formal relations with the Catholic Church. The loyalty of French Quebec rested, Grey explained for the benefit of the colonial secretary, in a somewhat skewed reading of Canadian history and Quebec geography, upon the liberties given the Catholic Church:

> The consecration of the Plains is acceptable to Canadians of French descent because the Battle of Ste. Foy fought on the Plains in 1760 secured for them for all time the full and absolute right to the enjoyment of their own laws and religion. There is no part of the world where the RC Church has greater privileges than it enjoys in the Province of Quebec. That fact explains the loyalty of Quebec to British rule.

For the monarchy to sink deeper emotional roots into the soil of Quebec, the prince would have to be seen to show due respect to both the mother church and its episcopacy. But he would have to do so without alarming or causing excitement in the ultra Protestant English quarters. It was a delicate matter, especially on Sunday. Grey himself was not averse to having the prince attend the open-air mass, however briefly, but that got scotched immediately. Though desired by many in Quebec, the prince at a mass would be 'mal vue by the Protestant population of Western Canada.'[34] The prince would have to attend divine service in the Anglican Cathedral.

But this potentially distancing event that emphasized religious differences was dramatically turned the next day when the prince embarked upon a seemingly innocent, relaxing, journey into the countryside. On Monday morning he and his party boarded a special train bound for

Chateau Bellevue at Petit Cap, an hour east along the north shore. It was another poignant moment for the prince as he entered the same CPR private car that he and Princess Mary toured Canada in seven years earlier: 'It did remind me of you so much, I feel quite sad.'[35] It did not help much that the years had not been kind to the furnishings or now slightly shabby upholstery. Somewhat out of character, the weather was windy, cold, and disagreeable. At Petit Cap, the summer retreat of the Seminary of Quebec, the prince, in an overcoat, was guest of honour at a picnic luncheon spread out under the trees in the garden. In this rustic setting, in the bosom of the Quebec folk, removed from the press and public, the Catholic Church received the prince and the prince paid due respect to the church. There he was greeted by Monseigneur Sbarretti, Archbishop Bégin, and Monseigneur Mathieu of Laval. Accompanied by priests, the prince strolled through the grounds chatting amiably with 'the peasants who had come to catch a glimpse of the royal visitor.'[36] In the company of his hosts, he toured an old chapel at St-Joachim built by Monseigneur Briand in 1779, where the gathering posed briefly for a picture.

This trip served a double purpose. First it placed the prince unequivocally in the arms of the church, though far from public view. Secondly, the leisurely tour back to Quebec in an open automobile allowed the ordinary people of Quebec to see their prince. It was a mutual curiosity. According to a press account, 'The trip was an informal one and gave His Royal Highness not only a rest but [also] an opportunity to see at closer range the French Canadian subjects of Britain. He could now gaze at the habitant and his family,' now constructed in the tercentennial publicity as virtuous folk rather than backward peasants. They in turn gazed back. Every now and then as he slowly made his way along this line of brightly coloured cottages and barns, past wayside crosses, and through small villages, the prince ordered a halt to talk to small groups. At Ste-Anne-de-Beaupré the procession of automobiles stopped so that the prince could tour the famous shrine and see the piles of abandoned crutches. All along the way, according to press reports, the cheering crowds reflected the bonhommie, hospitality, faithfulness to church and loyalty to the British crown for which the French-Canadian habitant were renowned.[37]

The prince, then, was an actor too, putting on a performance for his people. The moment he arrived in Canada he made a special effort to seek out Champlain's Habitation. His route to the Citadel took him past

The Prince of Wales passing through the streets of Quebec in a landau escorted by a troop of Royal Northwest Mounted Police.

the new statue of Laval, which he paused to observe, and in which he was seen to take an animated interest. He endured the interminable speeches at the Champlain monument in good humour, laid a ceremonial wreath, and he waited patiently for the historic procession to pass. His public appearances were carefully planned and mapped out in advance.[38] It was not by chance that his many engagements took him through almost all of the sections of the city; he did not confine himself to his battleship and the Citadel. Like the Host at the Laval fête, he traversed the city, but the manner of his conveyance distanced him. He did not walk, he rode in a carriage or an automobile. He was guarded fore and aft by soldiers on horseback; he surrounded himself with dignitaries, mainly Englishmen, and for security reasons he passed by at a fairly high rate of speed. He put himself on display in the popular quarters, and in the countryside, but he could not be incorporated into the community. He paid attention to popular beliefs, including the miracle of the cures at the local Lourdes. He spoke French, steered clear of the traps; in short, he did everything he could to cultivate the love of French as well as English Canadians. 'I have done my best to try to be civil to everyone,' the prince confided to his wife, '& I hope perhaps that I have succeeded.'[39]

All of the evidence suggested he did. Colonel Denison refers to the prince in his diary in personal, familiar terms. On 28 July he notes: 'I went to the Victoria Park to see the prince plant a tree. Had a few minutes chat with him.' Later that evening at the prince's dinner on the *Exmouth*, Denison observed: 'It was, a very handsome function, had a short chat with the prince.'[40] From this close-up perspective the prince was more or less a member of the family.

Ethel Chadwick's relationship with the prince, though formed from a greater distance, was much more emotional and intense, more like a courtship than cousinship. On Saturday, after the prince had watched the historic pageants, he and Earl Grey took to their cars, stopping first at the nearby monument to the fallen Wolfe. Then immediately it was on to the Monument des Braves to pay homage to the heroes of the Battle of Ste-Foy. The four Ottawa women, still in their pageant costumes, stationed themselves to watch the celebrities on their return route. 'Just as the Prince of Wales drove past with His Ex,' Ethel wrote, 'we four Anna, Marguerite, Lola & I all curtsied low, His Ex pointed us out to the prince, and he bowed and smiled at us.'[41] From the theatrical court of Henri IV to the mass court of the future George V, these women were playing the part of citizens in a modern monarchy. Whether as a friend and trusted confidant, Prince Charming, or in some other form, the monarchy insinuated itself into the popular imagination. For such a people what could be sweeter than a real royal smile? The looking-glass looked back.

Afterwards, in an advanced state of self-congratulation, Earl Grey could scarcely contain his glee. To the colonial secretary he marvelled at both the public relations triumph and the faultless execution of the tercentenary events: 'What is remarkable about the week just passed is that with the exception of the annoyance caused to the French Catholics by the "free-thinking" character of the French Mission (an incident which is not to be regretted as it turned to our advantage) there was not a single contretemps or peril or hitch of any sort. Everything went like clockwork.'[42]

The prince was undoubtedly the centrepiece of the tercentenary in the press. His presence turned a historic commemoration into an act of public homage. And in his presence, Earl Grey exulted in a seven-page letter

The Prince of Wales in a top hat takes his seat in the centre balcony for the royal presentation of the historical pageants. Earl Grey, standing, welcomes him. On the rooftop platform the director, Frank Lascelles, is seen standing just to the left of the date 1908.

to King Edward VII, a people fondly saw their own reflection in him: 'The Prince & People have been delighted with each other & have enthused each other – the manifestations of enthusiasm evoked by His Royal Highness' presence, wherever he went, were a surprise to everyone acquainted with Quebec.' At the tercentenary, 'The Prince of Wales has taught the people of Quebec how to cheer,' Grey happily reported to the king. The tercentenary had, as he hoped, 'warmed the hearts of the People towards the Crown.' With perhaps pardonable exaggeration, he added: 'It has also kindled in their hearts a new consciousness of their own strength. It has levelled, at any rate for a time, the wall which separates Canadians of French and British descent, and has given them an opportunity of knowing and liking one another.'[43] That, at least, was the plan.

To the princess, Grey reported that her husband 'sent an electric thrill through the whole population, and caused them to manifest their pent up loyalty in gestures and expressions of whole-hearted enthusiasm which I do not believe have ever been witnessed in equal degree for anyone who was not a French Canadian, and seldom if ever for anyone of French descent.' Thanks largely to the prince, the tercentenary had been a force of great and permanent good: 'It has helped to fuse the Canadians of French and British descent into a United People, to consolidate the Dominion, to unite the Empire to strengthen the Entente Cordiale with France and the United States, and to strengthen the Crown.'[44]

The enthusiasm impressed the prince: 'The loyalty to the Throne & to the Mother Country was never stronger,' he wrote to his wife. Steaming back across the Atlantic aboard the *Indomitable*, the prince privately congratulated Grey on 'the triumphal success,' and for the opportunity 'of meeting & talking with so many of Canada's public men.' With some relief and justifiable exhaustion the prince confided to his diary in the privacy of his cabin:

> I am indeed thankful that all the functions & ceremonies are over & that they all went off so well but it was indeed a strenuous week, but I hope my visit has done good, especially in helping to improve relations between the English & French Canadians, which have never been so good as they are now.

On arrival he told the correspondent for the London *Times* that 'he was profoundly moved by his experience in Canada.' He returned convinced of the need to make the people of Britain better acquainted with the greatness and opportunities of Canada and to make visiting Canadians feel more at ease in the 'vastness of London's social life.'[45]

The aura of the new monarchy was 'made' in public appearances, tours, and staged spectacles of which the tercentenary was a typical example. For his part, the prince had to work at being the next king and it was tiring. He had to learn to be a modern monarch, travelling, bringing the monarchy to the people. And that rarely meant having things his own way. By reaching out to the people of his far-flung empire he hoped to create a personal bond and attachment that transcended governments and politics. His people in turn, he hoped, would see an image of their better selves in him.

The sun of the monarchy had cast everything else into its long shadow at Quebec. The prince eclipsed all others, Grey boasted, in a slighting reference to the lingering vice-president of the United States' profession: 'The dentist could not be seen in Quebec after the departure of your Royal Highness.' Grey's other metaphor was perhaps more fitting for a festive celebration. The royal departure, he confided to the prince, 'took all the fizz out of our Quebec champagne.'[46]

11. SOUVENIRS DE QUÉBEC

Allegory

Being there was not enough. Presence had to be declared or acknowledged with a memento. Fittingly, the Prince of Wales returned home with the most magnificent souvenir of all, a golden cigar box containing the address of the city of Quebec, presented during the speeches at the Champlain monument. The city wanted to give him a gift he would use, not something to be tucked away. Thereafter, as the prince frequented his humidor, and wreathed himself in sweet smoke, Quebec's politicians hoped he would drift in reverie back to this celebration and think fondly of his subjects at Quebec. The decoration of the box declared that the city fathers wanted the prince to remember their founder, the striking geography and natural resources upon which the commerce of the city depended, their flourishing arts and industries, and above all their own devotion to him. They said as much in words in their address, and again for lasting effect in symbols etched in enamel and gold. Their gift spoke, in French only, of a thriving, surviving community.[1]

At a small ceremony in London in June of 1910 Lord Strathcona, Canada's high commissioner, who was himself very much in evidence at the tercentenary, presented Frank Lascelles with a magnificent silver sculpture of the *Don-de-Dieu*. Grey had taken a personal interest in both its design and the execution by the silversmiths.[2] In whorls of silver it depicted the drama of venturing, the peril of small vessels in rough seas, the exotic encounter with the new world. The *Don-de-Dieu*, contemporary with Shakespeare, thus bore faint allusions to the *The Tempest*; its billowing sails also gestured towards the heroics of Drake and Nelson.

It was customary to mark a memorable occasion by striking a medal. There is power in this gesture – giving an order to the mint – a hint of majesty. Surprisingly the strongest impetus for a commemorative medal came from the members of the local committee working through Garneau, who in turn persuaded the National Battlefields Commission. E.E. Taché, the multi-talented deputy minister of lands and forests in Quebec, was commissioned to design the medal. Casts were prepared and reviewed by the commission, and in the fall of 1909 the firm of M. Henri Dubois of Paris struck 6 gold and 750 bronze medals from the dies. Gold medals were presented to those contributors of the highest rank – the Prince of Wales, the prime minister, Earl Grey, Sir Lomer Gouin, Sir George Garneau, and the lieutenant-governor of Quebec, Sir Louis Jetté, the last probably as consolation for being dropped from the honours list. Bronze medals were distributed to the tercentenary notables, the living descendants of Wolfe, Montcalm, Lévis, and Murray, major contributors to the Battlefields Fund, members of the various committees and, of course, the commissioners themselves.[3]

We have already encountered one such medal in Clare Denison's collection, given to her father in recognition of his services to the National Battlefields Commission. The medal is in its own way a minor masterpiece of the engraver's art. Samuel de Champlain, the model Christian knight, ventures bravely forth, penetrates the wilderness, takes peaceful possession, and founds a colony on a rock. On the reverse two maidens, one French and one English, preside over the cultivation of the domestic arts. They represent innocence, fidelity, and purity of motive. The words and the symbols boldly proclaim that what had begun French now thrived under British management.[4]

When organizations spoke of their aspirations, gratitude, and achievements on precious metals they used the language of allegory. It was a language of classical allusion and heraldic symbols. Quebec City, for example, on its golden casket equated the symbols of the heir to the throne with the coat of arms of the municipal corporation; to embody itself the city used a draped female form surrounded by the symbols of industry, prudence, abundance, and fortitude. The National Battlefields

Commission also had recourse to this arcane language of signification. On their gifts they struck a symbolic pose between romance and allegory, Champlain the knight, the storm-tossed barque, the virtuous maidens in their Garden of Eden.

Romance

The Midsummer Night's Dream that had come and gone would be permanently inscribed for elite participants in bronze, silver, and gold. But there were souvenirs too for the masses, available for pennies. They spoke in other visual vocabularies.

The tercentenary of Quebec was the occasion par excellence for the manufacture of souvenirs. Long before excited tourists and proud residents of Quebec put pen to postcard, a small industry set itself in motion to diffuse the memory of what had not yet taken place. Tourists had to be enticed to come with attractive advertisements. The postcard companies had to design, print, and distribute commemorative images by the thousands for sale in a crowded marketplace. During the festivities, photographers hauled about their bulky equipment to frame and freeze dramatic moments. These images would then be printed in postcard format, or for newspapers, weekend supplements, and stereoscopic slides.

Mass produced to be consumed and discarded, an astonishing variety of ephemera survives as debris from the tercentenary. From this store of texts and images Ethel Chadwick and Clare Denison selected the items for their scrapbooks. Ironically these most disposable of things survive in surprising abundance. To some it is junk, to be tossed out during the cleaning out of grandmother's attic. To others these tattered objects provide direct connection and communion with the past, an authentic link to a former time. For yet others these items are simply commodities to be hoarded, bought and sold for their monetary value alone. Guarded in archives or for sale on the open market, these ephemeral leavings become grist for the historian's mill.[5] These mass-produced popular objects provide other ways of imagining the event.

The railway companies sent out thousands of posters and brochures advertising the spectacle and, of course, their excursion fares. The Intercolonial Railway produced the coloured lithograph by the young C.W. Jefferys of Champlain we first encountered on the opening page of

Clare Denison's scrapbook. Its original blue envelope featured an image of a buckled, heavily laced, art nouveau Champlain being paddled ashore in a birchbark canoe by two naked, muscular natives, an enigmatic expression framed by the upswept brim of his feathered hat (see colour illustration no. 1). In the CPR poster the canoe bearing the explorer has just touched shore. The Indians have shipped their paddles. Champlain stands heroically, one foot on the sand, his right arm brandishing a flag of possession. The image alludes vaguely to the famous painting, widely diffused in lithographic reproductions, of Washington crossing the Delaware. Here, then, was Canada's defining moment.[6] Jefferys's Champlain bore the distinct stamp of the arts and crafts medieval revival style, including the Gothic typography. It is meditative, enigmatic.

Once at Quebec City, visitors could buy small lapel buttons bearing the familiar face of Champlain, commemorative plates, or a special linen handkerchief of the Prince of Wales and his family surrounded by dreadnoughts. But by far the most popular vehicle for the mass dissemination of imagery on this occasion was the postcard. The Edwardian era was the golden age of the postcard. It was still something of a novelty, depending as it did upon mass tourism. The postcard served in the place of the tourist's camera in the era before cheap amateur photography. That accounts for the profusion of images generated for and of the tercentenary by several competing companies. Cards ranged from dull, lifeless monochrome drawings to elaborate, coloured, gold-framed exemplars of the art. Many had to be designed and printed long before the tercentenary. Others, such as the scenes from the procession, pageants, and the royal visit, were photographed, printed and put into circulation during or immediately after the celebration.[7] Approximately one hundred and fifty different postcards were issued on this occasion, approximately half of which were drawings of historical scenes. The others were mainly photographs of the pageants, the city, ships, dignitaries, and the processions.

The postcard imagery spoke primarily about the past, of course, or of a present infused with pastness. The cheapest and least interesting were the series of monochrome vignettes of Canadian history sold by the Illustrated Post Card Company. The series begins with a three-quarter portrait of Champlain, the drapery behind him parting to reveal his ship before the rock at Quebec. This series then shifts the focus forward in time. Depending upon preference, a purchaser could choose from among

The CPR poster advertising the Quebec tercentenary.

illustrations of the death of Wolfe, Montcalm being carried mortally wounded to the Ursuline Convent, or medallion portraits of 'Victors and Vanquished in the Struggle Resulting in the Conquest of Canada.'

Champlain appears on several fine postcards. In a variant on the 'Washington Crosses the Delaware' iconography with a French-language inscription, Champlain is seen standing in a great *canot de maître* paddled by twelve Indians. Beside him a companion grasping a huge flag gestures towards a landing place. John F. Walsh & Company of Quebec City issued a delightful coloured impression of Champlain's Habitation like a French château complete with a formal French garden on the left, cliffs rising behind, and a wild, windswept landscape on the right. Another postcard image captures Champlain, with plans, calipers and charter laid out on a sea chest, surveying the townsite.

The set of six official souvenir postcards authorized for the occasion (French on the front, English on the back), although colourfully framed by a rich gold border, draped in flags and centred under the coat of arms of the city, were nevertheless lifeless tinted photographs of historic monuments and the city (see colour illustration no. 2). These unimaginative plinths and shafts of stone opened up a great deal of opportunity for other enterprising companies to compete with livelier designs.

The Valentine Publishing Company of Montreal put out a much more visually successful series, borrowing the gold frame of the official cards but substituting the French flag for the gold-on-white fleur-de-lis, the Union Jack for the ensign, and the coat of arms of Canada for those of Quebec. These scenes of the city emphasized verticals, the heights, walls, tiny streetscapes. They said in their own way that Quebec was a city from another time, definitely not a flattened, commercialized grid. The same company used the same shield, flags, and inscribed gold frame for a second series of postcards on a related theme, called Habitant Life Studies. These hand-tinted photographs portrayed rural Quebec as an archetypical folk society. The focus is on home, the hearth, fields and a simple faith. A woman and her daughter in straw hats hoe the garden; a bullock pulls a cart loaded with children, a familiar scene in Quebec province; three women kneel before a roadside calvary surrounded by a neat picket fence in evening devotions (see colour illustration no. 3).

These two sets of cards published by the Valentine Company dramatically attempt, in warm yellows, reds and pastels, to represent Quebec as a historic city – marked by gated, narrow streets, filled with monuments

The Illustrated Post Card Company's 'Death of Wolfe.'

The companion card showing the arrival of a fatally wounded General Montcalm at the doors of the Ursuline Convent.

A carte postale with French inscriptions. According to the English handwriting on front and back, Charlotte Lloyd of Quebec is sending John C. Beal in Pembroke 'this historic card dated & stamped during the Tercentenary celebration.' The stamp is one of the commemoratives.

and buildings of undoubted antiquity and linked to an extended past. Here was an explicitly anti-modern set of images deployed for specifically modern purposes – the promotion of tourism.[8] These images suggested that the tourist had visited not just another place, but also another time. The Habitant Life Studies recast the people of Quebec not as backward, unprogressive farmers, but rather as true folk: honest sons and daughters of the soil, living according to time-honoured traditions.[7] The framing of the work, the coloration, and the caption give the otherwise ambiguous image meaning. These were not peasants presented in a derogatory way, but rather living survivors of a simpler, purer, nobler age who could be casually observed everywhere on any visit to Quebec.

Some of these postcards in the archives still bear their original postage stamps (not to mention messages of greeting) and therein lies a tale of a new form of souvenir – 'the commemorative.' The Quebec tercentenary was the occasion for the first issue in Canada of a commemorative historical stamp. Commemoratives had been issued earlier, on the occasion, for example, of Queen Victoria's Diamond Jubilee. But these featured only a portrait of the monarch. Early in the planning for the tercentenary Thomas Chapais had planted the idea of a special stamp to commemorate the occasion. The postmaster general, Rodolphe Lemieux, subsequently championed the idea.[10] In all, the Post Office issued more than 62 million stamps with a value of $1.2 million. The half-cent stamp used for postcards featured portraits of the Prince and Princess of Wales in a dull sepia; Cartier and Champlain are paired on the dark blue-green one cent stamp, and the king and queen on the rose-hued first-class letter stamp published in the greatest quantity. Beyond that, higher denomination stamps printed in much smaller runs represented the Habitation against a blue background, Montcalm and Wolfe under columned olive arches, a violet Quebec in 1700, the departure of Champlain for the west in orange, and Cartier's three ships in dull brown.

Demand for these stamps was extraordinary, according to the postmaster general's annual report. Part of their popularity stemmed from the fact that these were the first scenic stamps issued in Canada and the first on which the French language appeared. All bore the inscription 'IIIe Centenaire de Québec.' Note that only one of the eight dealt with the most touchy issue of the tercentenary, the battlefields, and on it an English and a French general were paired.[11]

An event as elaborate and complex as the tercentenary required a

Three of the commemorative stamps issued on the occasion of the tercentenary.

program explaining what to see, where to stay, who was who, when and where things took place, and why it was happening. From the very outset, the National Battlefields Commission concerned itself with ensuring that programs of suitable quality be available so that visitors did not have to depend upon cheap, tacky programs filled with tasteless advertisements. Accordingly they commissioned the Cambridge Corporation of Montreal to produce 'proper' programs in English and French.

First came a handy pocket program published in both languages providing a day-by-day schedule of events, the order of the historical procession, and a listing of the scenes in the historical pageants. A page of text offset an opposing photograph of monuments, vistas, public buildings, gates, historic sites, and prominent geographical features of the region. The last photo is of the engraving of 'Le Chien d'Or' made famous by the novel of William Kirby in English and Pamphile Le May in French. These Quebec scenes closely resembled the postcard photos of the city, stressing the formal gates, soaring heights and narrow, old-time streets.

Under the auspices of the commission the Cambridge Company also published a larger twenty-five-page brochure. This is the document, with the colourful red and blue English and French soldiers facing one another on the cover, in Clare Denison's collection of tercentenary memorabilia. A proper program, in the eyes of the commissioners, should be earnest and comprehensive. It stressed clarity; it created discrete categories of things and it ensured that the niceties of rank and protocol were minutely observed in the extensive listing of the official guests, military ranks, and committee members of the festival.

But that was not proper enough in other people's terms. Afterwards what use would such a document be? Flimsy and insubstantial, it would likely be tossed out. Above all, it should explain the *meaning* of things. Sensing that the tercentenary might come off without a high-quality

1. Art nouveau facing of the envelope printed by Mortimer Press in Montreal for the Intercolonial Railway. The envelope contained the coloured version of the C.W. Jefferys illustration on p. 7.

2. A view of Quebec City in the official souvenir postcard series.

3. A typical farm scene as represented in the Valentine & Company series, 'Habitant Life Studies,' issued at the same time and using the same borders as the tercentenary series.

4. Cover illustration of the official program of the tercentenary.

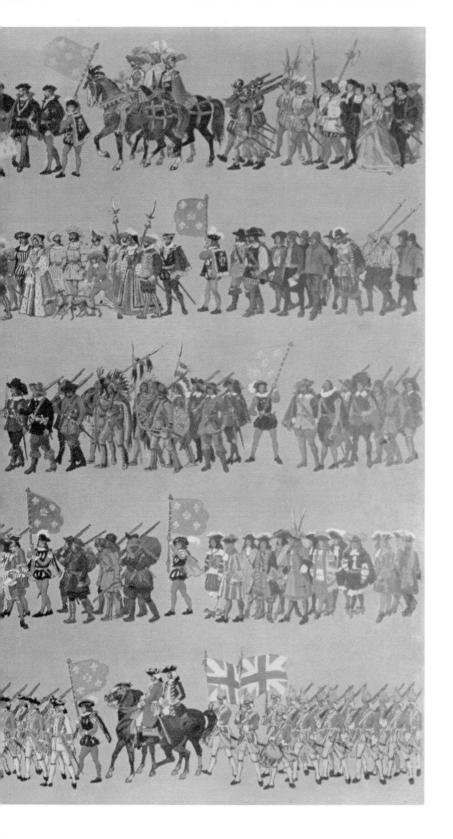

6. The Angel of Peace above Quebec: cover illustration on the Montreal *Standard* tercentenary souvenir issue.

5. (preceding pages) Henri Julien's impression of the historical parade, printed as a fold-out to the Montreal *Standard* Tercentenary Souvenir Number, 25 July 1908.

7. Charles Huot's costume designs. a) A colonial family from the 'heroic era.'

b) A mousquetaire from the time of Louis XIII.

c) A young noble accompanying the Duc de Tracy.

8. George Reid, 'The Arrival of Champlain.'

9. Frank Craig, 'Bishop Laval Receives the Marquis de Tracy.'

textual explication that would live on in libraries and be of value afterwards, Arthur Doughty seized command. As he explained later to his friend George Wrong, 'in order that the event should not pass without some sort of a book as a Souvenir I had to take the matter out of the hands of the local committee and rush it through the press without consulting them much. They are not very pleased with me for doing this, some of them thought the little vest pocket program was all that was necessary and many of them hinted that I was doing all this to see what I could get out of it.'

During the run up to the tercentenary Doughty held the post of joint secretary of the commission, together with Chouinard. Thus under the auspices of the National Battlefields Commission, Doughty arranged to have published what amounted to his own program for the tercentenary: he wrote it, edited it, oversaw the translation, and marked up the proofs for the publisher. A proper program, in Doughty's aesthetic, had to be a history; it had to be beautifully designed and elaborately illustrated, it had to be substantial enough for a bookshelf, didactic, and filled with moral purpose.[12]

The distinctive typography on the cover, a caligraphic medieval revival typeface, established a visual link between Doughty's souvenir booklet and a William Morris Kelmscott House arts and crafts publication. Like Morris and Burne-Jones, Doughty too was romantically engaged in a 'Crusade and Holy Warfare against the Age.'[13] Like Lascelles with his pageantry, Doughty sought here to re-enchant modern life with the chivalry and heroic spirit of another era through history (see colour illustration no. 4).

Doughty's cover stands in striking contrast to the other commission-sponsored documents. A solitary bronzed Indian, hands resting on his loosened bow, gazes at a cross planted on a rocky shore, set off against green undulating hills in the background. Something is coming. Something is passing. One form of nobility is to be supplanted by another. The Indian appears stoical, accepting of his fate. The cover announces that prehistory is over; history is about to begin.

Turning the page exposes a technicolor cavalcade of Wolfe, Montcalm, Lévis, and Murray on horseback, an illustration of the famous last scene of the pageant. Behind them in mingled ranks stand their armies. Behind the generals and their armies on the river the guns of the great fleet send up puffs of white smoke. Golden twilight brightens the horizon.

Pictures of the king and queen, followed by the prince, provide a fanfare for a historical introduction. 'In pride, but not with boasting, Canada turns towards the rock of Quebec,' Doughty begins. Then in sixteen pages the reader is led from Columbus to the Conquest. The final section, dealing with the conflict in 1759 and the transfer of power from France to England, opens with this remarkable 'presentist' assertion that offers insight into Doughty's conception of the meaning of Canadian history and the political goal of the tercentenary:

> It is the chief characteristic of our life to-day that in one state two races should be working for the advancement of Canada. Under a flag which is not the banner of Frontenac or Montcalm, French and English enjoy the same protection and the same citizenship. In other words the ideal for which Colbert and Talon strove was impracticable and has given way. Instead we find English and French co-operating, and if, three hundred years after Champlain there is no French King in Canada, there is a French prime minister.

A dramatic photograph of Louis-Philippe Hébert's truly extraordinary statue 'Sans Merci' brings the historical introduction to a gruesome close. A harvester, stripped to the waist, and a native writhe in mortal combat in a grainfield. The right arm of the habitant is raised, gripping a wicked-looking sickle. According to the caption, civilization is fighting barbarism, the moment frozen in a chilling fusion of muscle. We all know, however, that the blade is about to descend.

After the historical introduction, the remainder of the booklet is given over to a detailed description of each of the pageant scenes with accompanying historical notes on the events and persons depicted. The text is illustrated with snatches of printed music for popular songs, photographs of buildings and monuments, and numerous lithograph portraits of major historical figures. The program thus concentrates entirely upon the history of New France from Cartier to 1759 as a prologue to the present. In the final pageant, the program notes: 'There floats up out of the distance a full-throated rhythmical song and, as its volume swells, there appear regiment by regiment, marching shoulder to shoulder, two great and victorious armies.' As they march past the grandstand, the program explains, 'the present is joining hands with the past to glorify a splendid future.' Before the tercentenary, the commission and the pub-

The photograph of Hébert's statue 'Sans Merci' that appeared in Doughty's program for the tercentenary. The original, in slightly damaged condition, is on display at the Musée de Québec.

lisher wrangled over a sharing of the profits from the sale of this 'quality' program. Afterwards, this being a Canadian publishing venture, they had to negotiate a sharing of the losses.[14]

In different ways these ephemera conveyed the coded messages to visitors to help them see and understand the scenery, the ceremonies, and the pageants. Quebec as a province was being given a new 'reading' as a folk society and the city as a *lieux de memoire*, a place of memory, or a 'historic site.' This past, which could be seen and felt, or at least seen and felt after it had been read about or looked up, had a clear set of meanings. Canada was the product of two conquests. The violence of one conflict could not be openly acknowledged; the conquest of native people however could be acted out in graphic detail – though it should be noted that the example of Dollard illustrated in the pageants was of a native victory. The image of the native, like that of the female form, became more idealized as a symbol when it became less visible in the public sphere. Because the Indian was supposedly vanishing, thus reaffirming European superiority, the stoic primitive facing his fate became a nostalgic symbol of self-justification. An image of an Indian could appear on the cover of Doughty's official program and appear noble because inside, in Hébert's sculpture and the drama of historical pageantry, native people were effectively subdued. The violence of the encounter, amply depicted in theatre and art, gave the lie to the notion of peaceful conquest. The marginalization of native people from contemporary public life meant, among other things, that the violence could at least be acknowledged as a regrettable consequence of a tragic inevitability.

Much as some extreme imperialists might want to create a similar symbol out of French Canada through conquest, French Canada resisted. The Conquest could not be played out, not even as theatre. Moreover, there were many Canadian intellectuals, Arthur Doughty among them, who sought to transcend conquest imagery in order to make one nation out of two noble peoples. Thus his message that the passion of those essential struggles had long since died away. Native people had succumbed, been subjugated. They were now lost to history but beloved of the theatre and the novel. The two peoples of European origin now formed a united army marching forward, two peoples under a British king and a French prime minister singing in unison what would become their unofficial national anthem, with the audience in the grandstand checking their program for the words:

Ton histoire est une épopée
Des plus brillants exploits.
Et ta valeur, de foi trempée
Protégera nos foyers et nos droits.

Realism

The nineteenth century is said to have been 'the most visual period of Western culture,' when sight was favoured over the other senses.[15] Diderot justified the profusion of engravings in his encyclopedia with the argument 'a glance at an object or its representation says more than a page of discourse.' Translated from the French, we know this aphorism as a picture being worth a thousand words. The nineteenth century gave rise to a number of institutions of the visual, most notably the museum and the exhibition. Museums came into prominence and attracted patrons as well as audiences as superior means of public instruction. The immediacy of direct contact, the play of the eye and the imagination upon the object, and the connections drawn to other objects were much better ways of teaching than words and books. 'Things,' in Asa Briggs's memorable phrase, 'were there to teach.'[16]

The enormous success of the Crystal Palace exhibition in 1851 proved that seeing, if not believing, was fascinating for a mass audience. Surveying the sequence of extravagant international exhibitions in the later nineteenth and early twentieth centuries, Robert Rydell, the American historian of world's fairs, viewed them as artifacts of 'a fundamental cognitive shift' towards the visual arts.[17] G. Brown Goode, an assistant secretary at the Smithsonian Institution, once observed: 'There is an Oriental saying that the distance between ear and eye is small, but the difference between hearing and seeing is very great.' It followed that visual teaching and learning were more effective than verbal or literary modes. The goal of a fair as much as a museum should be the presentation of 'an illustrated encyclopedia of civilization.'[18] Louis Napoleon Parker and Frank Lascelles simply transferred this set of ideas to the theatre under Lascelles's succinct slogan: 'Things seen are more powerful than things read.'

If what distinguished the late Victorian era was its fascination with objects and belief in their didactic power, then the camera was its handmaiden; the photograph was a more authentic representation of that reality and disseminator of knowledge than a description. The photograph affirmed involvement; it captured rich moments, above all it showed others, thereby multiplying the audience. The images of exhibitions possessed a power at a distance not unlike that of the exhibitions themselves. More people visited the Chicago Exposition by stereoscope, postcard, photograph, and illustrated guidebook than ever travelled there by train. Images created expectations about what an exhibition ought to be.

The tercentenary of Quebec drew from these deeper reservoirs of western philosophy as it moved swiftly forward on the shallower surface currents of institutional promotion. It was part of the tremendous explosion of bric-à-brac, objects, things, of seeing. The photograph, taken, produced, reproduced, jostled in circulation with thousands of other photographic images, was at once the means, evidence, remembrance, and extension of seeing. You hadn't been there if you did not have a photograph of it. If the organizers tried to control the production and diffusion of photographic images of the tercentenary events – and there is some slight evidence they did try for commercial reasons – they utterly failed. For in one way or another, unauthorized photographers and numerous amateurs seized their opportunities. It seems that several companies either purchased or were given permission to take and sell photographic images of tercentennial events. Professional photographers such as J.E. Livernois made a good business taking formal portraits of actors in their historical costumes and pageant scenes. In some cases he took family portraits with each member dressed for different parts. The postcard, the photographic reproduction, or better yet, the Kodak snapshot taken with your own camera showed what the tercentenary had been really like.

But there were problems with realism. This most visual event did not always photograph well. Or rather, the event emphasized the limitations of photography as a means of expression. The broad scope of the event meant it was almost impossible to capture the dramatic sweep of the scenes without reducing the objects to miniatures. As the camera pulled back to capture the entire scene, the central figures were reduced to ant-like proportions, mere black dots on a grey field. Everything became flat and two dimensional.

That, of course, raised the second major limitation of film technology, its lack of colour. The tercentenary was a riot of colour; the camera

A photographic portrait, taken by the Livernois studio, of Mr W.H. Wiggs and family in their pageant costumes.

reduced everything to a dull grey. Here is where some of the postcard publishers had an advantage. To appeal to this taste for a more authentic reproduction, they colorized familiar images. Heavy reliance upon warm yellows and reds, with a surround of gold, framed these scenes as pastoral.

There were, however, other limitations to the technology of the day that diminished the camera's eye somewhat as a reliable recorder. The bulky equipment of the professional as well as the portable box cameras of the tourist required bright light. That ruled out capture of the dramatic scenes late in the pageants, and all indoor activities. Nor could the slow film speed capture or stop motion effectively. Thus the camera artificially stopped action, as if everyone had to pause for the picture to be taken. This removed from the pictures all sense of spontaneity, of a moment frozen in passing. Most photographs, especially of large groups, seemed static and staged. Moreover, the images did not explain themselves. From a photograph it was not always clear what was happening. This was particularly true when the photograph was of a representation of the past, the actors in costumes. A picture sometimes needed a thousand words if a non-participant were to make any sense of it, or rather, obtain the sense intended of it.[19]

Within its limitations, however, the camera faithfully recorded the light it captured through the shutter. That too was something of a problem. Some of the pictures looked too real. By accurately recording actors in costume, showing them indeed to be actors in costume, the illusion of history was thereby stripped away. The Livernois Studio in Quebec photographed and published a large number of images of Quebeckers in their pageant costumes.[20] Some of the leading figures suited their images better than others. Cartier, Champlain, de Tracy, Frontenac come to mind. But others seemed like youngsters dressed up in other people's clothes – Bishop Laval, for example. The blinking eye of the camera took in all that it surveyed; the scene could only be partly controlled. Thus anachronism crept in unawares: Indian tepees in the background of French court scenes, glimpses of the grandstand. Far from replacing 'art' as a recorder of events, photography at this point underscored the need for it.

The sense of experience most easily captured by photography, depth of field, the perspective of three dimensions, *could* be captured by the camera, or rather by a highly specialized camera, the stereoscope. Essentially, by mounting two cameras side by side, images taken by these cameras when viewed through a stereoscopic viewer gave the illusion of three dimensions. Some objects seemed to stand out in front of others; images jutted off the slide towards the viewer. A stereoscopic viewer was an almost universal element of a middle-class Edwardian parlour. A highly organized network of photographic publishing houses, some national and many small and regional, supplied the demand for arresting and exotic images to slip into these viewers. The Quebec tercentenary, at a geographically dramatic site, in a decorated city, with its people massed in ordered ranks or columns, or arrayed on stage, was made for the stereoscope.

The Keystone View Company, a major American publisher of stereo-scopic slides, obtained a contract to reproduce a huge set of slides of the tercentenary. All told, Keystone published 128 images, each with a caption below and three paragraphs of explanatory text on the back (in English). Keystone's major rival, Underwood and Underwood, published only a dozen or so slides.[21] The stereoscope worked best for well-lit subjects emphasizing the vertical and the linear. Thus the Keystone collection begins with dramatic geometric images of the battleships, their sharp bows leaping towards the eye. The parades and processions work well. The illusion works best when the camera is reasonably close to its

Portrait of Abbé Vachon as Monseigneur Laval. The photograph shows him to be one of the characters who did not fully fill his role.

subject, and when the image thus fills the frame. For the massed spectacles, the military review, and the pageants the technique did not produce
quite the same dramatic results. However, close-up images of portions of
scenes, and individual actors or groups of actors did work. For that
reason, some of the most striking visual images are of the native encampments, lines of warriors in front of their tents, groups of costumed
Indians at ease.

The story of the tercentenary could be 'read' from the numbered
slides. The reading metaphor was heightened by the packaging of the
collection in a box resembling two leather-bound books, and the extensive text explaining each scene on the back of each slide. The slides could
be looked at in order, or, even better, the viewer could jumble the images,
focusing on the most interesting or arresting.

The stereoscope captured the illusion of depth at the expense of
breadth. Here too another modification of photographic technology
made it possible to reproduce scope. At the turn of the century the
panoramic photograph was at the peak of its popularity. At least three
professional panoramic photographers worked the tercentenary, taking
sweeping views of the fleet in the river, the military review, and especially
the scenes from the pageants. The photographer arranged the actors on
the circumference of a huge semi-circular with the camera in the centre.
As the camera swung from left to right, it exposed a long, narrow
negative within. To capture the pageant scenes, for example, the actors
would be arrayed in an arc from one wing of the stadium to the other. In
this kind of photograph a circle became a straight line. The panorama
sacrifices detail to breadth. The eye cannot take in the whole picture at
once; it must sweep across the image.[22]

Many prints of these panoramic photographs survive. The most popular subjects for panoramic photography, of course, were the richly costumed and heavily peopled court scenes in the pageant. The court of
Henri IV is captured in its glory. If you look very carefully, de Tracy can
be seen kneeling to kiss Laval's ring in the focal point of a very busy
photograph of Pageant 5. Similarly, Frontenac can be discerned delivering his memorable rebuff to Phips's envoy in another. But what is more
notable about all these scenes is not a story being told, but rather the
sheer massing of figures and costumes in a tableau. Sometimes this did
not work as effectively in photographic form. Two scenes, the arrival of
Champlain and the arrival of the Ursulines, both taken from higher up

in the grandstand, do not fill the frame; a third of the photograph is empty. The last scene of the historic armies, however memorable it may have been to spectators, could not be easily photographed by any of these techniques. It involved movement, colour, it came late in bad light. Thus the panoramic photograph of the two armies lined up across a shallow valley proved a distinct disappointment. However formidable the British thin red line might have been to the enemy, someone viewing a four-foot-long black and white photograph of a straggling line of men in different uniforms received an entirely different impression.

Events that filled the frame worked best for the panoramic photographer. The military review panoramas – two different moments have been frozen in time – do provide a sense of the massive numbers of people involved. Thousands of black dots spread across the huge field, but here what is lost is detail. What exactly is going on is somewhat obscure. The ferris wheel and the jail in the background, however, catch the eye. An unusual panoramic image of the messe solennelle by H.O. Dodge ironically places the emphasis upon those in attendance protecting themselves with umbrellas from the sun in the vast grandstand. The altar itself, off to the right amidst a crowd and surrounded by shrubbery, looks more like a gazebo in the outfield.

By their very nature, these huge images could not be widely reproduced. In the first place they were expensive. Usually organizations commissioned these massive images: the Department of the Marine, for example, sponsored the panoramic photographs of the fleet. The National Battlefields Commission bought several of these large-scale images for its own collection and as gifts to foreign and colonial governments who had sent greetings. Four of these panoramic photographs were given to the Prince of Wales as gifts to take home to show his family: the fleet, the military review, and the Henri IV and the Frontenac scenes.

These elongated images could not be reproduced easily in newspapers or books unless in the form of fold-out. Cropped versions, however, were printed on pieces of stiff paper and sold as oversize postcards. Both Ethel and Clare have examples of the pageant scenes pasted in their scrapbooks. Ethel identifies herself and Lola on the far left of the frame by writing initials under the costumed figures.

Still, the magic of the event eluded the camera. None of these techniques captured motion. For that reason Grey insisted that a moving picture film be made of the dramatic last scene. He even put words in the

Prince of Wales's mouth to this effect. By wireless from *Indomitable* came the telegraphed words of the prince more or less commanding a motion picture of the parade of the historic armies. Such a film was made for the National Battlefields Commission, and afterwards shown to various women's groups and men's clubs who had been involved in the fund-raising effort. For many years it lay in the archives' vaults, but at some point in time it disappeared – perhaps it disintegrated. Only a brief flickering movie image of the event survives in the Library of Congress, but it shows nothing of the final scene of the pageant. Rather, this newsreel footage focuses on the Prince of Wales, riding in his carriage, laying a wreath on Champlain's statue, receiving the salute of the fleet, and watching the troops pass by on jerky parade in the military review.[23]

Impressionism

Ironically, the limitations of photography as a medium opened up opportunities for traditional artists. To capture mood newspapers supplemented photographic images with artists' sketches. The artists' drawings worked best with caricature. A stroke of a pen exaggerated a feature, creating a stereotypical image. Artwork illustrated lighter moments, ironic juxtapositions, confusions. The chaotic jumble of the cartoon frame rendered the surreal, kaleidoscopic sense of the event better than the literal photographic image.

Some of the tercentenary was pure illusion that could only be grasped in the imagination and skill of the artist. At the same time, the long lead times of rotogravure journalism required renderings in advance of the event. So artists, attending rehearsals, could anticipate outcomes and frame the elements as they chose. Their images are all closer to the eye; they fill the frame, and on the cover and inserts seize the imagination with colour. The juxtaposition of two forms of art, sketches and photography, created the impression of past and present being one and the same; Champlain becomes Wolfe becomes modern Quebec constructed as a historic site. Art and design created the illusion of a heroic age in which all events occurred simultaneously and time stood still – a once upon a time.

The weekend rotogravure magazines covered the tercentenary in extenso. Here, too, the editors chose to illustrate events with artists' interpretations as well as photographs. The *Canadian Pictorial* featured drawings of Wolfe's Cove and the 'Death of Wolfe' after Benjamin West, intended to show how 'Pageants will reproduce stirring events of Canadian History.' As this magazine went to press before the celebration, it depended heavily upon scenic photographic views of Quebec, an essay by Frank Lascelles (profile photo and line drawings of military figures), and a charming collection of Livernois photos of Quebeckers posing as historical figures and watercolour drawings of the costumes.[24] The Montreal *Standard,* the leading pictorial magazine of the time, employed many of Canada's leading graphic artists in its studios. Henri Julien, Marc Aurèle de Foy Suzor-Coté, and Ralph Seward attended the tercentenary for the *Standard,* producing charcoal sketches and ink drawings, mainly of pageant scenes. In the special tercentenary souvenir number of The *Standard* a portrait of an older, reflective Champlain appears on the first page surrounded by halberdiers, musketeers, courtiers, a fur trader, an Indian, and a herald. Images of contemporary Quebec as seen by the camera are interspersed with drawings by the staff artists of scenes from the pageants. A dramatic drawing of Cartier reading prayers after planting his cross contrasts with photographs of this actual scene, by bringing all of the characters fully into the frame in a hierarchical order.

Like the tercentenary itself, not all the images in the magazines followed a chronological sequence. Time is collapsed; events are anachronistically juxtaposed, creating in the eye of the viewer one undifferentiated pastness interspersed with and thereby connected to photographs of the present. The Cartier scene, for example, is followed by a drawing of Bigot's palace ('as it was in Wolfe's time') and a photograph of the Quebec legislature (was the irony intended?). Ralph Seward's sketch of Champlain at court in the Louvre bowing before Henri IV precedes photographs of Duberger's model of Quebec City and its gates, leading to a page of photographs of Quebec streetscapes. The sequence stresses the continuity of past and present.

Some original art of very high quality was produced by commercial artists for the weekly rotogravure newspapers. At this time Suzor-Coté, a personal friend of the prime minister, had a commission to paint some historical panels in the House of Commons. He had made a name for himself initially as a landscape painter and portrait artist. However, he too had begun to take up historical subjects, perhaps sensing that there was a market for such paintings in the public sector peopled by his friends. Earlier, in his Paris studio, he had already painted a gloomy

Ralph Seward's impression of the scene in which Henri IV commissions Champlain.

earth-toned representation of the 'Death of Montcalm.' This extraordinary image, consciously presented in opposition to Benjamin West's 'Death of Wolfe,' is bled of almost all colour and light. Montcalm, a figure in white, lies dying in bed in a cavernous chamber surrounded by mourners and ecclesiastics. This lights from tapers pierce the gloom. The eye is drawn up past a standing bishop and a kneeling nun, past the candles, to a dim cross. Wounded soldiers frame the scene on either side. You can almost smell the incense. The painting might equally be titled the death of a pope.

Around the time of the tercentenary, Suzor-Coté completed a large oil painting of a conquistador-like Cartier, surrounded by soldiers in gleaming armour, taking possession of the new world for France. He reworked this theme for a popular audience in a deft charcoal sketch for the *Standard.* Afterwards he would paint a large canvas of Champlain's landing in 1608. However, when he failed to interest any gallery in it he cut it up in a rage.[25] At about this time, Suzor-Coté's friend, the sculptor Alfred Laliberté, cast a bronze head of Champlain, a copy of which remains on display at the entrance to the archives in Quebec City.[26]

Events of the festival were thus worked up into high art. At the same time these artists worked to diffuse images of the tercentenary as popular art in mass circulation formats. Henri Julien, better known as an editorial cartoonist, put his talents to work in a Wild West rendition of the Iroquois overrunning Dollard's fort. Besides his notable sketches of action scenes in the pageants, Julien also executed a remarkable poster illustrating all of the major constituent elements of the historical procession which appeared as a colour fold-out supplement to the souvenir issue of the *Standard.* Julien turned Canadian history into a veritable Bayeux Tapestry. Five lines of figures stretching out into a single column, broken into five parts, illustrate the march of Canadian history from Cartier to Wolfe and Montcalm's armies. It was in many ways an apt and evocative model to work from: a French invasion of England lending authority to the French occupation of Canada. In a curious twist, since the religious figures did not march in the procession, Julien's rendering of Canadian history leaves out the ecclesiastical and ultramontane themes that figured so prominently in the pageants themselves. Julien dropped dead in a Montreal street of a heart attack soon afterwards, it was said, exhausted by this extra tercentenary work.[27] This remarkable lithograph, of which only two known copies survive, was his masterpiece as a histori-

Henri Julien's Wild West version of Dollard's martyrdom at the Long Sault drawn for the Montreal *Standard*.

cal illustrator (see colour illustration no. 5).

One last image deserves attention. The Angel of Peace, who would never tower above Cap Diamant to raise Canadian eyes to her from the muck and moil of modernity, did nevertheless live in the mind's eye of the artist. An unknown artist captured the image of Earl Grey's phantasmagoric colossus for the cover of the *Standard* (see colour illustration no. 6). She can be seen floating like a Pre-Raphaelite chimera over Quebec, in gauze-like drapery, lightly grasping a palm of peace. This is a truly stunning image. The red and white armies and banners of England and France mingle in the foreground. Across the band of river rises a golden city on a hill. Above it hovers the angel against clouds and blue sky.

The well-known local Quebec City artist Charles Huot, retained to design the costumes for the pageants, had made a study sometime earlier of traditional French costumes of the seventeenth and eighteenth centuries. He engaged at least one assistant, Miss W. Bonham. The watercolour designs for costumes produced by this pair of artists were used by seamstresses and tailors to make the costumes for the pageants. Some of these sketches appeared in the *Canadian Pictorial* magazine. Afterwards most of these sketches became the property of the National Battlefields Commission. Perhaps not so strangely, the costume designs for the principal actors have disappeared, the suspicion being that the actors arranged with Huot to obtain the watercolours as mementos. This hoard of about one hundred and thirty drawings, most by Miss Bonham if the rancorous correspondence in the archives after the fact is to be believed, have lain virtually untouched and unseen for ninety years[28] (see colour illustration no. 7).

One of Canada's leading artists, the Torontonian George Agnew Reid, also managed to be present at Quebec. Reid had made his reputation in Canada in the 1890s after study in Philadelphia and Paris with a series of large paintings capturing intense moments – some might say melodramatic moments – in the lives of ordinary people: 'Forbidden Fruit,' a boy reading a book in a hayloft; 'The Other Side of the Question,' a young man pleading his case before bearded elders; 'Mortgaging the Homestead,' a wife with her baby looking away as the lawyers sign the papers; 'Family Prayer,' mother and daughters on their knees, faces in their hands, father praying behind them before a window. His academy style, described by critics at the time as sympathetic realism, dripped with emotion.

In the mid-1890s Reid's art took a historical turn. A century earlier, historical painting had been considered the highest form of art in the European aesthetic. In Canada at the turn of the twentieth century, historical painting enjoyed a brief revival as artists sought ways of expressing in visual and symbolic terms the meaning of an emergent Canadian citizenship. George Reid and a group of fellow artists mounted a campaign to decorate the many new public buildings in the country with 'public art' to promote patriotism. In Quebec City Charles Huot had begun to brighten the interior of the new Legislative Buildings with historical illustrations. Suzor-Coté had been commissioned by Sir Wilfrid Laurier to decorate the Parliament Buildings in Ottawa. In Toronto, as a demonstration project, George Reid painted two murals for Toronto's new City Hall as prototypes of a more ambitious program of civic historical art. Only two paintings were completed, but they can be seen still, overpowered somewhat by a glowing stained-glass window opposite. Overhead, flanking the main doorway, Reid's murals focus on ordinary people as the title, 'Hail to the Pioneers,' would suggest.

Reid began to conceive of art not simply as an object of beauty or a crystallized emotive moment, but also as a force in civic edification. Art could also teach; it could tell the story of history more effectively than books. In this respect he, too, was a missionary of the visual over the textual. Public buildings should, in his view, be adorned with these images in order to develop a citizenry fully informed of its past and, by implication, of its national character. As citizens scurried about attending to their taxes or atoning for their petty crimes before the police magistrate, their ancestors would peer down from above, reminding them of their debt and their destiny. An art gallery would thus not only elevate public taste, but also be a school of citizenship.[29]

At this time Reid was busy attempting to organize a national gallery for Canada which would, among other things, be in his mind a treasure house of historical images in paint. To this end, he himself contributed a large oil painting to the National Gallery once it was launched, a painting worked up from his 1908 sketches depicting Champlain's arrival at Quebec (see colour illustration no. 8). In this heroic canvas, Champlain's ship, in golden hues, towers deck upon deck over the native canoes swarming about in the water below. In art at least, European technology exudes power and wealth; in historic reconstruction, European technology as represented by Champlain's ship, the *Don-de-Dieu*, seemed so diminutive on the St Lawrence, dwarfed both by the landscape and the behemoths of the modern navy. The natives in this representation raise their paddles in an ambiguous gesture; is it welcome or resistance?[30]

George Reid was, as might be expected, captivated by the historical pageants. Sitting in the grandstand with Lascelles he executed sketches and rapid pastel renderings of several key scenes, several of which survive. The National Archives Picture Division houses a panoramic triptych of the Cartier at Fontainebleau scene. It has a misty, dreamlike quality entirely appropriate to the scene. Cartier, left centre and surrounded by feathered native captives, addresses François I. The king and his queen on horseback are shaded by a golden canopy. The court stretches into panels on the left and right. Woodland nymphs and dancing sylphs are spread out in the centre foreground. It is a blur of shimmering colour dancing across the three panels like northern lights.

Reid also composed a memorable image of the Iroquois returning after the massacre of Dollard and his company. In the background the fort flames and smokes; in the foreground fierce contorted red faces, scalps raised overhead, howl defiance. Two sketches of fur-trading scenes, and a sketch of Champlain in blue, seated at the window of his Habita-tion, looking wistfully out at the *Don-de-Dieu* anchored in the river, con-veys something of the sadness of discovery, the guilt of possession, and of separation from home represented by the ship.[31]

Reid was but one of a half-dozen or so of Canadian artists who at-tended the tercentenary to enrich his visual palette. This, of course, was particularly important to a painter who placed so much emphasis upon the uplifting, civic aspects of historical art. The tercentenary fired his imagination, and for years afterwards he would return to these scenes to paint them in public buildings for the edification of subsequent generations.[32]

Under the influence of Suzor-Coté in French Canada and Reid in English Canada, Canadian painting took a 'historic turn' during the first decade of the twentieth century. Painters and sculptors joined historians, novelists, poets, and dramatists in teaching through art. The tercente-nary provided an occasion for these artists to diffuse their historical vision to a much wider public. At the same time its dramatic form, particularly the pageant, provided them with a whole new range of opportunities for visual representation. High art and popular art came momentarily together, in magazines, postcards, stamps, and graphic images. Photography by its limitations curiously re-emphasized the dra-matic power of art.

The imagery of the tercentennial came from many sources; it was not controlled from the centre by one powerful creator. Many hands and eyes conspired to visualize the meaning of the festivities in several styles and media. Some images were created in the eye of eternity; others were disposable. It would be a mistake to try to reduce all of this to a common theme, or some underlying irreducible truth. We can, however, see some tendencies in this tremendous outpouring of imagery.

Two images of native people co-existed: the Indian as symbol (noble, doomed, pre-historic) and the Indian as actor (alive, potent, menacing).

From the special issue of the Montreal *Standard*, a black-and-white charcoal sketch by Suzor-Coté of his painting of Cartier's landing. The painting is on permanent display at the Musée de Québec.

Native people retain their power and their historicity in many of these images. Native children particularly attracted the camera lens, sending a coded message to predisposed observers. But most images de-centre the natives, literally moving them to the margins as Europeans occupy the focal point, landing, erecting crosses, trading. In some works the Indian as symbol and actor appears simultaneously. In Suzor-Coté's famous painting and sketch of Cartier's landing, the contorted subhuman forms of the crouching natives grow out of the forest foliage on the left-hand side of the picture. They are nature, but also untamed. Fully erect Europeans in the centre of the picture possess human shapes; Cartier gestures open-handed in trusting supplication, but his colleague has his sword drawn and poised. At the same time the Indians carry clubs; they might be cowering in awe, but they are also ready to spring. In imagery, then, the fate of the native remained undecided. Symbol or actor, the message was not clear.

Culturally and historically the French and English were equals: that was the second theme in the imagery tourists mailed home on postcards or encountered in books and magazines. This can be seen in the subjects chosen for postcards, program illustrations and stamps. Wolfe is invariably paired with Montcalm, as are the flags of Britain and France. Symbolically, at least, French and English were represented as having arrived at some cultural equilibrium. Taken together, the images on the ephemera subtly echo the allegory of the tercentennial medal: France represents the past, the arts, and religion; Britain represents power, the future, and commerce.

The graphic artists reinforced the textual message of a heroic, romantic past. History was a costume drama, full of colourful, dramatic gestures. Canada was thus the work of giants, bold explorers who penetrated and brought light to the dark forest, fearless soldiers, heroic martyrs, brave citizens. These were a devout people following a divine purpose, led by their church. On the fields of battle French and English fought to an honourable draw. Now united, they formed part of a broader imperial force.

Finally, photographs and artwork conspire to leave the impression that the past is not over; it lives on in the streets, stones, and faces of Quebec. Past and present mingle on the pages of the glossy magazines. The walls and gates of the old city survive; you can walk where Champlain, Wolfe, and Montcalm once trod. The folk were still there, living in warm families and communities, baking, going to church, tilling the fields, and praying, a gold-hued human archive of essential wisdom to give renewed life to the enervated society around them. You could, if you wished, go visit it.

12. LANDSCAPE OF MEMORY

Landscape Architecture

Before the tercentenary of Quebec had even begun, that indefatigable scribbler, Arthur Doughty, had launched a campaign to perpetuate it with a history. He proposed to shape the contours of memory with words and images. Even before that, of course, the concept of permanent memorialization had been built into the festival. Champlain would be honoured by the creation of a historic park – Canada's first – literally, a landscape of memory.

Like Doughty, many other people felt that the event should be permanently recorded, especially after all the excitement. Thus several memories and meanings sought expression in remembrance just as they did in performance. The tercentenary gave rise, then, to a battle of the books, as different factions strove to set the record straight in print.

Memory had also to be inscribed on the land. Creating a historic park was not as simple as it first seemed. There were limits to what might be done. Much of the land was already occupied. Some owners could be bought out or dispossessed, some could not be. Some things were more fixed and immovable than others. Golf courses, rifle ranges, observatories, and such like could be relocated. But the space already appropriated and covered with housing, for example, would of necessity have to remain permanently private. Redemption of this 'sacred' site meant more than buying the land, placing it in public trusteeship, or even removing offensive structures. The land once nationalized had to be shaped, marked, transformed. The Plains of Abraham were not there to be found; they had to be created. To preserve this historic site, it first had to be made.

Paper and Ink

'I regard the forthcoming celebration as one of the most important events in Canadian history, the full significance of which we do not at present realize,' Arthur Doughty wrote to Edmund Walker, an Ontario member of the National Battlefields Commission, as anticipation mounted in July of 1908. To the governor general he feigned amazement that even 'the most enlightened' people he talked to had failed to grasp the significance of the event or its deeper meaning for Canada. Quebec city would be thronged and the participants in the celebration would most certainly be overwhelmed. Nevertheless, comparatively few members of the population would be able to experience the tercentenary directly. And certainly the world needed to be told. A celebration of this importance deserved to be recorded in 'a book that will illustrate the splendour of the past and may be accepted as evidence of our intellectual status.' But such an important matter should not be left to local initiative; a cheap fifty-cent booklet would be the result. Nothing less than a five-dollar volume would do, Doughty insisted, 'something that anyone would be glad to get.'

Archivists and historians think that way. For an event to be well and truly held, it must be encased within a book. Lives lived are marked by obituaries and graves; ideas and events get interred between covers and live forever in libraries. Events did not interpret themselves or explain themselves on their own. History determined that something of importance had taken place; the historian decided what it had meant. The point was not simply that a work of history, like a punctuation mark, brought closure to an important happening, but rather that the book of memory, through a process of literary transubstantiation, became the thing itself.

Doughty knew well that he was preaching to the converted. On 10 August 1908 the governor general summoned him to Rideau Hall for an extended and fretful monologue. As Doughty explained later that

The Dominion archivist, Arthur Doughty, in his office, *c.* 1908.

same day in a letter to Edmund Walker:

> He said that he was greatly disappointed that there was absolutely nothing
> with the exception of the hastily prepared book of the pageants that was fit
> to send away. Here we have had a celebration that was worthy of travelling a
> thousand miles to see, & which people would have travelled five times the
> distance to witness if they had been given an idea of what was prepared for
> them, & all we have to offer them as a memento is a five cent post card and
> a fifty cent book of the scenes.'[1]

Edmund Walker, a noted bibliophile and patron of the arts, readily
agreed that a permanent and complete record must be left.[2] He even
suggested several models that might be followed, all of them as extravagant as the governor general's idea. In the privacy of his study, Grey

sniped to Doughty that it would not do to leave this to Quebec because 'local patronage will spoil everything.' Modesty did not prevent Doughty from seeing a role for himself in the production of the literary monument that had now become Earl Grey's enthusiasm.

A shadow suddenly fell across Doughty's project. Frank Carrel, the publisher of the Quebec *Telegraph*, wrote to ask Doughty if he would contribute something to a commemorative history of the tercentenary he was proposing to have printed. This was the very kind of flimsy thing Doughty feared. Doughty offered encouragement in a guarded fashion, but warned Carrel that the commission might not support the publication of two histories. When the two men met in Quebec in the days leading up to the celebration, they optimistically agreed that there would be room for both kinds of books. Reassured, Doughty even agreed to supply a preface.[3]

H.-J.-J.-B. Chouinard also felt the need to make history. Whereas Doughty's motives were ideological and Carrel's commercial, Chouinard had another purpose. He felt shunted aside, especially once the tercentenary had concluded. After all, he had thought up the idea, nursed it through the years of indifference, and toiled night and day with the various local committees and latterly the National Battlefields Commission to bring it to fruition. He harboured a grievance that the thing had been wrenched away from him when the Ottawa crowd moved in. And that was no doubt true. He had his future to think of as well.

So, before the Dominion archivist could get his great literary project aloft, or Frank Carrel could start his presses, Chouinard launched his own pre-emptive historical strike. As city clerk he had taken the minutes of all of the important meetings and had written all of the briefs and letters. He gathered up all the documentation in his possession and had it printed in a 270–page book under the title *Fêtes du Troisième Centenaire de la Fondation de Québec par Champlain: Projets – Délibérations – Documents.*[4] It bore a charming cover, the medallion portrait of Champlain superimposed over a reproduction of his Habitation.

Like all covers, this one misled because there was nothing charming, or artful, inside. Chouinard's *Fêtes* was essentially a book of documents, reports of committees, minutes of meetings, texts of briefs leading up to the festival, a program of activities, lists of committee members. Though it appeared to be a collection of diverse materials, it nevertheless had a clear purpose and message. This was, in a very real sense, history as self-

The cover of Chouinard's history of the tercentenary.

justification. History begins, in this version, with Chouinard's letter to the *Daily Telegraph* in 1904 and events unfold under Chouinard's patient nudging.[5] The documents established that Chouinard had been the inspiration and guiding force in the planning, that Champlain was the sole object of memorialization, and that the tercentenary's success depended upon these local initiatives.

Chouinard had his friends in the Saint-Jean-Baptiste Society to think of. On that flank he wanted to show how much the local people had done to keep the focus on Champlain; by implication the rest had been imposed from outside. To his employers at City Hall he wanted to demonstrate the essentially civic nature of the process and the role he had played as mover and shaker. But he had another audience: Chouinard sensed that he occupied a very precarious position vis-à-vis the commission. His boss, the mayor, Sir George Garneau, had been named chairman of the federal commission with a handsome salary. Chouinard had acted as an on-site administrator-secretary during the festival on a small retainer, first from the city and then from the commission, but he had no permanent appointment. His services as the local administrator during the run-up to the celebration, though valued by some, had not met with universal satisfaction. Edmund Walker and Colonel Denison, as concerned commissioners, had had to curb his independent spending authority in the spring before scandal ruined things. Nor did he seem to be up to the clerical tasks required. Lascelles complained bitterly of his lax habits, and Doughty found him prickly and difficult to get along with. Chouinard obviously sensed danger. So he compiled his documentary collection to protect himself, the implication being that he, too, ought to be appropriately rewarded with a comfortable sinecure.

It was to no avail. In 1910 the National Battlefields Commission thanked him profusely, paid him a substantial honorarium, bid him a fond farewell, and appointed someone else in his place as permanent secretary. Wounded and feeling betrayed, he drafted a long memorandum to the prime minister (in English), detailing his own version of the history of the tercentenary, placing, of course, the greatest emphasis upon his inspiration and championship. Those in power saw things differently. He had already been honoured, paid, and indulged beyond the limits of patience. It was not his ability as an organizer that was in doubt, but rather his administrative competence. And there was the delicate matter of his political affiliation. After the election of 1908, with Quebec safely back in the Liberal fold, the tercentenary mercifully over without calamity, Chouinard could be dispensed with. But he would not go without a struggle, nor would this be his last word.[6]

Frank Carrel was the publisher of the *Daily Telegraph*, the English-language Liberal newspaper in Quebec City. He had eagerly opened its pages early on to the promotion of the tercentenary; indeed, it could be said that the idea had been born in the pages of the *Telegraph*'s Christmas number in 1904. Carrel thus had a paternal interest in the event. He was also a businessman. Paid announcements from the commission and advertisements from merchants put him in a warm frame of mind about the festival. And from a news point of view, the tercentenary was the biggest thing to happen in Quebec in living memory. It sold a lot of newspapers. A commemorative volume naturally recommended itself to him. His newspaper stories could be recycled and easily supplemented; speeches and documents could be quickly set in type. He had within his reach hundreds of photographs to occupy many pages. Moreover, literally thousands of people had taken part and even more had looked on. The potential market for a souvenir volume was very large.

Carrel and his team actually produced an elegant, leather-bound 176-page chronicle of spectacle early in the fall of 1908, the *Quebec Tercentenary Commemorative History*. It was no flimsy knock-off. Carrel drew his illustrations and photographs from a wide range of newspapers and pictorial magazines. He reproduced some of J.E. Livernois's studio portraits of pageant participants. He commissioned colour portraits by C.W. Jefferys of Champlain wielding his sword, Montcalm on horseback, Wolfe leading the charge on foot, and Montgomery struggling through the blizzard.

Doughty's preface emphasized that: 'The festivities at Quebec have shown us, as nothing else could have shown, how great a debt we owe to the men sent forth from France.' History had blessed the Dominion with a dual heritage; two peoples, two languages, one country. He believed the spectacle would induce a greater interest in Canadian history and help with 'the creation of an historical literature worthy of the country's past.'

Carrel's chronicle took the reader through the tercentenary day by day in a spacious double-columned format. The reportage carried the narrative briskly forward while ample use of photographs broke up the text and lightened the page. As a good newspaperman, Carrel understood the importance of getting everyone's name in the account. Though it did not make for gripping prose, and it tied up many pages with lists in tiny print, every name was a potential subscriber.

Probably to Doughty's chagrin, this was not the 50-cent production he anticipated. For most people, Carrel's *Commemorative History* was probably deemed to have done the job quite satisfactorily. It was a visually attractive book, with text and illustrations nicely balanced. The photographs mixed the various genres, formal portraits, candid shots, crowds, streetscapes, personalities, costumes, architecture, spectacle. The last quarter of the book amounted to an illustrated presentation of the pageants. Carrel's book seemed to catch the Sunday-afternoon-parlour spirit quite nicely – just enough text, just enough illustration, and a dash of colour lithography tipped in. Stately and dignified, yet not intimidating. Frank Carrel's *Commemorative History* was in every respect a record worthy of the event.

It was not, however, in Arthur Doughty's mind, a proper history. Clearly it succeeded as a description of what had taken place and a record of proceedings. But a description is not an explanation of what happened. Nor did it pay sufficient attention to the history of the country which the tercentenary celebrated. Neither could it be considered a book; it was simply a glorified newspaper report, though a very good one, to be sure.

Thus, even with Chouinard's documents and Carrel's commemorative chronicle, Doughty and his friends believed that the tercentennial still needed another history. In August, with the full flush of success working in his favour, Doughty pressed his campaign. The governor general was keen; Walker sympathized, but as a member of the National Battlefields Commission he had to acknowledge there was a problem.

In all times and in all places, a government body with a large budget exerts a powerful attraction. The National Battlefields Commission, with its dual mandate of putting on a big show and creating a national park, was such a sweet honey-pot. From the very beginning, the commission had been inundated with requests from individuals to sponsor books, pamphlets, and other works, however distantly associated with the celebration. In an early mood of generosity, the commission had subsidized the publication, for example, of Ernest Myrand's booklet of the pageants, Arthur Lavigne's hymn, 'God Bless the Prince of Wales,' and P.B. Casgrain's pamphlet on 'The Plains of Abraham.' These at least, it could be argued, would make a direct contribution to the festival or to the public understanding of the proposed battlefields park. But the commission turned down requests from Ulrich Barthe who proposed a popular edition of Champlain's *Voyages,* and J.E. Logan, who had a detailed account of Champlain's explorations already in manuscript. When Dr Albert Watson of Toronto sought support for his musical composition, 'Canada,' at the end of June 1908, the members impatiently called a halt, resolving firmly 'that the Commission cannot patronize any literary or musical publication.'[7]

In effect, by the time Grey and Doughty were working themselves up to making a pitch for a lavish production heavily subsidized by the National Battlefields Commission, the commissioners had taken what amounted to a self-denying ordinance against such activities. That kept the pamphleteers and songsters at bay, but alas also the putative official historians. Grey, as usual, would not be deterred. He himself would raise the funds necessary for a history. As Doughty confidently informed his friend George Wrong at the beginning of August, 'We are going to get up a gorgeous book of the whole celebrations at probably $25 a copy. All the guests in the city have subscribed to it. G. Drummond, Edmund Walker and a few others will provide the funds.'[8] There were advantages to this course of action. Untroubled by politics or local committees, Grey and Doughty could produce the book they wanted.

What distinguished a proper history of the tercentenary? It should be an advertisement for the intellectual aspirations of the country. That meant a doorstopper, an example of the bookmaker's art, possibly more than one volume, lavishly illustrated, designed with great care as to binding, endpapers, paper, with appropriate patronage. It had also to be a history of Canada, noble, stirring, and patriotic. It should be dignified and lyrical in tone. It should possess fine illustrations, themselves memorable works of art. In short, it should be a beautiful book produced by and for a cultural elite in the English language.

Doughty and his historian friend Colonel William Wood divided responsibility for the text: Doughty would write the historical section, Wood was commissioned to write a glowing account of the tercentenary festivities. Doughty scoured his archives for engravings, and wrote to the Wolfe and Lévis families for suitable portraits. Grey took a personal interest in the illustrations. Nothing he had seen satisfied him. Photographs could not convey either the emotion or the colour. The occasion called for the hand of a skilled painter.

As Doughty and Wood cobbled together their texts, Grey sought out suitable artwork. C.W. Jefferys would do, but Carrel had already used his pale cartoon-like drawings. Knowing that George Reid had been present, Grey appealed to him for material. Reid's blurred pastels captured the immediacy and the drama of the spectacle, but these hastily prepared sketches hardly measured up to the grandeur of the occasion. Grey wanted something bold, heroic, even magnificent, for his book. No one in Canada came immediately to mind. So in the fall he readily seized Frank Lascelles's parting offer to locate a suitable artist upon his return to England and work with him on appropriate pictorial renderings of key pageant scenes in oils.[9]

Thus, when it came time to write a book about the tercentenary to record it for all time, the editors and publishers of this English-language production avoided photographs. The camera was reserved mainly for portraits. Rather than present dim black-and-white images of what actually happened, Earl Grey chose instead to illustrate in colour the spirit of the occasion in art. On his return to England, Lascelles found an artist friend, Frank Craig, a relatively unknown book illustrator who had shown a few oils at Royal Academy exhibitions, who was willing to work with the director of the pageants in the artistic reconstruction of six memorable scenes.[10] Doughty supplied the artist with photographs; Lascelles helped him with costume colours and composition. When the first painting arrived in Ottawa in May of 1909, Doughty was impressed with the colour, the composition, and the possibilities of photo-reproduction. Indeed, as he told Earl Grey, 'I believe that the pictures alone without the text would make a first rate souvenir of the Celebration and that we should have them in any event.' On seeing Craig's painting of Champlain, the governor general enthusiastically commissioned five more pictures, suggesting the scenes he thought most suitable.[11]

The extraordinary excitement generated by the tercentenary stirred literary ambitions amongst the francophone intelligentsia of Quebec City as well, out of which a fourth history would eventually emerge. Frank Carrel's English *Commemorative History* published in the autumn of 1908 had the predictable effect. Over the next winter a Publications Committee took shape, nominally under the aegis of the civic Executive Committee, for the purpose of publishing a comparable French-language commemorative volume. The first task of this committee, which consisted of G.-A. Vandry as president, Chouinard inevitably as secretary, A.-J.

Painchaud as treasurer, and the scholars Monseigneur C.-O. Gagnon, Thomas Chapais, and l'Abbé Camille Roy, was to raise the necessary money. With the help of Mayor Garneau, the City Council was persuaded to finance the project using some of the remaining funds from the promised $100,000 municipal grant to the celebration. The city, wishing to control its contribution to the tercentenary directly, had not allowed its money to be included in the contribution administered by the National Battlefields Commission. Abbé Roy, the energetic, young, literary historian and member of the Royal Society, agreed to edit the book on the understanding that other members of the committee would provide documents and write separate chapters.[12] Thus during 1909 and 1910 two histories of the tercentenary were in production in Quebec and in Ottawa, one English and one French.

When these books, *The King's Book of Quebec* and *Les Fêtes du Troisième Centenaire de Québec: 1608–1908*, finally appeared after much delay in 1911, they were a study in contrasts. In form, structure, illustration, and interpretation they differed significantly. Both were substantial literary productions; the former in two volumes and 392 elegantly printed pages, the latter a single 630 page volume. Doughty had only five hundred copies printed on heavy hand-cut paper and bound in calf. He intended his book should have scarcity value. The Quebec production, though handsome, looked much like a conventional history book intended for wide distribution. Both were lavishly illustrated, though in different ways. Both books strove in lyric prose to ensure that an event that had made such a deep emotional impression should remain permanent in memory.

The titles of the two books suggest one of the main lines of difference. When everything was in readiness to go to press, Arthur Doughty suggested to Earl Grey that 'the success of the celebration was due largely to the interest taken in it by His Majesty, and as it is your wish to dedicate the volume to the King, I think it quite proper that it should be called "The King's Book."'[13] Doughty's patron obviously agreed and so *The King's Book of Quebec* it would be, even though the title offered no hint as to the contents. The Comité Livre-Souvenir adopted a much more straightforward, descriptive title. It was as if the sole audience for the one book was the king; the Quebec City book was written for a community. Doughty's book assumed that the king had 'made' the event, given it meaning; Abbé Roy's volume by implication argued that the initiative and success was due to the collective effort of Quebeckers. The frontispiece of *The*

King's Book was a full-page portrait of King George V; the frontispiece of *Les Fêtes* was an engraving of Champlain.

Casual readers leafing through these volumes when they arrived long after the event would gain their first and perhaps most lasting impression from the illustrations. In keeping with the lofty ambition of the authors and the deep pockets of their sponsors, *The King's Book* contained a greater volume of illustration and, significantly, ten colour plates of original art. The black-and-white illustrations in *Les Fêtes* were less numerous, and depended more on woodcuts, old engravings, and photography.

The images of monarchy weigh down the front end of *The King's Book*. First comes the king, then his late father, followed by Queen Alexandra – all by page 4. The king and queen do not appear until page 64 of *Les Fêtes*. But after this monarchical introduction, attention shifts in *The King's Book* to Champlain, the *Don-de-Dieu*, and scenes from the pageants, and photographs of dignitaries. Illustrations selected for *Les Fêtes* kept the focus on the city itself and the pageants. Woodcuts of the gates, ramparts, and old buildings at the head of each chapter stressed that this was a celebration of a city. Reproductions of engraved views of the city sustained this theme. Public figures tended to appear in pairs: the king and queen, the governor general and Sir Louis Jetté, Laurier and Gouin, Monseigneur Bégin and Mayor Garneau, Laval and Marie de l'Incarnation. There is a federal-provincial, church-state balance implied by the arrangement.

The use of panoramic photography, however, was the distinguishing feature of the illustrations in *Les Fêtes*. About two-thirds of the way through the text, at about the point where a description of the pageants commenced, glossy panels folded out once, and then again, to reveal full-scale panoramic views. On the first panel Cartier's greeting upon landing is paired with his encounter with François I in the gardens at Fontainebleau. Further along, the scene of Champlain's return to Quebec with his young bride shares the page with an overhead view of the arrival of the Ursulines. Next the dancers in the sumptuously costumed Henri IV scene float above a panoramic scene showing the newly arrived Governor de Tracy kneeling to kiss the ring of Bishop Laval before an immense throng. Near the end of the book a page folds out to reveal the messe solonnelle in the grandstand under which is to be found the three navies anchored in harmony in the river below Quebec. Visually the editors of *Les Fêtes* thus strove to capture the immense sweep of the festivities using a new technology, to put France and New France on terms of courtly equality, and to stress the glory of Rome as well as the power of empire.

The King's Book aimed at an entirely different effect. Where the editors of *Les Fêtes* strove to use pictures to capture the breadth of the festivities, Doughty, Wood, and Grey used art to capture intense moments in the pageants, and by extension Canadian history – moments of commission, piety, encounter, arrival, founding, submission, and accommodation. The stunning coloured illustrations would immediately arrest the eye: Frank Craig's Champlain bowing before a group of ladies of the court in deep seductive curtsies; George Reid's *Don-de-Dieu*, glowing golden in the dawn of discovery, dwarfing the war-bonnetted Indians in their canoes below (colour illustration no. 8). Reid's pensive Champlain looks out over the river. In Craig's most striking painting, Marie de l'Incarnation and the Ursulines float on a green field, their faces, framed by white cowls, wreathed in an aura of religious ecstacy. Craig's interpretation of the march-past of the historic armies is less successful. In the classic structure of military portraiture, he has Wolfe on a white charger, its nostrils flaring and eyes bulging in fear. The ground-level view exaggerates the horses and diminishes the riders, making them somewhat indistinguishable – though that, of course, was the point.

In volume two of *The King's Book* the coloured illustrations are grouped as a climax near the end. Craig's magnificent rendering of Cartier comes first, kneeling in the foreground in a flowered meadow before François I. The king and queen on horseback under a golden canopy soar above him but in shadow. The final climactic image, Frank Craig's visually and emotionally striking encounter of Laval and de Tracy, ends the series. Altar boys in white surplices shade the bishop, whose head is tilted only so slightly in greeting. Standing just to the right of centre, de Tracy returns the salutation bareheaded, his plumed hat in his left hand, his right hand across his heart. The smirk of the Intendant Talon, dressed all in black between these two figures, suggests something of the condescension of the aristocrats (see cover and colour illustration no. 9).

Craig composed his subjects on a flattened colour field, usually green. He suggested a mass of people in the background, but he always kept a few figures prominent and carefully assembled in triangles in the foreground or along a rising diagonal. He painted intense moments, using light and shadow to sharpen power relations. Emotion drips from the

Arrival of the Ursulines. Painting by Frank Craig.

canvas: the religious transport of Marie de l'Incarnation; the haughtiness of de Tracy, the mock humility of Laval. These pictures vaguely resemble in style the paintings of Arthur Rackham, whose career had just begun to flourish at this time. Occasionally these oils suggest decorative poster-art realism. Craig's painting may have been influenced by Burne-Jones and the William Morris group, but the brightness of the palette and the dramatic composition of the figures on the field put Craig in a school of his own.[14]

There were also profound differences in the text of *The King's Book* and *Les Fêtes*. After an opening chapter (drafted most certainly by Chouinard) tracing the origins of the festival from 1904 to the arrival of the ships of the three navies below Quebec, *Les Fêtes* proceeded with a day-by-day account of the main events, quoting extensively from all the principal speeches. Chapter 11 offered an extensive plot summary of the pageants, scene by scene. A lengthy set of appendices reprints the pope's letter on the occasion, the circular letters of the archbishop of Quebec, and a list of ancient families. These were matters not given much emphasis in the English-language volume.

The King's Book of Quebec was something else entirely, a history of Canada as well as an account of the events. Following a fawning full paragraph of dedication to the king, and a brief prologue by Earl Grey written in long, rolling periods extolling the goals of the festival, then came history, 126 pages of it.

Doughty opened with a statement that flowed logically from Craig's wonderful paintings: 'In a very real sense Canada is the child of the Renaissance.' He was then off tripping lightly over the master narrative of Canadian history. In Canada, unlike the United States, religion tempered commerce in the work of colonization. The explorer, the priest, the settler, soldier, and administrator each receive their due. New France is shown bravely resisting for much longer than anyone expected the gathering force of the enemy before it inevitably fell. But, Doughty is quick to observe, 'No war had happier sequels,' as French Canadians rallied in 1775 and again in 1812 to the defence of their new king and old country. The War of 1812, with which his narrative ended (not, it should be noted, 1759) 'proved to Canadians their national obligation of self-defence, the necessity for a nucleus of regular troops, and the supreme importance to Canada of British command of the seas.' Then he leapt forward, with a D'Artagnan-like flourish: 'Here, after all, are the essen-

tials of Empire as British statesmanship conceive it; national responsibility combined with Imperial obligation; one for all and all for one.' The
past was thus a prologue: 'Fifty years later Quebec saw that meeting of the
Fathers of Confederation out of which Canadian nationality arose, and
the event of 1867 was nothing so much as the carrying one step further of
a power which took its definite direction in the War of 1812.' For Grey
and Doughty, history spoke of greatness, heroic bloodlines, superior
character. It preached the accommodation of the two founding peoples
by diminishing the Conquest, by stressing its happy issue. Above all, it
pointed towards a future for a new nation within a greater Empire.

Doughty could dance lightly over the military events of 1759–60 perhaps because he knew that Wood, the leading authority on the subject,
would follow him. And indeed, Wood opened his essay on the tercentennial events with a powerful argument that the truth of the fall of New
France made both communities free. The lesson of history was there,
Wood believed, for all to see and it was not the suppression of one people
by another:

> Thus four races fought on five Quebec battlefields. The Americans were on
> the victorious side once, the British-born twice, and the Canadian-born no
> less than four times. When we consider further that the winning side was
> always composed of two races, and that the losing side never suffered the
> slightest dishonour in defeat, we can fully understand, not only that there
> is nothing to fear from the truth, but that all four races have at Quebec the
> unique souvenir of such an *entente cordiale d'honneur* as the whole world
> beside has never possessed since history began.[15]

With that settled, Wood confidently marched on with a sprightly account
of the planning, preparations, principal events of the celebration and
a brisk summary of the historical pageant. In Wood's hands, history
served present purposes, in particular the harmonization of relations on
more equal terms of the relations of French and English in Canada. It
should be noted, however, that in both pieces by Doughty and Wood, the
native 'race' disappears; it was not, apparently, a presence on the fields of
honour.

L'Abbé Roy and his colleagues drew different but not fundamentally
dissimilar conclusions from their account of the tercentenary. *Les Fêtes*
brimmed with pride. The citizens of Quebec had put on an extraordi-

nary spectacle before the eyes of the world, the like of which would not likely ever be seen again. Such a triumph deserved never to be forgotten. But the tercentenary had been more than a mere entertainment, however grand the scale. This fête represented a moment of recognition for French culture. French Canadians had done something that had earned the respect and admiration of others. That was the lesson that should always be remembered.

The success of the fête, especially the pageant, had opened the eyes of the young in a way heretofore not possible to the heroic origins of a people. Memories of these astonishing scenes would live deep in the souls of all who saw them or, in this instance, could relive them in the words and photographs of this livre-souvenir. The tercentenary acknowledged that Quebec had a glorious history before 1760. Citizens from other parts of the country and from abroad had applauded French-Canadian heroes. The tasteful closing scene represented 'a virtual homage rendered by this generation to the proud dignity and unshakeable patriotism of our ancestors.' The tercentenary had celebrated not only the 'Frenchness' of the Canadian past, but also its Christian and Catholic character: 'Laval, our missionaries, our nuns passed before us as guardian angels of the colony.'

But the tercentenary held lessons for the future. The welcome accorded the Prince of Wales and the British fleet demonstrated that Quebec felt completely at home under the British flag. Quebeckers rejoiced 'to live happily guarded by the redoubtable powers of the Lion of England.' The tercentenary showed the possibility of a genuine entente cordiale within Canada. As the English showed unstinting admiration for French-Canadian heroes, so too could French-Canadians give ample testimony to their affection for the larger nation and lay claim to its grandeur as their own: 'It is because we respected one another at the feet of Champlain's statue that we can clasp one another in fraternity. This embrace should continue: it should not loosen as long as the races jealously guard and respect each other's rights.'[16]

Thus, though the two books put the emphasis in different places, they nevertheless came to a similar conclusion. Earl Grey's claim that the tercentenary had served 'to draw Canadians of British and French descent closer to each other and to the Crown,' and thereby assisted Laurier in his efforts to harmonize the different elements of the country, could in large measure be supported by the evidence of these two commemorative volumes.[17] Whether this was actually true or not, whether the historians read the evidence correctly, whether the words represented some deeper reality, is another matter. But in the world of the literary imagination, saying it made it true.

There was an ironic footnote to this interment between covers of the literary remains of the tercentennial day. It was as if a light blinked on sometime in the early fall of 1908. Edmund Walker and his academic friend, the historian George Wrong, woke up to the significance of what they had done in founding the Champlain Society a few years earlier, a Canadian version of the British Camden and Hakluyt societies. The Champlain Society intended to reprint in fine editions the key texts of the discovery and exploration of Canada. With some effort Wrong and Walker had rounded up the 250 bibliophiles needed to support this venture. They had already undertaken to print an English translation of Marc Lescarbot's *History of New France*, and more volumes were planned.

The tercentenary of Champlain's founding of Quebec ought surely to be memorialized, they reasoned, with a variorum edition of the voluminous *Voyages of Champlain*, the explorer who had given the society its name and, providentially, to whose honour the National Battlefields Commission had been dedicated. These works existed in a modern edition in French, but not in English. The Champlain Society would undertake the publication and annotation of a bilingual edition. Wrong appears to have first seized the opportunity; Doughty offered encouragement and suggested possible editors and translators. Walker, the guiding financial spirit of the society, readily concurred with these enterprising scholars. Such a project would be expensive, far beyond the means of a subscription society that was already stretched to publish an occasional volume. That is where the tercentenary and the National Battlefields Commission came in.

Walker first prevailed upon his colleague on the commission, Colonel Denison. Together they squared Sir George Garneau. And thus, at a meeting on 29 March 1909, with Garneau, Denison, Turgeon, and Walker present, the commission voted a subsidy of $5,000 to the Champlain Society of Toronto to publish Champlain's works.[18] So much for the policy of not supporting literary endeavours. But let not these ironies and conflicts of interest diminish the accomplishment. This cabal, using funds provided for the celebration at Quebec and the creation of a national historic park, provided an impetus to one of the great monuments of Canadian historical scholarship in the early twentieth century, the collective effort under H.P. Biggar's direction that resulted in the publication in six volumes of Champlain's *Voyages*. This incidental gesture by the National Battlefields Commission would result in a more lasting literary monument to Champlain than any of the four works of commemorative history. However, having committed their funds, the commissioners must have despaired of living to see the day when these books would ever be finished. The first volume did not appear until 1922! They might have feared the same thing about the park they were charged to create.

Grass and Trees

Once the grandstand had been taken down, the ferris wheel carted away, and the open-air altar disassembled, the Plains of Abraham reverted to their former appearance – rough, open fields. Here and there clumps of scrub and rough rock outcrops gave it a desolate, drab, windswept appearance. To be redeemed, sacralized, nationalized, or imperialized as Earl Grey would have it, meant that the Plains of Abraham would have to look like something else, something other than what they were.

It mattered little that the Plains had little real connection to Abraham Martin, dit l'Écossais, one of Champlain's pilots. His allotment above the town gave rise to the name of a path which carried the name over time and connected it to other places in the vicinity. What mattered most was that in 1759 both the recently arrived French generals and the invading British believed themselves to be manoeuvring their armies across a space above the river casually known as the Plains of Abraham or the Heights of Abraham. And thus the name, with its Old Testament allusions, comes down to us through history even though there might be more direct claimants to the topographical nomenclature.[19]

Upon what principles would the Plains be reconstructed? No one could be quite sure what the Plains looked like in 1759–60. Surviving accounts speak of unkempt pastures, and scattered grainfields. So a historical model would not do. Besides, no one could reasonably propose the restoration of the Plains of Abraham as they were at the time of the Seven Years' War because most of that land had subsequently been covered with buildings, including the provincial legislature. The ground on which the centre-right of Montcalm's army clashed with the centre-left of Wolfe's had long since been turned into prime real estate. The Ste-Foy battlefield had only recently been subdivided. During the nineteenth century the territory colloquially known as the Plains of Abraham had been systematically reduced by urban encroachment to that space between the Grand Allée on the north and the cliffs on the south, the Citadel on the east, and the Ursulines' Merici school to the west. The park would have to be built upon this residue.

This space, however, was far from being empty. The land showed marks of heavy use, of previous and continuing occupation. Close to the Citadel a fourteen-hole golf course could be seen lacing its way between the rocky mounds. At the crest near the Citadel the boxy stone shape of the Naval Observatory sat up improbably against the skyline. Here and there trenches from an old firing range could be seen. Rickety fences wandered aimlessly over the hills. Across from the entrance closest to the city squatted the hump-roofed skating rink that doubled as an agricultural hall. Not far away, the low buildings of the new Ross Rifle factory nestled behind a knoll. On lower ground nearby, a ragged picket fence enclosed the scattered buildings of the cartridge works, sunken and embanked to protect against explosions. And, of course, smack dab in the middle of the space, squatting like a giant toad, stood the grim fortress of the provincial jail, built in 1867. A mile away the white shaft of the Monument des Braves stood in splendid isolation in the middle of a subdivision.[20]

It was, allegedly, in Champlain's memory that this coveted and neglected piece of real estate was to be turned into Canada's first national historic park. The urge to build a park came from several different and sometimes conflicting sources. Even those who objected to the ideology behind this particular park nevertheless believed urban parks a necessity. From New York's landmark Central Park, constructed in the 1860s, a North American ideal had developed that each great city needed a large park at its centre. As a green space amidst concrete it would serve as the lungs of the city, bringing air and light to the people. As a civic venture it provided the working classes with the green space and pleasure grounds that previously only the rich could afford. Building and maintaining a park provided jobs, especially in times of economic distress. Parks acted as a moral force on the city, softening its rigidities and commercial anxieties with the curves and balm of nature. While parks occupied valuable space, they had the magical effect of making the land around

A view looking west from the Citadel of the Plains of Abraham before 1908. The observatory is on the left and the jail on the right. Note the rail fences.

them more valuable. Green space could also disguise those amenities necessary to public health, safety, and sanitation, such as reservoirs and sewers. For boosters, parks became the symbolic image of cities, the spaces cities were known by and tourists came to envy.[21]

Complex social coalitions of businessmen, professionals, and labour leaders loosely formed behind this aesthetic of parks. In North America the second half of the nineteenth century was the moment for the construction of urban parks, most notably in Chicago, San Francisco, Vancouver, and Montreal – where Frederick Law Olmsted as one of his last commissions developed the master plan for Mount Royal Park.[22] To a large extent, therefore, local support for the creation of a park on the Plains of Abraham rested on these fairly typical political foundations. The difference in Quebec, however, was that the city did not have to pay, and thus had less to say about its location or design.

Responsibility for creating a national park in the heart of Quebec City rested with the National Battlefields Commission, an agency of the federal government. It had been provided with a statutory foundation and $300,000 by the Dominion government; the provinces added $260,000. Earl Grey's campaign, spearheaded by the Quebec Battlefields Association appeal, raised an additional $300,000 from various sources. Out of this total the commission had to deduct expenses incurred for the tercentennial celebrations which, when all the bills came in, added up to $339,038.92. That left the commission with roughly $560,000 to acquire land from private owners and build the park.[23]

To make the park, as much land as possible had first to be secured. This in itself was no easy task, as the commission quickly discovered. Land prices shot up. Without powers of expropriation, the commission fell prey to the machinations of local speculators. Nor could all of the land in public hands be readily assembled into a single parcel adminis-tered by the commission. Neither the province of Quebec nor the federal goverment, both of whom owned extensive properties within the bounds of the putative park, would vacate without either compensation or alter-native local sites.

These were the problems to which the commissioners turned their minds once the dust had settled from the tercentenary and everyone had been paid off. It fell to them to decide, within their political, aesthetic, and financial means, how the land would be reshaped to honour the memory of Champlain on the one hand and the fallen heroes of the battles of 1759–60 on the other. But how precisely could this landscape be made 'to speak its eloquent message?' What would it be meant to say?[24]

The Quebec Literary and Historical Society, one of the first advocates of a park on the Plains, thought in terms of a public garden.[25] Apart from purging the site of the loathsome jail and the nuisance of the rifle factory, Earl Grey conceived of the place largely as a setting for his symbolic Angel of Peace; he did not give a great deal of thought to the design of the terrain. His minion, Arthur Doughty, in his first memorandum on the subject, considered the place as primarily the site for a historical museum and a statue.[26] At some point in conversations with the governor general in 1907, Laurier mentioned his desire at some future point to see the Plains of Abraham turned into a park much like the Gettysburg National Military Park in Pennsylvania. It is not clear whether Laurier had himself visited Gettysburg, or had only heard of it. Picking up on this lead, Grey despatched Doughty, General Lake, and Colonel Wood to Gettysburg in November of 1907 to investigate. In brief, these three men believed that the program of reserving land, restoring it to its 1863 condition, and marking the battle lines with unobstrusive markers would be well suited to the Quebec situation. They also thought the battlefields would be just the beginning of a larger historic park.[27]

Earlier in 1907 the Quebec Landmarks Commission (Langelier, Taché, and Wood) had also recommended that the Plains of Abraham and the Monument des Braves become an urban park. In their minds that meant that it would resemble the Bois de Boulogne, Hyde Park, the Tiergarten, or Central Park and serve similar public purposes: public heath, sanitation, rest and relaxation from the daily struggle for survival, and a glorious inheritance of precious space to future generations. Treed and landscaped, this park would give the city 'a magnificent crown,' its easy winding drives would form a veritable pilgrimage, a promenade unrivalled in the world. It would also give it a soul, according to the commission: 'These few famous acres are no dilettante souvenir of a dead and buried past, but the living embodiment of her ancestral spirit at a zenith of its aspiration and achievement.' Langelier, Taché, and Wood believed that there was a scientific connection between a heroic history and the present vitality of the country. Accordingly, a landscape of this nature would directly serve both spiritual and economic progress by fostering historical consciousness:

> It is the mark of all great peoples; it is taught by the faith of all religion, by the records of all history, and by the most modern science of heredity. Science and history also prove that the same essential energy assumes different forms to meet different needs. So it is no idle sentiment, but a scientific fact, that most of the national energy now displayed in bridging the St. Lawrence at Cap Rouge, building new transcontinental railways and transoceanic steamers, prospecting and surveying and pioneering far and wide, repatriating French-Canadians in the Quebec hinterland, or directing towards the waiting prairie the full flood tide of human life that surges so eagerly through Winnipeg Station – it is a scientific fact that most of this transmuted energy is inherited from the national heroes of the Plains of Abraham.[28]

Reverence for the past thus fed present purposes and ensured future greatness.

The commission reissued this report somewhat defensively with a revised preface correcting a few errors, and addressing some omissions in the first edition (such as the need to relocate the rifle works). For clarity, the commissioners stressed: 'The word "Park" does not imply any tricking out of the battlefields in flower-beds and other artificial incongruities. The "gardening" and "laying out" should never interfere with the natural aspect of the historic sites, which should be marked with unobtrusive tablets that the whole ground should be read like an open book.'[29]

In the spring of 1908, the Quebec Battlefields Association had plainly modelled its appeal to the people of Canada on the Gettysburg Battlefield Monuments Association that had privately spearheaded public preservation, but it remained quite vague about its precise goals for the site. The pamphlet spoke of consecration as a means of reconnecting modern society with the bloodied heroism of the past. After much fervid prose about the battles themselves and the glory that must live forever, the pamphlet concluded lamely that the park 'will include the best of what must always be known as the Plains of Abraham, and the best of every other centre of action that can be preserved in whole, or part, or only in souvenir by means of a tablet.' The pamphlet regained its lofty syntax, however, with a concluding panegyric on the massive Angel of Peace statue soaring above the scene, her folded wings pronouncing a benediction on the scene.[30]

That is as far as any thinking got on the subject of the landscape of memory before the tercentenary. It should have an open, natural appearance and not be a formal French or English garden. It should be accessible through winding drives which would open onto uplifting vistas, and permit different angles of view onto the park. The ground should be cleared of incongruous intrusions such as factories, rifle ranges, golf courses. There should be unobtrusive markers on the ground so that people might guide themselves through the past. Clearly the Quebeckers and park promoters were under the unconscious influence of the prevailing North American 'naturalistic landscape' aesthetic. When they thought of a specific model for this first Canadian national historic park, Gettysburg came immediately to mind. Thus democratic and republican landscape ideals became gradually adopted to a monarchist, Canadian nationalist and imperial purpose.

After the tercentenary, as the National Battlefields Commission plunged ever deeper into the morass of Quebec City real estate acquisitions, it hired Frederick G. Todd, a young American landscape architect who had recently moved his practice to Montreal, to devise a plan to make the earth speak.[31] Todd had in fact been trained in Brookline, Massachusetts, and had then migrated to Canada to work for an early precursor of the National Capital Commission devising a master plan for the Ottawa region. Quickly he became the leading landscape architect in the country. His services were in particular demand in the blossoming cities of western Canada whose municipal councils wished to emulate the grand parks and elegant residential neighbourhoods of the east.

The commission gave Todd the somewhat contradictory instructions to develop a master plan that would transform the Plains of Abraham 'into a national park, in order to ensure their restoration and permanent conservation, without altering their beauty or historic aspect.' He replied with a proposal, subsequently adopted, that draped the site in the full raiment of the American 'natural picturesque.' The main contours of the land would be retained, though smoothed and softened with shrubbery and vast lawn. Todd emphasized the 'natural' landscape, though nature would be subtly reshaped to appear natural. Curvilinear drives would make looping figure eights through the space, affording ever-changing views of the undulating land. Promenades along the top of the cliff would afford spectacular views of the river and lead to a curved terrace overlooking Wolfe's Cove, with space there reserved for the Angel of Peace statue. Trees native to the region would be planted to shield the park from the city, to break the vast expanse, bring the eye to several points of focus, and mark natural features, folds in the land, knolls, and ravines. A treed boulevard would frame a large green where the race course and pageant grandstand once stood. These same shade trees would then march down a long avenue connecting the Plains of Abraham to the Monument des Braves about a mile away. Discreet stone markers, bearing brief inscriptions, would mark strategic points in the battles. Visitors would thus be able to guide themselves over the ground, from place to place, to receive a physical sense of the situation, reading the land like a book.

But all was not battlefield. The five different zones of the park the set off by greenery and driveways were each intended to serve different purposes and each received slightly different treatment. The area closest to the Citadel, with its Martello tower of 1812 and many rocky outcrops, was left open and somewhat rough; it was a place to walk and take in the vistas. The flat semi-circle west of Wolfe's monument became a vast curving lawn on which parades, reviews, and spectacles might be held.

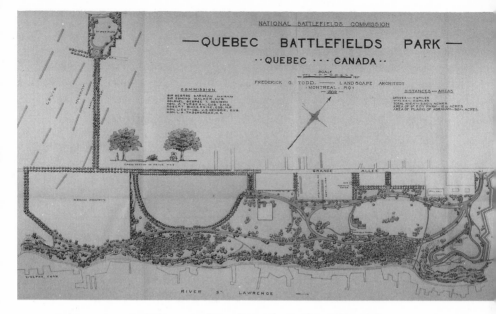

A plan for the Quebec National Battlefields Historic Park, prepared by Frederic Todd, as it appeared as a fold-out in *The King's Book of Quebec*.

The third zone, the broad ravine sloping down towards the river, was to be reforested and provided with meandering trails so that the exploits of the troops scaling the cliffs to the heights might be emulated in more gentle circumstances. A birds-eye view of this spot could be had from the semi-circular terrace. The cliffs, which were to remain more of less inaccessible, became a site for botanical restoration and the extensive planting of wild flowers. A sloping picnic ground with planted margins provided a picturesque setting for the Monument des Braves.[32]

The commission formally adopted Todd's plan in 1911. It then took what must have seemed like an eternity to create the park. Until the mid-1920s the Plains of Abraham most closely resembled an abandoned construction site. Works begun were interrupted for long periods by war or for budgetary reasons. In the 1930s the city of Quebec excavated a huge underground reservoir on the Plains to help solve a perennial water problem. This introduced a blunt, flat, geometric shape into an area Todd had left lumpy and uneven. A modern parking lot on the surface emphasizes this intrusion. The Department of National Defence reoccupied the terrain during the Second World War, surrendering it only in 1952.

The commission slowly acquired properties, but to do so it had to be equipped with powers of expropriation to bring opportunistic owners to accept reasonable estimates of the value of their properties. Public agencies could be even more obdurate and the weapon of expropriation did not work against them. The federal government itself only slowly surrendered its real estate to the commission for parks purposes, and then in times of emergency resumed occupancy. The famous Ross Rifle factory and the Cartridge works remained firmly ensconced within the proposed boundaries of the park until 1939.[33]

It would take more than a lifetime for the commission to assemble the land and realize Todd's plan. Much of what he proposed may be seen when you walk on the Plains today. It was not always this verdant, tree-marked meadow. Todd subtly reshaped the terrain to make it seem to resemble what ought to have been there in 1759. He kept buildings to a minumum or hid them away. Picturesque ruins from a later period were retained, most notably the Martello tower from 1812. The slope of the land and the avenues gently bring the visitor to the point of British penetration. The landscaping led the visitor to Wolfe. Todd tried in vain to link physically the site of the Battle of Ste-Foy to the Plains of Abraham with his long straight avenue; but try as he might, the Monument des Braves proved difficult to integrate and remained something of a forgotten appendage to the park. Todd's landscape spoke most eloquently of 1759.

Some things would not appear according to the plan; others would not disappear. The crenellated gate, echoing the rebuilt fortifications of the city, would not be erected. The viewpoint over Wolfe's Cove, named Earl Grey Terrace when it was completed in 1916, still lacks its colossal Angel of Peace, though the pedestal is there waiting for it to descend.[34] The ailing Earl Grey, when he received photographs from Sir George Garneau of the landscaping and the terrace that bore his name, could not resist one last blast at his favourite monstrosity in his letter of thanks: 'The only blot on the photographs is the existence of that detestable gaol, which I hope it may be possible for the Provincial Government to transfer as soon as opportunity offers. I shall be very grateful to you if you will let me know if there is the slightest chance of this being done in the approximately near future.'[35] Were he alive, he would still be waiting.

The jail that drove Earl Grey to distraction remains, a grim fortress on grey days, though it has lost much of its horror and grown quaint in autumn light. Ironically it serves a dual purpose now, neither of which Earl Grey would have approved of: it is both a museum of the macabre arts of penology, and it has become the interpretive centre for the National Battlefields Park – which must surely be a stinging rebuke of the ages! It is to this jail with its video displays that tourists must come to understand fully what Todd's landscape is saying.

CONCLUSION: FORGETTING

The Denisons raced home on the overnight train to prepare Heydon Villa for Lord Roberts's arrival. They were to be his hosts during his much anticipated side-trip to Toronto. He would never arrive; overcome by the midday heat and his exertions on the Plains of Abraham the old soldier had to be taken directly home to England. All of Toronto was disappointed.

Clare Denison carried with her in her bag a large parcel of photographs, souvenir programs, and her own sweet memories of her coming out in the presence of the Prince of Wales before all of Canadian society. The Toronto newspapers were waiting for her at Heydon Villa with a more measured budget of reportage and illustration. For days afterwards, she patiently cut out articles, corrected some errors in the captions, and organized these objects in order in her special scrapbook. There in these pages her Toronto friends might see more clearly the sights she could only breathlessly and meagrely describe in words. Later, when the oversize *Quebec Tercentenary Commemorative History* arrived with estimable speed from the presses of the enterprising Mr Carrel, she and her family could relive what for her were surely some of the happiest days of her life when, like her, the country seemed young and full of promise.

Ethel Chadwick and Lola Powell mooned about Quebec for a few days with Forbes Dennis and Frank Lascelles in melancholy contemplation of *temps perdu*. Together they went on a wistful journey down the St Lawrence striking poses aboard the Prices' yacht. The more interest Forbes Dennis showed in Ethel, the more withdrawn and moody Lascelles became. Dennis gave Ethel the pin the Iroquois had given him as a memento when they parted. At first she teased him about where he had bought the trinket, only to become mortified afterwards when she learned the truth. Thus it was with aching romantic regret at the necessary passing of all things that Ethel Chadwick, Lola Powell, and company made their tearful way back to Ottawa.

The Prince of Wales could not have been happier. The seas were calm, the *Indomitable* was bounding across the Atlantic at the astonishing speed of twenty-five knots, and he was on his way home to his wife and family. On Friday off the coast of Newfoundland he had briefly visited the engine room to observe preparations for the speed trials. Now, as the ship swallowed up vast quantities of fuel to maintain her headway, everyone had to do a turn below to help the overworked colliers in the stokeholds and bunkers. Dirty and disagreeable it might be, but everyone pitched in, including the prince. On Saturday night at 6:00 p.m. he too descended into the depths to shovel coal for half an hour: 'got pretty dirty, fine exercise, quite good fun' he scratched in his diary afterwards. With the forced draught of the furnaces whipping up coal dust down below, and cinders raining down on the deck from the black plumes of smoke pouring out of the funnels, there was no escape from the dirt and grime. But in the excitement of an attempt on a record crossing no one complained. Quebec now lay far behind the Prince of Wales. By Monday morning at 5:00 a.m. the coast of Ireland was sighted; by noon they were off the Scilly Isles, and at 9:45 in the evening the *Indomitable* dropped anchor off Cowes. The average speed of 25.13 knots between Belle Isle and Fastnet was most certainly a record for a heavily laden man-of-war, but the times set by the luxury liners *Lusitania* and the *Mauretania* had not been broken.[1]

For those returning home from the tercentenary, words seemed somehow inadequate to convey the excitement that had poured in simultaneously through every sense. It was almost impossible to explain to friends what it had been like, to hear the earth-rending roar of the cannons and the competing bands, to smell the cordite and perfume, to see colour and gaiety and society wherever one looked, to be among handsome soldiers and sailors, to be enchanted by the spectacle of the pageant, to be *in* the pageant, to feel a frisson of fear as the Iroquois attacked, to thrill to the marching troops, to dance and flirt, and to see and be seen by really important people. It was a message that simply could not be

The Prince of Wales, centre with the shovel, about to go below to assist in heaving coal during HMS *Indomitable*'s attempt at an Atlantic crossing speed record.

transmitted. Moreover, friends and neighbours who hadn't been there did not seem much interested.

Pictures too proved a disappointment. So dull and grey, so diminutive. The camera reduced spectacular things to distant dots. Everything seemed frozen, staged, even a bit odd, all motion and colour drained from the event. The thrusting prows of the ships jumped dramatically out of the stereoscope, but the crowds seemed thinner than they were in memory. And what of the balls, the fleeting glimpses of the Prince of Wales as he passed en route to a public engagement? Pictures didn't convey feelings. Pasting pictures in scrapbooks brought back some of the sensation, but precious little. And the pictures took so much explaining for friends to make any sense of them.

August, September, October brought new concerns: the general election in Canada, the naval scare in Europe. Still, occasional reminders of the tercentenary cropped up unexpectedly. Every now and then word of some new scandal having to do with land assembly for the Plains of Abraham Park caused a temporary sensation in the press. Premier Whitney gave a dinner for his Quebec counterpart late in 1909 at which the good feelings of the tercentenary were rhetorically revisited. The governor general, ever the optimist, believed 'that this rapprochement between the two provinces is a direct result of the Quebec Celebrations last year.' He hoped that the two thousand Orange militiamen from Ontario would spread the word of the charms of Quebec on their return: 'all that is required to make the Ontario Orangeman and the Quebec Roman Catholic love one another is intercourse, with more frequent opportunities of making friends.'[2]

At home, the stereoscopic slides were much admired at first. The arrival by mail of the tercentennial medals, and afterwards, the fat, pretentious, much-delayed ceremonial books, put the event firmly in the past. Memory had become enshrined, thus buried. By that time the Prince of Wales had been crowned King George V.

Programs and postcards sifted to the bottom of piles and the backs of drawers until it was time either to throw them out, or stuff them into boxes along with old photograph albums and scrapbooks. Letters and memoranda were filed away, to be sorted and picked over later. Memory faded; only the ephemeral residue remained packed away in boxes until much later, in old age or by children and grandchildren, it was given to the archives.

Despite the elaborate public effort at remembering, the country gradually forgot the tercentenary and whatever meanings it might have had. Public memory, so theatrical, intense, vivid, and spectacular, vanished in the gusts of controversy. The naval debate, and renewed wars of language and religion, revealed that deep currents of suspicion and animosity swirled not far beneath the surface of public civility.

The country flourished, but the imagined nation of the tercentenary never appeared, for better or for worse. A master narrative for a nation can be glimpsed in performance, but it was not echoed in belief and behaviour. The tercentenary of Quebec did not, therefore, begin anything. It did not produce the Angel of Peace, a national symbol, like the Statue of Liberty or France's Marianne. The imagined sharing of a common vision of the past between two peoples did not take place. And the third nation, now the first, struggled without success to find its place in the picture without being a symbol of a vanishing race.

Personal memory is a constituent of, but not identical with, public memory. People at Quebec came away with quite different recollections, some of pride in accomplishment, some of anger and shame at slights real and imagined, some of indifference, some of business, some that the message was being heard, some with regret that the proper impression had not been made, some with relief that disaster had been averted, some with hope that the future might be much brighter because of it. For many, the tercentenary was not a moment to build upon, but rather one to endure, enjoy, and let pass.

As the tercentenary showed, and as we have discovered many times since, Canadians would not be as easily made as Italians – but perhaps that exaggerates the speed and completeness of the fusion of regional peoples into a European state. Goldwin Smith, the sage of the Grange and great smiter of Canadian pretensions, spelled out the attributes of nationhood to demonstrate that Canada could never become a nation like the others; it lacked a singular identity, a common history, and a shared destiny. His pessimism perhaps erred in the other direction. Canadians found enough common ground at Quebec to go on with the show. Moreover, they took considerable pride in their performance as they revised and negotiated their past to meet their present needs. They convinced themselves that what they had to do was not only necessary, but also right and true. They also politely agreed to disagree and chose to ignore some important, pressing matters. But at root Goldwin Smith was right. Because of a persistent pluralism that refused to be reduced to a single story or language, a much better fate than integral nationalism lay in store for Canadians. A history of the Quebec tercentenary, which was a prototype of many subsequent attempts to cultivate a national identity, must be faithful to the many voices on that occasion, as well as the silences and the omissions.

Art involves wilful deception. The artist creates illusions; the audience suspends disbelief. The tercentenary of Quebec spun an illusion of nation based upon a plausible past. Some found the whole inspiring. Others savoured the parts selectively. That there was an official program does not imply that a single-minded purpose lay behind the event, nor that everyone in attendance responded similarly to the multiple mes-

Crowds disperse across the Plains of Abraham after the historical pageant. Note the jail in the background.

sages. It is important in looking back at this event, and others like it, that this essential pluralism and multivocality of the experience be recognized. Earl Grey wanted to teach French Canada about imperialism. The several French Canadas taught back. Native people, initially consigned to the margins, pushed themselves forward into the centre of the picture. We can glimpse, however momentarily, some bonne ententiste possibilities in this event, and some surprising moments of agreement amidst the exhilarating theatrics and spectacle. Some things could be admired in theatre that could not be admitted politically. But in retrospect this harmony between two peoples in a new nation has a movie-set flimsiness to it; utterly convincing when seen through the lens, but illusory when one looks at it from the back.

From the uncertainties as well as the overbearing confidences of the late twentieth century, we look back at the documentary evidence of this event with perhaps some slight condescension. To us it may seem like the springtime of our innocence. How much of this have we thankfully put behind us? How much of it is still the history that burdens us? At the same time, we might wonder how this generation of Canadians could not see and deal with their differences, so clearly visible in the symbolism, but so cunningly cloaked in this mask of ceremony and professed amity? The posed figures in the stereoscope stare out at us like figures from a jerky old newsreel. There were once other possible futures, but we know in hindsight that tragedy of sorts, disappointment, and the exasperating business of muddling through lay ahead. In that sense, we all feel the loss of the great statue of the Angel of Peace, knowing we could not build it, then or now. We cannot be that people. Looking back through time, these documents speak to us in a way they could not to the participants. They saw things we cannot easily know. We see some things they couldn't; they saw and felt in a way we can only imagine. Once upon a time these images and possibilities lived.

It is not that the fantasy ended and history began again. Rather, history, which had been part of this all along, simply continued in a more prosaic way.

NOTES

INTRODUCTION   The Memory Box

1 Ontario Archives, MU2365, Quebec Tercentenary Papers. This collection
  was presented to the Ontario Archives in 1954 by Mrs Woodburn Langmuir,
  née Clare Denison.
2 Colonel Denison storms through the pages of Canadian history, a larger-
  than-life figure, seen variously as a military sage, francophobe, anti-Ameri-
  can, punctilious Toronto police magistrate, essayist, and ideologue of
  Canadian imperialism. He features in Carl Berger's *Sense of Power* (Toronto:
  University of Toronto Press 1970), and David Gagan's family portrait, *The
  Denison Family of Toronto, 1792–1925* (Toronto: University of Toronto Press
  1973); he makes cameo appearances in books and articles dealing with
  Canadian military policy before the First World War. A prodigious pam-
  phleteer and commentator, his most famous book, *A History of the Cavalry
  from Earliest Times*, first published in 1877, was reissued as recently as 1977.
  He is also author of *Modern Cavalry* (1868), *Soldiering in Canada* (1900), *The
  Struggle for Imperial Unity* (1909), and *Recollections of a Police Magistrate* (1920).
     Clare Denison, the only child of his second marriage to Helen Amanda
  Mair, seems to have been largely responsible for preserving Colonel
  Denison's papers and giving them to the National Archives of Canada. She
  married Archibald Woodburn Langmuir in 1915, and the couple had three
  children. I am indebted to her son, Gavin Langmuir, Professor Emeritus of
  the Department of History, Stanford University, for information about her
  recollections of Quebec in 1908, and her later life.
     There are a couple of feisty letters from Clare in the Baldwin Room,

Metropolitan Toronto Public Library, G.T. Denison Papers, Clare Langmuir to Miss Firth, 26 August 1962 and 8 September 1964, complaining about the calendar of her father's papers. She describes the reverie induced by reading the archival inventory despite its mistakes:

> The general effect of a great part of the list was extremely nostalgic with its references to so many of the chief figures of my childhood – my father, my kind big brother (G.T.D. 4th), my dear Grandmother (who spoilt me dreadfully), a very large number of uncles, aunts, cousins of all degrees, and great uncles and aunts, most of whom at the time lived about five minutes' walk from Heydon Villa. I was carried back so vividly to the atmosphere of 1900 that I am only just returning to that of 1962. The difference is somewhat startling.

3 NA, Robert Sutherland Papers, MG27 II, E9, vol. 1. The map shows him four places from the prince, opposite the premier of Quebec and between the captains of the *Exmouth* and the *Albemarle*.

CHAPTER 1   A Midsummer Night's Dream

1 NA, George Taylor Denison Papers, MG29, E29, vol. 29–30, Diary, 9–10 July 1908 (hereafter NA, Denison Papers). The colonel was as terse to his diary as he was to the miscreants who appeared before him in Toronto police court. The entire tercentenary celebration takes up only three pages.
2 NA, Ethel Chadwick Papers, MG30, D258, vol. 2, Journal, 18 July 1908 (hereafter NA, Chadwick Journal). Ethel Chadwick was one of a bevy of Ottawa beauties who fluttered around Government House, attracted by the handsome ADCs and the faintly erotic scent of vice-regal power. Lola Powell, her closest friend, eventually was captured by a dashing equerry and spirited off to England in 1911, but only after a series of ill-starred love affairs, one with the governor general himself. Ethel, a devout Catholic, also flirted discreetly with members of the governor general's entourage, and was Earl Grey's favourite squeeze – quite literally. However, entangled in a complicated emotional attachment to D'Arcy Scott, a married man from a distinguished Catholic family, she never married. As she aged she slipped into not-so-genteel penury, and recycled the diaries of her halcyon days in Ottawa newspapers.

The activities of this Rideau Hall set are chronicled in Sandra Gwyn's delightful books, *The Private Capital: Ambition and Love in the Age of Macdonald and Laurier* (Toronto: McClelland and Stewart 1984) and *Tapestry of War: A Private View of Canadians in the Great War* (Toronto:

McClelland and Stewart 1992). These books taught me many things about the social life of Ottawa in the late Victorian and Edwardian eras I did not know. I would like to publicly acknowledge my debt to Sandra Gwyn, in whose pages I discovered the Chadwick diaries.

Ethel Chadwick, in contrast to Colonel Denison, chatted voluably to her diary. A typical daily entry covers pages. The tercentenary, which she attended and in whose historical pageant she participated, takes up about forty densely written pages of her 1908 journal.

3 This interpretation of the events of the Quebec tercentenary is based primarily upon newspaper accounts in the Liberal *Le Soleil*, the Conservative *L'Événement*, the Liberal Quebec *Daily Telegraph* and Conservative *Chronicle*, and three commemorative histories of the tercentenary: a handsome hard-cover souvenir volume published by Frank Carrel, *The Quebec Tercentenary Commemorative History* (Quebec: Daily Telegraph Printing House 1908); Earl Grey, Arthur Doughty, and William Wood, *The King's Book of Quebec* (Ottawa: Mortimer 1911), and l'Abbé Roy, G.-A. Vandry, H.-J.-J.-B. Chouinard, A.-J. Painchaud, Monseigneur C.-O. Gagnon, and Thomas Chapais, *Les Fêtes du Troisième Centenaire de Québec, 1608–1908* (Québec: Laflamme & Proulx 1911).

4 This composite account is reconstructed from newspaper accounts on 20 July 1908 in *Le Soleil*, *L'Événement*, the Quebec *Chronicle* and *Telegraph*, and the Montreal *Gazette*. *La Vérité* devotes its front page on 25 juillet to George Baril's address. The several accounts do not match precisely; the fullest transcript in *L'Événement* is garbled by misplaced lines of type.

5 Royal Archives, Windsor Castle (hereafter RA), Prince of Wales to Princess of Wales, 17, 19, 22, 24 July 1908, GV CC4/4. This twelve-page episodic letter, begun at sea, was completed and sent off several days later after the prince's arrival.

6 NA, Chadwick Journal, 22 July 1908.

7 RA, GV AA27/48, Prince of Wales to King Edward VII, 17–24 July 1908.

8 *Commemorative History*, pp. 41–7, provides transcripts of the addresses which correspond to most of the press accounts in English and French.

9 RA, GV CC4/4, Prince of Wales to Princess of Wales, 17–24 July 1908. He made similar observations in his letter to his father noted above and in his diary entry for that day; see RA, King George V's Diary, Thursday 23 July 1908, from the Citadel.

10 Ernest Myrand, *Pageants du Tricentenaire de Québec* (Québec: Laflamme & Proulx 1908), p. 36.

11 A full account of the pageants is provided in the *Commemorative History*, pp. 130–62; see also Myrand, *Pageants*, for the script. This text appeared first in

instalments in *L'Événement.* See also the National Battlefields Commission's official *Historical Souvenir Book of the Pageants* and its French-language counterpart written by Arthur Doughty; see NA, Doughty Papers, MG30, D26, vol. 3, file 7, and below, chapter 11. The programs, of course, were written before the event. The newspapers contain lengthy accounts of the pageants as they were presented, which have been used to check against the printed text.

12 *Commemorative History,* pp. 77–80. The English-language press carried the fullest descriptions of the military review: see, for example, the 25 July 1908 issues of the Quebec *Chronicle,* the Montreal *Gazette,* and the Toronto *Telegram* for a particularly breathless account. *Le Soleil* and *L'Événement* provided only perfunctory coverage by comparison.

13 As the prince had not yet arrived on the first Sunday, this potential problem did not arise. Church parades of sailors from the fleets and soldiers from the camps were the order of the day. Different regimental and national groups attended different churches. In honour of the delegation of Catholic sailors from the British fleet who marched to the Basilica, the sermon was read in English for the first time ever. This policy of elective religious affirmation, which dispersed events across the town, caused no difficulties except for an occasion after service when three marching bands arrived in a square from different directions playing different music. That accident perhaps symbolized the day's events.

14 NA, Chadwick Journal, 26 July 1908. It reminded her 'of the mass celebrated years ago by Laval.' Afterwards she rejoined her friends at the Château Frontenac for iced drinks and gossip.

15 *Le Soleil,* 27 juillet 1908; *L'Événement,* 27 juillet 1908; and the *Commemorative History,* pp. 105–6. There is some confusion as to whether or not a detachment of Montcalm's army attended as part of the honour guard. The *Commemorative History* mentions them but the newspaper accounts do not. Grey uniforms are visible in the panoramic photograph of the messe solennelle in *Les Fêtes* opposite p. 464.

16 RA, GV CC4/5, Prince of Wales to Princess of Wales, 29 July 1908.

17 See *Proceedings and Transactions of the Royal Society of Canada,* third series, vol. II, 1908, pp. vii–x for the correspondence between Mayor Garneau inviting the Royal Society to meet in Quebec and Dr S.E. Dawson, president, agreeing to a special meeting at Quebec rather than a relocation of the regular May meeting. *Proceedings,* vol. III, 1909, pp. vi–xlviii contains a transcript of the opening session message of the Ontario Historical Society, the papers of Judge Routier and Chancellor Burwash, and the poem of Zidler read by Adjutor Rivard. To attract the Royal Society, the National

Battlefields Commission provided a $500 subsidy; NA, National Battlefields Commission Records, vol. 3, Minutes, 26–27 June 1908.

18 NA, Denison Papers, Diary, 23 July 1908. The sentence 'I went to see the Govr Genl in the morning to decline the decoration C.V.O.' is obviously added later as it was squeezed in between two lines. Is it possible he was unhappy with the honour given to his nemesis, General Otter?

19 Ibid., 25 July 1908.

20 RA, GV CC4/4–5, Prince of Wales to Princess of Wales, 17–24, 29 July 1908; GV Diary, Saturday July 25, 1908.

21 NA, Chadwick Journal, 24 July 1908. The reference to D'Arcy is to D'Arcy Scott, an Ottawa lawyer who, though married, was her frequent companion.

22 RA, GV CC4/5, Prince of Wales to Princess of Wales, 29 July 1908.

23 As well as her scrapbook, Clare Denison kept a diary of her own. I am indebted to her son, Professor Gavin Langmuir, who has shared the relevant portions of it dealing with the tercentenary by letter.

CHAPTER 2   Patriotism

1 The special Christmas number of the Quebec *Daily Telegraph* has not, unfortunately, survived and was not microfilmed with the rest of the paper on the version I examined in the Library of the Quebec National Assembly. However, in subsequent memoranda, reports, and letters Chouinard quoted extensively from this early text and it is from those later versions I have pieced together this account. After the festival, Chouinard gathered together for publication all of the preliminary documents generated by the various committees, including several of his early memoranda; see H.-J.-J.-B. Chouinard, *Troisième Centenaire de la Fondation de Québec, Berceau du Canada par Champlain, 1608–1908* (Québec: Laflamme & Proulx 1908). Archives de la Ville de Québec (AVQ), *Préliminaires de la celebration du 3ᵉ centenaire de la fondation de Québec* (Comité Centenaire), Procès Verbeaux, Comité Executif, Comité d'Action, 1906–1908, contains the minutes of the municipal body that took over planning of the celebration. Most of these documents are reprinted in Chouinard, *Troisième Centenaire.* Later still, Chouinard had his version of events published in the French-language commemorative volume printed by the city, *Les Fêtes du Troisième Centenaire de Québec, 1608–1908* (Québec: Laflamme & Proulx 1911), pp. 1–40. He also provided a memorandum on his role as initiator of the festival in support of his unsuccessful application for the position of permanent secretary to the National Battlefields Commission in 1909; see NA, Laurier Papers, C884, 163985, Chouinard to Laurier, 20 December 1909. A memoir in his hand,

composed apparently sometime in 1909, provides a version of events up to 1906 and can be found in Archives Nationales de Québec (ANQ), Fonds Société Saint-Jean-Baptiste du Québec, dossier no. 12. In this version Chouinard traces the origins of the fête to a 1902 conversation with Mayor Parent at a Université Laval celebration. Chouinard's own papers in the Archives du Séminaire de Québec (ASQ), Fonds Chouinard, preserve about ten file folders of notes, letters, and memoranda generated in the planning for the festival. Photographs of Chouinard and his office are from AVQ, neg. 478 and neg. 10891 respectively.

2 ANQ, *Annuaire de l'Institut Canadien de Québec, 1875*, no. 2, 'La Pologne: Ses Origines, Sa Gloire, Ses Malheurs,' pp. 39ff (CIHM 05718); ANQ, *Centenaire de l'Assaut de Québec par les Américains*, compte-rendu de la séance solennelle donnée par L'Institut Canadien le 30 décembre 1875 (Québec: Coté & Co. 1876) pp. 1–12 (CIHM 25051); ANQ, *Annuaire de L'Institut Canadien, 1881*, no. 8, 'Paul de Chomedey, Sieur de Maisonneuve, Fondateur de Montréal,' pp. 31ff (CIHM 00632). Biographical information from the Royal Society of Canada, *Mémoires*, 1929, pp. iv–v; W. Stewart Wallace, ed., *The Macmillan Dictionary of Canadian Biography* (London and Toronto: Macmillan 1963), p. 137; Pierre-Georges Roy, *Les Avocats de la Region de Québec* (Lévis 1936), p. 97; J.K. Johnson, ed., *The Canadian Directory of Parliament, 1867–1967* (Ottawa: Public Archives of Canada 1968), p.118, and a lengthy front-page obituary published in *Le Soleil*, 27 novembre 1928.

3 H.-J.-J.-B. Chouinard, *Fête Nationale des Canadiens-Français* (Québec: Coté & Cie. 1881); *Fête Nationale des Canadiens-Français, 1881–1889* (Québec: Beaulleau & Cie. 1890); *Inauguration du Monument Champlain à Québec le 21 septembre, 1898* (Québec: Le Soleil 1902), CIHM 06195; *Annales de la Société St. Jean Baptiste de Québec*, 4 vols. (Québec: Le Soleil 1903).

4 For such an important social and political organization, the Saint-Jean-Baptiste Society has not been much studied. It is an organization more frequently alluded to – as if everyone knew – than systematically examined. Bibliographies of Quebec history contain only a few references, among them Robert Rumilly's chronicle of the Montreal branch of the organization, *Histoire de la Société Saint-Jean Baptiste de Montréal: des Patriotes au fleur-de-lisé, 1834–1948* (Montréal: L'Aurore 1975).

5 Joseph-Israel Tarte was one of the most mercurial political figures in late nineteenth-century Canadian politics. He began his career as a Conservative, turned on his party during the McGreevy scandals, joined forces with Laurier in the 1890s, contributed significantly to the 'Liberalization' of Quebec politics, only to part company with Laurier once in power over participation in the Boer War. A man of great ability and charm, always to

be found manoeuvring in the shadows of a back room, Tarte was a formidable adversary and a not entirely trustworthy friend. He inspired more fear than respect among his contemporaries and does not enjoy a good reputation among historians. The 'Judas' reference is to his reputation for political treachery and is taken from the title of a famous 1903 pamphlet, *Judas Iscariote Tarte: sa carrière politique d'après divers auteurs* (no publisher 1903). For Tarte's career, see Laurier LaPierre, 'Joseph Israel Tarte and the McGreevy-Langevin Scandal,' Canadian Historical Society *Annual Report* (1961), and 'Politics, Race and Religion in French Canada: Joseph Israel Tarte' (PhD thesis, University of Toronto 1962).

6 The best account of this paradigm shift in Quebec politics remains H. Blair Neatby, *Laurier and Liberal Quebec* (Toronto: McClelland and Stewart 1973), an edited version of his 1956 PhD thesis. Michel Lévesque and Robert Comeau have compiled a useful bibliography, *Le Parti Libéral du Québec* (Québec: Bibliothèque de l'Assemblée Nationale 1991). A recent and quite lively book by Patrice Dutil, *Devil's Advocate: Godfroy Langlois and the Politics of Liberal Progressivism in Laurier's Quebec* (Montreal and Toronto: Robert Davies 1994) surveys this period from the progressive left wing of the party.

7 ANQ, Fonds Garneau, boîte 5, 'Notes sur les projéts d'embellissement Dufferin,' n.d. (été 1905).

8 Chouinard, *Troisième Centenaire*, pp. 1–21; ANQ, Fonds Garneau, boite 5, Société Saint-Jean Baptiste à Garneau, 20 mars 1906.

9 *Les Maires de la Vieille Capitale* (Québec: Gouvernement du Canada et les Archives de la Ville de Québec 1980), pp. 53–5; Paul E. Parent, *Le Bottin du Parlementaire du Québec* (Montréal 1962), pp. 245–7, 289–90, 318–19. The best account of Liberal factionalism is Neatby, *Laurier and Liberal Quebec*, pp. 172–3.

10 *Les Maires de la Vieille Capitale*, pp. 37–9.

11 Ibid., pp. 60–1.

12 On the relative economic decline of Quebec City, see G.A. Nader, *Cities of Canada* (Toronto: Macmillan 1975), vol. 1, pp. 224–32, and vol. 2, pp. 89–90; and Jean Hamelin and Yves Roby, *Histoire Économique du Québec* (Montréal: Fides 1971), pp. 291–303. As the weight of total population shifted westward toward Montreal during industrialization, the east around Quebec became proportionately more francophone. On this displacement westward, and francicization eastward, see Fernand Ouellet, 'Canadiens français et non-francophones dans les villes québécoises et ontariennes, 1851–1911: une perspective comparative et régionale,' in J. Cotnam, Y. Frenette, and A. Whitfield, eds., *La francophonie ontarienne* (Ottawa: Nordir 1995), pp. 148–55.

13 The reconstruction of medieval Avignon and Carcassone in France oc-
    curred at about the same time. The most accessible brief account of Lord
    Dufferin's influence on the re-walling of Quebec is André Charbonneau,
    Yvon Desloges, and Marc Lafrance, *Québec: Ville Fortifiée du XVIIe au XIXe
    Siècles* (Québec: Éditions du Pélican et Parcs Canada 1982), pp. 452–7.
    Judging from her diary, Lady Dufferin did not share her husband's archi-
    tectural enthusiasms; see *My Canadian Journal* (Toronto: Longmans 1969).
14 ANQ, Fonds Garneau, boîte 4, Garneau to Laurier, 17 mai 1906; there is
    also a memorandum in Chouinard's hand in boîte 5, 'Notes sur les projéts
    d'embellissement Dufferin,' referring to Earl Grey's forthcoming 1905 visit
    and urging the municipal officials to seize the opportunity to further the
    reconstruction.
15 President Roosevelt had recently committed the U.S. Government to the
    support of a celebration to mark the three hundredth anniversary of the
    first settlement at Jamestown, akin to the 1876 Philadelphia Centennial of
    the Revolution, and created a commission to organize the event. See
    Michael Kammen, *Mystic Chords of Memory: The Transformation of Tradition in
    American Culture* (New York: Random House 1993), pp. 130, 145, 267, 496.
16 Chouinard, *Troisième Centenaire*, pp. 22–57; *Les Fêtes du Troisième Centenaire*,
    p. 15.
17 The best biography of Laurier in English remains O.D. Skelton's *Life and
    Letters of Sir Wilfrid Laurier*, 2 vols. (Toronto: Oxford 1921) and in French,
    Robert Rumilly's *Sir Wilfrid Laurier* (Paris: Flammarion 1931). Joseph
    Schull's *Laurier* (Toronto: Macmillan 1965) updates the received version
    with action verbs. Richard Clippingdale's illustrated *Laurier: His Life and
    World* (Toronto: McGraw-Hill Ryerson 1979) is Laurier lite. Laurier
    LaPierre revisits scenes from his early academic career in search of the
    'soul' of Laurier in *Sir Wilfrid Laurier and the Romance of Canada* (Toronto:
    Stoddart 1996). Though sound and insightful, this undocumented popular
    biography focuses on Laurier's personal relationships and slights public
    policy. A recent biography of Laurier in French is Réal Bélanger, *Wilfrid
    Laurier: quand la politique devient passion* (Québec: Presses de l'Université
    Laval 1986). R.C. Brown and Ramsay Cook provide the best account of the
    history of the period in *Canada: A Nation Transformed* (Toronto: McClelland
    and Stewart 1974). Paul-André Linteau, René Durocher, and Jean-Claude
    Robert do something similar for Quebec in *Histoire du Québec Contemporain*,
    vol. 1 (Montreal: Boréal Express 1979). Volume 13 of Robert Rumilly's
    Histoire de la Province de Québec: Henri Bourassa (Montréal: Fides 1959) covers
    this period of federal-provincial relations from a point of view sympathetic
    to Bourassa.

18 Chouinard, *Troisième Centenaire*, Comité Exécutif, 4, 19 juin 1906, pp. 59–
65. The petition had been prepared by a special committee consisting of
Monseigneur Gagnon, Reverend F.G. Scott, and the Honourable Thomas
Chapais. See also ANQ, Fonds Garneau, boîte 5, memorial, 1 juin 1906.

19 Chouinard, *Troisième Centenaire*, Comité Exécutif, 25 septembre, octobre 24
1906, pp. 66–84; AVQ, Procès Verbeaux, Comité Exécutif, quoted re: 'un
cachet national de la Fête,' 24 octobre 1906. ANQ, Fonds Garneau, boîte 5,
contains the report of the program committee; see boîte 4, Garneau to
Grey, 20 November 1906, summarizing the planned program and identifying the need for federal support.

20 NA, Laurier Papers, C840, 115996, Garneau to Laurier, 21 novembre 1906;
116124, Garneau to Laurier, 28 novembre 1908; NA, Grey Papers, vol. 1,
Grey to Laurier, 19 December 1906, quotes Casgrain on the disappointment abroad in Quebec; ANQ, Fonds Garneau, boîte 4, Garneau to
Laurier, 28 novembre, 13 décembre 1906.

21 Chouinard, *Troisième Centenaire*, Comité Exécutif, 17 janvier 1907; AVQ,
Comité Centenaire, Procès Verbeaux, 17 janvier 1907.

22 ANQ, Fonds Garneau, boîte 5, *Premier Rapport de la Commission d'Histoire et
d'Archeologie nommée par son honeur le maire de Québec* (Québec: 1907). The
text is dated 22 décembre 1906. The core of this report on the best means
of celebrating Champlain's tercentennial is a detailed account of the Battle
of the Plains of Abraham, obviously the work of Wood.

23 ANQ, Fonds Garneau, boîte 5, Memoire pour entrevue avec Sir Wilfrid
Laurier, 24 mars 1907.

24 NA, Laurier Papers, C846, 122331, Garneau to Laurier, 3 mars 1907;
123165, Garneau to Laurier, 25 mars 1907.

25 Chouinard, *Troisième Centenaire*, Comité Exécutif, 10 avril 1907, pp. 105–14;
AVQ, Comité Centenaire, Procès Verbeaux, 10 avril 1907. ANQ, Fonds
Garneau, boîte 5, Garneau to Laurier, memorandum of their interview,
24 mars 1907. The rector of the seminary received information on
Laurier's commitment from Chouinard on 10 April 1907; see ASQ, *Journal.*

CHAPTER 3   A Knight's Quest

1 NA, Laurier Papers, C1161, 203095–3114, Grey to Laurier, 23 June 1905. In
the Laurier Papers this letter is misfiled with the 1908 correspondence. A
copy of it is in its proper place in NA, Grey Papers, vol. 1.

2 The earliest Canadian scholarship on these matters adopted a Liberal
Nationalist interpretation, hostile to the governor general's 'meddling' and
wholly sympathetic to Laurier's interpretation of the responsibilities of

government and governors general; see, for example, O.D. Skelton, *Life and Letters of Sir Wilfrid Laurier*, 2 vols. (Toronto: Oxford 1921), especially vol. 2, *The Flood Tide of Imperialism*, pp. 59–118. Subsequent scholarship based upon a fuller range of documentation arrived at a less partisan, more nuanced but nevertheless similar judgment; see, for example, Blair Neatby, *Laurier and a Liberal Quebec* (Toronto: McClelland and Stewart 1973); Norman Penlington, *Canada and Imperialism, 1896–1899* (Toronto: University of Toronto Press 1965); John Kendle, *The Colonial and Imperial Conferences, 1887–1911* (London: Royal Commonwealth Institute 1967); Desmond Morton, *Ministers and Generals* (Toronto: University of Toronto Press 1970). Subsequently Carl Berger freed the Canadian imperialist impulse from the realm of caricature to reveal it as a form of aspiring Canadian nationalism in *The Sense of Power* (Toronto: University of Toronto Press 1970). Carman Miller has restored Minto's reputation slightly, arguing that he could – and did – learn from his mistakes, in *The Canadian Career of the Fourth Earl of Minto: The Education of a Viceroy* (Waterloo: Wilfrid Laurier Press 1980), and *Painting the Map Red: Canada and the South African War, 1895–1902* (Montreal and Kingston: McGill-Queen's University Press 1993). The editors of Lord Minto's papers do not go quite so far as Miller by way of exculpation; see Paul Stevens and John T. Saywell, *Lord Minto's Canadian Papers*, 2 vols. (Toronto: Champlain Society 1981, 1983). For something completely different, Sandra Gwyn brilliantly captures the snobbery, social climbing, dalliances, and gossip of the vice-regal circle in Ottawa in *The Private Capital* (Toronto: McClelland and Stewart 1984).

3 This evaluation of Earl Grey is based primarily upon the thesis by the late Mary Elizabeth Hallett, 'The 4th Earl Grey as Governor General of Canada, 1904–1911' (PhD thesis, University of London 1966). My reading of only a portion of the Laurier and Grey correspondence supports her interpretation. Chapter 5 of Hallett's thesis provides an excellent account of Lord Grey's involvement in the tercentenary. See also 'The Quebec Tercentennial: Lord Grey's Imperial Birthday Party,' *Canadian Historical Review*, 54 (1973), pp. 341–52. The entry for Grey in the *Dictionary of National Biography, 1912–1921* (Oxford: Oxford University Press 1927), pp. 227–8 stresses his accomplishments in Canada, 'a most happy combination of office and man.'

4 Hallett, 'The 4th Earl Grey,' pp. 136ff.

5 NA, Doughty Papers, M2244, Grey to Doughty, private, 27 August 1905. Grey had similar if less-developed plans to develop a historic site around the ruins of the fortress at Louisbourg.

6 Minto bitterly protested what he called the 'vandalism' being perpetrated

on the Plains of Abraham, especially the location of the rifle factory. In his correspondence he claimed Laurier was 'miserable' about it as well. See Miller, *The Canadian Career of the Fourth Earl of Minto,* p. 178, and Stevens and Saywell, eds., *Lord Minto's Canadian Papers,* vol. 2, p. 533.

7 NA, National Battlefields Commission Papers, RG 90, vol. 1, Arthur Doughty to Lord Grey, 15 June 1906; NA, Doughty Papers, vol. 10, Arthur Doughty to Lord Grey, 15 June 1906.

8 NA, Doughty Papers, vol. 19, Grey to Laurier, 16 June 1906.

9 ANQ, Fonds Garneau, boîte 1, Grey to Garneau, 3 November 1906; boîte 4, Garneau to Grey, 5 November 1906, boîte 4, Garneau to Grey, 20 November 1906 sending draft program.

10 ANQ, Fonds Garneau, boîte 5, *Premier Rapport de la Commission d'Histoire et d'Archéologie* (Québec 1907).

11 This oversight on the part of the committee was corrected after the fact with the addition of a new preface containing a brief paragraph linking the removal of the factory to suitable relocation arrangements for the workers; see NA, National Battlefields Commission Papers, M1991, *Report of the Quebec Landmarks Commission* (Quebec 1907).

12 NA, Laurier Papers, C1161, 204035–48, Grey to Laurier, 19 December 1906 enclosing Grey to Casgrain, draft letter, 19 December 1906. In his letter to Casgrain, Grey repeated what was becoming his mantra on the subject of the Quebec jail:

> Have you ever considered the difference between the entrance to New York and to Montreal? The first welcome which the immigrant to the US receives on coming within sight of land is the great Statue of Liberty in New York harbour, with its message of new hope. What is the corresponding message the immigrant to Montreal receives? He looks up at the bare steeps of Cape Diamond from his steamer and sees no Statue of Liberty with a message of hope, but the Gaol! It is unnecessary to say more.

13 NA, Grey Papers, vol. 1, Laurier to Grey, 22 December 1906.

14 The campaign, led by the Quebec Literary and Historical Society and subsequently the Royal Society of Canada, began in 1899 and the saga continued until at least 1904 when the deeds were finally made out. Properties mysteriously changed hands shortly before the negotiations and the asking price shot up. The mayor and one of the new owners seemed to be in cahoots, though nothing could be documented. Rumours of extravagant land valuation, some spread by Richard Dobell, a renegade minister without portfolio in Laurier's own cabinet, could not be fully contained. Dobell was silenced and did not run again. J.-A. Charlebois handled the

land transactions, the last and most controversial aspect being the settlement of his exaggerated fee.

The unsavoury story can be followed in NA, Laurier Papers, C765 to C799. The Ursuline side of the story is recounted in Marie-Emmanuel Chabot, *Le Petit Mérici (1902–1930)* (Québec 1994), pp. 9–12. See also Literary and Historical Society of Quebec, *Transactions*, 1899, 'Appeal by the Society to Preserve the Plains of Abraham as Historic Grounds,' and 'A Memorial to Sir Wilfrid Laurier that Historic Grounds be preserved to the public'; and Royal Society of Canada, *Mémoires*, sect. 2, 1899. For a lavishly illustrated history of the National Battlefields in English in which these matters are barely touched on, see Jacques Mathieu and Eugene Kedl, eds. *The Plains of Abraham: The Search for the Ideal* (Quebec: Septentrion 1993).

15 NA, Grey Papers, vol. 28, Grey to Garneau, 23 March 1907. The Ross Rifle expansion controversy can be followed in the correspondence between Laurier and Garneau in their respective papers. This saga has yet to attract its historian, but a brief introduction can be obtained from Ronald Haycock, 'Early Canadian Weapons Acquisition: "That Damned Ross Rifle",' *Canadian Defence Quarterly* 14 (1984–5), pp. 48–57, and Alain Gelly, 'Importance et Incidence de l'Industrie des Munitions sur la Structure Industrielle de Québec, 1879–1946' (MA thesis, Université Laval, 1989), pp. 34–9.

16 NA, Grey Papers, vol. 1, Laurier to Grey, 23 October 1907.

17 Quebec Literary and Historical Society, *Transactions*, 1899, for H.R. Casgrain's paper on the Battle of Ste-Foy, 28 April 1760, and a print of the Monument des Braves.

18 The battles of 1759 and 1760 are most authoritatively and economically presented in C.P. Stacey's admirable little book *Quebec, 1759: The Siege and the Battle* (London: Pan Books 1973).

19 The wooing began with three letters to the bishops in October which are treated below in chapter 5.

20 NA, Grey Papers, vol. 28, Grey to Garneau, 7 November 1907, asking for estimates on the removal of the jail and other buildings, the purchase of additional land, the construction of a museum of the old regime, a seven-mile driveway, and 'a colossal statue of the Goddess of Peace.' This was what he called his 'big plan.'

21 Ibid., Grey to Whitney, 22 March 1907; Grey to Whitney, private, 26 March 1907.

22 The best and most accessible account of the collapse of the Quebec Bridge is to be found in Henry Petroski, *Engineers of Dreams: Great Bridge Builders and the Spanning of America* (New York: Knopf 1995), chapter 3. The

engineers simply underestimated the stresses bearing down upon the light structure during construction. The redesigned bridge was and is much heavier than the ill-fated first attempt, but it too suffered a major mishap before its final completion in 1917.

23 NA, Laurier Papers, C853, 130852, Garneau to Laurier, personnelle, 23 octobre 1907; NA, Fonds Garneau, boîte 1, 25 octobre 1907.

24 ANQ, Fonds Garneau, boîte 4, Garneau to Laurier, 28 octobre 1907; PAC, Laurier Papers, C854, 131076, Garneau to Laurier, 28 octobre 1907.

25 ANQ, Fonds Garneau, boîte 4, Laurier to Garneau, 30 octobre 1907.

26 Ibid., Garneau to Rodolphe Lemieux, 6 novembre 1907.

27 NA, Laurier Papers, C1161, 204570–73, Grey to the King, draft, 21 October 1907

28 Ibid., C1162, 204594–626, Grey to Laurier, 25 October 1907 with enclosures.

CHAPTER 4   C'est Trop Jesuite

1 NA, Laurier Papers, C1161, 204570–73, Grey to King, draft, 21 October 1907. On Grey's tutoring of Edward in India, see Christopher Hibbert, *Edward VII: A Portrait* (London: Allen Lane 1976), and Dana Bentley-Cranch, *Edward VII: Image of an Era* (London: HMSO 1992).

2 NA, National Battlefields Commission Records, vol. 1, Governor General's Appeal through Women's Canadian Club of Montreal, December 12, 1907. On Grey's social agenda in Montreal, see Mary Elizabeth Hallett, 'The 4th Earl Grey as Governor General of Canada, 1904–1911 (PhD thesis, University of London 1966), pp. 138–9.

3 NA, National Battlefields Commission Records, vol. 2, clipping files; see, *inter alia, Daily Telegraph*, 14 December 1907, 'Wolfe's Victory on the Plains of Abraham/ Final Struggle for Canada/ English and French Heroes'; Toronto *Globe*, Saturday, 30 November 1907, and John A. Ewan, 7 December 1907, 'The Plains of Abraham: One of Canada's Holy Places,' and 'Save the Plains of Abraham as a National Memorial'; *Le Soleil*, 14 décembre 1907, 'Metton Nous à l'oeuvre'; Montreal *Gazette*, 20 December 1907, story and editorial; Montreal *Star*, 16 December 1907, 'Earl Grey on Canadianism'; Ottawa *Free Press*, 14 December 1907, 'A National Memorial'; *The Times* (London), 16 December 1907, 'The Battlefields of Quebec'; Ottawa *Journal*, 13 December 1907, 'Enlightened Womanhood/ and the Part She Must Play in the Development of Canada/ Earl Grey at the Women's Canadian Club of Montreal/ Refers to the Dominion Memorial on the Plains of Abraham'; Ottawa *Citizen*, 14 December 1907, 'Wants Colossal

Statue on Heights of Quebec: Earl Grey suggests Angel of Peace of Huge Proportions to Greet New Arrivals/ King Sends Money and Sympathy towards New National Park/' and editorial, 'An Inspiring Project'; Montreal *Star*, 13 December 1907, 'The King Approves of Tercentenary'; Montreal *Witness*, 13 December 1907, 'The Women's Canadian Club's Auspicious Inauguration'; Ottawa *Citizen*, 30 December 1907, editorial 'The Quebec Memorial Park'; Quebec *Daily Telegraph*, 17 December 1907, 'A Patriotic Speech'; Montreal *Star*, 16 December 1907, editorial, 'Earl Grey on Canadianism'; Winnipeg *Telegram*, 31 December 1907, 'To Preserve Battlefields of the Plains of Abraham'; Winnipeg *Free Press*, 31 December 1907, 'Tercentenary of Quebec's Founding'; *La Presse*, 18 décembre 1907, 'Les Plaines d'Abraham'; and Toronto *Mail and Empire*, 19 December 1907, editorial, 'To Hallow a Great Battlefield.'

4 NA, National Battlefields Commission Records, vol. 1, printed brochure, Quebec Battlefields: Earl Grey's Appeal, Mass Meeting at Russell Theatre, Ottawa, 15 January 1908.

5 Ibid., undated, Grey to Rex Burston, Eton; Harry Lewison to Grey, 13 December 1907; Francis D'Aley Osborne Wolfe Murray to Grey, 16 December 1907; Lord Derby to Grey, 19 December 1907; A.J.Dawson to Grey, 15 February 1908; NA, Grey Papers, vol. 28, 7279, Grey to Lord Strathcona, 11 December 1907, 7411 Grey to Lord Strathcona, 11 March 1909; vol. 28, 4763, Grey to the king, 26 March 1908.

6 NA, National Battlefields Commission Records, vol. 1, Alphonese Desjardins to Grey, 7 October 1907, sending cheque for one dollar; James Dunsmuir to Grey, 28 December 1907; Barlow Cumberland, president, Ontario Historical Society to Grey, 4 January 1908; Arthur W. McCurdy, Victoria, BC, to Mr Templeman, 16 January 1908; G.C. Coldwell, minister of education, Manitoba to Grey, 7 April 1908; Arthur F. Sladen, secretary to Grey, to Doughty, 7 April 1908; Arthur F. Sladen to Courtney, 9 April 1908; Bursar, University of Toronto to Courtney, 16 April 1908, sends $572.30 collected by students.

7 NA, Grey Papers, vol. 28, 7290, Grey to Mrs Chapin, 8 January 1908; NA, Quebec Battlefields Association Papers, vol. 2, George S. Wade, sculptor, to Lord Grey, 15 February 1908, including samples from his portfolio: 'Should it not be an armed 'Peace' with sword in sheath at her side & in the one hand a sickle & the other wheat-olives? Standing perhaps on a hemisphere with draperies slightly swayed by the winds?'

8 ANQ, Fonds du Département du Procureur Général, no. 1206, 1908; 12 février 1908, Deputy Attorney General, Quebec, to Laurier, telegram informing him that the cabinet had decided at the next session to ask the

legislature for a $100,000 contribution to the tercentenary. Of course, an election stood between this promise and the next session.

9 NA, Grey Papers, vol. 12, 3924, Grey to Lord Elgin, 3 March 1908.

10 Ibid., vol. 2–4, Grey to Laurier, 25 January 1908; Grey to Laurier, 8 February 1908, on his trip to Toronto and announcement he hoped to make; Grey to Laurier, 15 February 1908, regarding a telegram on the urgency of scheduling the trip of the Prince of Wales; Laurier to Grey, 16 February 1908, explaining an oversight in the draft legislation and the likelihood the festival would absorb the whole of the grant; Laurier to Grey, 26 February 1908: 'The Battlefields will surely be taken up tomorrow even if we have to sit up all night.' For the other side of the correspondence, see NA, Laurier Papers, C1181, for the 4:00 a.m. letter, Grey to Laurier, 2 March 1908. See also 205086-92, Grey to Laurier, 29 February 1908, thanking the P.M. for the news that an announcement would be made the next day: 'I am sorry to think that any action of mine should have committed you to a course of policy in which you apprehend possible danger – that was very far from being my intention – I am with you heart & soul in desiring union, harmony & peace & I trust even the most violent ultramontane may not kick very hard against a proposal the object of which is to bring money from across the seas for the benefit of the City of Quebec & the RC Church.'

11 *Statutes of Canada*, 7–8 Edw. VII, chaps. 57, 58, Acts Respecting the National Battlefields at Quebec. For the debate on these bills, see House of Commons, Debates, 1908, vol. III, 5 March (4376–4401), 6 March (4497–4536); and vol. VII, 1 July (13496–13506). Other than Armand Lavergne's backhanded support for these bills, there were no other notable contributions. Quebec named its minister of justice, L.-A. Taschereau, to the commission and Ontario a prominent member of the provincial cabinet, J.S. Hendrie.

12 NA, National Battlefields Commission Records, vol. 3, for the minutes; NA, Grey Papers, vol. 2, 817, Grey to Laurier, 13 March 1908, reporting on the first meeting of the commission; NA, Denison Papers, vol. 11, 5309, telegram, ADC, Lord Grey to Denison, Ottawa, 7 March 1908, inviting Denison to meeting of a commission that had yet to be created. Denison was understandably incredulous; 5312, telegram, Laurier to Denison, undated ('Recommendation sent to Council. Order will be passed today and signed. Walker and you should go by all means'); 5313, telegram, Arthur F. Sladen to Denison, 19 March 1908, reporting Grey has approved the minute of Privy Council appointing Denison a member of the commission. University of Toronto Fisher Rare Books Collection, Sir Edmund Walker Papers, vol. 20, Grey to Walker, 29 January 1908.

13 This organization was launched with a $400 preliminary grant by the

National Battlefields Commission at its fourth meeting, NA, National Battlefields Commission Records, vol. 3, Minutes, 13 April 1908. NA, Quebec Battlefields Association Papers, vol. 1, contains organizing correspondence, subscription lists, and memoranda; vol. 2 retains samples of printed material and newspaper clippings. The Dominion Central Committee consisted of the following: Honourable Raoul Dandurand, Speaker of the Senate, Honourable R.F. Sutherland, Speaker of the House of Commons, senators R.W. Scott, L.G. Power, A. Lougheed, P. Landry, H. Bostock, J. Wood, and members of Parliament Wilfrid Laurier, F.D. Monk, R.L. Borden, Samuel Barber, Charles Marcil, F.F. Pardee, and messrs. P.B. Taylor, Gordon Edwards, James W. Woods, and Hamnet Hill.

14 NA, Quebec Battlefields Association Papers, vol. 1, W.L.M. King to Gerald Brown, House of Commons, 23 May 1908: 'We had fine meetings at Winnipeg, Regina and Calgary and I think you may count on the Canadian Clubs of these cities taking a very active interest in the matter of raising subscriptions. The attendance at all the meetings was large, and the project appeared to be enthusiastically received.'

15 Ibid., Canadian Club of Fort William to Courtney, 27 April 1908; Imperial Order Daughters of the Empire, head office, national chapter to Courtney, 8 July 1908 (sending cheque for $2,483.75); Woodstock Canadian Club to Gibson, 2 June 1908; Halifax Canadian Club to Gibson, 9 June 1908; Moncton Canadian Club to Gibson, 10 June 1908; official statement, Douglas M. Gibson, 19 June 1908 (started local organizations for the purpose of collecting money to further the nationalization of the battlefields in about two hundred of the more important towns of the Dominion. Canadian Clubs in the west carried out active campaigns, similar organizations in New York, Boston, Pittsburgh, special appeal issued to the mayors throughout the province of Quebec); Lieutenant-Governor D.A. Mackinnon, Prince Edward Island, to Lord Grey, 12 May 1908, enclosing contribution from PEI schools; Douglas Gibson to Courtney, 2 July 1908, enclosing note from F.S. Meighen of Montreal whose committee raised $30,000. The *Globe* reported that Toronto raised $30,237.70.

16 Ibid., vol. 2, files 2–6 to 2–12, newspaper clippings; file 2–13, magazine clippings; file 2–14, printed material. See also Elsie Reford, Montreal branch of Quebec Battlefields Association, 'Appeal' (as premier city Montreal must take the lead); John Francis Waters, Ottawa, 'The Tercentenary Celebration at Quebec,' undated clipping; extract from *The Times*, 22 April 1908, 'The Consecration of Quebec's Battlefields'; 'The Plains of Abraham and Canada's Place in the British Empire,' lecture given by Mr H.J. Macinder, director of London School of Economics at Eton, 22

February 1908. Some of the poetry is collected in the back of the *Quebec Tercentenary Commemorative History*, pp. 171ff.

17 NA, National Battlefields Commission Records, vol. 1, Laurier's private secretary to Courtney, 13 July 1908, enclosing letter received from J.R. Dickson, forester, chief of party, Riding Mountain Forest Survey, Laurier, Manitoba, to Laurier.

18 NA, National Battlefields Commission Records, vol. 1, Montreal City, Extrait du procès-verbal de l'assemblé special du conseil municipal, 6 juillet 1908 (sent $10,000 following a mass meeting of citizens on 26 May).

19 CO42 Despatches, War Office, Treasury, reel B2246, Arthur Grenfell to Rt. Hon. Winston Churchill, 7 March 1908: 'I find that the majority of people are not inclined to assist in the purchasing of the Plains of Abraham.'

20 NA, Grey Papers, vol. 28, 7284, Grey to Lieutenant-Governor Sir William Clark, Ontario, 28 December 1907:

> To tell you the truth I am not a little proud of having accomplished what up to now has been impossible, namely to do honour to Wolfe and to please the French at the same time! That difficulty, up to now insuperable, has been successfully overcome, and if I am now defeated in my attempt to do honour to Wolfe's immortal achievement, which gave half a continent to the English, and to the United States their independence, by the lack of national sentiment among the people of Toronto, and the Province of Ontario, where I specially looked for support, I shall be bitterly disappointed.

21 Ibid., vol. 8, 2082, James Bryce to Grey, 28 December 1907; 2179, Bryce to Grey, 16 March 1908 on Clouston's visit.

22 NA, Quebec Battlefields Association Papers, vol. 1, Printed Booklet, *Canadian Tercentenary, Wolfe and Montclm Memorial Contributions from Great Britain to the Wolfe and Montcalm Memorial*, Mansion House, 15 May 1908.

23 NA, National Battlefields Commission Records, vol. 1, Courtney to Byron Walker, 26 May 1908; Walker Papers, vol. 7, Courtney to Walker, 6 April 1908, worrying about income and expenditures.

24 Walker and Denison, supported by Drummond, insisted upon keeping control over all expenditures in Ottawa. Much to the indignation of the Quebec City representatives, no expenditures other than those previously authorized by the commission would be paid. Laurier would have been proud of them. See NA, National Battlefields Commission Records, vol. 3, Minutes, 23 March 1908. The Quebec people received only $2,000 for incidental expenses, for which they were expected to provide receipts. This was something of a blow.

25 NA, Quebec Battlefields Association, vol. 1, Gibson to George Wilson, secretary, Toronto Branch, Quebec Battlefields Association, 26 June 1908; R. Home Smith, honorary Secretary, Toronto Branch to Gibson, 7 July 1908.

26 NA, Grey Papers, vol. 30, 7798, Sir Hugh Graham, Hotel St Regis, New York, to Grey, 12 May 1908; 7802, Graham to Grey, 17 May 1908; 7809, Grey to Graham, 20 May 1908; 7812, Grey to Graham, 21 May 1908; vol. 28, 7476, Grey to Sir George [Drummond], 19 May 1908, announcing receipt of anonymous $10,000 contribution from New York; vol. 28, 7478, Grey to Graham, 21 May 1908; 7482, Grey to Graham, 6 June 1908, thanking him for splendid article in *Star* of 2 June 1908.

27 NA, National Battlefields Commission Records, vol. 1, Walker to Grey, 23 May 1908.

28 Ibid., Quebec City Archives, Accounts of the Quebec Battlefields Association, 1908, F.J. Turnbull, list of contributions to Quebec Battlefield, total $462,163.91 – all names listed by province, cities, institutions, societies, commercial and financial, clubs, military corps, churches, general subscriptions, English, Quebec Battlefields Association, making a grant total of $766,087.17. See also ibid, vol. 2, Deputy Minister of Finance Boville to Courtney, enclosing a reply to a question from House of Commons, 22 February 1909. The two accounts differ slightly, the calculation of bank interest being the main discrepancy. The City of Quebec did not make a contribution to this fund, but spent its donation as it saw fit during the celebrations; see ibid., vol. 1, Courtney to Mrs Reford, 19 August 1908: 'As for the city grant I have never seen it or never shall – at a very early stage in the game I was told it would be spent by the city authorities in their own way apart from the Commission.' The local government was miffed that the other governments did not simply hand the money over to them to spend. See Walker Papers, Courtney to Walker, 6 April 1908: 'I am afraid that, with all due respect, if it is left to the local people who have never had any experience of such business, that we might not get all the advantages that we should.' How delicately put. The final accounting is discussed below in chapter 12.

CHAPTER 5   Debauchery

1 NA, Grey Papers, vol. 28, 7246, Grey to Monseigneur Bégin, 6 October 1907; 7248, Grey to Monseigneur Bruchési, 8 October 1907; 7250, Grey to Monseigneur Mathieu, Laval, 8 October 1907. Each letter was modified slightly. The letter to Bégin, for example, made it seem as if Bruchési had already given his approval and Bégin could safely come onboard.

2 Mona Ozouf, *L'École, l'Église at la République, 1871–1914* (Paris: Armand Colin 1963), and Eugen Weber, *Peasants into Frenchmen: The Modernization of Rural France, 1870–1914* (Stanford: Stanford University Press 1976).

3 My understanding of late nineteenth century ultramontanism is drawn from, among others, Roberto Perin, *Rome in Canada: The Vatican and Canadian Affairs in the Late Victorian Age* (Toronto: University of Toronto Press 1990); Jean Hamelin et Nive Voisin, *Les Ultramontains canadiens-français* (Montréal: Boréal Express 1985); Philippe Sylvain et Nive Voisin, *Histoire du catholisism québecois: Réveil et consolidation, 1840–1898* (Montréal: Boréal Express 1985); and Jean Hamelin et Nicole Gagnon, *Histoire du catholicism québecois: Le XXᵉ siècle, 1898–1940* (Montréal: Boréal Express 1993).

This battle between the forces of light and darkness is the stuff of Canadian Whig historiography. For the most recent retelling of Laurier's undeniably courageous youthful tilting against ultramontanism, see Laurier LaPierre, *Sir Wilfrid Laurier and the Romance of Canada* (Toronto: Stoddart 1996), pp. 60–106. The church side of the story is set forth in Sylvain et Voisin, *Histoire du catholicism québécois*, pp. 161–201, 365–96.

4 H. Blair Neatby, *Laurier and a Liberal Quebec* (Toronto: McClelland and Stewart 1973), pp. 92–9. The Quebec school question was as difficult for Laurier at home as the Manitoba School Question. Neatby shows the Liberals in Quebec backing away from their promise of education reform under pressure from the bishops and Rome.

5 ASQ, Université 168, No. 52, Sbarretti to Mathieu, 12 novembre 1905, regarding the inevitable invitation to France.

6 The journal of the seminary kept a careful record of all public meetings regarding tercentenary planning; see ASQ, *Journal Seminaire*, vol. VII, p. 34. In one instance, Chouinard is specifically mentioned as providing Mathieu with information regarding the likely federal contribution; *Journal Seminaire*, vol. VIII, p. 39.

7 ASQ, Université 168, no. 52, Sbarretti to Mathieu, 12 novembre 1905, repeating Mathieu's reassurances.

8 Ibid., no. 26B, 29 juin 1906, Sbarretti asks Mathieu if England and France will take part in the festivities; no. 26C, juillet 1906, Mathieu replies he thinks not; no. 28A, Sbarretti to Mathieu, 4 juillet 1906, notes that it was fitting that 'France catholique' ought to be represented; no. 28B, 2 octobre 1906, Mgr Alfred A. Sinnott to Mathieu; no. 26D, 28 décembre 1906, Sinnott to Mathieu, asking what is being done to prevent invitations to England and France? no. 26H, 19 January 1907, Sinnott writes Mathieu in English, quoted (emphasis in the original); no. 26L, 18 février 1907,

Sinnott to Mathieu, do everything possible to prevent an invitation to France.

9 Sylvain et Voisine, *Histoire du catholicism québecois*, vol. 2, pp. 365–96; Hamelin et Gagnon, *Histoire du catholicism québecois*, vol 3, pp. 53–5, 65–7, on Bégin's outlook following *Affari Vos* and a portrait opposite p. 61. For Laurier's relations with the bishops during this time see LaPierre, *Sir Wilfrid Laurier*, p. 236; Joseph Schull, *Laurier* (Toronto: Macmillan 1965), pp. 375, 506; O.D. Skelton, *Life and Letters of Sir Wilfrid Laurier* (Toronto: Oxford 1921), vol. 2, pp. 20, 41–4; Blair Neatby, *Laurier and a Liberal Quebec*, pp. 82–99. LaPierre quotes Bruchési reporting to Rome sometime in 1899 on the conflict in Quebec City between the church and Laurier's government: 'The warfare which went on there goes on still, with this difference, that it has become undercover in place of open.'

10 NA, Letterbooks of the governor general's civil secretary, J. Hanbury-Williams, RG7, G17C, vol. 49, 1908, Hanbury-Williams to L.P. Sirois, 7 avril 1908, thanking him for the invitation to the G.G. to attend the Laval fête; Hanbury-Williams to Sirois, 20 mai 1908, 'Son Excellence accept avec plaisir l'invitation du Comité du Monument Laval à assister aux cerémonies de l'inauguration le 22 juin, et á devoiler le monument.'

11 On this subject see, for example, Stephen Davis, 'Empty Eyes, Marble Hands: The Confederate Monument and the South,' *Journal of Popular Culture* 16 (1982) pp. 2-21; Thomas L. Connelly, *The Marble Man: Robert E. Lee and His Image in American Society* (New York: Knopf 1977); Daniel J. Sherman, *Worthy Monuments: Art Museums and the Politics of Culture in Nineteenth-Century France* (Cambridge: Harvard University Press 1991); and G. Mosse, 'Caersarism, Circuses, and Monuments,' *Journal of Contemporary History* 6 (1971), pp. 167–82; Maurice Agulhon, 'La "Statuomanie" en Histoire,' *Ethnologie français* 18 (Septembre 1988), pp. 146–72; and for Quebec, Bruno Hébert, *Monuments et Patrie* (Québec: Les Éditions Pleins Bords 1980). See also Pierre Nora's monumental edited collection of essays dealing with the construction of public memory in France, *Les Lieux de Mémoire: La République* (1 vol.), *La Nation* (3 vols.), and *Les France* (3 vols.) (Paris: Gallimard 1986–). In that collection, Antoine Prost's 'Les Monument aux morts,' (*La Républic*, pp. 195–225), and June Hargrove, 'Les Statues de Paris' (*La Nation* 3, pp. 243–82) deal directly with this phenomenon.

12 Bruno Hébert, a descendant of the sculptor, has written a meditation on the phenomenon of 'commémoration par le monument historique,' *Monuments et Patrie* which focuses upon the work of Philippe Hébert. The Laval statue is illustrated and discussed briefly on pp. 50, 97, 173.

13 Eight volumes of documentation pertaining to this Laval Monument are to

be found in Les Archives de l'Archdiocèse de Québec (hereafter AAQ), 4A, Evêques et archevêques de Québec, Monuments Commémoratifs, Au Bienheureux de Laval: vol. 1, minute books of the committee and official documents; vol. 2, correspondence with Hébert regarding the design; vol. 3, documentation of the subscription campaign; vol. 4, documents from the unveiling ceremony; vol. 5, the souvenir book; vol. 6, expenditures and receipts; vol. 7, press clippings; and vol. 8, documents pertaining to the transfer of the statue to the City of Quebec, 5–7 November 1908.

14 AAQ, 4A, vol. 1, Comité du Monument Laval, Procès verbeaux des Assemblées du Comité, 28 avril 1907, pp. 62–6. Present for the debate were the following in the order and in the form noted in the minutes: P.-P. Sirois, president; Monseigneurs C.-A. Marois, O.-E. Mathieu, H. Têtu, C.-O. Gagnon; Judges Routhier and Langelier; Mm. E. Gagnon, S. Lesage, E. Foley; les abbés V. Huard, L. Lindsey, P.-E. Roy, C. Roy; notaries Charlebois, Grenier, Savard; doctors H. Lessard, F. Dorion. Mms. Th. Béland, A. Galipeault, C.-J. Magnan, and l'abbé Garneau, secretary. *La Semaine Religieuse de Québec*, vol. XIX, no. 38, 4 mai 1907, reports the decision ('à la presque unanimité des assistants') to stay with the 1908 date.

15 All the papers gave full and on the whole favourable reports of this discussion; see *L'Événement, Le Soleil*, the Quebec *Chronicle*, and the new church newspaper, *L'Action Sociale*, 14 janvier 1908.

16 *Le Soleil* and *L'Événement*, 22 juin 1908. The Quebec *Chronicle* and the *Telegraph* also carried full front-page coverage emphasizing the willingness of all races and creeds to join in the spirit of the celebration.

17 My reading of this parade is influenced by Roberto da Matta's suggestive essay, 'Carnival in Multiple Planes,' in John J. MacAloon, ed., *Rite, Drama, Festival, Spectacle: Rehearsals Toward a Theory of Cultural Performance* (Philadelphia: Institute for the Study of Human Issues 1984), pp. 208–40.

18 *Le Soleil, L'Événement*, Quebec *Chronicle*, 24 juin 1908. See also AAQ, *La Semaine Religieuse*, vol. XX, 4 avril 1908, p. 531; 20 juin 1908, pp. 709–10; 27 juin 1908, pp. 722–36. Enterprising merchants were able to gain some publicity from the event. Paquet & Cie., the department store, used an engraving of the clergy surrounding the monument in its daily advertisement. A front-page ad in *Le Soleil* showed a woman at her chores using a De Laval cream separator. The festivities were darkened somewhat by reports the same day of a devastating fire in Trois Rivières.

19 NA, CO42, Canada 1908, vol. 920, reel B241, Earl Grey to the Colonial Office, 4 July 1908, enclosing a letter received from the archbishop of Quebec, 26 June 1908.

20 NA, Grey Papers, vol. 14, 4044, Grey to Crewe, 24 June 1908.

21 Copies of these replies are to be found in ibid., vol. 28, Monseigneur Bégin to Lord Grey, 11 October 1907; Archevêché de Montréal to Grey, octobre 14 1907; Mgr Mathieu to Grey, 9 octobre 1907. Grey forwarded copies to the prime minister, where they can be found also in NA, Laurier Papers, C1161, 204618–24.

22 AAQ, *Mandements: Letters Pastorale et Circulaires des Evêques de Québec, Nouvelle Série*, Circulaire au Clergé No. 49, 1 mai 1908, pp. 179–94. NA, Grey Papers, vol. 14, 4001, Grey to Lord Crewe, 18 May 1908.

23 NA, Grey Papers, vol. 14, 4044, Grey to Crewe, 24 June 1908, enclosing two speeches in French. AAQ, *Mandements*, Lettre Pastorale, no. 53, 24 juin 1908, p. 218.

24 Quebec *Chronicle*, 30 June 1908; *Le Soleil*, 30 juin 1908 on the pastoral letter of Monseigneur Bégin.

25 NA, Grey Papers, vol. 14, 4001, Grey to Crewe, 18 May 1908; NA, CO42, vol. 919, reel B2241, Grey to Elgin, 3 June 1908 (Norfolk has accepted).

26 Arundel Castle, Sussex, Duke of Norfolk's Archives, Correspondence of the 15th Duke, Grey to Duke of Norfolk, telegram, 17 May 1908. I am grateful to the archivist, Dr Robinson, and the assistant librarian, Mrs Rodger, for their assistance.

27 NA, Crewe Papers, Grey to Crewe, 3 June 1908; Crewe to Grey, undated, July 1908, reporting he will 'talk to Norfolk before his departure to ensure he understands the situation and his role.'

28 Arundel Castle, Duke of Norfolk's Archives, Correspondence of the 15th Duke, Grey to the Duke of Norfolk, 2 August 1908. NA, Grey Papers, vol. 14, 4075, Grey to Crewe, 31 July 1908.

29 NA, Chadwick Journal, 26 July 1908. In truth she was rather more excited by her visit later in the afternoon to the *Exmouth*, where she met all the lieutenants.

30 Ursuline Archives (hereafter UA), *Journal*, 1908, pp. 79–98 (Norfolk: 'chef des catholiques anglais, un des plus éminents catholiques de l'Europe'), pp. 93–4; Archives des Augustines, *Annales de l'Hotel-Dieu de Quebec*, vol. 3, 1902–11, pp. 196–9; *Lettre Annuelle du Monastère de l'Hôtel-Dieu de Québec*, 1908, for the visit of the Duke of Norfolk; *Lettre Annuelle du Monastère de l'Hôtel-Dieu du Sacre Coeur de Québec*, 1908: 'Quant aux solennites du 3ème centenaire ... les faibles échoes qui en sont parvenus à notre cloître, me permettent de vous redire qu'elles aussi ont été splendides et dignes de leur objet.' These documents in the two archives make it abundantly clear that the Laval fête was for the religious communities a far more important and imposing event.

31 *La Vérité*, 25 juillet 1908, 'M. Herbette'; 1 août, 'La Parenté est brisée';
    1 août 1908, 'Oncle Zélé,' 'L'Oncle et ses Neveux,' 8 août, 'Sur l'Herbette.'
    Toronto *Telegram*, 28 July 1908, 'France Should Not Have Sent Anti-Clerical
    Leaders to Canada.' The appointment placed the bishops in a difficult
    dilemma: 'They had to choose between disloyalty to their church and
    incivility to the French delegate. They chose a policy dictated by every
    consideration of sincerity and self-respect.'
32 NA, Denison Papers, vols. 29–30, diary, 17 July (paid call to French admi-
    ral), 27 July (Helen and Clare attend dance on the *Léon Gambetta*). Clare's
    own diary concentrates understandably upon parties, dances, and balls,
    although Profesor Langmuir vaguely recalls his mother telling him that
    'some of the official contingent from France spent a lot of time with them
    because (many of) the French Canadians viewed the French Government
    as a bunch of godless atheists, or words to that effect' (private communica-
    tion). Colonel Denison would not have minded the company, being
    indifferent to religion himself.
33 According to *La Vérité*, 1 août 1908.
34 *L'Événement*, a popular Conservative paper with its close ties to the hierar-
    chy, called this an 'extraordinary' delegation when it was announced on
    20 juin 1908. Not deserving of contempt, it was plainly a delegation that
    under the circumstances would suffice by causing the proper offence.
    Originally Jauréguiberry was to command the *Montcalm*, but for some
    reason that did not work out. Perhaps the government of France knew how
    to play the game as well.

CHAPTER 6   Papineau Trouble

1 NA, Grey Papers, vol. 14, 4001, Grey to Lord Crewe, 18 May 1908; 3924,
   Grey to Elgin, 3 March 1908; NA, Crewe Papers, A1645, Grey to Crewe,
   3 June 1908.
2 I am indebted to Arthur Silver's introduction to the translation of Jules-
   Paul Tardivel's separatist novel, *For My Country/Pour la Patrie* (Toronto:
   University of Toronto Press 1975) and Pierre Savard, *Jules-Paul Tardivel, la
   France et les États-Unis, 1851–1905* (Québec: Les Presses de l'Université Laval
   1967). As the title suggests, Savard deals only with two main themes of
   Tardivel's thought, the problem presented to Quebec by the materialism of
   the United States and the secularism of Republican Franc. Silver illumi-
   nates the heated excesses Savard overlooks, in particular the anti-semitic,
   conspiratorial, credulous, brawling aspect of Tardivel's journalism. The two

accounts must be read together for a fully rounded picture of Tardivel. Silver and Savard broadly agree on their interpretation of Tardivel and his influence. The quotation is from Silver's introduction to *For My Country*, p. xv. Réal Bélanger shows how Tardivel's nationalism influenced his thinking about religion in 'Le nationalism ultramontain: le cas de Jules-Paul Tardivel,' in Nive Voisine et Jean Hamelin, eds., *Les Ultramontains Canadiens-Français* (Montréal: Boréal Express 1985), pp. 267–303, without giving much consideration to the darker, xenophobic aspects of his nationalism.

3 *La Vérité*, 9 mai 1908, 'Bovril, Canayens et Crachats!'

4 Ibid., 5 novembre 1887, quoted in Silver, ed., *For My Country*, p.xxvi.

5 This debate can be sampled in Ramsay Cook, ed., *French-Canadian Nationalism* (Toronto: Macmillan 1969), pp. 147–51.

6 *La Vérité*, 27 décembre 1907, Paul Tardivel, 'Lord Grey et la Fusion des Races.'

7 Ibid., 1 février 1908, Canadien, 'Les Fêtes du Troisième Centenaire.'

8 Ibid., 15, 29 fevrier, 7, 21 mars; 4, 11, 18, 25 avril; 9, 16, 23, 30 mai; 13 juin; et 18 juillet.

9 *Le Soleil*, 11 avril 1908.

10 *La Vérité*, 21 mars, 'La Campagne de Lord Grey'; 11 avril, 'Les Champs de bataille' and 'Haro! Haro!'; 18 avril, 'Supercherie Impérialiste'; 25 avril, 'Têtes Chaudes! Cerveaux Brulé.' With the fêtes safely out of the way, in August *La Vérité* then published a long review of Earl Grey's previous career, drawn from a profile by the British journalist W.T. Stead. It pounced upon scraps of evidence, such as Grey's interest in religious and social reform, to show the undoubted influences of the Masonic Order. Grey had gone to serve as Cecil Rhodes's 'fixer' in South Africa and become a jingo whose imperial conquests only enriched powerful Jewish interests. This was the man who now trained his talent for intrigue and propaganda on French Canada. 29 août, 'Lord Grey Impérialiste.'

11 *Le Soleil*, 8 février 1908: 'Cessons donc pour une fois ces guerres vaines qui ne servent qu'a semer des germes de défiance et de discorde. La solidarité n'est pourtant pas déjà si excessive chez nous. Unissons-nous à ceux qui s'efforcent de promouvoir de nobles et grandes idees.' See also 'Un Appel aux Citoyens,' 21 avril; 'A l'oeuvre patriotes,' 22 avril. The pages of *Le Soleil* and the *Chronicle* are filled with advertisements regarding the festival. See, in particular, the ads for Faguy, Lepinay & Frere.

12 Quebec *Chronicle*, 22 May 1908, 'Appeal to Press.'

13 *Le Soleil*, 28 mars 1908. This appeared in a letter from Victor Olivier,

expounding a general defence of the benefits of British liberty.

14 ANQ, Fonds Garneau, boîte 5, clipping from *Action Sociale*, 17 mars 1908, and Circulaire au Clergé, 1 mai 1908. Chapais's intervention earned him the undying admiration of Lord Grey; see NA, Grey Papers, vol. 28, 7484, Grey to Chapais, 9 September 1908.

15 Chapais's essay was printed in its entirety in the new Montreal nationalist newspaper, *Le Nationaliste*, 22 mars 1908. *Le Soleil* and *L'Événement* also took note of it.

16 I read a much marked-up and underlined offprint of this article in ANQ, Fonds Garneau, boîte 5. The mayor obviously took great comfort from the essay. It is also noted in Grey's correspondence.

17 *L'Événement*, 22 juin 1908.

18 Bourassa to Goldwin Smith, 26 June 1908, quoted in Hallett, 'The 4th Earl Grey,' pp. 173–4. For his part, Smith admired the spectacle but wondered too whether it was Wolfe and not Champlain who was being honoured; he praised the forbearance of the French Canadians in the face of such bad taste, and he doubted that the 'assimilationist' impulse behind the whole affair would work, *Le Nationaliste* quoting the *Weekly Sun*, 9 août 1908. Smith wrote a long letter to Edmund Walker, a member of the National Battlefields Commission, admonishing him for celebrating war and its consequences. See the Walker Papers, Fisher Rare Book Room, University of Toronto, box 7, Goldwin Smith to Walker, 6 April 1908. In his reply, Walker stressed somewhat disingenuously that this was a celebration of Champlain.

19 *Le Nationaliste*, 26 janvier 1908, 'La Statue des Plaines d'Abraham'; 23 février, 'Les Plaines d'Abraham'; 15 mars, 'Le Tricentenaire'; 22 mars, 'Tricentenaire ou IIIᵉ Centenaire.'

20 Ibid., 15 mars 1908, 'Le Tricentenaire.' This article was signed 'A.B.' Omer Héroux moved to Montreal to edit this newspaper following the death of his wife in the spring.

21 This is a canard. Laurier, ever conscious of language issues, insisted upon bilingual presentations. The English press reported that he spoke in both languages; the nationalist press insisted he spoke English only. That seems unlikely under the circumstances. The Prince of Wales in his diary and letters home comments on Laurier's bilingual greeting, as it required him to reply in kind.

22 *Le Nationaliste*, 26 juillet, 'Labarrière aux fêtes de Québec'; this one was signed 'P.-M.-B.'

23 Ibid., 19 juillet 1908, 'Charlebois et le prince de Galles à Québec,' provides a description of many of the cartoons. The drawings may be found in

various issues of *Le Nationaliste*. I found a copy of the pamphlet, *Le Prince de Galles aux Fêtes du 3ᵉ Centenaire de la Fondation de Québec: Album de Dessins Inédits par J. Charlebois* (Montréal 1908) in the Archives de la Ville du Québec, Fonds du Tricentenaire.

24 *Le Nationaliste*, 26 juillet 1908. *La Vérité* reprinted most of this as 'Le Vrai Sentiment National,' 1 août 1908. See it also noted in the admirable account of the tercentenary in J. Castell Hopkins, *Canadian Annual Review of Public Affairs, 1908* (Toronto: Annual Review Publishing 1909), pp. 238–60.

25 *La Vérité*, 8 août 1908, 'Il n'était pas la!' Tardivel considered the Jeunesse Catholique homage to Champlain *the* event of the fêtes.

CHAPTER 7   Pageanting

1 Frank Lascelles had acted on the London stage with Sir Herbert Tree but, as the great actor generously recalled later in a tribute to his friend, it was he who studied with Lascelles. Earl of Darnley, ed., *Frank Lascelles: "Our Modern Orpheus"* (Oxford: University of Oxford Press 1932), p. 106.

2 Quebec *Chronicle*, 13 April 1908, printed a verbatim transcript. *Le Soleil*, 13 avril 1908, provided a front-page translation of the speech, which was given in English. *Saturday Night*, 20 June 1908, on Lascelles visit to Toronto, offered a profile as well of his acting career.

3 David Glassberg, *American Historical Pageantry* (Chapel Hill: University of North Carolina Press 1990), p.4. See also Michael Kammen, *Mystic Chords of Memory* (New York: Vintage 1991), pp. 279–80. The standard work on the subject is Robert Withington, *English Pageantry: An Historical Outline* (Cambridge, Mass.: Harvard 1918, reprinted 1963).

4 Louis Napoleon Parker, *Several of My Lives* (London: Chapman and Hall 1928), pp. 278ff. Parker also contributed an essay on the principles of historical pageantry to the *Journal of the Society of Arts* 54 (1905) from which Glassberg and Withington quote.

5 Withington, *English Pageantry*, vol. 2:195ff, for a full chapter on the Parkerian pageant; see also Glassberg, *American Historical Pageantry*, p. 44, for a perceptive commentary.

6 *The Times Annual Index*, 1908, pp. 803–4, 915–16; Darnley, ed., *Frank Lascelles*, p. 106; G.K. Chesterton, 'The Mystery of a Pageant,' in Chesterton, *Tremendous Trifles* (Philadelphia: Dufor Editions 1968). This essay, first published in 1909, draws irony and amusement from the fact that the person playing the theologian William Paley kept changing.

7 Quebec *Chronicle*, 7, 13 January 1908. See also an undated and unidentified clipping from a Montreal newspaper in the NA, Quebec Battlefields Association Papers, vol. 1, part 2 (these were probably gathered by Colonel Hanbury-Williams for Grey), headlined: 'Pageant Possibility: An Interesting Suggestion Has Been Made that England's Recent Craze Should Be Introduced.' The article echoed the *Chronicle* piece quoted above on the subject of lowering distinctions and leads to the thought that there may have been a calculated campaign on the part of Grey and Hanbury-Williams to launch pageantry in Canada. As to substance, this article noted:

> ... in view of the fact that Canada, although one of the youngest nations of the world, nevertheless possesses a page of history bright with chivalrous deeds, splendid achievements and noble martyrdoms; in view of the associations that cluster around the 'Gibraltar of Canada' and its environments, the suggestion has been made that it would be well to lend a truly picturesque aspect to this year's celebration by portraying in the form of pageants and tableaux some of the commanding incidents in Canadian history that are unfortunately but little thought of in this day of bustle, competition and commercialism.

Internal evidence suggests this piece probably appeared sometime in January of 1908.

8 These phrases are drawn from Chouinard's early proposal; see AVQ, Chouinard to the Comité Executif, 26 octobre 1906.

9 Chouinard, *Troisième Centenaire*, Rapport du sous Comité d'histoire et d'archéologie, 23 janvier 1908, pp. 183–96; see also the reports in *L'Événement*, *Le Soleil*, and the Quebec *Chronicle*, 1 février 1908. The members of Chapais's committee were Mgr. C.O. Gagnon, G.M. Fairchild, Mgr. Hamel, l'abbé Gosselin, Philéas Gagnon, Dr Hubert Neilson, H.M. Price, Cyrille Tessior, Ernest Gagnon, Rev. F.G. Scott, l'abbé Camille Roy, Sir James Lemoine, P.-B. Casgrain, l'abbé L. Lindsey, Eugene Taché, Dr N.-E. Dionne, E. Joly de Lotbinière, Dr Harper, and Dr Bacon.

10 AVQ, Comité Centenaire, Procès Verbeaux, 19, 24 février 1908. Lascelles did not ask for a fee, only expenses. Neverthless, these were considerable as he brought with him his personal assistant, Forbes Dennis, and a valet. Inevitably there would be problems regarding the prompt payment of these expenses and submission of receipts. Chouinard, who handled payments at the Quebec end, drove Lascelles wild with his casual disregard of these matters ('Chouinard leaves the accounts lying about his office for some days before sending them on and refers, forsooth, to my *salary*!!! which irks

me some deal.') NA, National Battlefields Commission, vol. 1, private and
confidential, Lascelles to Courtney, 23 June 1908.

11 *La Verité*, 21 décembre 1907; 1, 8, 15, 27, février 1908; *Le Soleil*, 8 février
1908: 'Cessons donc pour une fois ces guerres vaines qui ne servent qu'a
semer des germes de défiance et de discorde. La solidarité n'est pourtant
pas déjà si excessive chez nous. Unissons-nous a ceux qui s'efforcent de
promouvoir de nobles et grandes idees.'

12 NA, National Battlefields Commission Records, vol. 1, Courtney to Walker,
6 April 1908; Courtney to T.C. Boville, Deputy Minister, Finance, 6 April
1908; Frank Lascelles, 'A Rough Estimate of Expenditure on Pageants,
April 4, 1908':

Grandstand,	$15,000
with fencing	$30,000
Uniforms for army (1,500 at $25)	$36,000
Dress court gentlemen	$36,000
Ladies dresses	not charged
Two thousand wigs	$10,000
Fifteen hundred hats	$7,500
1500 muskets at $3	$4,500
1500 swords at $3	$4,500
50 halberds at $3	$150
Bows, arrows, personal properties	$1000
100 flags at $3	$300
Cannon	$500
50 drums at $5	$250
50 bugles	$150
Scenery and properties	$5,000
Indians	$5,500
Horses	$2,000
Horse trappings	$2,500
Printing and tickets	$5,000
Music	$5,000
Total	$155,850

13 Quebec *Chronicle*, 13 April 1908, printed a verbatim transcript. *Le Soleil*
13 avril 1908.

14 Many years later when Lascelles's health had deteriorated, his friend, the
Earl of Darnley, gathered together a collection of tributes to the man and his
art from the many people he had worked with in his pageant projects at
Oxford, Quebec, South Africa, Calcutta, London, Wembley, Bath, Bradford,
and Bristol. Included in these appreciations of his work were accounts of the
Quebec tercentenary from Sir Wilfrid Laurier, Sir Robert Borden, Sir
George Garneau, Earl Grey, Colonel William Wood, Lord Strathcona,

Monseigneur Mathieu, the Bishop of Quebec, the Duke of Norfolk, Earl Roberts, and General Sir John Hanbury-Williams. Mark Twain contributed a short rave about the Oxford pageant. Participants in that early venture spoke with particular warmth about Lascelles's ability to prod the stuffy Oxford dons into theatrical attire and overcome the resistance of the university authorities. Sir George Garneau also emphasized Lascelles's determination in the face of adversity and his unfailing optimism. See Darnley, ed., *Frank Lascelles*, privately printed by Oxford University Press in 1932.

15 NA, National Battlefields Commission Records, vol. 1, Lascelles to Courtney, 28 April 1908 enclosing receipts.

16 Ibid., Minutes, 27–8 April 1908. The Ladies' Auxiliary submits bill for $5,000 for one thousand dresses; the commission votes $2,500 for five hundred. Quebec *Chronicle* 11, 30 April, 11 May 1908; *Le Soleil*, 11 avril, 8, 23, 27, 30 mai, 6 juin 1908. Mrs Champlain began to get quite a lot of attention in the women's pages of *Le Soleil*.

17 *La Vérité*, 16 mai 1908.

18 Quebec *Chronicle*, 11 June 1908; *Le Soleil*, 11 juin 1908. See also ASQ, Fonds Chouinard, for the actual list.

19 NA, National Battlefields Commission Records, vol. 1, private and confidential, Frank Lascelles to Courtney, 23 June 1908. Lascelles's legendary ability to charm sceptics into becoming believers approached the apocryphal in the hands of an imaginative journalist such as W.T. Stead:

> To go to the capital of French Canada, into the midst of a population of which eighty per cent. at least is Catholic in religion and French in speech and origin, in order to re-enact on the historic Plains of Abraham the decisive battle which tore Canada for ever from the hands of France and made Quebec over to the Protestant Briton – that was a commission that might well have cowed any man. But it only stimulated the master to greater effort. Landing in Quebec a total stranger he found popular feeling bitterly hostile both to him as an Englishman and to the pageant as a commemoration of a defeat which dethroned the fleur-de-lis. But before he had been a month there Quebec was crazy for the pageant. Everybody wanted to act. It was impossible to employ all who applied. And so bitter was the feeling of disappointment on the part of those whose services were rejected that the grand stand had to be guarded by soldiers night and day to prevent it being set on fire by disappointed applicants. (Darnley, ed., *Frank Lascelles*, pp. 5–6).

20 *Le Soleil*, 10 juin 1908. At this point, most of the papers had daily bulletins on tercentenary progress.

21 Montreal *Daily Witness*, 21 July 1908.

22 *Le Soleil*, 17 juillet 1908; Quebec *Chronicle*, 17 July 1908.

23 'On the Plains of Abraham, with the St. Lawrence's silver surfaces beyond, and the green, fir-clad hills of Canada piled high above the stream, in the fading lights of the far Northern summer evening, the scene was incomparably beautiful.' Quoted in Kammen, *Mystic Chords of Memory*, p. 279. Robert Withington's, *English Pageantry: An Historical Outline*, vol. 2:240–4, comments on the 'historical importance' of the Quebec pageant in its chapter on the transfer of pageantry to the United States. Quebec's success inspired subsequent efforts in the United States, most obviously at Lake Champlain a year later. It is no coincidence that Vermont was the site where Chauncey Langdon and Virginia Turner presided over the full flowering of American community historical pageantry in 1910. See also the contemporary guide to pageant-making, Ester Willard Bates, *Pageants and Pageantry* (New York: Ginn 1912), pp. 5, 6, 14, 15, 19. The 'grand effects' of the massed armies were thought to be especially striking. It also left a lasting mark on Quebec popular theatre. The local legacy is dealt with briefly in Rémi Tourangeau, *Fêtes et Spectacles du Québec* (Québec: Nuit Blanche 1992).

24 The names of the individual participants are listed in Frank Carrel, *The Quebec Tercentenary Commemorative History* (Quebec: Daily Telegraph Printing House 1908), pp. 130–62. The list, though long, is obviously not complete; whole groups of participants are missing from the roster. The most obvious omissions are the names of the native performers (with the exception of American Horse) and the orphans who greet Champlain and the Ursulines. For the municipal data I have used the mean of the 1901 and 1911 census counts, *Census of Canada, 1901*, vol. 1, pp. 380–1, and *Census of Canada, 1911*, vol. 2:372.

25 These points are made in greater detail in my earlier essay, 'Historical Pageantry and the "Fusion of the Races" at the tercentenary of Quebec, 1908,' *Histoire sociale/Social History* 29, no. 58 (1996), pp. 391–415.

26 Mrs Thomas Chapais and others kept the nuns fully informed by means of postcards. See UA, *Journal*, 1908, pp. 85–6. See also 90–1: 'Tous ces dialogues et discours étaient l'oeuvre de M. Ernest Myrand, de Québec, qui a fait connaître et aimer d'avantage l'histoire de son pays de concert avec M. Lascelles (protestant) il montre a tous la noblesse et l'héroïsme des fondateurs de notre race.'

27 *L'Événement*, 20 juillet 1908.

28 Ernest Myrand, *Pageants du Tricentenaire de Québec* (Québec: Laflamme & Proulx 1908), p. 33.

29 *Le Soleil*, 9 juillet 1908.

30 RA, King George V's Diary, Saturday, 25 July 1908, and the Prince of Wales to Princess Mary, 29 July 1908. NA, Grey Papers, vol. 14, 4092, Crewe to Grey, 23 September 1908. Vols. 38 and 31 contain his exchange of correspondence with the Prince of Wales and the king. The *Commemorative History* contains a sample of Canadian and overseas press reaction. Immediately following the event, the Quebec papers carried extensive reprints of evaluations of the tercentenary from other papers. Invariably the focus fell upon the pageants.

31 NA, Chadwick Papers, Journal, 20 July 1908.

32 AAQ, L'abbé V.-A. Huard, directeur, *La Semaine Religieuse de Québec*, vol. XX (Québec 1908), pp. 804–7.

33 Quebec *Chronicle*, 17 July 1908; *Le Soleil*, 17, 21 juillet 1908.

34 *Le Soleil*, 8 août 1908.

35 See NA, National Battlefields Commission Records, vol. 1, for a gift in gratitude for Lascelles's services; E.A. Forbes Dennis to Courtney, 15 September 1908; vol. 2, Grey to Courtney, 24 February 1909; ANQ, Fonds Garneau, boîte 1, Grey to Garneau, 1 January 1910; NA, Doughty Papers, M2224, Strathcona to Doughty, 6 June 1910.

36 NA, Grey Papers, vol. 28, 4794, Grey to Edward VII, 30 July 1908.

37 AVQ, Tercentenary Files, Lascelles to Chouinard, on board S.S. *Cedric*, 8 October 1908.

CHAPTER 8   Dressing Up

1 NA, Chadwick Journal, 29 July 1908.

2 John J. MacAloon, ed., *Rite, Drama, Festival, Spectacle: Rehearsals Toward a Theory of Cultural Performance* (Philadelphia: Institute for the Study of Human Issues 1984), p. 1. See also Greg Dening, *Performances* (Chicago: University of Chicago Press 1996).

3 MacAloon, ed., *Rite, Drama, Festival, Spectacle*, p. 246.

4 See, for example, Mona Ozouf, *Festivals and the French Revolution* (Cambridge: Harvard University Press 1988); E. Hobsbawm and T. Ranger, eds., *The Invention of Tradition* (Cambridge: Cambridge University Press 1983); John Bodnar, *Remaking America: Public Memory, Commemoration and Patriotism in Twentieth Century America* (Princeton: Princeton University Press 1992); John R. Gillis, ed., *Commemorations: The Politics of National Identity* (Princeton: Princeton University Press 1994).

Recently Canadian scholars have made notable contributions to this literature; see, for example, Jacques Mathieu et Jacques Lacoursière, *Les Mémoires Québécoises* (Québec: Les Presses de l'Université Laval 1991);

Norman Knowles, *Inventing the Loyalists: The Ontario Loyalist Tradition and the Creation of Usable Pasts* (Toronto: University of Toronto Press 1997); and Peter Pope, *The Many Landfalls of John Cabot* (Toronto: University of Toronto Press 1997).

5 ANQ, Fonds Garneau, boîte 5, Memoire pour entrevue avec Sir Wilfrid Laurier, 24 mars 1907.

6 Robert Rydell, *All the World's a Fair* (Chicago: University of Chicago 1984), pp. 48–71; David Nasaw, *Going Out: The Rise and Fall of Public Amusements* (New York: Basic Books 1994), pp. 62–79; Douglas Cole, *Captured Heritage* (Vancouver: Douglas and McIntyre 1985), pp. 122–40; Curtis M. Hinsley, 'The World as Marketplace: Commodification of the Exotic at the World's Columbian Exposition, Chicago, 1893,' in I. Karp and S.D. Lavine, eds., *Exhibiting Cultures* (Washington: Smithsonian Institution Press 1991), pp. 344–65, and Richard White, *'Its Your Misfortune and None of My Own': A History of the American West* (Norman: University of Oklahoma 1991), pp. 109–17, 613–32.

7 Elsbeth Heaman, 'Commercial Leviathan: Central Canadian Exhibitions at Home and Abroad during the Nineteenth Century.' (PhD thesis, University of Toronto 1995).

8 Jacques Mathieu and Eugene Kedl, eds, *The Plains of Abraham* (Montreal: Septentrion 1993), p. 145.

9 L.G. Moses provides the best account of this cultural phenomenon in *Wild West Shows and the Images of American Indians, 1883–1933* (Albuquerque: University of New Mexico Press 1996). Walter Battice, a native actor in this show, wrote his impressions of the Jamestown show which Moses quotes on pp. 178–9. Unfortunately I have not been able to find a native account of the Quebec tercentenary. On the production and popular consumption of wild west mythology, see Christine Bold, *Selling the West* (Bloomington: Indiana University Press 1987) and Richard W. Etulain, *Re-Imagining the Modern American West* (Tucson: University of Arizona Press 1996).

10 Judging from contemporary reports in the *New York Times*, the Jamestown tercentennial from 26 April to 31 November 1907 was not a great success. It suffered from poor weather, disappointing attendance, a bad press, and management turmoil. Reports suggest that it was primarily a show of modern technology, notable for its lack of historical representation. It was more overtly a celebration of the past through praise of the present than Quebec. It closed with a debt of $2.5 million.

11 Don Smith, *Le Sauvage: The Native People in Quebec Historical Writing on the Heroic Period (1534–1663) of New France* (Ottawa: National Museums of Canada 1974). For an analysis of European perceptions of native people

during the seventeenth century with the emphasis upon Canada and France, see Olive P. Dickason, *The Myth of the Savage and the Beginnings of French Colonialism in the Americas* (Edmonton: University of Alberta Press 1984), and Julie Schimmel, 'Inventing "the Indian,"' in William H. Truettner, ed., *The West as America* (Washington: Smithsonian Institution 1991), pp. 149–90.

12 Terry Goldie, *Fear and Temptation: The Image of the Indigene in Canadian, Australian, and New Zealand Literatures* (Montreal: McGill-Queen's University Press 1989). Goldie's synchronic analysis of writing in English does not differentiate imagery by period, but his generalizations do correspond with the diachronic analysis of native imagery in popular magazines by Ronald Haycock in his *The Image of the Indian* (Waterloo: Wilfrid Laurier University Press 1971), part I, 'The Poor Doomed Savage.'

13 Here I am following Robert Berkhoffer, *The White Man's Indian* (New York: Knopf 1978), the more recent Canadian counterpart by Daniel Francis, *The Imaginary Indian* (Vancouver: Arsenal 1992), and the contributors to S. Elizabeth Bird's collection, *Dressing in Feathers: The Construction of the Indian in American Popular Culture* (Boulder: Westview Press 1996); see, in particular, the introductory essay by Bird; Sally Jones on mid-nineteenth-century theatrical representations; Frank Goodyear on the photographic iconography of Sitting Bull's surrender; Jeffrey Steele on native images in advertising; Peter Geller on Indian participation in the 1920 Hudson's Bay Red River Pageant; and Alison Griffiths on the native in early films.

14 Quebec *Chronicle*, 29 June, 13, 14 July 1908; *Le Soleil*, 14, 18 juillet 1908. Some of the native people had been voyageurs on the expeditionary force up the Nile. Mr Armstrong claimed to possess a peace pipe 'brought from the same red stone as Hiawatha obtained his.'

15 I can now see that my reading of the native participation in the tercentenary, arrived at independently, corroborates that of Moses's interpretation of the opening that Buffalo Bill's Theatre of the West gave to native people. See Moses, *Wild West Shows*, pp. 8, 272–7. Richard White has partially rehabilitated Buffalo Bill's reputation as a historian in 'Frederick Jackson Turner and Buffalo Bill,' in James R. Grossman, ed., *The Frontier in American Culture* (Berkeley: University of California Press and the Newberry Library 1994), pp. 7–66.

16 See the Duke of Norfolk's contribution to the Earl of Darnley's collection of tributes, *Frank Lascelles 'Our Modern Orpheus'* (Oxford: University of Oxford Press 1932), p. 25, which captured Lascelles in one of his more outrageous moments at Quebec:

In the evening we took part in a gathering at which our present King was the guest, and in the midst of it all I was alarmed to see a Red Indian with the fiercest stripes approaching me, tomahawk in hand. It was an Iroquois chief, and the traditions of their race are that they are the most cruel and bloodthirsty of all the Red Indian tribes ... I afterwards discovered Frank Lascelles beneath his war-paint.

17 *Who Was Who*, vol. 3: *1929–1940* (London: Adam and Charles Black 1941), p. 781.

18 See *The Historical Record of the Imperial Visit to India, 1911* (London: John Murray 1914), pp. 256–8, for details of the Calcutta pageant. See also John Fortescue, *Narrative of the Visit to India of Their Majesties King George V and Queen Mary and of the Coronation Durbar held at Delhi, 12th December, 1911* (London: Macmillan 1912), pp. 236–41.

19 NA, Maurice Arthur Pope Papers, MG27, III, F4, vol. 1, Address of the Quebec Indians to the Prince of Wales on the occasion of Quebec tercentenary celebrations, 1908.

20 Jacques Cartier's changing character in historiography is brilliantly treated by Jacques Mathieu, 'Un événement fondateur: la découverte du Canada: Le Personage de Jacques Cartier et son évolution,' in Claire Dolan, ed., *Événement, Identité et Histoire* (Québec: Septentrion 1991), pp. 255–67. See also the splendid illustrated collection, *Le Monde de Jacques Cartier* (Montréal: Libre Expression 1984), a joint France-Quebec publication to mark the 450th anniverary of his voyages. See especially pp. 295–305 for a discussion of the 'invention' of a hero.

21 Compare this theatrical representation in 1908 with Patricia Seed's imaginative reading of contact rituals in *Ceremonies of Possession in Europe's Conquest of the New World, 1492–1640* (New York: Cambridge University Press 1995). In her comparative reading, French rites of possession were more processional than textual, more a dance than prose. The 1908 representation seems more like a mass than a masque.

22 NA, Chadwick Papers, Journal, 20 July 1908.

23 Francis Parkman, Introduction to *France and England in North America, Pioneers of France in the New World* (Toronto: George N. Morang, Frontenac Edition 1900), vol. I: xcviii–xcix.

24 For a post-modern interpretation that emphasizes François-Xavier Garneau more than Parkman and tends to de-emphasize clericalism, see Mathieu et Lacoursière, *Les Mémoires Québécoises*, pp. 274–5, 313–25. See also Manon Brunet, 'La constitution d'une tradition littéraire québécoise par l'institution littéraire en formation au XIX⁰ siècle,' in P. Lanthier et G.

Rouseau, eds., *La Culture Inventée* (Trois-Rivières: Institut Québécois de Recherche sur la Culture 1992), pp. 23–44. Gérard Bouchard's essay in the same collection, 'Sur les perspectives de la culture québécoise comme francophonie nord-américaine,' pp. 320–1, touches briefly on the social basis of this elite view of Quebec history.

25 Carl Berger, *The Writing of Canadian History* (Toronto: Oxford University Press 1976), pp. 18–19.

26 Frank Basil Tracy was a journalist with the *Boston Transcript* (he would later become its editor) and an amateur historian. Born in the far west, educated and inducted into the newspaper business in the midwest, Tracy moved to Boston about 1897. According to his entry in *Who's Who in America*, vol. 7, *1912–13*, he contributed articles on contemporary social issues to magazines such as the *Forum*, the *North American Review* and the *Fortnightly Review*. His *Tercentenary History* was published in New York in 1908 by P.F. Collier. It was reissued after Tracy's death in 1913 with an epiloque by Britton B. Cooke. This ambitious work goes unremarked in the standard works on Canadian historiography. I am indebted to one of my readers for the reference. I am further indebted to Richard Landon of the Thomas Fisher Rare Book Room at the University of Toronto Library for finding this letter from Frank Tracy to George Wrong, 22 March 1906 in the Wrong Papers. The English writer Tracy had in mind was W.B. Munro, a professor at Harvard University.

CHAPTER 9   On Parade

1 NA, Grey Papers, vol. 14, 3918, Grey to Elgin, 2 February 1908; 3919, Grey to Elgin, 27 February 1908.

2 My interpretation of parades has been influenced by Mary Ryan, 'The American Parade: Representations of the Nineteenth Century Social Order,' in Lynn Hunt, ed., *The New Cultural History* (Berkeley: University of California Press 1989), pp. 131–53; Susan Davis, *Parades and Power: Street Theatre in Nineteenth Century Philadelphia* (Philadelphia: Temple University Press 1986); John J. MacAloon, 'Introduction: Cultural Performances, Culture Theory,' and Roberto da Matta, 'Carnival in Multiple Planes,' in John J. MacAloon, ed., *Rite, Drama, Festival, Spectacle* (Philadelphia: Institute for the Study of Human Issues 1984), pp. 1–15, 208–40; Peter Jackson, 'The Politics of the Streets: A Geography of Caribana,' *Political Geography* 11 (1992), pp. 130–5; and Peter Goheen, 'Symbols in the Streets: Parades in Victorian Canada,' *Urban History Review* 18 (1990), pp. 237–43.

3 The story of the militia in Canadian politics can be read in: Norman

Penlington, *Canada and Imperialism, 1896–1899* (Toronto: University of
Toronto Press 1965); Richard Preston, *The Defence of the Undefended Border*
(Montreal and Kingston: McGill-Queen's University Press 1977); Desmond
Morton, *The Canadian General: Sir William Otter* (Toronto: Hakkert 1974),
and Carman Miller, *Painting the Map Red: Canada and the South African War,
1899–1902* (Montreal and Kingston: McGill-Queen's University Press 1993);
Desmond Morton, *Ministers and Generals: Politics and the Canadian Militia,
1868–1904* (Toronto: University of Toronto Press 1970); and Stephen J.
Harris, *Canadian Brass: The Making of a Professional Army 1860–1939*
(Toronto: University of Toronto Press 1988).

4 For several assessments of Canadian military preparedness, see NA, War
   Office Papers, WO 106/40, reel B3079, 'A Study of the Strategic Considera-
   tions Afffecting the Invasion of Canada by the United States,' Lt.-Col. H.J.
   Foster, military attaché, Washington 1904; 'The Defence of Canada,'
   13 December 1904, General Staff, War Office; 'Canadian Military Policy,'
   Colonel Kirkpatrick, 1905; 'Canada and the United States, Defence and
   Military Resources,' January 1906:

   > The active militia is excellent. But the general standard of efficiency for
   > the non-commissioned officers and men is not up to that of our average
   > Volunteers and Yeomanry, while only a certain proportion of the officers
   > undergo training equal to that of our Militia Officers. The old soldier
   > element is almost totally wanting, because, although the period of service
   > is nominally 3 years very few men serve more than one training ...
   > Canada could not at the present moment arm and equip a force of more
   > than 50,000 men without receiving additional arms from GB.

5 Lord Dundonald reporting on an interview with Laurier, quoted in
   Morton, *Ministers and Generals*, p. 176.

6 NA, Denison Papers, vol. 11, W. Wallace, Lt.-Col., 36th Peel Regiment to
   Denison, 15 May 1908, urging him not to neglect the rural regiments:
   'While it may be admitted that the City Corps possibly make a better
   showing than the Rural Corps owing to their greater facilities, yet a man is a
   man for all that, and when it comes to the real duty of a soldier the Rural
   Corps have never been found wanting. Feathers and furs do not make
   soldiers.'

7 This waffling by the military brass can be followed in Militia Council,
   Minutes, vol. IV, 1908: 25 February (50 per cent of authorized establishment
   to attend); 10 March (too costly, over $900,000); 18 March (A Canadian,
   Brigadier Otter, to command troops); 17–18 April (detailed cost estimates
   for 24,500 men of $973,900); 6 May (perhaps rural corps from Quebec to

assemble); 11 May (permanent force alone to attend at a cost of $85,000); 2 June (Mayor Garneau asks for 12,000 militia, decision to send city regiments and rural corps close to Quebec totalling more than 10,000 men and 900 horses at a cost of $142,127).

8 Otter had some experience with this sort of thing. During a visit of this same Duke of York in 1901, he had hurriedly mustered 10,000 militiamen on the Garrison Common in Toronto, at that time the largest mobilization of troops in Canadian history. See Morton, *The Canadian General*, p. 252.

9 The frantic preparations can be followed in detail in NA, RG9, II D1, Department of Militia and Defence Records, Quartermaster's Letterbooks, vol. 68, reel T409, and vol. 69, reel T410, the correspondence of H.W. Brown, director of contracts with various suppliers.

10 Toronto *Telegram*, 21 July 1908.

11 Ibid., 27 July 1908.

12 *L'Événement*, 16, 21 juillet 1908.

13 York University Library, Special Collections, Keystone Stereoscopic Slide Collection, the Tercentenary of Quebec. Quebec's Archives Nationales also has a complete set. Of the 128 views, seventeen were of this military parade through the streets of Quebec. Another sixteen stereoscopic slides documented the military review on the Plains of Abraham the next day, but the focus was upon dignitaries observing the event.

14 Frank Carrel, *The Quebec Tercentenary Commemorative History* (Quebec: Daily Telegraph Printing House 1908), p. 71.

15 *L'Événement*, 24 juillet 1908.

16 RA, George V Diary, Friday, 24 July 1908.

17 NA, Admiralty files (MG12,) Adm. 1, file 8992, reel B3643, C.P. Lucas to Foreign Office, 24 June 1908; Lord Crewe, secretary of state for the colonies, to Earl Grey, 18 June, 8 July 1908; Crewe to Grey, draft telegram, 8 July 1908, pointing out that the vice president of the United States should at all times take precedence over the French delegation led by an admiral; however, on the occasion of the military review the French Blue Jackets could come ahead of the Americans.

18 Desmond Morton reserves some of the finest prose to describe the tercentennial military events at which his grandfather distinguished himself, *The Canadian General*, pp. 237–8, 282–8. Professor Morton has generously shared his collection of images of the military review at the tercentenary and given permission for the reproduction of the artist's sketch of the occasion that hangs on his office wall (see illustration on p. 209).

19 NA, RG9, II B1, Adjutant General's Correspondence, Re: tercentenary, Vols. 488–93. Quebec City's waterworks broke down under the strain. Many

troops became ill from drinking contaminated water, giving rise to the rumour that many died of dysentry. Private Roberts's death may or may not have been caused by poor sanitation; certainly the authorities responded by assuming it had been and issued orders to pay closer attention to sanitary arrangements. Many people returned from Quebec with stomach complaints, Edmund Walker among them, which gave credence to suspicions that Quebec's water supply had not been what it should have been. See NA, Archives Records, RG37, vol. 190, Arthur Doughty to Walker, 15 August 1908, expressing regret at Walker's illness: 'I do not know what is the cause but I have seen paragraphs in the paper about the number of people who were either ill at Quebec, or since their return home. The Quebec water is supposed to be exceptionally good. It comes from Lake St. Charles.'

20 RA, George V Diary, Friday, 24 July 1908; W.8/38, Earl Grey to the King, 31 July 1908; NA, Grey Papers, vol. 14, telegram, Grey to Colonial Office for His Majesty the King, 25 July 1908, and his longer despatch of the same date.

21 The standard work on this subject remains Arthur Marder, *From Dreadnought to Scapa Flow: The Royal Navy in the Fisher Era, 1904–1919*, 5 vols. (Oxford: Oxford University Press 1961–70). Vol. 1, *The Road to War,* covers these events. Paul Kennedy widens the focus and the concept of seapower by taking other factors into account in his analysis of naval mastery, *The Rise and Fall of British Naval Mastery* (London: A. Lane 1976); see also D.M. Schurman, *The Education of a Navy: The Development of British Naval Strategic Thought* (Chicago: University of Chicago Press 1965). In many ways the most accessible introduction to these matters is Robert Massie's book of dreadnought proportions entitled *Dreadnought: Britain, Germany and the Coming of the Great War* (New York: Random House 1991) where the naval race and the crisis of 1908 are dealt with on pp. 459–514.

22 Grey to Lord Elgin, 25 August 1906, quoted in Mary Hallett, 'The 4th Earl Grey' (PhD thesis, University of London 1966), p. 259.

23 John Kendle, *The Colonial and Imperial Conferences, 1887–1911* (London: Longmans 1967).

24 The standard works are Gilbert C. Tucker, *The Naval Service of Canada, Its Official History*, vol. 1 (Ottawa: King's Printer 1952), and R.A. Preston, *Canada and Imperial Defense* (Durham, NC: Duke University Press 1967). Recent contributions have corrected and added nuances to the received version, among them, Michael Hadley and Roger Sarty, *Tin Pots and Pirate Ships: Canadian Naval Forces and German Sea Raiders, 1880–1918* (Montreal and Kingston: McGill-Queen's University Press 1991), pp. 20–9, which is especially good on the implications of torpedoes; Nigel D. Brodeur, 'L.P.

Brodeur and the Origins of the Royal Canadian Navy,' in James A. Boutelier, ed., *The RCN in Retrospect, 1910–1968* (Vancouver: University of British Columbia Press 1993), pp. 13–32, which implies that Brodeur prepared the ground for public policy, and Paul Kennedy, 'Naval Mastery: The Canadian Context,' in W.A.B. Douglas, ed., *The RCN in Transition, 1910–1985* (Vancouver: University of British Columbia Press 1988), pp. 15–33, which, by looking more broadly at the elements of naval power, sees more to Canadian policy than foot-dragging.

25 NA, Admiralty Files, MG12, Adm. 1, file 8992, reel B3643, Memorandum, 2 March 1908; telegram to Commander-in-Chief, Atlantic Fleet, 3 March 1908, contains the formal orders; Memorandum for the First Sea Lord, 7 March 1908, initiates the visit.

26 Ibid., 1 June 1908, Orders – Admiralty.

27 NA, CO42, reel B2246, Treasury, Memorandum, 1 April 1908, Treasury to Colonial Secretary. The Admiralty files document the elaborate arrangements for the 'naval entertainments at the Tercentenary.' See, for example, C.P. Lucas to Secretary of Treasury, 18 March 1908 (formal request to Treasury); G.H. Murray, Treasury to Colonial Office, 1 April 1908 (agreement in principle for suitable entertainments); 7 May 1908 (draft order for one of the ships to pick up the Admiralty barge); 16 May 1908, Vice-Admiral Commander-in-Chief to Secretary of Admiralty (coal); letter of Commander-in-Chief, Atlantic Fleet, 15 May 1908. The sheer novelty of the occasion led to a special order, Embarkation of Live Stock – 3 July 1908, to which the following minute was added: 'Note: This order was issued for information as Commander in Chief has not seen live bullocks on board one of HM ships since 1870.' The detailed order spells out loading techniques, care, feeding, and killing instructions along with regulations regarding the auctioning off of the tongue, liver and heart to the crew.

28 NA, Admiralty Files, MG12, Adm. 1, file 8992, reel B3643, C.P. Lucas to Secretary of Admiralty, 7 March 1908; Louis Mallet to Under Secretary of State Colonies, 9 March 1908; telegram to Mr Bryce from FO, 11 March 1908; Monsieur Pichon to Sir Francis Bertie, UK Ambassador, Paris, 22 mai 1908 (accepts invitation to celebration, delegate to be the officer commmmanding the naval division, and Mr Louis Herbette, Conseiller d'état, Mr Loynes, Consul General); Pichon to Bertie, 11 juin 1908, sending *Léon Gambetta*, 12,500 tons and another cruiser of 10,000 tons, Vice-Admiral Jauréguiberry, commandant en chef de l'escadre du nord – chef de mission officielle française; C.P. Lucas to Foreign Office, 24 June 1908; Crewe, Secretary of State for Colonies, to Grey, 18 June 1908.

29 RA, George V Diary, 16–22 July 1908; GV CC4/4, Prince of Wales to
    Princess of Wales, 17–24 July 1908: 'Thank God darling you did not come
    with us, you would indeed have had a time of it and been miserable. The
    ship being new & never having been in bad weather ... produced leaks in
    most of the cabins which is also most disagreeable; so not only would you
    have been sea sick, but wet besides.'

30 RA, George V Diary, Saturday July 25, 1908.

31 *Commemorative History*, pp. 85–6, 108–12; NA, Chadwick Journal, 25 July
    1908; Toronto *Telegram*, 27 July 1908.

32 *Le Soleil* reported the arrival and departure of the ships and not much else.
    The *Chronicle*, by contrast, reported on both the naval review and the
    aquatic contests on 27 and 28 July and the fireworks in 29 July, as did the
    Telegraph. The Montreal *Gazette* put the fleet in its headlines on 15, 21, 27,
    28, and 30 July.

33 NA, Admiralty Files, MG12, Adm. 1, file 8992, reel B3643, Orders,
    Confidental, 8 July 1908, Commander-in-Chief Atlantic 'On the return
    journey it is left to your discretion for HMS *Indomitable* to steam at full
    power for such a distance as you may think fit, taking into account the state
    of the weather, the condition of the boilers & engines & other attendant
    circumstances.' See also Harold Nicolson, *King George the Fifth* (London:
    Constable 1952), p. 99, and Kenneth Rose, *King George V* (London:
    Weidenfeld and Nicholson 1983), p. 72.

34 NA, Admiralty Files, MG12, Adm. 1, file 8992, reel B3643, General Letter
    No. 29, *Exmouth* at Berehaven, 7 August 1908, Curzon-Howe, Vice-Admiral
    and Commander-in-Chief to Secretary of the Admiralty, REPORT ON QUEBEC
    VISIT.

35 RA, Diary of George V, Friday, 31 July 1908; GV CC4/5, Prince of Wales to
    Princess of Wales, 1 August 1908.

36 O.D. Skelton, *Life and Letters of Sir Wilfrid Laurier* (Toronto: Oxford 1921),
    vol. 2:320–4 for this debate and the text of the resolution. See Brodeur,
    'L.P. Brodeur and the Origins of the Royal Canadian Navy,' pp. 24–6, for
    Grey's pressure.

CHAPTER 10   Of Cabbages and Kings

1 NA, Laurier Papers, 204632, Grey to Laurier, 30 October 1907; NA, Grey
   Papers, vol. 28, 7284, Grey to Sir William Clark, Ontario, 28 December
   1907; 4773 Grey to Bigge, 24 June 1908.

2 NA, Grey Papers, 4769, Grey to Bigge, 18, 24 June 1908.

3 O.D. Skelton, *Life and Letters of Sir Wilfrid Laurier* (Toronto: Oxford 1921),

vol. 2, pp. 307–8. Opposite p. 304 there is a charming picture of Botha, Laurier, Asquith, and Ward seated surrounded by children.

4 NA, Crewe Papers, Grey to Crewe, 3 June 1908.

5 Benedict Anderson, *Imagined Communities* (London: Verso 1983); Eric Hobsbawm and Terrance Ranger, eds., *The Invention of Tradition* (Cambridge: Cambridge University Press 1983); Eric Hobsbawm, *Nations and Nationalism since 1780* (Cambridge: Cambridge University Press 1990); David Cannadine, 'The Context, Performance and Meaning of Ritual: The British Monarchy and the "Invention of Tradition",' in Hobsbawm and Ranger, *The Invention of Tradition*, pp. 101–64, and his introduction as editor to *Rituals of Royalty* (Cambridge: Cambridge University Press 1987); Linda Colley, *The Britons: Forging the Nation, 1707–1837* (New Haven: Yale University Press 1992); Patrick Joyce, *Visions of the People* (Cambridge: Cambridge University Press 1991) and especially *Democratic Subjects: The Self and the Social in Nineteenth-Century England* (Cambridge: Cambridge University Press 1994) – a book initially entitled *The Fall of Class*; Raphael Samuel, *Theatres of Memory* (London: Verso 1994); and Philip Corrigan and Derek Sawyer, *The Arch of the State* (Oxford: Oxford University Press 1985).

6 On this, see John M. Mackenzie, *Propaganda and Empire* (Manchester: Manchester University Press 1984), a book that has inspired an entire series, Studies in Imperialism, several of which touch on this subject. See, in particular, John M. Mackenzie, ed., *Imperialism and Popular Culture* (1986) and John M. Mackenzie, ed., *Popular Imperialism and the Military* (1992). The feminist literary critic Mary Poovey comes at this subject from quite a different direction but makes a similar point about the formation of what she calls 'a social body' – a phrase I owe to her – through various representations of society and popular imperialism in differing literary genres; see *Making a Social Body: British Cultural Formation, 1830–1864* (Chicago: University of Chicago Press 1995).

7 See Penny Summerfield, 'Patriotism and Empire: Music Hall Entertainment, 1870–1914,' in Mackenzie, ed., *Imperialism and Popular Culture*, pp. 17–48; Peter Bailey, ed., *The Victorian Music Hall: The Business of Pleasure* (Milton Keynes 1987) and 'Conspiracies of Meaning: Music-Hall and the Knowingness of Popular Culture,' *Past and Present* 144 (1994), pp. 138–70.

8 The imperialist ladies reported in some distress to the governor general that after a visit by Henri Bourassa the French ladies agreed with their guest that once Canada had become a great nation it would break its tie with Great Britain. Mary Hallett, 'The 4th Earl Grey' (PhD thesis, University of London 1966), pp. 137–9.

9 NA, Crewe Papers, A1645, Grey to Crewe, 16 June 1908.

10 NA, Grey Papers, vol. 2, 912, Grey to Laurier, 18 June 1908, and 913, Laurier to Grey, 19 June 1908, complaining the list of honours was too long.

11 NA, Crewe Papers, A1645, Crewe to Grey, 19 June 1908, private and personal. The king wanted to make Grey a member of Privy Council. Beyond that, Crewe reported: 'HM willing to make one to two knights who must be connected with the *celebration* not merely people of general merit.' See also Grey to Crewe, 14 July 1908, complaining that Australia has outdone Canada in birthday honours – four knights against two for Canada, three KCMGs to Australia and none to Canada after rejecting Clouston.

12 The quotation is from Grey's letter to Crewe of 16 June 1908. This sub-plot can be followed as well in the Laurier Papers; see, for example, C1162, 205361, Grey to Laurier, 18 June 1908; 205382, Grey to Laurier, 20 June 1908, reporting failure to get a knighthood for Clouston, who nonetheless received one later in the year.

13 Respectively Brigadier-General William Otter, Sir George Drummond, Edmund Walker, Adélard Turgeon, and Joseph Pope (Companions of the Victorian Order). The ADCs, Colonel Percy Sherwood and Colonel Alexandre Roy, received the Victorian Order, and Chouinard was made a Companion of St Michael and St George.

14 The story shared the front page of the Conservative *Chronicle* on Friday, 24 July. The same day *Le Soleil* filled its full front page with the story and pictures of Gouin, Grey, Garneau, Turgeon, and line drawings of Chouinard, Otter, and Roy, who received a CVO. The story carried on for three more pages inside.

15 Carl Berger, *Honour and the Search for Influence* (Toronto: University of Toronto Press 1995).

16 *L'Événement*, 24 juillet 1908 for a full account of the Royal Society meeting, in particular Thomas Chapais's address; the *Chronicle* covered the meetings in a column on p. 10 on 25 July 1908.

17 *The Commemorative History*, pp. 29, 74, 81–2, 102, 110.

18 William H. McNeil, *Keeping Together in Time: Dance and Drill in Human History* (Cambridge, Mass.: Harvard University Press 1996).

19 I have consulted the file in the National Library Special Collections, Music Division, on the composition, modification, copyright protection, and eventual nationalization of Canada's now official national anthem. See also Helmut Kallmann, *A History of Music in Canada, 1534–1914* (Toronto: University of Toronto Press 1960), pp. 137–9, 247, and the biography of Calixa Lavallée in Helmut Kallmann, ed., *The Encyclopedia of Music in Canada*, 2nd ed. (Toronto: University of Toronto Press 1992), pp. 532–3.

20 This story, quoted from one of Jones's papers on the psychology of popular monarchy, can be found in Philip Ziegler, *Crown and People* (London: Collins 1978), p. 18. To a man who, as a boy, waited late into the night for the royal train to squash his pennies beneath its wheels on the rails, these things do not have to be explained. To his children, they do.

21 Ibid., pp. 21–3, (emphasis in original quotations).

22 On Edward VII, see Dana Bentley-Cranch, *Edward VII: Image of an Era* (London: HMSO 1992), which is particularly good on his imperial tours; Christopher Hibbert, *Edward VII* (London: Allen Lane 1976), which offers the best detail of Grey's observations on his tour of India; and Kinley Roby, *The King, The Press and the People* (London: Barrie & Jenkins 1975).

23 Harold Nicolson, *King George the Fifth* (London: Constable 1962), p. 86; Ziegler, *Crown and People*, p. 30.

24 In addition to Ziegler and Nicolson on this point, see also Kenneth Rose, *King George V* (London: Weidenfeld and Nicholson 1983).

25 RA, GV, CC4/4, Prince of Wales to Princess of Wales, 17–24 July 1908.

26 NA, CO42 Canada 1908, vol. 918, reel B2240, Grey to Crewe, 22 June 1908, secret; NA, Crewe Papes, Grey to Crewe, 9 June 1908, private; Crewe to Grey, 19 June 1908, private and personal, warning against 'awkward customers amongst the Irish Americans.' One Canadian-Irish partisan, John Nolan, allegedly murdered two people in Ireland before emigrating and made threats on the life of Lord Crewe and a companion. Laughing past the graveyard, Crewe added mordantly: 'But I suppose we were not worth it.'

27 NA, Grey Papers, vol. 14, 3903, Elgin to Grey, asking about the line to be taken in the tercentenary and wanting in particular to know what to say when the prince asks: 'Tell me exactly what I am expected to do.' On Sir Edward Grey's conversations with the French ambassador, Paul Cambon, see Robert Massie, *Dreadnought* (New York: Random House 1991), p. 589.

28 NA, Grey Papers, 3983, Sir F. Hopwood to Grey, private, 18 April 1908.

29 NA, CO42, Grey to Elgin, 23 May 1908; NA, Grey Papers, 3988, Grey to Crewe, 4 May 1908; 4001, Grey to Crewe, 18 May 1908; NA, Crewe Papers, Crewe to Grey, 11 June 1908, private and personal.

30 NA, Grey Papers, 4779, Grey to Bigge, private Quebec, undated (1908); 4769, Grey to Bigge, 18 June 1908; 4771, Grey to Bigge, 20 June 1908; 4773, Grey to Bigge, 24 June 1908; 4777, Grey to Bigge, 30 June 1908; 4784, Lord Crewe to Grey, 14 July 1908; NA, CO42, vol. 918, Grey to the Colonial Office, 28 June 1908 (reports cabinet has met and approved the Prince of Wales's address); vol. 920, reel B241, Grey to Colonial Office re addresses on arrival, 6 June 1908; Grey to Colonial Office, 6 July 1908, re king's

telegram; letter from the king to Colonial Office, 13 July 1908, approving text. There are several other communications in this file on the delicate matter of the text of various addresses. The British officials saw the text of the Canadian addresses in advance as well.

31 NA, Grey Papers, 4777, Grey to Bigge, 30 June 1908.

32 NA, Crewe Papers, A1645, Grey to Crewe, 9 June 1908; NA Grey Papers, vol. 14, 4041, Crewe to Grey, 19 June 1908, notes that he sees the importance of 'laying emphasis' on the Champlain part of the ceremony.

33 NA, CO42 Canada 1908, vol. 918 (Reel B2240), Grey to Elgin, 12 June 1908; Crewe to Grey, 15 June 1908.

34 NA, Grey Papers, vol. 14, Grey to Crewe, 4 May 1908.

35 RA, GV, CC4/5, Prince of Wales to Princess of Wales, 29 July–3 August 1908.

36 *Commemorative History*, p. 107.

37 Ibid., pp. 107–8; *L'Événement*, 28 juillet 1908, 'le Prince de Galles à St.-Joachim: Une Belle Reception par S.E. Mgr Sbarretti, S.G. Mgr Bégin et les messieurs du Séminaire'; RA, George V Diary, Monday, 27 July 1908.

38 Eight maps of the prince's progress through the city and a detailed itinerary for each day can be found in NA, RG7, G23, vol. 16, Prince of Wales Royal Visit 1908.

39 RA, GV, CC4/4, Prince of Wales to Princess of Wales, 29 July–3 August 1908.

40 NA, Denison Papers, vol. 29–30, Diary, 28 July 1908.

41 NA, Chadwick, Journal, 25 July 1908. On 9 October 1923 Ethel revisited these pages of her diary to squeeze this note in the margin: 'I was at a dance last night for the Present P of W, son of this one.'

42 NA, Grey Papers, vol. 14, 4075, Grey to Crewe, 31 July 1908; vol. 28, 4805, Grey to the Duke of Connaught, 14 August 1908.

43 Ibid., vol. 28, 4794, Grey to Edward VII, 30 July 1908; RA, GV RA W.8/38, Grey to King Edward VII, 30 July 1908. The king's reply from Marienbad expresses satisfaction with the prince's performance and Grey's skillful handling of a difficult situation; Vol. 31, 8002, King Edward VII to My Dear Albert, 15 August 1908.

44 NA, Grey Papers, vol. 28, 4788, Grey to the Princess of Wales, 30 June 1908; 7996, reply, 13 August 1908.

45 London *Times*, Toronto *Telegram*, 28 July 1908; NA, Grey Papers, vol. 31, 8001, Prince of Wales to Grey, 31 July 1908; RA, George V Diary, Wednesday, 29 July 1908; GV CC4/4, Prince of Wales to Princess of Wales, 17–24 July 1908.

46 NA, Grey Papers, vol. 28, 4791, Grey to the Prince of Wales, 31 July 1908.

CHAPTER 11   Souvenirs de Québec

1 *The Quebec Tercentenary Commemorative History* (Quebec: Daily Telegraph Printing House 1908), p. 58.

2 NA, National Battlefields Commission Records, vol. 2, Secretary of the Governor General to J.M. Courtney, 24 February 1909; vol. 3, Minutes, 11–13 September 1908; ANQ, Garneau Papers, boîte 1, Grey to Garneau, 27 December 1909; NA, Doughty Papers, M2244, Strathcona to Doughty, 17 June 1910.

3 NA, National Battlefields Commission Records, vol. 3, Minutes, 13–14 April 1908; 29–30 May 1908; 17 December 1908; 26 November 1909 (distribution of six gold and 750 bronze); 10 January 1910; 1 March 1910 (three more gold medals, ordered struck). A formal description of the medals, probably written by Taché himself, appears in *Les Fêtes du Troisème Centenaire de Québec, 1608–1908* (Québec: Laflamme & Proulx 1911), pp. 22–4. A complete list of persons who received medals can be found in the archives of the Quebec office of the National Battlefields Commission, files and notebooks of medals sent.

4 Earl Grey, after he got over the shock of the richness of the gift, shot off a letter wondering where the money for it had come from and reminding the National Battlefields commissioners that the governments of France, the United States, and Ontario had also incurred great expense for the tercentenary and thus deserved equal recognition. Grey reminded Garneau that it cost the British $100,000 to send the fleet; the French and American costs would have been proportional. The commission faithfully struck three more gold medals, one each for the presidents of France and the United States and the third for the vaults of the Dominion Archives. See ANQ, Garneau, boîte 1, Grey to Garneau, 1 January 1910. The medals cost the commission $4,125, which it paid out of its general accounts. The silver sculpture for Lascelles cost $1,500. The commission also had a bust of Earl Grey sculpted – possibly by Lascelles himself – for which it paid $850. See also NA, Doughty Papers, M2244, Lévis de Mirepoux to Doughty, 22 November 1910.

5 For one example, see UA, Quebec Central Railway, *Quebec Tercentenary Celebration, 1908*. This is essentially the daily itinerary, the order of the historical procession, and the scenes from the pageants printed on the back of a fold-out train timetable.

6 I am indebted to my colleague Mary Williamson for a photograph of this poster and for much guidance in my bewildering descent into the under-world of ephemera.

7 I have benefited from the beautifully illustrated study of this genre by
Jacques Poitras, *La Carte Postale Québécoise: Une Aventure Photographique*
(Laprairie: Éditions Broquet 1990). In this publication, however, the
tercentenary cards do not elicit the analysis they deserve; there is only a
passing mention on p. 34 and an unremarked colour reproduction on
p. 162. Allan Anderson and Betty Tomlinson, *Greetings from Canada: An
Album of Unique Canadian Postcards from the Edwardian Era, 1900–1916*
(Toronto: Macmillan 1978), shows an example of the Habitant Life Studies
and another of the Château Frontenac from the tercentenary series.

8 T. Jackson Lears, *No Place of Grace: Anti-modernism and the Transformation of
American Culture* (New York: Pantheon 1981).

9 The construction of Quebec as a folk society about this time deserves a
study all its own. I have been helped considerably in my thinking about this
subject by Ian McKay's splendid book, *The Quest of the Folk: Antimodernism
and Cultural Selection in Twentieth-Century Nova Scotia* (Montreal: McGill-
Queen's University Press 1994). This subject is touched upon in Carole
Carpenter, *Many Voices* (Ottawa: Canadian Centre for Folk Cultural Studies
1979), and in Richard Handler, *Nationalism and the Politics of Culture in
Quebec* (Madison: University of Wisconsin Press 1988), pp. 67–80. Handler
relies a good deal upon Carpenter for the earlier period. Both, however,
are interested primarily in the way folklorists and anthropologists constructed the notion of a folk society after Marius Barbeau. As these images
clearly reveal, commercial forces were hard at work constructing a folk
society before the academics. David Whisnant, in *All That Is Native & Fine*
(Chapel Hill: University of North Carolina Press 1983), describes the
contemporaneous reconstruction of Appalachia by folklorists.

10 H.-J.-J.-B. Chouinard, *Troisième Centenaire* (Québec: Laflamme & Proulx
1908), p. 87; CO42, Canada 1908, vol. 918, reel B2240, Postage Stamps file,
Grey to Elgin, 4 March 1908. Apparently the king had no objection provided the issue was for domestic use only and not for international service,
in keeping with an international postal convention.

11 *Report of the Postmaster General Rodolphe Lemieux for the Year Ended March 31,
1909* (Ottawa: C.H. Parmelee, King's Printer 1909), Sessional Paper no. 24,
pp. xii–xiii. To save time, the likenesses of the Prince and Princess of Wales
were copied from two earlier 1899 Newfoundland stamps. For two beautifully mounted sets of stamps, see the NA, Philatelic Collection, Gerald E.
Wellburn, Canada: Vol. 25, 1908 – Quebec Tercentenary Issue, HE 6185
C24B4 W46 1949. Wellburn claims the scenes were selected by Lemieux
and designed by Jose A. Machado, chief engraver of the American Bank
Note Company. He adds: 'The beautiful stamps were in use for about three

months and were current when this collector started collecting nearly 60 years ago.' See also in the same collection the Rosemary J. Nickle Collection, the Quebec Tercentenary Issue 1908, December 1984, HE 6185 C24B4 N54, c.2. She lists the individual engravers names and includes a collection of stamped postcards in her volume, most to overseas destinations. For reproductions, see, for example, *Darnell Timbres du Canada 1997* (Montréal: Éditions Darnell 1997), p. 28, nos 82–9. See also C.E.C. Shipton, 'The Quebec Tercentenary Issue,' *Maple Leaves,* vol. 4 (1951), pp. 4–6. At current prices a mint set would be worth about $1,800. Then they cost just over 60 cents.

12 *Historical Souvenir and Book of the Pageants* (issued under the direction of the National Battlefields Commission, Montreal: The Cambridge Corporation 1908), and *Souvenirs du Passé et livret des Spectacles Historiques* (Commission des Champs de Battailes Nationaux, Montréal: Cambridge Corporation 1908). The English and French texts are essentially the same. Arthur Doughty seems to have written the text from notes provided by Quebec collaborators on the Committee on History and Archeology, and overseen the correction of the proofs in both English and French. The marked-up galleys are to be found in NA, Doughty Papers, vol. 3–4, file 7, Quebec Tercentenary. See also NA, RG37, Archives Records, vol. 189, Doughty to George Wrong, 1 August 1908, thanking him for compliments on the book of the pageants: 'I returned to Quebec Saturday to attend the state dinner and make myself agreeable to Wolfe, Montcalm and a few others.' He adds: 'I may tell you that I have not been paid a cent for anything I did for the Commission. If anything I did helped to insure the success of the celebration this is all I ask.' He subsequently received a small honorarium for his work.

13 Katherine Lochnan et al., *The Earthly Paradise: Arts and Crafts by William Morris and His Circle from Canadian Collections* (Toronto: Art Gallery of Ontario, Key Porter Books 1993). The quotation is from p. 2. The typography of the Kelmscott Press is discussed by Richard Landon and illustrated on pp. 248–75.

14 NA, National Battlefields Commission Records, vol. 1, Cambridge Corporation to Courtney, 3 September, 1908. The publisher printed 25,000 books in English; 17,982 remained on hand afterwards. It claimed that the market for a high-quality publication of this sort had been undercut by unauthorized commercial guides. The commission paid the $4,000 indemnity without protest; see vol. 3, Minutes, 29–30 May 1908, 11–12 September 1908, for the contract and the aftermath.

15 Martin Jay in his recent book *Downcast Eyes: The Denigration of Vision in*

Twentieth-Century French Thought (Berkeley: University of California Press 1994) analyses the apogee of 'occularcentric hegemony' in a chapter entitled 'Dialectic of EnLIGHTenment.'

16 Asa Briggs, *Victorian Things* (Chicago: University of Chicago Press 1988), p. 89.

17 Robert W. Rydell, *All the World's a Fair: Visions of Empire at American Industrial Expositions, 1876–1916* (Chicago: University of Chicago Press 1984).

18 Juli K. Brown, *Contesting Images: Photography at the World's Columbian Exposition* (Tucson: University of Arizona Press 1994), pp. xii–xvi, for Goode's objectives at expositions, and Rydell, *All the World's a Fair*, pp. 44–5, for the quotation and his ideas about teaching with objects in museums.

19 I have been influenced in different ways in my reading of the photographic images by John Berger's elegant little books, *Ways of Seeing* (London: Penguin 1972) and *Another Way of Telling* (New York: Pantheon 1983); by Susan Sontag, *On Photography* (New York: Dell 1977); and somewhat in reaction to John Tagg's overpowering social control analysis in *The Burden of Representation* (London: Macmillan 1988).

20 On the Livernois family and its images, see Michel Lessard, 'Le Studio Livernois 1854–1974: Un Commerce Familial d'Art Photographique à Québec' (Thèse de Doctorat, Université Laval, 1986), and the same author, *The Livernois: A Family of Photographers* (Québec: Musée du Québec 1987).

21 One complete set of these slides, gathered in a small coffer in the shape of a two-volume leather-bound book, survives in the Archives National in Quebec. A second collection, better preserved, but seven slides short of a complete set, arrived at York University with the Ducharme Collection, and it may be seen in the Rare Books and Special Collections Department. Underwood and Underwood's published images are interleaved with the photographs at the National Archives of Canada. The Picture Division also holds the Underwood and Underwood archive containing many more unpublished photographs. William Darrah, *Stereo Views: A History of the Stereograph in America* (Gettysburg, Pa.: Times and News Publishing 1964); see also for this particular event, the brief account of Robert G. Wilson, 'Canada Through the Stereoscope: Quebec Tercentenary Celebraton,' *Photographic Canadiana* 10 (1984), pp. 5–6. These photographic publishers are treated in Turner Browne and Elaine Partnow, eds., *Macmillan Biographical Encyclopedia of Photographic Artists and Innovators* (New York: Macmillan 1983).

22 Diana Edkins, 'An Introduction to Panoramic Photography,' in The Grey Art Gallery and Study Center publication, *Panoramic Photography* (New York: New York University Press 1977), pp. 2–7, and the fascinating history of the

panoramic image by Ralph Hyde in *Panoramania!* (London: Trefoil Publications and the Barbican Art Gallery 1988).

23 Frank Lascelles arranged for the final scene to be filmed by the Garamond Company. Correspondence regarding payment of this invoice can be found in the National Battlefields Commission Records, vol. 1. As for the second film, I am indebted to Gene Allan, a CBC documentary historian, for finding this rare footage and providing me with a copy for study.

24 Archives of Ontario, Tercentenary of Quebec Collection, contains both the *Canadian Pictorial* and the Montreal *Standard* July 1908 special issues, the latter without its cover. I have been able to obtain an issue with a cover, but without the Henri Julien insert. Les Archives de la Cité de Québec has the best extant example of the Julien 'Historical Procession.'

25 His 'Cartier,' painted in 1906, did not find a home until 1923 when the government of Quebec bought it for its new museum on the Plains of Abraham, where it may still be seen on permanent display. Hughes de Jouvancourt, *Suzor-Coté* (Montréal: Stanké 1978), from which I have drawn this information, reproduces the 'Cartier' on pp. 130–1 and 139; for his 'Champlain,' see p. 72. See also *Le Musée du Québec, 500 oeuvres choisies* (Québec: Musée de Québec 1983), p. 142. Both the Cartier and Montcalm paintings are reproduced (poorly) in both books. The art critics are at some pains to point out the influences of impressionism on these early paintings, 'La Mort de Monctcalm' in particular. It is not so obvious to me. See also Dennis Reid, *A Concise History of Canadian Painting* (Toronto: Oxford University Press 1973), pp. 103–4, 129–30, and J. Russell Harper, *Painting in Canada* (Toronto: University of Toronto Press 1966), pp. 72, 130–1, 139, 143. I am especially indebted to Charles Hill, curator of Canadian Art at the National Gallery of Canada, for guidance on the turn-of-the-century historical turn in Canadian painting and in particular on the work of Suzor-Coté; Charles Hill to author, 5 November 1997.

26 Nicole Cloutier, *Laliberté* (Montreal: Montreal Museum of Fine Art 1990), and *Les Bronzes d'Alfred Laliberté* (Québec: Musée du Québec 1978). Laliberté taught Suzor-Coté the art of sculpture and their work, especially of heads, bears a strong resemblance. They both mined a rich vein of historical and folk studies that has ever since sustained a subsidiary flood of habitant wood carvings onto the tourist and curio markets.

27 Paul Gladu, *Henri Julien* (Montréal: Lidec 1970); Marius Barbeau, *Henri Julien* (Toronto: Ryerson Press 1941); and Harper, *Painting in Canada*, pp. 223–4. The scope and variation in Julien's work can be sampled in a posthumous collection of his drawings, in the *Album* published in 1916 in York University, Special Collections.

28 NA, National Battlefields Commission Records, Quebec City Archives, Charles Huot's Sketchbook. Huot had already made a study of peasant costumes in Britanny during 1907. Lascelles and Chouinard seem to have provided him with some particular references on historical dress. Considerable recrimination followed upon the presentation of the bill. Lascelles thought his work unsatisfactory. He insisted that Miss Bonham receive the same compensation as Huot for the work. Huot has a few interiors and landscapes in the collections of the Musée du Québec and the National Gallery. These costume watercolours do not resemble his extant work. See, in addition to the catalogues of those collections, Jean-René Ostiguy, *Charles Huot* (Ottawa: Galerie Nationale du Canada 1979); David Karl, *Dictionnaire des Artistes de Langue Française et Amérique et Amérique du Nord* (Québec: Musée du Québec 1990), pp. 403–4; and Reid, *A Concise History of Canadian Painting*, p. 102.

29 Rosalind Pepall, 'The Murals in the Toronto Municipal Buildings: George Reid's Debt to Puvis de Chavannes,' *Journal of Canadian Art History* 9 (1986), pp. 142–62; Marylin McKay, 'Canadian Historical Murals, 1895–1939: Material Progress, Morality and the "Disappearance" of Native People,' *Journal of Canadian Art History* 15 (1992), pp. 63–83; Reid, *A Concise History of Canadian Painting*, pp. 99–102, and Robert Derome, 'Charles Huot et la peinture d'histoire au Palais législatif de Québec (1883–1930),' *Bulletin of the National Gallery of Canada*, no. 27 (1976).

30 National Gallery of Canada, George Agnew Reid, 'The Arrival of Champlain at Quebec,' RC223, no. 115.

31 NA, Picture Division, 'Fur Traders at Montreal,' C-11013A; 'Fur Traders at Montreal,' C-11014A; 'Arrival of Champlain at Quebec,' C-11015A; 'Champlain,' C-11016; 'Return of the Indians from Long Sault,' C-3137; and 'Jacques Cartier erects a Cross,' C-96999. The Picture Division also contains a panoramic triptych, 'The Pageants at Quebec for the Tercentenary Celebration, 1908,' which is a representation of the magnificent Fontainebleau court scene, C-142814-6.

32 George Agnew Reid's drawings are mainly located in the National Archives of Canada, Picture Division. However, his papers at the Art Gallery of Ontario, E.P. Taylor Reference Library, contain many sketches drawn at the time of these scenes, and subsequently worked up on different occasions. A sample of his historical paintings is to be found in Fern Bayer, *The Ontario Collection* (Toronto: Fitzhenry & Whiteside 1990). These historical paintings were purchased by the Government of Ontario as part of a civic art collection.

CHAPTER 12   Landscape of Memory

1 University of Toronto, Fisher Rare Book Library, Walker Papers, box 7, Doughty to Walker, 12 July 1908; Doughty to Walker, 10 August 1908. NA, RG27, Archives Records, vol. 190, Doughty to Grey, 13 July 1908.

2 NA, Doughty Papers, M2244, vol. 1, Walker to Doughty, 15 July 1908; Walker to Doughty, 6 August 1908; Walker to Doughty, 12 August 1908.

3 NA, RG37, Archives Records, vol. 190, Frank Carrel to Doughty, 20, 30 July 1908; vol. 189, Doughty to Carrel, 22 July 1908.

4 The title page differs, *Troisième Centenaire de la Fondation de Québec, Berceau du Canada, Par Champlain, 1608–1908: Travaux Préliminaires – Délibérations – Documents* (Québec: Laflamme & Proulx 1908).

5 ANQ, Fonds Societé Saint-Jean Baptiste du Québec, dossier 12, 'Les Fêtes de IIIᵉ centenaire de la fondation de Québec, 3 Juillet, 1608–1908.' This document, in Chouinard's hand and written for his colleagues in the society, pushes the inspiration ahead to his 1902 meeting with Parent at Laval. This goes unmentioned in the document collection.

6 Archives de la Seminaire de Québec, Fonds Chouinard, file 2, Chouinard to Garneau, 17 June 1907; file 3, Finance Committee resolution 7 June 1907. NA, National Battlefields Commission Records, vol. 1, private and confidential, Frank Lascelles to Courtney, 23 June 1908; Minutes, 13–14 April 1908 and 21 March 1910, when Charles Edouard Gauvin was appointed permanent secretary at a salary of $2,500. NA, Laurier Papers, C884, 163985, Chouinard to Laurier, memorandum, 20 December 1909; NA, RG37, Archives Records, vol. 192, Doughty to Garneau, 4 April 1910: 'We knew at least a year ago he would not be the permanent secretary.'

7 NA, National Battlefields Commission Records, vol. 3, Minutes, 13–14 April, 27–8 April, 12–13 June, 26–7 June, 11–12 September 1908.

8 NA, RG37, Archives Records, vol. 189, Doughty to Wrong, 1 August 1908; NA, Doughty Papers, M2244, vol. 1, Walker to Doughty, 21 August 1908; (dined with Grey in Toronto last night who proposed a guarantee fund of $10,000. Walker thought Mackenzie, Mann etc are good; Sir George Drummond, despite his initial refusal could probably be persuaded to give $5,000); Walker to Doughty, 30 October 1908; ANQ, Fonds Garneau, boîte 1, Grey to Garneau, private, 9 September 1908 ('I am happy to tell you that I see my way to obtain the sum of $10000 to be used for meeting the expenditure incidental to the preparation of a Souvenir Volume of the tercentenary and that I propose that this volume shall be got up in a manner worthy of the occasion.')

9 NA, RG37, Archives Records, vol. 190, Archives Letterbook, Walker to Doughty, 21 August 1908; vol. 189, Doughty to Walker, 13 August 1908; Doughty to Walker, 15 August 1908 ('Mr Reid spent a good deal of time on the Plains and was on the Stand several days with Lascelles. I know that he made a good many sketches'); Doughty to Walker, 22 August 1908; Doughty to George Wolfe, 2 November 1908.

10 Royal Academy Library, Catalogue of Royal Academy Exhibitors, p. 190; Guildhall Library, Grant W. Waters, *Dictionary of British Artists Working 1900–1950* (Eastbourne: Eastbourne Fine Arts 1975), p. 79. Frank Craig is identified as a genre and historical painter, trained at Lambeth School of Art, Cooks Schools, and the Royal Academy. As a book illustrator he was known for his illustrations of Kipling. He died of tuberculosis in 1918 at Sintra, Portugal, a favourite artists' haunt.

11 NA, RG37, Archives Records, vol. 189, Doughty to Walker, 2 November 1908; Doughty to Frank Lascelles, 2 November 1908, asking for a preliminary sketch; Doughty to Lascelles, 23 December 1908, agreeing to provide photographs to Craig; Doughty to Lascelles, 28 December 1908, reporting that Craig will paint pictures for forty-five guineas each; Doughty to Craig, 29 December 1908, sending a copy of the Montreal *Standard* souvenir number; Doughty to Monseigneur Mathieu, 11 February 1909, promising a French edition; vol. 192, Doughty to Frank Craig, 31 May 1909; Doughty to Craig, 3 August 1909; Doughty to Grey, 5 June 1909; Doughty to Craig, 17 December 1909, sending cheque for $500.

12 Archives de la Seminaire de Québec, Fonds Chouinard, dossier 4, handwritten report of the Publication Committee, to the Executive Committee no date; *Journal Seminaire*, 8 mars 1909; *Les Fêtes du Troisième Centenaire de Québec: 1608–1908* (Québec: Laflamme & Proulx 1911), pp. 9–10. At thirty-eight, Abbé Camille Roy was one of Quebec's most noted literary scholars and historians. By 1909 he had already published a history of French-Canadian literature and several critical studies as well as some local history.

13 NA, RG37, Archives Records, vol. 189, Doughty to Grey, 11 November 1910, and vol. 191 for the paintings. As the project neared completion, Doughty had to fight off an effort by someone on the commission to take it over as an official publication. Doughty would have none of it, as he explained firmly to Wood on 12 October 1910: 'My intention was to publish about five hundred copies of the book and make it quite a scarce publication, but if it becomes any way official it must be distributed to those who are on the offficial list and at least two thousand copies would have to be published. I am quite sure however that the commission would insist on more being

said about the local organization, and for many other reasons I think it is desirable that it should be [free] of every form of official assistance.'

14 The original paintings remain cryptically catalogued in the Picture Collection of the National Archives of Canada. They have not, so far as I am aware, been seen publicly since Craig painted them and Grey donated them to Doughty's archive. It was a moment of intense excitement for me to be ushered into the storeroom at the heart of that dull grey building one day to see all six of these paintings propped up in their ornate gilt frames against a wall. NA, Picture Division, Paintings by Frank Craig: C10622, C10618, C10621, C10619, C100073, and C1549.

15 *The King's Book of Quebec*, vol. 1: pp. 126, 146.

16 *Les Fêtes*, pp. 455–71.

17 *The King's Book of Quebec*, pp. iii–iv.

18 NA, Doughty Papers, M2244, vol. 1, Walker to Doughty, 2 November 1908; NA, Denison Papers, 5422–24, Edmund Walker to Denison, 15 December 1908, repeating his telephone call and including a copy of George Wrong's proposal to Sir George Garneau, 7 December 1908 ('Equal importance should be given to the French text and to the English translation'); University of Toronto Fisher Rare Book Collection, Champlain Society Records, vol. 66, Minutes, 10 May 1906, 6 April 1909; vol. 48, B.E. Walker to Laurier, 21 November 1907; ANQ, Fonds Garneau, boîte 3, contains letters from Walker in 1917 regarding publication of some of these volumes. NA, Records of the National Battlefields Commission, vol. 3, Minutes, 29 March 1909.

19 See Jacques Mathieu and Eugene Kedl, eds., *The Plains of Abraham: The Search for the Ideal* (Montreal: Septentrion 1993), pp. 25–33, for the best discussion of the origin of the name. Much of the land upon which the battle was fought was owned by the Ursuline Order. The name still rankles in the convent as I discovered during one of my research trips. The sister responsible for the management of the order's real estate produced an old ledger, pointed to the lease payments received from the government throughout the nineteenth century, made a photocopy of the page, and gave me a stiff argument for renaming the Plains of Abraham the Ursuline Plains. This issue is touched upon in Marie-Emmanuel Chabot, *Le Petit Mérici, 1902–1930* (Québec 1994), pp. 7–12.

20 For a sense of what this space looked like before the National Battlefields Commission took it over, see the *Proceedings and Transactions of the Royal Society of Canada 1899* (this was part of the earlier campaign to protect this space from urban development), and Mathieu and Kedl, eds., *The Plains of Abraham.*

21 The literature on this urban park movement is vast. Most valuable for these purposes are Laura Roper's serviceable biography of Frederick Law Olmsted, *FLO* (Baltimore: Johns Hopkins University Press 1973); Galen Ganz's monograph, *The Politics of Park Design* (Cambridge: MIT Press 1982), David Schuyler, *The New Urban Landscape* (Baltimore: Johns Hopkins University Press 1986), which is quite favourably disposed towards Olmsted, and the recent 'user-focused' history of Central Park by Roy Rosenzweig and Elizabeth Blackamar, *The Park and the People* (Ithaca: Cornell University Press 1992), which tends to elevate Calvert Vaux's republicanism over Olmsted's paternal federalism.

22 The literature on the park movement in Canada can be sampled in W.C. McKee, 'The Vancouver Park System, 1886–1929: A Product of Local Businessmen,' *Urban History Review* 3 (1978), pp. 33–49, and Robert A.J. Macdonald's essay '"Holy Retreat" or "Practical Breathing Spot"?: Class Perceptions of Vancouver's Stanley Park, 1910–1913,' *Canadian Historical Review* 65 (1984), pp. 127–53.

23 According to a National Battlefields Statement dated 12 January 1911 in the Quebec City National Battlefields Commission Papers, this final accounting went as follows:

Receipts

Government grant	$300,000.00
Pageant ticket sales	35,671.60
Other sales	3,367.32
Total Receipts	$339,038.92

Expenditures

Pageants	$157,681.48
Reception, Prince of Wales	43,794.04
Entertainment officers, men	9,805.55
Expenses	12,338.23
Contingencies	5,852.92
Le 'Don de Dieu'	9,716.50
L'Habitation de Québec	5,293.79
Champlain monument stands	3,505.12
Military review stand	5,324.10
Decorations	18,733.10
Fireworks	16,178.00
Musical program	5,993.60
Press	1,926.34
Athletic sports	5,000.00
Men-of-the-watch	1,837.50
Tablets	4,858.50
Local entertainment of officers	15,000.00

Posters	6,139.42
Medals	4,150.30
Champlain Society	5,000.00
Earl Grey bust	817.63
Total Expenditures	338,996.21
Cash in bank transferred to Land Account	42.71

It was politically important to show that no money raised from public subscription went to finance the festivities at Quebec. Taking these additional funds into account, the National Battlefields Commission had in its treasury after the celebration the following contributions for the acquisitions and construction of the Battlefields Park:

Provincial Governments

Ontario	100,000.00
Quebec	100,000.00
Nova Scotia	10,000.00
New Brunswick	7,500.00
Manitoba	10,000.00
British Columbia	10,000.00
Prince Edward Island	2,500.00
Alberta	10,000.00
Saskatchewan	10,000.00
Subtotal	260,000.00

Private Contributions

Canadian Municipalities	17,864.00
Gift of New Zealand	4,865.00
School contributions, Canada and abroad	3,752.17
Literary and historical societies	785.56
Corporate contributions	16,396.53
Associations in Canada and abroad	4,181.05
Military organizations	1,243.78
Religious societies	346.36
Individuals in Canada	15,278.47
Individuals in England	5,385.45
Anonymous, England and Canada	19,735.34
English subscriptions special	34,439.89
Quebec Battlefields Association	84,574.44
Sub Total	468,821.04
Bank Interest	94,005.02
Total	$562,826.06

24 This phrase is taken from E.T. Linenthal's concluding paragraph on the history of Gettysburg in *Sacred Ground: Americans and Their Battlefields* (Urbana and Chicago: University of Illinois Press 1993), p. 118.

25 NA, Laurier Papers, C 785, 55888, James Le Moine to Laurier, 4 May 1901, for the Quebec Literary and Historical Society.

26 NA, National Battlefields Commission Records, vol. 1, Doughty to Grey, 15 June 1906; see also Doughty Papers, vol. 10, and Laurier Papers, C1161, 203756ff, Grey to Laurier enclosing Doughty's letter, 23 June 1906.

27 NA, Grey Papers, vol. 1, Laurier to Grey, 22 December 1906; Laurier Papers, C1162, 204556, Grey to Laurier, 4 October 1907, on the Doughty-Lake-Wood mission. See NA, Quebec Battlefields Association Papers, vol. 1, for their brief report, 'Quebec: Reservation of the Battlefields and Historic Sites, Report by General Lake, W. Wood and A.G. Doughty on the Methods adopted at Gettysburg Pa.,' Ottawa, 14 January 1908.

28 *Premier Rapport de la Commission d'Histoire et Archéologie Nommée par Son Honneur le Maire de Québec* (Québec 1907), especially pp. 5, 17–18, located in ANQ, Fonds Garneau, boîte 5.

29 NA, National Battlields Commission Records, M1991, Report of the Quebec Landmarks Commission with a new preface.

30 NA, National Battlefields Commission Records, vol. 1, *The Quebec Battlefields: An Appeal to History* (Ottawa 1908), pp. 7–8; *Les Champs de Battaile de Québec: La Voix de l'Histoire* (Québec 1908), pp. 46–7.

31 Todd had approached the Quebec Battlefields Association early in 1908; see NA, Quebec Battlefields Association Papers, vol. 1, Frederick G. Todd, landscape architect to Col. J. Hanbury-Williams, 27 January 1908, asking about the park contract and listing his planning experience. On 17 December 1908 the commissioners felt that the time had come to retain a professional landscape architect. Todd made a presentation to them at their next meeting on 26 March 1909. On 15 May the commission retained him, and he reported to them on 26 November 1909. He was then engaged to supervise the works on an ongoing basis. See NA, National Battlefields Commission Records, vol. 3, Minutes, these dates.

32 NA, MG30, E35, Frederick G. Todd Papers, Report, National Battlefields, Quebec, 1911 (sends Lord Grey this copy of plan for National Battlefields approved by the commission, report submitted 15 November 1909). See also Mathieu and Kedl, *The Plains of Abraham*, pp. 215–24. On Todd's career, see Linda M.M. Dicaire, 'The Rideau Canal Driveway: Founding Element of Ottawa's Evolving Landscape,' *Ontario History* 89 (1997), pp. 141–59.

33 Mathieu and Kedl, *The Plains of Abraham*, pp. 227–37; this chapter is called 'A Lengthy Undertaking.'

34 But the Plains did receive a gift of another female saint, Joan of Arc. During the late thirties a benefactor donated a small equestrian statue of

the French heroine most beloved by both the French and the romantic English. Though she has nothing to do with the place, her heroic martial spirit, expressing equal defiance towards English aggression and condemnation of French cowardice, commands a small formal French garden tucked away on the north side of the park.

35 ANQ, Fonds Garneau, boîte 1, Earl Grey to Garneau, 5 January 1917: 'Your photographs have arrived this morning and I cannot express to you the immense pleasure they have given me. The fact that you should have associated my name with the National Battlefields Park in the prominent and dignified way you have, will enable me to go to my grave with a consciousness that my life has not been altogether in vain.'

CONCLUSION   Forgetting

1 RA, George V Diary, Friday, 31 July to Tuesday, 4 August 1908; GV, CC4/5, Prince of Wales to Princess Mary, Saturday 1 August to Tuesday 4 August, 1908.

2 NA, Grey Papers, vol. 28, 7339 Grey to Sir James Whitney, 17 December 1909. When Whitney sent him a picture of this historic meeting of the 'brother Premiers' in Toronto, Grey replied: 'I am hanging it opposite my big photograph of the Review on the Plains of Abraham, in which as you will remember that abominable gaol is the central feature. I shall find, in the picture of the Premiers, opposite the Goal, an assurance that their joint influences will be successful in removing from the Plains of Abraham that polluting spot ... which was one of the chief objects of the Celebrations.' This would not, he realized, happen during his term; vol. 28, 7486, Grey to Whitney, 14 January 1910.

ACKNOWLEDGMENTS

My most lasting debt is to the Social Sciences and Humanities Research Council of Canada. The support of the Council over several years allowed me to work in collections that I would otherwise never have seen, and conduct research which, I believe, has enriched my understanding of the subtleties of the Quebec tercentenary.

The gracious permission of Her Majesty the Queen allowed me to visit the Royal Archives at Windsor Castle to read the Prince of Wales's diary and letters. The registrar, Lady Sheila de Bellaigue, advised and accommodated me; the deputy registrar, Pamela Clark, located material, and her assistant, Jill Kelsey, helped me with it. Frances Dimond, curator of photographs, and her assistant, Helen Gray, showed me the Princess of Wales's photograph albums of an earlier Canadian trip, and the images the Prince of Wales brought back from Quebec.

Many busy and patient archivists in Canada and in England put up with my requests and helped me find obscure material essential to this project. In England I am also grateful to Dr J. Robinson and Mrs Sara Rodger, in the Duke of Norfolk's archives at Arundel Castle, for permission to examine parts of the 15th Duke's correspondence. I especially enjoyed working in Les Archives des Ursulines de Québec, under the gentle guidance of Soeur Marie Marchand OSU, archiviste. There by the fireplace, under the low ceiling of the oldest part of the convent, with the Journals of the Order, and postcards and memorabilia of an event the nuns never witnessed spread out on a table before me, I too began to imagine the baroque splendour of the festival.

At the National Archives of Canada I owe a special thanks to the staff of the Visual and Sound Archives Division who, over the years, have helped me find and see the imagery of this event, in particular Peter Robertson, Diane Martineau, Irene Van Bavel, Joy Houston (for permission to videotape the panoramas, and borrow the Reid transparencies), and Martha Marleau of the Art Acquisition and Research Section, who arranged for me to see the luminous paintings by Frank Craig. Roanne Mokhtar in the Philatellic Collection assisted me in finding illustrations of the tercentenary commemorative set of stamps, three of which are reproduced with the permission of Canada Post Corporation.

At Les Archives du Ville de Québec the archivist, Martine Ménard, located documents and pictures and showed me the huge flag of the *Don-de-Dieu* that survives in the collection. Mariette Chantall helped me obtain copies from the magnificently organized photograph collection. Jacques Morin and Raynald Lessard of the Photography and Iconography Division of Les Archives Nationales du Québec helped me with the Livernois images and the stereoscopic slide collection. At Les Archives de l'Archdiocèse de Québec, Monsieur Armand Gagné, archiviste, opened the collection of documents pertaining to the Laval celebration. Soeur Juliette Cloutier AMJ, archiviste, Archives des Soeurs Augustines de la Miséricorde de Jésus, Monastère de l'Hôpital Géneral de Québec, welcomed me, gave me a tour, and provided photocopies of relevant sections of the Journal of the Order. At Les Archives de la Séminaire de Québec, Monsieur Laurent Tailleur, directeur, made it possible for me to see the Chouinard papers as well as the records of the seminary. Marie Cantin gave me access to the papers of the National Battlefields Commission at Quebec and allowed me to make copies of the remarkable Huot watercolours of the pageant costumes. France Duhamel at the National Gallery of Canada helped me find the George Reid paintings in the collection. Archivists and librarians at the British Museum, the Guildhall Library, and the Public Record Office in England, the National Library in Ottawa, the Metropolitan Toronto Reference Library, and the Fisher Rare Book Room of the Robarts Library at the University of Toronto went out of their way to find obscure things. Sandra Guillaume and Leon Warmski at the Ontario Archives guided me in that collection and at the Art Gallery of Ontario Maia-Mari Sutnik gave me permission to examine George Reid's sketchbooks and notes in the E.P. Taylor Reference Library.

My own library at York University demonstrated time and again that most of what I wanted was right there under my nose. Mary Williamson, in addition to helping me with many other matters, alerted me to the existence of the stereoscopic slides in the Ducharme collection. Kent Howarth in Special Collections found it, and made it available for viewing. The Interlibrary Loan Department found newspapers on microfilm. Ellen Hoffmann, chief librarian, took a direct interest in my project. My friend John Dawson, from the Division of Instructional Technology, worked with me on the images and taught me to see them through a photographer's eye. Kelly Parke and Bob McKenzie helped me visualize the pageantry by recreating it in the Video Studio.

At York University I am especially blessed with colleagues in many quarters who have helped and encouraged me at various stages, especially Beverly Diamond, Mary Jane Warner, and Joyce Zeamans in the Faculty of Fine Art; Carole Carpenter in Humanities helped me with the historiography of folklore; my colleagues Nick Rogers and Adrian Shubert organized a conference, 'Spectacle, Monument and Memory,' that brought me into contact with a large, interdisciplinary group of cultural historians at a key moment. Fernand Ouellet, Susan Houston, Jack Saywell, Marcel Martel, and Marlene Shore in the Department of History listened to me as I struggled with ideas, and they also commented on papers and answered queries. Roberto Perin read the sections on the church, and Ian Wilson, the archivist of Ontario, read those dealing with Arthur Doughty and reassured me of my interpretation. My graduate student assistants Jacqueline Warwick, Maxine Paabo, Lori Pucar, Chris Elsner, and Matthew Evenden taught me more than they know and kept me organized. I tried out some of these ideas on students in my course, the Uses of the Past, and in seminars at the universities of Windsor, McMaster, Carleton, and York.

Without the help of Michèle Brassard, of the *Dictionary of Canadian Biography*, I would have been hopelessly lost in the archives of Quebec. Her experience and enthusiasm for the project turned up a wealth of material in the most unlikely places. A longshot communication with Dr Gavin Langmuir, Professor Emeritus, Stanford University, proved immensely illuminating about his mother's recollections of the tercentenary and in subsequent letters I have benefited from his helpful criticism. Professor Brian Dippie of the University of Victoria gave me some advice about the Wild West material, and Charles Hill, curator of Canadian art at the National Gallery of Canada, took a lively and helpful interest in my pictures. Maria Tippett encouraged me in this venture into cultural history and helped make my visit to the Royal Archives possible; she and Peter Clarke also entertained me royally in Cambridge and took me to see Benjamin West's 'Death of Wolfe' at Ickworth.

At the University of Toronto Press Gerry Hallowell talked me out of Plan A and pointed me towards a more realistic Plan B long before I had a manuscript. When I eventually delivered the manuscript he gave it a thorough critical reading, advised me regarding illustrations, and generously arranged for this splendid publication. His associates, Emily Andrew and then Frances Mundy, skilfully managed the editorial and production process. Diane Mew, who edited my first book more years ago than we both care to remember, brought her professional skills to bear on my overwrought prose once again. The designer, Val Cooke, and the staff at UTP have made this a model of the bookmaker's art.

I am particularly indebted to the three anonymous readers of the manuscript whose criticism has greatly improved the book. My friend Barbara Wilson read all of the manuscript, sharing with me her knowledge of military history and the royal family, and spared me much embarrassment in the process. My long-suffering colleagues Christopher Armstrong and Ramsay Cook tolerated my infatuation for 'visual history,' fought their way through the typographical horrors of earlier versions of the manuscript, and gave me sound advice and encouragement when I most needed it. Diane Nelles helped me revise and rethink the early chapters. I hope all of these people can see some of their efforts in these pages and take some pleasure in the results.

History remains a branch of literature. Moreover, in the modern era the novel has provided the pattern for historical narrative. Recently Canadian fiction has taken a historical turn, drawing heavily upon the past for characters and themes. This book represents my attempt to borrow back, to engage in dialogue with contemporary writing, especially on matters of form and structure. Fiction, like a forbidden fruit, inspires and tempts historians like me. It also intimidates us, for our imaginations are constrained by our evidence. Novelists arrive at historians' conclusions from different directions. As I was reading the proofs for this book, what a startling surprise to discover a novelist working with similar material, making essentially the same point with more flair and ribaldry than my skill or evidence would permit. On the subject of historical commemoration the novelist, in this case Julian Barnes, surely has written the last word: 'It was like a country remembering its history: the past was never just the past, it was what made the present able to live with itself.'

Toronto, Christmas 1998

ILLUSTRATION CREDITS

167 (PA24132), 175 (PA194728), 178 (PA24127), 180 (PA194729), 183 (PA24147), 191 (PA165499), 208 (C31402), 214–5 (PA165609), 217 (C14042), 220 (PA194747), 225 top (Ethel Chadwick Papers), 225 bottom (PA138386), 248 (C19928), 250 (C2181), 271 (PA24129), 287 (C51653), 298 (C1549), 305 (PA29235), 318 (PA194716)

Royal Archives, Windsor Castle: 315 (80/1997)

Colour Section:

Archives de la Ville de Québec: plate 5 (11199-1)

Author's collection: plates 1–4

Montreal *Standard*: (25 July 1908): plate 6

National Archives of Canada: plate 8 (C11015), plate 9 (C10621)

National Battlefields Collection, Québec: plates 7a–c

INDEX